P9-ECQ-062

**ON STAGE, EVERYONE** ☆☆☆

On

GRACE BARNES
MARY JEAN SUTCLIFFE

# *Stage, Everyone*

THE MACMILLAN COMPANY
NEW YORK

## ☆☆☆ ABOUT THE AUTHORS

**Grace Barnes** formerly Beverly Hills High School, and University High School, Los Angeles, California, and supervisor of training for secondary school drama teachers, University of California, Los Angeles

**Mary Jean Sutcliffe (Mrs. Paul E. Weaver, Jr.)** Santa Monica City College, Santa Monica, California, and supervisor of training for secondary school drama teachers, University of California, Los Angeles



PRINTED IN THE UNITED STATES OF AMERICA

## ☆☆☆ ACKNOWLEDGMENTS

Grateful acknowledgment is made to the authors and publishers who have generously granted permission for copyrighted material to be used in this volume. Copyright notices in general appear at the end of quotations or at the foot of the first page of each scene or play quoted. A scene has also been reprinted from the following play:

*Our Hearts Were Young and Gay,* copyright 1946 by The Dramatic Publishing Company. Based upon the book of the same title, copyright 1942 by Dodd, Mead & Co., Inc.

# FOREWORD ☆☆☆

HERE IS a book that has grown up in the classroom. Its content has developed and its organization has taken form in connection with its use in many high school classes of all types, sizes, and make-up. Its writers for many years have searched for and tested diligently a mass of material to find what it is that best develops the skills of expression essential for modern living. They have examined the available texts and other written materials bearing on the subject; they have observed and queried many teachers in both high schools and colleges. As supervisors of student teachers from the University of California, Los Angeles, preparing to be teachers of oral English and dramatics, they have had ample opportunity to see how teachers with little or no experience respond to various teaching materials and use them in actual teaching situations.

While much of the book is pointed toward the activities of pupils as identified with acting and the stage—and this is carried out sufficiently so that it may be used as the basis of a curriculum in drama—its chief value is its provision for the development of qualities of expression, poise, and conduct necessary to young people if they are to be successful in their contacts with each other and with society generally. The book provides a wealth of information and experience in an area in which the pupil is interested and for which he recognizes his needs. Of special importance, the content is organized into a sequential form of experience so that the interest of the pupil can be maintained at a high level.

The book fully reflects not only the insight of these writers into the thinking and needs of young people, but also their understanding of the broad responsibilities of the secondary school. This book fulfills a real need. A long life of usefulness may be predicted for it.

The above constitutes the foreword of the 1954 edition of this book. The book has indeed been well received and extensively used in secondary schools. But in spite of this the authors have not been satisfied. They have sought suggestions and criticisms pertaining to possible additions and revisions which would make the book even more helpful to teachers and students. They have made further observations of theatre-arts activities in the classroom. They have made additional analyses of the place and purpose of oral experiences in the modern and changing school. The results of these studies by the authors are reflected in the new edition. The book has been brought up to date.

Scenes from best plays in present-day theatre, with suggestions for adapting and using the scenes, have been added. How to do "Central Staging;" how to adapt the content of the course to the learning needs of all students; how to put general suggestions into specific classroom activities. These are some additional points of emphasis in the revised edition. Another feature is the inclusion of a chapter on theatre history which will help the student to better understand the modern theatre. And, of most importance, the new edition continues to stress student activity.

Again we may predict a uniformly enthusiastic reception for this, the latest edition of ON STAGE, EVERYONE.

Jesse A. Bond
*Director of Teacher Training*
*University of California, Los Angeles*

# PREFACE ☆☆☆

"On stage, everyone!" is the call of the director when he wishes to assemble his cast for instructions. So ON STAGE, EVERYONE is our call to those who have "always wanted to be in a play." Drama is fun! Its appeal is universal and has existed through the ages.

Just as a greater knowledge of the rules makes any game more interesting, so does a greater knowledge of the basic principles make any art more enjoyable. After hearing repeatedly, "Drama has meant more to me than any other subject I have ever studied," the authors are encouraged to offer methods and materials tested through the years with hundreds of students, hoping that thereby more young people may thrill to the joys of artistic expression through acting.

The maximum development of the personality and character traits of the individual is of paramount importance in any study that is undertaken. No subject in the curriculum leads more effectively and pleasantly to this goal than does drama. Since the actor's medium is himself—his voice, body, mind, senses, and emotions—all training must first be directed toward his personal improvement. Until he has acquired beautiful speech, he is not ready to attempt dialects. Until he has a controlled, coordinated body, he is not ready to assume mannerisms. Until he has trained, acute senses, he cannot portray human emotions faithfully. And until he has a disciplined, alert, inquiring mind, he is not ready to interpret the works of the great dramatists. In the final analysis, it is the actor as a whole, of which everything that has ever happened to him is a part, that is the instrument of acting.

We propose, then, a study of acting which takes into consideration the whole individual. Whether behind the footlights or in that greater theatre of daily living, with its varied and complex social relationships, the lessons of the stage will prove equally valid. Integrity and truth are indispensable ingredients, but an expressive personality is needed to project them to the world. To aid in this development is the aim of ON STAGE, EVERYONE.

## OUTLINE OF THE BOOK

Acting is primarily an activity, not an academic study. Students enter the drama class with a desire to act. To capitalize upon this natural interest, the methods and materials in this book have been organized around acting projects.

Chapters 1, 2, 3, 4, in which the four beginning acting projects are set up, present an over-all view of all phases of the subject. Each project is more difficult than the preceding one, and all training is summarized in the one-act play.

Chapters 5, 6, 7, 8, 9, 10 each present separately and in detail one phase of the basic training. While all are a part of every acting activity, each one must, at some time, receive major emphasis. Technique is learned as needed in connection with any project.

### BASIC TRAINING EMPHASES

1. The Modern Scene—senses and emotions (5), technique (9)
2. The Character-Opposite Scene—the body (6), senses and emotions (5)
3. The Shakespearian Scene—the voice (7), history (8)
4. The One-Act Play—play production (10), technique (9)

Chapters 11, 12 provide scripts for class study.

Chapter 13 lists suitable material to supplement the text.

Chapter 14 outlines Courses of Study for three semesters, incorporating all the elements of basic training, giving time allotment, sequence of projects, and the student activity.

Chapter 15 gives detailed assistance to teachers in developing the Courses of Study, and is designed to be of particular help to the less experienced.

Perhaps the special contribution of the book is the emphasis it places upon personality development as one of the chief benefits of educational dramatics. Practical features, too, are the methods suggested for integrating all the different phases of the subject, and the inclusion of sufficient acting material to provide ample and varied outlets for the talents of any beginning group.

Since the portrayal of real people is the major part of acting, great sensitivity and sympathetic understanding will always be the actor's most prized possessions. It is the authors' hope that through the use of this book vistas will be opened to aspiring young actors that will help to make life's journey one of confidence, service, and joy.

The authors express their gratitude to the following directors for pictures of their productions: Roger C. Anderson, Roosevelt High School, Des Moines, Iowa; Rosemary Burns, Portland High School, Portland, Maine; Amy Sutton and Norman H. Kirschbaum, Central High School, Omaha, Nebraska; Aristelle Macdonald, Roosevelt High School, Seattle, Washington; Wanda B. Mitchell, Evanston Township High School, Evanston, Illinois; Laurlene Straughn Pratt, Forest Park High School, Baltimore, Maryland; Gene Nielson Owen, Santa Monica City College; and to Elladora Hudson Furbush, Production Coordinator, Eagle Rock High School, Los Angeles, California.

The authors acknowledge with gratitude the aid of Ann Sughrue, drama instructor, Flagstaff High School, Flagstaff, Arizona, for testing new material and for editorial criticism; Gene Nielson Owen, head of the theatre department, Santa Monica City College, Santa Monica, California, for editorial criticism on central and flexible staging, theatre history, and teaching methods.

Sets and costumes for productions at Beverly Hills, Eagle Rock, and University High Schools were designed and constructed by students under the direction of Elladora Hudson Furbush.

# CONTENTS ☆☆☆

# ON STAGE, EVERYONE ☆☆☆

# Prologue

*Law office of Stuart and Lincoln on the second floor of the Court House in Springfield, Illinois.*

(ABE *is sitting, slumped in his chair, staring at his desk. He has his hat and overcoat on. A muffler is hanging about his neck untied.* JOSH SPEED *is half-sitting on the table at the right. He is reading a long letter with most serious attention. At length he finishes it, refolds it very carefully, stares at the floor.*)

ABE. Have you finished it, Josh?

JOSH. Yes.

ABE. Well—do you think it's all right?

JOSH. No, Abe—I don't. (ABE *turns slowly and looks at him.*) I think the sending of this letter would be a most grave mistake—and that is putting it mildly and charitably.

ABE. Have I stated the case too crudely?

(ABE *is evidently in a serious state of distress, although he is making a tremendous effort to disguise it by speaking in what he intends to be a coldly impersonal tone. He is struggling mightily to hold himself back from the brink of a nervous collapse.*)

---

JOSH. No—I have no quarrel with your choice of words. None whatever. If anything, the phraseology is too correct. But your method of doing it, Abe! It's brutal, it's heartless, it's so unworthy of you that I—I'm at a loss to understand how you ever thought you could do it this way.

ABE. I've done the same thing before with a woman to whom I seemed to have become attached. She approved of my action.

JOSH. This is a different woman.

(*He walks over to the window, then turns again toward* ABE.) You cannot seem to accept the fact that women are human beings, too, as variable as we are. You act on the assumption that they're all the same one—and that one is a completely unearthly being of your own conception. This letter isn't written to Mary Todd—it's written to yourself. Every line of it is intended to provide salve for your own conscience.

ABE. (*Rising; coldly.*) Do I understand that you will not deliver it for me?

JOSH. No, Abe—I shall not.

ABE. (*Angrily.*) Then someone else will!

JOSH. (*Scornfully.*) Yes. You could give it to the minister, to hand to the bride when she arrives for the ceremony. But—I hope, Abe, you won't send it till you're feeling a little calmer in your mind . . .

ABE. (*Vehemently, turning to* JOSH.) How can I ever be calm in my mind until this thing is settled, and out of the way, once and for all? Have you got eyes in your head, Josh? Can't you see that I'm desperate?

This scene from *Abe Lincoln in Illinois* is an excellent example of effective drama. If you were to see it performed by accomplished actors you would share the anxiety and mental suffering of the characters and for a time be carried out of your own life to live with the people of the play. You would be in the shabby law office where

Abe is sitting slumped in his chair nervously awaiting the opinion of his friend; you would suffer with Josh as he slowly refolds the letter and tries to frame his answer in a way that will not hurt Abe. Their problems would be your problems, for you would believe in the reality of the scene of which you had become a part. You would be experiencing the magic of the theatre.

Every good actor wants to create such a perfect audience response at every performance. How can he accomplish this? What makes it possible for one person to move a theatreful of people to tears, to laughter, to fear, to any of the countless emotions that sway human beings?

What did the actors do in the scene you have just witnessed that made you, a member of the audience, participate? First, before a word was spoken, they so effectively made you aware of an emotional crisis that you yourself became emotionally stirred. Abe's long body slumped in his chair told plainer than words his utter dejection; Josh's restless moving revealed his indecision. When Abe finally spoke it was in a voice colored by the intensity of his emotion at the moment. Josh's tone, his carefully chosen words, his hesitancy in answering, made you understand not only that he disagreed with his friend, but that he was at the same time unwilling to hurt him. His moving away from his friend to the window heightened this feeling.

Thus analyzing the acting reveals that the actor's dramatic mediums are his own body and voice controlled by his mind and influenced by his senses and emotions. All of these are subject to training. Great artists, of course, have special gifts for which no amount of training can ever substitute. But in every art there are basic principles which can be learned and so well followed that the results, though not brilliant, are most satisfying. In the following pages you will be given a working knowledge of the actor's craft. Though, obviously, no one element of acting can be completely separated from the others, for purposes of study a single phase will be treated in detail in each of the chapters in Part 2. Through an intelligent use of this instruction you should be able to give competent and gratifying performances.

If, by rare good fortune, you are one of the gifted few, this preliminary training will serve as a stepping stone to great heights in acting.

Acting is a group activity, therefore you should begin at once to rehearse with a partner on acting material for group presentation. You need first to become acquainted with the stage and with being before an audience. Too much theory before this is accomplished may prove confusing and make your acting superficial. Over a period of months you should play a variety of parts, each one presenting a different problem and increasing in difficulty. The four acting assignments suggested in the following pages may be completed in one semester and are selected for specific reasons. As you work on them you will need to refer to the chapters in Part 2 for basic training, using as much of that material as you require. During the first week you should receive an evaluation of your posture and walk (as suggested on pages 83-84), and later on of your voice (pages 112-113). Then begin a daily practice of appropriate exercises for improvement.

In your first acting project you will develop a simple, but clearly defined, character in a modern scene. You will next attempt a more complex and detailed one in the character-opposite assignment. In your third portrayal you will progress to a completely well-rounded character drawn by the master dramatist, Shakespeare. As a summary of the course you will combine all your knowledge and skill in the presentation of a one-act play. You will learn not only from your own endeavors but from your fellow actors, provided that you train yourself to observe accurately and to evaluate correctly.

# Part 1

## ACTING

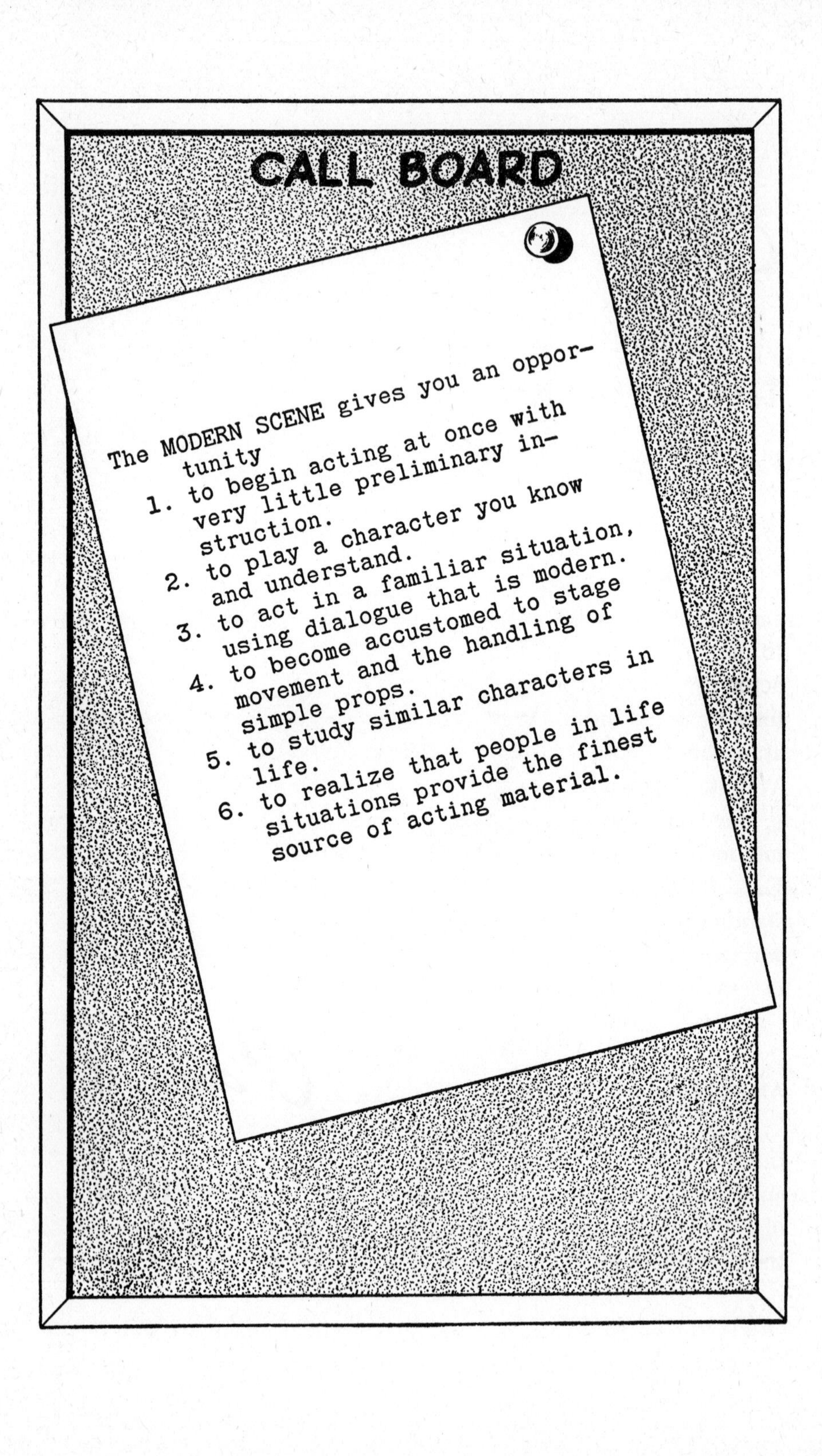
CALL BOARD
The MODERN SCENE gives you an opportunity
1. to begin acting at once with
very little preliminary instruction.
2. to play a character you know
and understand.
3. to act in a familiar situation,
using dialogue that is modern.
4. to become accustomed to stage
movement and the handling of
simple props.
5. to study similar characters in
life.
6. to realize that people in life
situations provide the finest
source of acting material.

# One

## THE MODERN SCENE ☆☆☆

Select a **Modern Scene**, from those in Part 3, that you would like to present. Nearly all are for two people only because the beginning actor usually finds it difficult to stay in character when he has no lines to speak and is not the immediate object of the other person's attention. Choose a partner who shares your enthusiasm for the scene. You are now ready to approach your role.

How does one go about this business of acting? There are many methods, and you will eventually develop the one that best suits you. Until then, here is a threefold plan which you can follow: 1) understanding the part; 2) rehearsing the part; 3) playing the part. Since you will follow this same routine in all your acting projects, a detailed description of it is given here. This you should review frequently.

### ☆☆☆ UNDERSTANDING THE PART

**ANALYZE THE PLAY** You will, of course, read the entire play several times, having a special objective each time: first, simply to understand the story; again, to determine moods and conflicts; and later, to concentrate on your character alone. Much of your skill in characterization depends upon your ability to analyze the script.

In order to understand a play thoroughly it is necessary for you to know something about play structure, and this takes you into the realm of playwriting, a highly specialized art. Later you will want to make a rather detailed study of it. For the present, the ideas here presented will provide a basis from which to work.

A play is a story presenting the conflict of two opposing forces, and designed to be presented by actors before an audience. Nearly always the dramatist has one main idea or proposition which he wishes to prove. This is his **theme** or premise. Usually the theme can be stated in a single short sentence.

The story which the author uses to develop his theme is arranged in a series of carefully planned situations which make up the **plot.** This is the particular way in which he expresses his theme. The same theme may be used for many different stories which can be plotted in hundreds of ways.

Since drama shows the **conflict** of emotions or will in action, you must determine the nature of the conflict in order to present it clearly. It may be mental or physical. It may be conflict within the individual, as in *Hamlet*. More often it is with another person, as in *Rebecca*. Or it may be with circumstances, with society, or with Fate, as in *Death of a Salesman*, or any of the Greek tragedies. "The pivotal character is the **protagonist**, the one who creates conflict and makes the play move forward."* The person most actively opposing him is the **antagonist**. All the important characters in the play are allied to one or the other of these people. Through this relationship of the characters, and their actions and reactions, the dramatist further reveals his ideas.

As the conflict in a play develops, an air of expectancy and excitement increases with each new situation and the audience is eager to know what the end will be. This is called **suspense** and is another essential ingredient of a well-written play.

The high point to which the plot consistently builds is the **climax**. Here the plot turns to a conclusion wherein the audience learns the

* Lajos Egri, *The Art of Dramatic Writing*. Simon and Schuster, 1946.

solution to the problem set up in the theme. In modern plays it is nearly always near the end. Although there are minor climaxes in every scene, the whole play builds step by step to this major one.

Each play has a **mood**, an emotional overtone. It may be essentially gay or tragic or mysterious, and it will change somewhat with each new situation. While being conscious of the over-all mood you must also detect the variations.

Other elements which will claim your attention are **tempo**, the speed with which scenes move, and **rhythm**, the pulse of the play. They are qualities of all movement and sound, including voice, and while varying from scene to scene will always be in harmony with those established for the play as a whole.

After you have analyzed the complete play, you must determine the relation of your scene to the others. To what extent does it advance the plot, or is it a part of a subplot? Is it vital to the development of the theme? Decide definitely how you want this scene to affect your audience, for the audience response must be consistent with this aim.

**ANALYZE YOUR CHARACTER** Before you can interpret your character you must know him. What kind of person is he? What is his *impelling motive,* the drive that makes him do what he does and say what he says? Is he brilliant or stupid, or a little of both? Is he jolly or sullen? Is he upright and honest, or are his ethical standards questionable? What of his family and home atmosphere? In what kind of community does he live? What does he do for a living? What are his principal interests; his hobbies? How does he look? Is he tall or short, fat or thin? How does he dress? How does he speak?

You will get the answers to these and many other questions from a number of sources—principally from the playwright's description; from what the character says and how he reacts; from what others say to him and about him, and from their reactions to him. But you will learn also from your knowledge of people like him; from your reading, especially of biography and history; and from your study of art. Often, too, you must call upon your own creative imagination, which will be active in direct proportion to your experiences, your study, and your observation of people and the world about you.

It is very important to realize at the outset of your training that the depth of your characterization is directly related to the amount of study and thinking that you employ in preparing your role. The sincere actor, interested in his own and his group's success, will spend much time and thought on each character analysis.

### CHARACTER ANALYSIS OUTLINE

1. What are his characteristics?

MENTAL — quick-witted, brilliant, average, stupid, dull?

EMOTIONAL — steady and poised or changeable; affectionate, confident, confused, gay, gloomy? Does he have a sense of humor? How does he respond to the people and situations he meets in the play?

SPIRITUAL — ideals, beliefs, religion, code of ethics? What is his attitude toward life and people in general?

PHYSICAL — Body: age, height, weight, coloring, posture; mannerisms of hands, feet, eyes, facial expression? Is he clumsy, slow, alert, fast-moving, tense, relaxed? Does he have much or little vitality? What is his general appearance; dress, shoes, make-up, hair?

Voice: quality, pitch, tempo, inflection? Does it show energy, boredom, illness?

2. What factors have determined these characteristics?

FAMILY — brothers, sisters, father, mother; childhood experiences; home atmosphere?

COMMUNITY — social standing, financial standing, work, friends? What is his adjustment to his environment?

EDUCATION — schooling, travel, hobbies, principal interests?

This outline is presented only to guide you in your character analysis. Do not burden yourself with details which would not be important in the play situation. Stay close to the dramatist's suggestions; make the most of what he has given you. But if he has not supplied you with enough material you must create for your character an imaginary background that will make logical everything he does and says. Write a complete description and analysis of every character you ever play.

Reread the script and pick out the moods through which your character passes, and the conflicts in which he takes part. Then, referring to your analysis, justify them by the background you have compiled. You may find that you must expand or change your original analysis in order to make it consistent.

**CREATE YOUR CHARACTER** Having analyzed your character you might start out on a Life Study trip to find people like him. (Chapter 5.) In this **Modern Scene** he will, no doubt, be much like someone you already know. As soon as you have a clear picture in mind you are ready to create him.

You will first try to take on his ways of thinking and feeling, and his emotional responses to people and situations. When this *inner* character is established, you will next assume the *outer* expression—his ways of standing, moving, and speaking. Heredity and environment will dictate certain characteristics which you must make more clear through costume and make-up.

In creating a character, as in preparing a speech, you collect much more material than you can possibly use. Through study, observation, and experience you will have many ideas of personal reactions, of mannerisms, of peculiarities of speech, of props, of costume details, and of make-up. From this collection you must select enough very telling items to make the character come to life in the manner in which the playwright intended that he should. This is the time to use your intelligence, and your taste in selection, and to practice **artistic economy**—not "How *much* can I do?" but "How *little* can I do and still best convey the ideas and emotions?" According to Sir Joshua Reynolds, the famous English painter, "Simplicity is the exact medium between too little and too much." Ruth Mason Rice expresses this same idea in "A Japanese Print."

A curve for the Shore
A line for the Lea
A tint for the Sky
Where the sunrise will be.

A stroke for a Gulf
A sweep for a Main
The skill to do more
With the will to refrain.

We have a right to expect from the artist not photographic reality, but interpretation. That is, he must never copy nature exactly but should use only such elements as he feels are essential to artistry. He must make a contribution; he must leave the stamp of his own personality through selection and emphasis. What he leaves out is as important as what he puts in. And the greater his skill, the greater his simplicity. For there is no such thing as reality on the stage; there is only the appearance of reality. The creative actor examines, selects, discards, combines, and evaluates his material. Then through his imagination, his sense of stage values, and his showmanship he evolves a character who appears vitally real to his audience.

**RELATE YOUR CHARACTER TO THE PLAY** What is the contribution of your character to the dramatic action? How is he connected with the basic conflict? Is he the protagonist or the antagonist or allied to either one? What is his relation to each person in the play and his general feeling toward them—admiration, loyalty, hate, fear? How does he feel toward them in your scene? What do other people think of your character? What do they say about him? What emotional transitions must he make between scenes as the play develops? What is each of his conflicts and how does he react to it?

**STUDY THE SPEECHES** After arriving at some definite conclusions about the play and your character, study carefully the lines which you are to speak. Find those speeches which are most essential to an understanding of the plot, for these must receive extra attention in interpretation and projection. Know the meaning of every word; be accurate in your pronunciations. Do not let one idea or syllable escape you. Study the script until you are sure of every thought expressed, then read between the lines to discover implied meanings, for lines must be padded with thoughts. Don't make the mistake of thinking that all the play is in printed form. That is only part of it; the rest is in the actor's mind and supplies the overtones, the undertone, the background for what he says. The actor is thinking definite, self-created speeches in answer to what others are saying to him. This colors his bodily response. It is part of his listening. So important is this that some actors write these thoughts into their scripts and memorize them with their speeches. This "talking back" mentally helps you not only to listen well but also to pick up your cues on time. Study your partner's lines as well, in order to develop appropriate reactions to them.

## ☆☆☆ REHEARSING THE PART

**SETTING** You will next devote your attention to the setting in which you are to act. Since nearly all movement on the stage is dependent upon the placement of the furniture, this becomes an essential factor in your planning. It is important to have a properly set stage for every rehearsal if you are to develop effective expression in both voice and body at the same time. Remember artistic economy and place no more furniture on the set than you intend to use. On the other hand, have enough to suggest good business and to balance the stage properly. (See page 178.) Many times you will find that your first stage arrangement is not adequate. Do not hesitate to change it. Keep experimenting until you find the one that best serves your needs. The sooner you solve such technical matters, however, the better.

**REHEARSAL PLANS** You can no more practice acting without a partner than you can learn to play tennis without an opponent. True, you can practice your serve by batting a number of balls over the net, but your serve is only part of your skill as a tennis player. You must learn to return the shots of your rival and to be prepared for whatever he does. So it is in acting. There is much that you can do alone to perfect your technique, but you can actually rehearse only with a partner.

In the following routine for practice it is suggested that your first walk-through be alone. This will enable you to get the feeling of your character without the distraction of another person's presence. But all other walk-throughs should be with your partner. Since your actions and reactions are largely dependent upon his, all interpretation, movement, and business become joint projects and should be so rehearsed. The give-and-take of a lively communication with another person is what gives purpose and reality to both your speeches and your reactions. These should not be faked but should be the result of compulsion—just as strong people by the force of their personalities make you answer them.

Use real or substitute props for every rehearsal so that you can work out the business as you go along. Be resourceful about props and make some if necessary. Plan a schedule for rehearsals at home. Use the same measurements for your stage there as you will have in the classroom and set your furniture accurately.

**REHEARSAL ROUTINE** So far your work has been confined to thinking and planning. Now leave your desk chair! It is time to *do* something—to begin to act!

1 **Walk-Through** Script in hand, enter into the mood of the situation, and walk through the scene reading your lines and letting your feelings flow undisciplined into the natural responses of the moment. Feel completely free and uninhibited. Imagine the setting in which you are to play; move, talk, respond with abandon. Make spontaneous responses to the speeches of your partner, which in this

first walk-through you will read silently. Don't think *about* your character, think *in* character. Keep the scene moving to the end with as few breaks as possible, and try to surrender to the mood as you move and read the lines.

2 **Think-Through** Relax! Perhaps you feel a trifle embarrassed after your emotional display. Well, it was good for you. You need that spirit of freedom. Doubtless you are disturbed about those passages which brought little response. That is good, too. You cannot play the whole scene with equal intensity.

Now is the time to sit down and analyze what you did. Forget emotion for the time being and let reason dominate. You were working more or less instinctively, using your own impulses in your walk-through. But uncontrolled emotion is not artistic creation, nor are your own emotional responses necessarily those of the character. You must learn to control and direct all your actions and responses, knowing exactly what you are doing and why. What seems spontaneous on the stage is really an evidence of fine technique.

As you evaluate your walk-through, check on each phase of your portrayal. Refer to the analysis outline which you made for your character. In what respects were you true to your original idea of the role? Some of the qualities which you possess are also those of the character. If this were not true you would be miscast. But how many attributes and mannerisms that you used were your own and had no relation to the character? These you must eliminate. What qualities should the character have which you do not possess? These you must develop.

Learning to move around the stage with grace and economy of movement is a fundamental part of every actor's training. Since these techniques are largely mechanical, it is suggested that you learn them in connection with each acting project, concentrating only on those which are required for your particular scene. Chapter 9, Technique, should be referred to constantly. For your Modern Scene you will need particularly to study and practice exits and entrances, sitting and rising, crossing, countering, opening and closing doors, and handling personal props.

Try creating and experimenting with bits of business and a variety of movements. Action makes a scene more interesting. During these early rehearsals, in order to gain ease and freedom on the stage, use an excess of movement and eliminate some later. You must, of course, have a reason, or motive, for everything that you do; therefore you will finally retain only such action and business as will make either the story or the character more clear to the audience.

Although the need for movement and action is being stressed, you are reminded that there are occasions for inactivity. An actor who can sit or stand completely quiet, but at the same time appear alive and interested, is said to exhibit **artistic repose.** This has been humorously called "the gentle art of doing nothing." It is indeed an art, the result of one's giving sympathetic attention to the action on the stage while presenting an outward appearance of calm.

Of particular importance is this repose when you are without lines to speak. Keeping in character without the aid of dialogue is primarily a matter of *thinking* in character, and this is the result of *listening* in character. "Nine-tenths of good acting is good listening" is an axiom often quoted in the theatre. In order to be as vital without speeches as you are with them you must plan how to be effective every second you are on the stage. Such planning calls for all the creative skill that an actor possesses. Responses should be controlled, however, and should never take the attention of the audience away from the character who is the center of interest.

Read through your speeches again, thinking the answers of your partner. Try different ways of reading the lines so as best to bring out the meaning. Paraphrase if you like, using your own words, in order to achieve a natural expression. Keep working from the feeling of the drive that makes your character act as he does, and try to grow in the power to reveal his thoughts and feelings simply and sincerely. From your analysis of the work of other actors, you will learn the meaning of dramatic effectiveness and the uses of both exaggeration and restraint. And after you have torn a scene apart in interpretation and analysis always put it back together again, letting thought and emotion dominate. Repeat the scene at once in its entirety to regain the feeling of unity.

3 **Repeat Walk-Through—Think-Through** Keep repeating this sequence as you rehearse the scene, discarding your script as early as possible. Ad lib where you do not have the speeches completely memorized, and always synchronize movement, business, and lines as you memorize in action. Place major emphasis on the succession of ideas and emotions, but keep going back to the script for more exact words after each practice of ad libbing. Not only do you owe the playwright the respect shown by your speaking his lines as he wrote them, but you have a further obligation to give your fellow actors the exact cues for their speeches. Finally, of course, all lines should be learned *verbatim,* word for word. If you have understood your character and his relationship to the scene, his thoughts, and his purposes, memorization will not be difficult; it will just happen as a result of much rehearsal. And never forget that *there is no substitute for rehearsal.*

In the case of a modern play that depends for much of its timeliness upon being up-to-the-minute in slang or in reference to current music and dances, it may be advisable to change certain words. But to change sentences just because you find them difficult is as inexcusable as it would be for a musician to change or omit a difficult run in a musical selection. It should be remembered that the speeches are those of the character, not the actor. If you develop the bad habit of changing words to fit your own form of expression, in time all your speeches will sound alike regardless of what script you are using. Naturally the playwright should be a sufficiently good writer to make it imperative for you to follow him exactly. If he is not, and the play can really be improved by rewriting, discard it and use something so well written that it is a challenge and an inspiration. For, although every good actor is, to some degree, a playwright, he should never usurp the author's place.

After a number of walk-throughs, when you feel that you are listening, thinking, and responding in character, you should turn your attention to **projection**. While in this early training it is better not to be too concerned with projection, at the same time you must recognize it as part of your acting technique. All that you have done up to this point is of little value unless it will carry to the far corners of the theatre and bring the response that you desire. For the reaction of the audience is your final test. What they get from your portrayal is what you have projected.

How can you project a character? By believing what you are saying; by being heard and understood; by being able to reveal, through voice and body, what the character is thinking and feeling, you will be able to bring a conviction of reality to your audience. And somehow (perhaps this is part of the magic of the theatre) it is possible through complete sincerity and personal magnetism to reach out over the footlights and carry the audience along on the flood of your emotions.

As you continue your rehearsals keep checking your scene for the following: Is my work marked by sincerity and simplicity? Am I observing artistic economy? Do I have variety and contrast in my speeches, actions, moods, responses? Are all of these intelligently motivated? Am I building to a climax? Am I projecting all of this with vitality?

4 **Follow-Through** After walking through and thinking through your part a great number of times, you are ready for the last step in your rehearsal routine; that is, playing the role as though there were an audience. In other words, the part is "made"; it is now to be "played." These are your full-dress rehearsals, and they should be as nearly like performances as it is possible to make them. There should be no stopping, and the show should be accurately timed. Obviously there should be several such rehearsals.

## ☆☆☆ PLAYING THE PART

With rehearsals over, you are now ready to play the show. ON STAGE, EVERYONE!

If you are presenting a scene from a three-act play, an introduction should be given telling enough of the story to make your scene intelligible. The introduction should contain these pertinent facts:

1. Name of the play and author
2. Setting and time

   (A useful device in the case of things impossible to reproduce on the small classroom stage is to say, "You are to imagine—" then include anything from the Dauphin's elegant throne room in *The Lark* to the grave that occupies the center of the stage in the scene from *Hamlet*. Audiences are always ready to imagine if you are definite enough.)
3. Characters and actors portraying them
4. The story up to the time of the scene, but nothing about the scene itself. (See *Holiday*, page 388.)

Before you make your first entrance, take some time to get into character, to give yourself up to his mood, mannerisms, and ways of thinking. This is the same as the warming-up process of the singer or athlete, neither of whom would think of going into action cold. You will do this every time you are about to begin a rehearsal or step onto the stage. If at this moment you are attacked by a case of stage fright, do not be alarmed. This invariably happens, even to experienced actors. Far from being a disaster, it usually means that through the stimulation and excitement which accompanies stage fright you will probably give a much more inspired performance than you would otherwise give. Take a few slow, deep breaths, forget about yourself, and become the character so fully that you have no time to think of anything else. Do not go over your lines; be relaxed but alert, and ready to enter on time.

At last you hear the magic word CURTAIN—and you are on! Now all your weeks of rehearsal will be rewarded. If you have been thorough in your early preparation, your subconscious mind and your muscular memory will execute the technical business, the lines, and the movement, so that you can forget almost everything except giving dramatic reality to your character. Although you, the actor, are always consciously in control of the character, you may be said, quite literally, to be living the role. From the moment you step onto the stage your one concern is to live with the other characters in the scene. Your first cue comes and your words say themselves. There is a spontaneous surge of emotion similar to that first outburst during the earliest rehearsals, only this time you are controlled and confident with the assurance of being in character. There is a natural freshness about the way in which your speeches are pouring forth as if for the first time. The excitement of the audience response gives an added spur to your reactions, and the scene takes on new meaning as you see it through the eyes of others for the first time.

Applause is ringing from somewhere. . . . When did the curtain go down? Suddenly you realize that the scene is over. You are elated and thrilled. Because the character was a person with whom you are familiar, you undoubtedly have every reason to be happy over the success of your performance. Perhaps you have played only a ten-minute scene, on a small stage, with a simple set, but for that space of time you have been another person; you have projected a characterization to an appreciative audience; you have been an actor!

## ☆☆☆ CRITICISM (EVALUATION)

In your training it is important, as in all growth and learning, to have repeated periods of performance followed by evaluation. The **critique** period is valuable not only to the performers but to those who participate as audience members, for through discussion all are learning to determine values. It is essential that comments be sincere, frank, and constructive. You must be told of your achievements and your needs. The two are equally important. The former give a sound basis on which to continue; the latter show on what phases to concentrate most work. At first *self*-criticism is possible to a limited degree only; one is inclined to be either too severe in self-condemnation, which destroys self-confidence, or else too satisfied and conceited, thereby losing perspective. Therefore you must rely quite largely upon the reports of others, especially during this early period.

Keep an open mind and weigh carefully all the advice and criticism given, but in the final analysis you must make your own decision as to what is true for you. Remember that your classmates, like you, are just beginning to learn the fine points of acting and do not have the knowledge and background that a more experienced person, such as your director, possesses. Nevertheless, because they are representative of the general untrained audience in the professional theatre, their criticisms are valuable.

As long as you are working in the theatre honest criticism is necessary to your growth, since in losing one set of bad habits you will acquire others. You will tend to repeat mannerisms and develop annoying speech patterns of which you are totally unaware. Rapid and continued progress can be made only if you have the benefit of fine criticism and will act upon it.

In your first performance the audience was particularly interested in whether or not the characterization was believable. In terms of your acting training, this is of greatest importance and should be the first point considered in every discussion. Possibly you were told that you could not be heard when you thought you were shouting, or that you turned so far away from the audience that your facial expressions could not be seen. These are usual first criticisms. One of the great advantages of beginning your training in a small room on a small stage is that you do not have to be greatly concerned about voice projection. That is particularly fortunate in this early period when there are so many things to learn and when you should be devoting most of your energies to character creation. If for even a few seconds the audience was convinced of the reality of your character, you have accomplished much in your first appearance on the stage. The highest compliment that you can receive is this: "You were convincing."

Although you learned much in rehearsal, the experience of playing should bring into sharp focus many of the ideas which before were hazy. Sudden, unexpected laughter at some point may cause you to re-examine your interpretation and change it slightly. The need of a longer pause here, a heightening of accent there, a pointing up of some bit of business or of a line which did not receive the desired response—these are the fine points that the experienced actor learns from his audience. These he can correct and will recall and use in developing his next role.

All audiences are different and from each you learn something new. They laugh at different places. Some grasp certain ideas more quickly than others. Some are warm and responsive, playing the scene with you; others are indifferent and undemonstrative. But whatever their reaction, always be a *steady* player. That is, play your show as you rehearsed it; do not let the audience run away with you. Good actors lead their audiences; they do not follow them. Many a beginning actor has repeated or added unrehearsed business because the audience became hilarious over something he did. This is no more legitimate than for the clarinetist in the orchestra to add a cadenza in the middle of the Overture just because, on the spur of the moment, he feels like it. If more actors realized that the exactness that is essential to the success of a musician is equally imperative in stage work, better shows would result. It would mean infinitely more detailed planning and rehearsal than go into most productions.

Being a steady player also means that you will not let a cold audience so deflate you that you cannot do your best. Provide your own motor power, have confidence in the worth of what you are doing, and always play to the utmost of your ability. Often a quiet audience is more understanding and appreciative than one that responds noisily. When watching a play in the theatre, sometimes take your attention from the stage and note the reactions of the people around you. You will learn much about what is transferable from stage to audience.

After you have worked on the criticisms that the class has given you, it would be ideal if you could present your scene again to the same group. Since the class schedule will probably not allow time for repeat performances, some students may wish to organize performance sessions outside of class time in which to perfect their scenes and to gain additional confidence and ease on the stage.

As the other scenes are presented you will want to add your criticisms to those of the other class members. Because criticism implies the ability to detect strength as well as weakness, your skill in recognizing both marks you as an intelligent reviewer. So form the habit of mentioning the good points first to build the self-confidence of the actor. Enter spiritedly into the discussions. Whether you agree or disagree with what others think is not important. But it is important that you honestly believe what you say and know why you believe it, and that you think and contribute constructive ideas.

#### CRITIQUE OUTLINE

In general, these are the points for you to consider in discussing each scene or play; but give greatest attention to the acting.

1. THE PLAY — What did it say? Was it well said? Was it worth saying?
2. THE PERFORMANCE — Was it convincing? Did it show teamwork? Did it build to a climax?
3. THE ACTING — Analyze each actor.
   Was his characterization complete, true to human nature, and believable?
   Mention points "well done" and "needs to improve" on each of the following:
   a. Body—characterization, movement, business, costume, make-up
   b. Voice—quality, distinctness, interpretation, projection
   c. Emotion—definite mood sustained, true reactions
   d. Technique—effective use of stage rules
4. THE PRODUCTION — Staging.
   a. Set—did it create the desired atmosphere for the play? Did it give maximum help to the actors?
   b. Lighting*—did it provide adequate visibility? Did it heighten the mood?
   c. Mechanics—were curtains, sound effects, and off-stage noises well handled?

* Omit discussion until the production of the one-act play.

5. THE AUDIENCE

a. What degree of interest and response was shown?

b. Were the responses consistent with the aim? (Page 9.)

All criticism should, of course, be given in a kindly, helpful spirit. It is better to say that certain things "need improving" than that they are "bad." Try to be as objective as the umpire who announces that the ballplayer is "out on first" because he honestly believes him to be. When the next scenes are given, note if the actor is improving. Be glad to tell him so. Everyone likes to know that he has done something well; but be sincere, don't gush. Cultivate, too, the admirable trait of humility in offering suggestions, as well as the attitude of the eternal student—seeking always to learn but never to impress others with his knowledge. Learn to distinguish between the acting and the production. Train yourself to see more and to hear more in every performance. Review all the instructions you have received in this course and use them in making your evaluations.

At the time of performance you will simply jot down ideas as they occur to you. Then for your written critiques add more to these first impressions as you think through the scenes again.

A good form for your written critique appears on the opposite page.

As you continue your work in the theatre, you will realize the increasing importance of being able intelligently to appraise performances and individual acting. In fact, this provides almost your only source of instruction. You will be aided in developing this critical faculty by reading the reviews of trained and reliable dramatic critics. Such reviews are found in the better magazines and in some newspapers. Who is the best critic whose reviews you can read? Make your own evaluation of the next professional play or good movie you see and then compare it with his. Do not accept every criticism at its face value, but use it as something with which to compare your own thinking. Each individual has a right to his own opinions, and no two

**CRITIQUE NOTES**

| WELL DONE | *Holiday* | NEEDS TO IMPROVE |
|---|---|---|
| good stage presence<br>seemed natural & poised<br>understood character<br>quite convincing<br>fairly good interpretation of lines<br>excellent pick-up of cues | Julia—<br><br>Patty Elton | voice—needs volume & richness<br>mispronounced "just"<br>listening<br>responses<br>had unmotivated gestures |
| good deep voice<br>engaging smile<br>suggested older man<br>good responses<br>had the spirit of joking | Johnny—<br><br>Bill Heath | coordination and ease in movement<br>assurance<br>broke character once<br>enunciation—especially final consonants<br>slurred "how do you do" |
| good contrast to Julia<br>effective entrance<br>clear speech & good voice quality<br>listened intelligently<br>gay spirit | Linda—<br><br>Beth Rowan | vitality in movement<br>posture<br>awkward handling of props<br>looked at floor sometimes<br>slow in topping speeches |

THE SCENE OR PLAY AS A WHOLE

Well-written play—amusing incident, distinctive characters, interesting dialogue. An entertaining comedy scene.
Good teamwork but didn't build strongly to the end.
Showed rehearsal—general movement good but individual business not well worked out.
Set adequate for action and business.
Curtain closing slow.
Audience interested and responsive—seemed to enjoy it.

people see things exactly alike. In *The Clocks of Gnoster Town* Edward Rowland Sill says:

> If ten think alike and you think alone,
> That never proves 'tis ten to one
> They are right, you wrong; for truth, you see,
> Is not a thing of majority.*

So have confidence in the value of your own opinions and at the same time realize that by keeping an open mind you will not only learn more but learn it faster.

## ☆☆☆ REVIEW OF AIMS

Before starting your new scene it might be well to review just what you are attempting to do in each of your characterizations.

### ESSENTIAL STEPS IN ACTING

PREPARATION
- An actor prepares for his role
  - by analyzing his script
  - by observing people and events
  - by experiencing through his trained senses

CREATION
- An actor creates a character
  - by developing an inner rightness
  - by acquiring convincing appearance and actions
  - by acquiring convincing speech

PROJECTION
- An actor projects ideas and emotions
  - through the medium of his body
  - through the medium of his voice
  - by means of such mechanical aids as technique, costume, make-up, and props

In this chapter the routines which you will follow in all the succeeding acting assignments have been established. You will need, therefore, to refer to it many times during the next few weeks. Keep

* Quoted by permission of Houghton Mifflin Company.

in mind the goals which you set up at the beginning of each project and check at the end to determine how nearly they have been reached.

#### CHAPTER HIGHLIGHTS

Understanding the part
Rehearsing the part
Playing the part
Criticism (evaluation)
Rehearsal and production routines

CALL BOARD

The CHARACTER-OPPOSITE SCENE gives you an opportunity

1. to analyze yourself.
2. to learn to understand types of people different from yourself.
3. to observe through Life Study the emotional responses of other people.
4. to give special attention to training your body as an instrument of dramatic expression.
5. to "stretch" your abilities by means of an especially difficult acting project.

# Two

## THE CHARACTER-OPPOSITE SCENE ☆☆☆

From the beginning, characterization has been stressed as being the most important function of the actor. However, in order to give you stage experience at once, it was suggested that you play a character much like yourself because in so doing you could become acquainted with the stage more readily. But with this second and more advanced role, your emphasis will be on the development of a much more complex characterization. This entails a greater understanding of what the individual actor brings to a role. Since no two people are alike, no two actors bring the same personality to the interpretation of a part. Each character in a play becomes a combination of the actor himself and the person created by the dramatist, for the art of acting is unique in that the actor is at the same time both the performer and the instrument of the performance. While being a distinct character as far as the audience is concerned, he must at all times, as himself, be watching and in control of that character. This dual role makes acting probably the most difficult and least tangible of all the arts.

In dramatic training the greatest emphasis is laid, quite naturally, upon the creation of the stage character. But at some point you need to concentrate on developing the other half of this dual personality—that is, on improving yourself. Trying to understand the thoughts and feelings of someone unlike yourself will make you a more sympathetic person. Not only will you be happier, you will also be a better actor.

So in preparing this more difficult acting project you will analyze not only the character, as you did for the Modern Scene, but also yourself. Using the following groups as a guide, make three complete and meaningful lists of your own characteristics.

#### PERSONAL ANALYSIS OUTLINE

First: those qualities which are definite assets: your best features in looks and disposition; your talents and abilities; all the *good* characteristics which make you a unique and pleasing individual. List them—all of them—and remember them in dark hours.

Second: those over which you have no control, which cannot be changed, which must, therefore, be accepted with good grace: perhaps your size, certain physical features, lack of ability along specific lines. Everyone has such negative qualities. List them completely just once, and then ignore them. Don't ever brood over them.

Third: those which are liabilities that can and should be changed: perhaps your voice, temper, lack of responsibility, annoying mannerisms. Don't just list these. Start right in to *do* something to replace them with characteristics that you can be proud to possess.

As a wise poet once said:

God grant me
The courage to change the things
I can change,
The serenity to accept the things
I can't change,
And the wisdom to know the difference.

—ANON

These ideas are only suggestive. Spend a good deal of time and thought on preparing the three lists. Refer to the character analysis outline on page 10 for additional help. Be as completely objective and honest as possible.

Some of the following statements may also stimulate your thinking. Answer Yes, No, or Sometimes.

1. I feel perfectly comfortable walking alone into a roomful of strangers.
2. I am nervous and self-conscious in front of a group of people.
3. I am very sensitive to what other people say and think about me.
4. I feel uncomfortable wearing new clothes for the first time.
5. I like to do or wear startling things so I'll be noticed.
6. I like to lead group activities and organize and direct others.
7. I seldom worry and feel quite capable of managing my affairs.
8. I prefer athletics to study.
9. I often have moody spells and prefer to be alone.
10. I usually do more listening than talking in a conversation with friends.
11. I am quick and impulsive and like excitement and noise.
12. I can laugh at my own boners.

Which of these statements suggests a very expressive, active person? Which are the reactions of a timid or thoughtful person? Which are those of a poised, well-adjusted person? Psychologists present a helpful way to classify these personality differences. They label the first group **extroverts,** the second group **introverts,** and the third group **normal.**

In bodily expression, extroverts have a tendency to be expansive, to use large, broad gestures radiating from a central body line and generally expressing positive emotions. Introverts, on the contrary, use small, cramped gestures, contracting toward a central body line, often the result of negative emotions. So-called normal persons present a poised, evenly balanced appearance and use gestures that are expressive but controlled. These are the bodily characteristics that you will wish to acquire first. (See Body, page 99.)

To be a happy, well-adjusted person is undoubtedly the desire of everyone. The normal person enjoys good health, is reasonably poised in all situations, and is well balanced emotionally. He is fairly objective about life's troubles and joys. He doesn't leap with hilarity at one moment and plunge into gloom at the slightest disappointment. However, everyone is a combination, in varying degrees, of both extremes. Not many are perpetual clowns, nor complete hermits. Everyone at some time feels free to express himself, at others is shy and retires to listen. Some of you will tend more to the extrovert side, others to the introvert. This should not be disturbing unless you are an extreme of either type. If everyone showed the same normal personality all the time there would be little color in our personal relationships; but this is not the case. The reason you recognize jealousy, hate, envy, admiration, love, tomfoolery, or anger in others is that you have experienced them all yourself and so can understand the moods and tempers of your friends.

After cataloguing some of your own traits, start on another Life Study trip to find people who exhibit the opposite ones. (See Chapter 5.) Since this assignment contributes to your growth as a person as well as an actor, you should play a character having those attributes which you need most to acquire for personal development. Remember, there is no one specific type that is your character-opposite; there are many, depending upon which of your physical, mental, or emotional traits you wish to contrast.

Because people are often judged by appearance, you may find it interesting first to analyze and contrast physical traits. Are you tall, ungainly, and lazy in movement? Find someone who is brisk, definite, and quick. What besides tempo makes his walk different from yours? Are you careless in your dress and grooming? Find someone who is neat, perhaps overly so. What particular things impress you as factors of his neatness? Are you apt to be unconcerned with the accuracy of your speech? Find someone who is a little too precise. What does he do that makes his speech sound stilted and formal?

Assuming the physical traits of a character will aid you in determining and portraying his emotional traits. Many actors make it an essential part of their earliest preparation of a role to take on these physical characteristics even to the point of wearing costume and make-up almost as soon as they have analyzed their character. They find that seeing themselves actually looking like the person tends to make them feel like him and definitely speeds up the creation of the inner character. Business and mannerisms seem to develop automatically under these circumstances. George Arliss, an English actor famous for the variety of his roles, said that unless, as he looked in the mirror before going on stage, he *looked* like the man he had visualized while studying the part, he could not play him with conviction.

As you study a great many people you will begin to realize to what extent bodily attitudes of standing and sitting, ways of walking, the tone of voice, and habits of speech give evidence of a person's thoughts and feelings. When you have the key to his emotions you have the key to his character. As a preparation for understanding the emotions of a character-opposite, try to find explanations for your own moods. What makes you happy, glum, sarcastic, shy, or bold? Recall experiences when you made well-defined responses which you can analyze. Then find someone making completely different responses to similar situations. Next, try to determine *why* he did so. Finding the reasons for responses is extremely difficult, but until you can discover them you do not know the character. This understanding of other people's emotions is not only fundamental in acting but invaluable in all human relationships.

When you have collected sufficient material through Life Study and have decided which of your own traits you wish to contrast, your next problem is to find appropriate acting material. Unless you are familiar with dramatic literature the selection of a suitable scene may not be easy. If at the bottom of your personal analysis outline (page 30) you will list the qualities you wish to find in a character, it will be possible for the director to assist you. Proper casting is essential to the success of this project, so it may be necessary to do considerable play reading in order to find exactly the right scene.

In general we might make the following suggestions:

A small, cocky, fast-talking man who is interested only in things that are quick-moving and noisy and who doesn't have much self-assurance in an unfamiliar situation should play a character who is poised, controlled, self-assured, and mature—such as Professor Shelby in *Blind Alley* or Drummond in *Inherit the Wind.*

A big, good-natured, ungainly man whose irresponsible actions demonstrate that he doesn't take life too seriously should play a character who carries himself well, has a sense of responsibility, commands respect and attention—such as Father in *Life With Father* or Colonel Purdy in *The Teahouse of the August Moon.*

An extremely dependable, overly serious, self-conscious girl who appears ill at ease in social situations should play a character who is gay, carefree, and uninhibited—such as Jean in *Stage Door* or Lady Teazle in *The School for Scandal.*

An easygoing, fun-loving girl who is usually inclined to let things drift and who seems to have no specific goal in life should play a character who is serious, strong, and a little hard—such as Mrs. Danvers in *Rebecca* or Mrs. Railton-Bell in *Separate Tables.*

No one will, of course, possess all these traits, but a complete listing of your own qualities and a similar listing of those of the character-opposite you are to play will aid you in developing your characterization. Check those which are yours alone, and hence must be submerged; those which are his alone, and therefore will demand the greatest development on your part.

Your Life Study should have convinced you that there are no set types, that within certain generalities of age, occupation, race, background, and like factors, all are distinct individuals. Suppose, for instance, you decide to play an old person. You would not immediately cloak yourself in the obvious mannerisms of old age—the faltering step, the hunched shoulders—for how many old people can you think of who have neither of these attributes? If you are to be true and convincing, you will study many people who are old to find the specific and universal evidences of long life. From your observations you may take a habit of speech from one, a mannerism from another, and peculiarities of several which can be consistently molded into the creation of a single person. Your playwright has given you a person with a distinct personality who happens to be old. In your portrayal you must bring out those traits that belong both to old age and to a separate individual.

Louis Calhern's portrayal of Justice Oliver Wendell Holmes in *The Magnificent Yankee* was a masterpiece of characterization, and the skill with which the actor gave evidence of advancing years was a superlative example of acting art. With the passing of time his body gradually took on more and more of the limitations of age. In the end he became so crippled that it was only through an almost superhuman effort that he was able to stand erect to greet his President. Through his shrewd observation of the revealing characteristics of age, as well as through his ability to project them, Mr. Calhern gave a living and unforgettable portrait of a great American.

What is the particular value of this assignment? It is to expand your acting range and to further your understanding of people, particularly those unlike yourself. Each time you attempt to play a different kind of role, you not only have added immeasurably to your abilities as an actor but have increased your knowledge of other people's motives and desires. This in the end means more intelligent and happier living for you. Just as you are richer for each new friend you earn and know, so you are richer for each new, varied characterization that you draw. So shake hands with this new stranger, your character-opposite! Know him as well as you know yourself. Know how he thinks, feels, looks, speaks, and acts.

In connection with this assignment, spend considerable time on the exercises in Chapter 6. If you have been practicing those which applied to your particular problems in posture and walk, suggested to you in the first week of the course, you are now ready for the **Daily Routine of Body Exercises** on page 95. Develop also some of the pantomimes for bodily training in characterization found in Chapter 6.

Follow the same routine that you did for the Modern Scene in approaching the development of this scene and characterization:

A. Prepare
   1. Read and analyze the play
   2. Analyze and create the character
   3. Work with a different partner
   4. Select a script that is appropriate for both partners
   5. Establish your setting
B. Rehearse
   1. Walk-through
   2. Think-through
   3. Repeat Walk-through and Think-through
   4. Follow-through
C. Play
   1. Introduction
   2. Production
   3. Critiques

It will take longer to develop this character, for it is much more difficult; therefore, plan more rehearsals than you had last time. You may wish to add more in the way of costume and setting; however, use only what is absolutely essential for your characterization, since that is your main objective and should occupy most of your time and thought.

You may, on the day of production, find that you have reverted to some of your own mannerisms instead of the ones you rehearsed. This often happens under the stress of performance. It means that you have not spent as much time in preparation as was necessary. Good actors often work on a role for a year and sometimes longer. But since it is advisable for a young actor to try a variety of roles early in his training, the time for this second project must necessarily be short. Perhaps you feel that you have done your best work to date in this scene. Often this indicates that you have a natural talent for playing character parts. If, however, you feel that you did not reach the goal you set for yourself, do not be discouraged, for this is an assignment that would tax the skill of many an experienced actor. Whatever the results, you undoubtedly felt more at ease on the stage and found it easier to stay in character than when you appeared the first time. Evidence of the accuracy of your Life Study observations, greater ease in stage movement, and a more expressive body should have been apparent in this performance. Listen carefully to all the criticisms of your work. Profit by your own and others' achievements and mistakes. Take pride in the fact that you are improving, and look forward with confidence to your next role.

#### CHAPTER HIGHLIGHTS

- Personal analysis
    - Desirable characteristics—to be retained
    - Characteristics that cannot be changed
    - Undesirable characteristics—to be changed to desirable ones
- Analysis of character types
- Emphasis on body training

# CALL BOARD

The SHAKESPEAREAN SCENE gives you an opportunity

1. to portray complete and well-drawn characters.
2. to increase your knowledge and appreciation of the finest dramatic literature.
3. to understand another age, the background of your own culture.
4. to create original business and movement, since none are indicated in the script.
5. to give special attention to training your voice as an instrument of dramatic expression.
6. to learn about period costumes and how to use them effectively.
7. to learn a distinct style of movement, manners, and customs.
8. to learn a unique type of staging peculiar to the period.

# Three

## THE SHAKESPEAREAN SCENE ☆☆☆

The finished product can never be any better than the material from which it is made. You would not expect to do fine embroidery on a piece of burlap or make a polished, inlaid table from the wood of a packing box. Nor can you do your finest acting in an inferior play. Since Shakespeare is the greatest playwright who has written in English you will, of course, want to try to interpret at least one of his well-drawn characters and to learn a little of what makes him great.

Do not, however, approach this assignment with awe and reverence. If you play a comedy scene you should have a rollicking good time. Broad exaggerated gestures and often even horseplay are needed to interpret many of Shakespeare's comedy characters. Remember that he wrote for the groundlings (those of the lower classes who stood on the ground near the stage), who loved his plays, as well as for the educated people of his time. If you play a tragedy you should have a genuine emotional experience, for Shakespeare created real people with intense emotions—robust people who lived life vitally and fully.

So real and universal are Shakespeare's characters that you could find their modern counterparts on your next Life Study trip if you were sufficiently discerning. The soldier pacing the ramparts of Elsinore in *Hamlet* has, no doubt, the same feelings about his job as the young man doing sentry duty today. Surely the Portia and Nerissa scene in *The Merchant of Venice* is familiar to every present-day schoolgirl. For who has not, at some time, enumerated the virtues and failings of all the young men she knows, to the amusement of her best friend?

As was customary in his time, Shakespeare used the same plots that were used by other writers—few of them were original. But his unique treatment of these time-worn tales made them seem new and unusual. His real genius, however, is constantly revealed in his character delineation. In the completeness of his many-faceted characters he offers actors unparalleled inspiration and challenge and has called for their best and most earnest efforts for three and a half centuries.

Logan Pearsall Smith enlarges upon this idea in his delightful book, *On Reading Shakespeare*:

> It seems safe to say that Shakespeare's characters were the result of observation, for they possess that convincing quality of characters drawn from life . . . Shakespeare's evident love of his characters, his delight that they should be exactly what they are, give warmth to the portrayal of their existence which helps them to exist in our imaginations, also. This habit of falling in love with his characters is one of the things which gave Shakespeare his power of identifying himself with them, of placing himself, as it were, in their skins and participating in all their thoughts and feelings.*

Something of Shakespeare's own power of thinking himself into the thoughts of others will be required in your interpretation of Shakespearean scenes. Consequently, you should first think yourselves back into the Elizabethan period and saturate yourselves with the flavor of Old England. Read the section in Chapter 8 that deals with Shakespeare's England. Read everything you can that will give you an understanding of Shakespearean drama, the theatre, the stage, the costumes, and the presentations.

Since you cannot give out what you have not taken in, it will require considerable study and cooperative group effort to piece together an

* Logan Pearsall Smith, *On Reading Shakespeare*. Harcourt, Brace and Company, Inc. Copyright 1933.

accurate picture of the England of Elizabeth's day. It is suggested, therefore, that you work in groups of three or four, and that your group select one of the following topics and collect research material to share with the rest of the class so that all may have a rich common background.

### ELIZABETHAN LIFE

1. ENGLAND rulers, writers, other notable people; politics, historical events, economics; spirit of nationalism, influence of medieval life, the Renaissance.
2. LONDON size, appearance, buildings, customs. (pictures, maps)
3. THE AUDIENCE classes, demands, specialties, participation, reactions.
4. THE THEATRES Globe, Hope, Blackfriars, Curtain, Fortune; location, size, development from innyard; acting areas, special effects, galleries, pit; admission prices, the flag, time of performances.
5. THE ACTING style: asides, soliloquies, duels, dances, songs, puns; poetic demands in speech and movement; women's roles.
6. THE ACTORS famous men: Richard Tarleton, William Kemp, Edward Alleyn, Richard Burbage, William Shakespeare, and others; famous acting companies: Lord Chamberlain's, The King's Men, Henslow's Company, Boys' Company; the children players, boy players.
7. COSTUME general outline, general characteristics, specific costume peculiarities of the period, accessories; convention of acting in contemporary dress.
8. WILLIAM SHAKESPEARE birth, family, education, Stratford days, marriage, career; patronage of the Earl of Southampton; London days, coat of arms, burial place.
9. SHAKESPEARE'S PLAYS comedies, tragedies, histories: number, titles, sources of ideas and plots; great characterizations; the First Folio.
10. MODERN SHAKESPEAREAN PRODUCTIONS AND ACTORS Stratford-on-Avon; Stratford, Connecticut; Stratford, Ontario; Ralph Richardson, John Gielgud, Michael Redgrave, Tyrone Guthrie, Laurence Olivier, Peggy Ashcroft, Judith Anderson, Margaret Webster, and others. Motion pictures: *Hamlet, Henry V, Macbeth, Romeo and Juliet, Henry VIII, Julius Caesar, Richard II, Richard III.*

After the reports have been given, you should have a fairly good picture of Shakespeare's time. Now you are ready to select your scene and begin rehearsals. (See Chapters 11 and 13.)

*Line drawing by Irwin Smith*
*of John Cranford Adams' Globe Playhouse Model*

You will find that it requires a richer, bigger voice to give Shakespearean lines than it does for ordinary speech, so extra attention should be devoted to voice training in connection with this unit. After an inventory of your voice needs (page 112) select the exercises that apply particularly to you. Add to these drills on "A Daily Routine for Speech Practice," on page 118, and practice other exercises for speech improvement found in Chapter 7 to gain skill in interpretive techniques. You will receive further help if you can hear some fine recordings of Shakespearean selections made by famous actors and actresses of our time. It will be particularly interesting to contrast some of the famous soliloquies, such as John Gielgud's and John Barrymore's "O, what a rogue and peasant slave am I," or hear other interpretations of *Hamlet* by Laurence Olivier and Maurice Evans.

It will be necessary to do considerable research on the meaning of the lines. Shakespeare "let his characters talk themselves alive," and you must understand his words if you are to transform yourself successfully into the person speaking them. His use of an obsolete word is often confusing. You will need to use a dictionary and a glossary of Shakespearean terms (see page 354) for those whose meaning is not absolutely clear to you. Shakespeare had an unusually large vocabulary even for a writer. He played with words; he used them with great skill to suggest motion, sounds, and color. He enriched this appeal to the senses by the use of vivid imagery which you must visualize if you are to understand your scene.

Although the idea in each speech is embroidered in poetry and is highly imaginative, if you emphasize the central thought you will discover the natural breaks in the long passages and the pauses to sustain. Of all types of poetry Shakespeare's blank verse is the most like ordinary speech. If you memorize exactly and read the lines with understanding, the poetic rhythm will take care of itself. Take plenty of time, but also keep the speeches moving. Bear in mind that you are still simply talking to someone, and that while giving the words full value you must be natural and convincing. That is the secret of such fine actors as John Gielgud, Ralph Richardson, Laurence Olivier, and Maurice Evans. Undoubtedly the best advice that can be given to you was written long ago by Shakespeare himself in Hamlet's advice to the Players before their performance at the court. (*Hamlet*, III, 2.)

HAMLET. Speak the speech, I pray you, as I pronounced it to you, trippingly on the tongue; but if you mouth it, as many of your players do, I had as lief the town-crier spoke my lines. Nor do not saw the air too much with your hand, thus; but use all gently: for in the very torrent, tempest, and (as I may say) whirlwind of passion, you must acquire and beget a temperance, that may give it smoothness. O! it offends me to the soul, to hear a robustious, periwig-pated fellow tear a passion to tatters, to very rags, to split the ears of the groundlings; who, for the most part, are capable of nothing but inexplicable dumb shows, and noise: I would have such a fellow whipped for o'er-doing Termagant; it out-herods Herod; pray you avoid it.

Be not too tame neither, but let your own discretion be your tutor: suit the action to the word, the word to the action, with this special observance, that you o'erstep not the modesty of nature; for anything so overdone is from the purpose of playing, whose end, both at the first, and now, was, and is, to hold, as 'twere the mirror up to nature; to show virtue her own feature, scorn her own image, and the very age and body of the time, his form and pressure. Now this overdone, or come tardy off, though it make the unskillful laugh, cannot but make the judicious grieve; the censure of the which one must, in your allowance, o'erweigh a whole theatre of others. O! there be players, that I have seen play, and heard others praise,—and that highly, not to speak it profanely,—that neither having the accent of Christians, nor the gait of Christian, pagan, nor man, have so strutted, and bellowed, that I have thought some of nature's journeymen had made men, and not made them well, they imitated humanity so abominably.

PLAYER. I hope, we have reformed that indifferently with us.

HAMLET. O! reform it altogether. And let those that play your clowns, speak no more than is set down for them: for there be of them, that will themselves laugh, to set on some quantity of barren spectators to laugh too; though in the meantime some necessary question of the play be then to be considered: that's villainous, and shows a most pitiful ambition in the fool that uses it.

Elizabethan Costumes

Since Shakespeare gives no direct instructions for reactions, for business or movement, you must watch for those that are indicated in your partner's speeches as well as in your own. In *Othello* (v, 2), for example, Desdemona says, "Alas! why gnaw you so your nether lip?" which indicates what Othello was doing. In *Romeo and Juliet* (I, 5) the Nurse says, "My back! o' t' other side," for Juliet is rubbing the Nurse's back. Definite props are also referred to in the same scene when the Nurse says, "What, have you dined at home?" for she sees evidence of food having been served. In *The Taming of the Shrew* (II, 1) Petruchio says, "In sooth, you 'scape not so," for Katharine has tried to leave. The script abounds in such hints of movement, business, and props. Be sure to find them all.

The distinctive carriage and posture of the Elizabethans was determined largely by the clothes they wore, so an understanding of the costumes of the period is necessary in order for you to plan your movements. Your problem will be to decide upon an appropriate costume, make or improvise it, and then learn to wear it with the same ease and assurance with which you wear your own modern clothes. (Page 182.) You will need to learn the Shakespearean manner of bowing, which men frequently used upon making either an entrance or an exit, and the technique of the curtsy which was executed by women. (Pages 167-168.)

The Elizabethan stage was unique in its design. With the extended platform, or forestage, which became any environment described in the speeches, the permanent inner stage, windows, and doors provided many combinations for enacting scenes. You may wish to play a street scene in front of the curtain on the stage apron, or use a U-shaped area with the audience sitting on three sides of the actors, duplicating the intimacy with which the players at the Globe acted. The staging should be planned to give the actors the greatest possible freedom of movement, whether the conventional set or a different arrangement of acting space is used. However, the stage setting, business, gestures, and costumes are merely accessories designed to heighten your characterization; they can never be a substitute for your understanding of the mental and emotional processes of the character.

Follow in your rehearsals the same routine that you did for both the Modern Scene and the Character-Opposite Scene:

A. Prepare
B. Rehearse
C. Play

Once again, rehearsals are over and the day of production arrives. Since you are using the greatest acting literature in the English language, you should find that now you are giving your best performance. Your reach has been high, your possibilities unlimited. Perhaps it has been especially difficult to give your speeches with seeming spontaneity once you had memorized them, but by concentrating on the *ideas* in each speech you have been able to make them sound real. It has been a challenge to keep true to the manners of the period and to handle your costumes and props, but every minute has been an absorbingly happy one. For the first time, possibly, you have realized the importance of energy. The color and excitement of Shakespearean scenes make great demands upon your physical vitality. Imagine playing with a Shakespearean troupe on a year's run! An actor must have vigor and reserve energy; yes, he must have physical fitness, and to have it he must keep in training as rigorously as the athlete does. Proper food, rest, and exercise will necessarily be a part of your daily dramatic routine.

The criticisms, as usual, will be first about your characterization, but your audience will note particularly voice quality and expression as well. By this time you should have made considerable improvement in enunciation and interpretation. You will be evaluated on your ability to project the meaning of the lines, to use the business indicated in the speeches, to create period movement, and to handle a suitable costume.

It has probably taken a great deal more work to prepare this assignment than it did to prepare either of the other two, but you have the great satisfaction of knowing that your time was well spent. One of the fascinating things about working with a Shakespearean script is that you can go right on working for years without exhausting its possibilities.

Through the introductions to the scenes, as given by your fellow students, you should know the plots of several plays as well as their leading characters. Now you may look forward to your next production, the complete one-act play, in which you can demonstrate all that you have learned and mastered to date.

### CHAPTER HIGHLIGHTS

Shakespeare's characters—modern and universal
Life in Elizabethan England
Interpretation of speeches
Creation of business and movement
Emphasis on voice training

## CALL BOARD

The ONE-ACT PLAY gives you an opportunity

1. to combine in a finished production all the knowledge and skill you have acquired.
2. to achieve the feeling of unity and completion in perfecting a whole play.
3. to develop greater teamwork in working with larger casts.
4. to assume more responsibility in managing, staging, and handling props, costumes, and sound effects.
5. to develop skill in organization and leadership.
6. to develop skill in play direction.
7. to prepare for work in a three-act play.

# Four

## THE ONE-ACT PLAY ☆☆☆

The **One-Act Play** is the last and most challenging acting assignment in the beginning drama course. Note the ways in which this differs from the three others you have just completed, and the particular contribution that it makes to your advancement.

Building a convincing characterization in single scenes was the main emphasis in each of the previous projects; at the same time one or two particular phases of acting were stressed. Although characterization is always your chief concern as an actor, in the **Modern Scene** the improvement of your own personality, in carriage, walk, poise, and naturalness on the stage, was an important part of the training. In the **Character-Opposite Scene** your ability to portray attitudes and emotions very different from your own was coupled with techniques to develop a more responsive body. In the **Shakespearean Scene** your study of period techniques of the Elizabethan Age, and costume management, was supplemented with special attention to the interpretation of lines and voice improvement. Now in the **One-Act Play** you can apply all that you have learned in presenting a finished production, with special emphasis on organization, teamwork, and responsibility. This unit should provide a rather adequate test of your theatre knowledge to date.

One of the greatest benefits you will derive from this project is the spirit of teamwork, both in acting and in production. Playing with a larger cast you will experience the lively give-and-take of a game where you are the center of interest one minute and in the background the next. Your previous training has been more of an individual affair, which, of course, comes first in logical sequence. But this is more like playing on the basketball squad or on the football team and having more than one opponent to deal with. Only by "playing your position" to the limit of your ability and resources can you help the "team" make the successful performance goal.

Your working approach to the one-act play will parallel that of the production procedures in a three-act play. The major difference will be that instead of separate departments handling the various staging responsibilities, the actors not only will be playing but also will be managing the show. For this reason, you will need to refer to Chapter 10, Play Production, and the section in Chapter 9 on Production Technique for technical information.

In the planning of a production there are several important steps. There are (1) the selection of the play, (2) the casting of characters, (3) the assignment of responsibilities, (4) the preparation of the prompt book, and (5) the scheduling of rehearsals. Inasmuch as the cast as a group is responsible for the finished production, the preliminary planning should be accomplished as a joint project with all working together in democratic fashion. One member of the group might act as secretary while you are organizing.

The play selected should be one in which everyone will enjoy working. (See one-act play list, page 342.) A play having not more than five or six characters is usually most satisfactory, since larger groups find it difficult to schedule rehearsals; moreover, a small stage is inadequate for the movement of many people. The characterizations should be stimulating to all members of the cast and, if possible, should offer parts which are quite different from those played previously.

As soon as you have decided upon your play you will need to order

*Painting by Norman Rockwell. Reprinted by permission of the artist and The Saturday Evening Post.*

CHARACTER TYPES: INTROVERT AND EXTROVERT

SET: LOST HORIZON *Eagle Rock High School, Los Angeles*

SET: SAINT JOAN *University of California, Los Angeles*

additional copies from the publisher. While awaiting the arrival of these you will have an opportunity to plan all the details of the production.

All production duties should be assigned to and agreed upon by a director, stage manager, prop manager, costume manager, sound and music manager, make-up manager, and business or publicity manager. The activities of all these managers must be coordinated and all plans should be included in the prompt book. The director will provide the leadership for the group as he guides the play through rehearsals. He should be especially interested in this phase of production and be willing to take the smallest role in order to devote more time to directorial duties.

Organizing the **prompt book** is one of the important techniques to be learned from this project. It is important because the production of a play is not a haphazard affair, but rather the result of organized planning, effective leadership, and coordinated responsibilities, without which there is chaos. The prompt book for a major production is compiled and kept by the director. It is a working handbook of all of the details connected with the play. (See page 199.) Although the prompt book which you will prepare will be greatly simplified, the general outlines are identical for all kinds of plays.

Additional "esprit de corps" may be given to the one-act play unit if each group works as a company, selecting a name and presenting their play under its banner.

### ORGANIZATION OF PRODUCTION DUTIES

*The Tea-Pot on the Rocks*—John Kirkpatrick (chapter 12)

| CHARACTER | ACTOR | DUTIES |
|---|---|---|
| May | Jean Baker | costumes, make-up |
| Daisy | Ruth Taylor | props |
| Mrs. Carstairs | Betty Randall | sound |
| Roy | John Cummings | publicity |
| Willie | Bob Murray | stage manager |
| Alec | Jack Hall | director |

I. Director

A. Supervise the preparation of the prompt book, which will contain

1. Cast of characters and staging responsibilities
2. Interpretation of the play—theme, mood, major conflict, climax
3. Style of production
4. Ground plan
5. Breakdown of play into scenes (page 57)
6. Rehearsal schedule (page 56)
7. Prop plot
8. Costume plot and costume sketches
9. Make-up plots
10. Cue sheets for curtain, sound, music, lights
11. Complete script with movement and business
12. Publicity management
13. Record of other details connected with production
14. Names, addresses, and phone numbers of entire cast

B. Supervise rehearsals

1. Conduct reading rehearsal (A), in which the play and character relationships are discussed and agreed upon.
2. Study the principles of movement and design; be responsible for unity, tempo, and projection.
3. Direct the following rehearsals: B, C, D, E, F, G (page 56).

II. Stage Manager

A. Draw the ground plan and make set sketch or model set if needed.
B. Set up the stage for rehearsals and production.
C. Supervise all backstage activity during rehearsals and production.
D. Hold the prompt book during rehearsals.
E. Be familiar with the movement and business of each character so that you can take an actor's place during rehearsal.
F. Make the cue sheet for curtain.

III. Prop Manager

A. Prepare for the set the prop plot, which lists all necessary props on stage and in the wings when the curtain rises.

B. Prepare the personal prop chart, which lists by character all props carried or handled by the actors.
C. Supervise the collection of necessary props and safe return of all borrowed items.
D. Supervise props used during rehearsals and productions.

IV. Costume Manager

A. Prepare the costume plot, do any necessary research on period costumes, and draw costume sketches for each character.
B. Coordinate the costume ensembles as to color and style.
C. Supervise the collection of costume articles, the making and pressing of costumes, and the safe return of all borrowed items.
D. Supervise the costume wardrobes during dress rehearsals and production. Establish and maintain clean, orderly dressing rooms.

V. Sound and Music Manager

A. Supervise the collection of sound-effect equipment.
B. Supervise the selection and collection of music effects:
    1. Music used to establish mood
    2. Music required in the script
C. Make the cue sheets for sound and music effects.
D. Operate the sound and music effects during rehearsals and production.
E. Be responsible for the safe return of all borrowed items.

VI. Make-up Manager

A. Design the make-up charts for each actor, specifying the exact materials used.
B. Acquire the necessary make-up materials.
C. Supervise the application of make-up.
D. Be responsible for the cleanliness of the make-up room and and for returning make-up supplies.

VII. Publicity Manager

A. Organize the development of publicity as to kind, amount, and time.
B. Make the poster and programs.
C. See that royalty is paid, if this is required.
D. Make necessary preparations if other classes or guests are to be invited.
E. Provide ushers, a host for invited guests, and an announcer for the production.

## SAMPLE CUE SHEETS AND PLOTS

I. Cue Sheets

A. Make separate cue sheets for each of the following: curtain, sound, music, lights.

B. Make cue sheets in the following form:

1. Typed with double spacing
2. Cue preceded by a half-page WARN
3. Action defined as to speed, duration, or volume

Example: a) curtain (fast)
b) phone bell (three times)
c) music (soft) *Serenade*—Schubert
d) lights (dim all very slowly)

The Tea-Pot on the Rocks

SOUND CUES

WARN - - I wouldn't marry him for anything on earth! (May)

CUE - - I DON'T WANT A FORTUNE. I WANT HARRY. (Daisy)

DOOR BELL JINGLES (once)

II. Costume Plot

A. List all articles of clothing worn by actors in each scene or act.

B. Follow this form:

| The Tea-Pot on the Rocks<br>COSTUME PLOT | |
|---|---|
| May Lovelace<br>(Jean Baker) | suit (very smart)<br>becoming hat<br>gloves<br>purse<br>high-heeled pumps |

Once these production details have been settled, only one organizational problem remains—the rehearsal schedule. You will note in the chart on page 57 that the one-act play *The Tea-Pot on the Rocks* has been divided into four sections and that rehearsals both in and outside of class have been planned. Most one-act plays will break into four or five sections of approximately equal length, usually by combinations of several scenes. (A scene, according to the French definition, is a section played by one group of actors. When a character leaves or another one enters you have a new scene.) This schedule provides for fifteen rehearsals in class and five outside of class, covering a period of three weeks. This should give adequate rehearsal time. Added to this will be the hours spent on home study, memorization, and the extra assigned duties. When your section is not called for rehearsal, you may study your lines or work with another actor who is not rehearsing.

Allowing one week for preparation and three weeks for rehearsing the play, designate the times and places for all outside rehearsals and have each cast member copy the schedule. The breakdown of scenes and full run-through rehearsals should be so arranged that the play develops logically to maturity, with all sections equally well rehearsed. It is better to repeat a short scene several times at one rehearsal, and so more or less "set" the action, than to cover a great deal of the script in early rehearsals. The following form for *The Tea-Pot on the Rocks* may be used in the organization of the production details, assignments, rehearsal schedule, and kinds of rehearsal for your play. You will note that the letters A, B, C, D, E, F, and G refer to the kind of rehearsal to be held during a given period. This is explained in the following pages.

**REHEARSAL SCHEDULE**

| In Class | | Outside of Class | | | |
|---|---|---|---|---|---|
| Date | Section | Date | Hour | Place | Section |
| Mon. 12 | Reh A | | | | |
| Tue. 13 | Sec. 1—Reh B | | | homes | |
| Wed. 14 | Sec. 2—Reh B | | | of | |
| Thu. 15 | Sec. 3—Reh B | | | | Reh B |
| Fri. 16 | Sec. 4—Reh B | 16 | 7:00 to 9:30 | Daisy | (Entire) |
| Mon. 19 | Sec. 1 & 2—Reh C | | | | |
| Tue. 20 | Sec. 3 & 4—Reh C | | | | |
| Wed. 21 | Sec. 1 & 2—Reh C | | | | |
| Thu. 22 | Sec. 3 & 4—Reh C | 22 | 7:00 | May | Reh D |
| Fri. 23 | Reh E | 23 | 7:00 | Roy | Reh D & E |
| Mon. 26 | Reh D | | | | |
| Tue. 27 | Reh E | | | | |
| Wed. 28 | Reh D | 28 | 7:00 | Willie | Reh F |
| Thu. 29 | Reh F | | | | |
| Fri. 30 | Reh G | 30 | 7:00 | Alec | Reh G |

A. Reading rehearsal
B. Movement and business rehearsal (blocking)
C. Developing rehearsal
D. Run-through rehearsal
E. Polishing rehearsal
F. Technical rehearsal
G. Dress rehearsal

**BREAKDOWN OF SCENES**

| SECTIONS | PAGES | |
|---|---|---|
| 1 | 305–309 | May, Daisy, |
| 2 | 310–312 | May, Daisy, Roy |
| | 313 | May, Roy |
| | 314 | May, Roy, Daisy |
| | 315 | May, Roy, Daisy, Carstairs |
| 3 | 316–317 | May, Roy, Daisy |
| | 318 | May, Roy, Daisy, Carstairs |
| | 318–319 | Roy, Daisy |
| | 320–321 | Roy, Daisy, May |
| 4 | 321–322 | Roy, Daisy, May, Willie |
| | 323–324 | Roy, Daisy, May, Carstairs |
| | 324–325 | Roy, Daisy, May, Alec |
| | 325–326 | Daisy, May |
| | 326–327 | May, Roy |

Leaving your production duties for the time being, you are now ready to begin rehearsals of the play as actors. Your first rehearsal is called a **reading rehearsal** (A), at which time the entire play is read and analyzed. Find the theme, the major and minor conflicts, the emotional moods and tempos of the various scenes, and the climax. Who is the protagonist, who the antagonist? What specific contribution does each character make to the plot? What are the elements of suspense and how will you create them? What is the general atmosphere? What is the dramatic style of the play? How will you stage it? What do you want your audience to get from your production? This analysis should be written and incorporated into the prompt book for frequent reference.

When the interpretation of the play has been established, each actor is ready to develop his own characterization. This character analysis should include a statement of your relationship to everyone in the play. Even though playing a so-called *straight* role you must make this new character a completely different individual. It is a great temptation for a beginning actor to repeat some of the traits of a previous character, especially if they have proved effective. You will retard your growth if you do this. Be especially careful to eliminate any speech peculiarities. In working with a greater number of actors you will find it necessary to make quicker and more varied emotional responses than ever before. Movement will be more complicated; stage grouping and pictures will take on importance for the first time.

Following the reading rehearsal, you should devote the second day to the **movement and business rehearsal** (B) of the first section of the play. With an additional section covered each day, the entire play will have been rehearsed by the end of the first week. This should be climaxed by an evening rehearsal, at which time problems will be solved as they arise. The second week you may devote to further developing characterizations and business through **developing rehearsals** (C) and to "setting" what was worked out the first week, rehearsing half of the play during each class period. This should be followed by an evening **run-through rehearsal** (D). A run-through rehearsal is one in which the play is given with no stops or interruptions, the actors playing the show as best they can while the director takes notes for the discussion period that follows. Such rehearsals sharply point up the weaknesses and strengths of the performance. During the run-throughs of the third week, the play should develop unity, proper tempo and rhythm, and build to a strong climax.

**Polishing rehearsals** (E) should be held after each of the run-throughs to work on sections which showed particular need.

Actual or substitute props and all sound and musical effects that are essential to action should be used at every rehearsal. There should be a prompter at all rehearsals and performances, even though the cast is letter-perfect as to lines. For this production the prompter's duties may be assumed by an actor who is not playing the scene.

During the last week, two **technical rehearsals** (F) should be held, at which time costumes may be checked, all sound and musical effects rehearsed, and any other technical problems solved.

A **dress rehearsal** (G) or two, which should be as nearly like the actual performance as possible, should assure a good production. At the home dress rehearsal you might invite your parents to watch. You will learn much from their reactions and friendly criticism.

Again you are reminded that *there is no substitute for rehearsal,* and you are urged to spend as many hours as you may need to do a finished piece of work. Be as faithful in meeting your outside rehearsal assignments as you are in meeting those in class; be on time and have lines memorized quickly. Your ability to take part in a well-run self-rehearsal marks you as a serious student of the drama. A businesslike attitude, cooperative teamwork, and a happy spirit are absolutely essential to a successful production.

Four weeks of planning and rehearsal are now behind you and the big moment is at hand. CURTAIN! Playing with assurance now, you find it easy to move and respond to the other characters. Like a well-trained athletic team, all are working together toward a single goal—the success of the play! Actions and reactions, speeches, movement, business—all seem spontaneous and natural. Scene follows scene smoothly and rhythmically as the play moves steadily to its climax. Once more the curtain is down. Once more the applause of a satisfied audience, sweetest music to an actor's ears, rings out.

The criticisms should be unusually fresh and stimulating, since this is the first time the audience has had an opportunity to go deeply into a discussion of production. The merits of the play itself, the performance as a whole, the set, and the mechanics of production will all be evaluated as well as the individual acting. This time, instead of using the former method of written critiques, try writing a journalistic review of the plays, comparable to the newspaper or magazine reviews of current productions which you have been reading. In discussing the actor, pay particular attention to any marked improvement in his work. In comparing his previous appearances with this one designate his greatest achievement to date. You may wish to single out for special recognition the boy and girl who have made the greatest improvement since they entered the class.

The one-act play should be the most exciting presentation in which

you have taken part, for this really is a show in every sense of the word. More than that, it marks the completion of one small portion of your training. Now you can look back and see how far you have progressed as a person and as an actor since the first Modern Scene. The extent to which the "team" functioned as a unit, with each member making his finest contribution, determined the final success of your play. May each of you be able to say with conviction, "This is the best acting I have ever done."

At this point you are no doubt eager to continue your theatre activities. If there is no opportunity to join a group in your community you can start an acting company of your own, as many students, after one or two semesters of drama training in school, have done. You may play out-doors in a garden or patio, on a terrace, a porch, or a hillside. Indoors a large living-room, a basement, an attic, a garage, or a barn will serve. You may use the conventional stage; your front curtain may be made of gunny sacks, dyed flour sacks, or odd bits of material in a patchwork quilt design. Or you can use screens that are easily moved as a substitute for a front curtain and for masking. You may prefer to play in central staging style (see page 184) with the audience seated on all sides, which requires no curtain or masking. Floodlights can be improvised from large electric globes with tin dishpans as reflectors; spotlights from small globes in coffee cans.

Create a festival spirit by adding imaginative touches that will make all your shows gala occasions. If you want to give plays there is no obstacle that you cannot surmount provided you are resourceful and willing to work hard.

#### CHAPTER HIGHLIGHTS

Selection of play
Organization of production duties
Sample cue sheets and plots
Form for Rehearsal Schedule
Breakdown of scenes
Kinds of rehearsals
Your own acting company

# Part 2

## BASIC TRAINING

# Five

## SENSES AND EMOTIONS ☆☆☆

Wherever people gather you have a drama laboratory, for the primary source of material for your character creations comes from your study of people in life situations. Norman Rockwell, the famous painter of homespun American types, may be said to have a "seeing eye," whereas a writer of dialogue must have a "hearing ear." Mr. Rockwell observes the self-conscious smile, the worried frown, or the awkward stance, and through his rare gift portrays it for everyone to see and enjoy. The writer, on the other hand, catches the phrase, or the exact word, that does the same thing through language alone. The alert actor has both the seeing eye, which observes the cocky walk, or the drooping shoulders, or the trembling hand; and the hearing ear, which catches the happy lilt, or the fatigue, or the trace of a dialect. These are priceless and often subtle bits of human behavior which tell volumes about a person.

### ☆☆☆ CREATING THE INNER CHARACTER

**LIFE STUDY** A great awareness of every phase of the world about you, an awareness which as an actor you need, can be developed through Life Study. Not everyone uses his faculties to the fullest. Much in modern living conspires against it. Indeed, if one were not able to shut out much that occurs about him he might lose his mind. Your object, then, will be to train yourself to turn your concentrated attention on and off at will, as you do when you listen to the theme or melody in a piece of music, ignoring all the other sounds. This is an acquired and highly desirable skill which is developed only through continual practice and concentration.

As an actor you are interested primarily in people. Your ability to understand and interpret them will depend upon how keenly you have observed and analyzed them in various emotional situations. Do you constantly watch people in buses, in stores, on the street, at school? Do you study the people who attend a rally, a lecture, or a fire? An actor notices the way people use their hands, heads, eyes, arms, legs; their ways of walking, standing, and sitting. He learns to detect mannerisms of age and traits which occupations develop. As an actor you need consciously to observe individuals in a variety of situations, to be alert to voice qualities, speech patterns, and physical poses. The results of these observations will be seen in every character you play.

George Arliss, the great English actor, made immortal his daily observation of people in the story of his acting career, *Up the Years from Bloomsbury.*

> I cannot pass over this period—my boyhood—without some further reference to the British Museum, because during my entire life on the stage I have been drawing upon the characters that I met or observed during that time, and I'm doing so still. . . . The museum was a regular meeting place for a picturesque and fascinating literary fringe—men who got a hand-to-mouth existence with their pen and lived Heaven knows where . . . I had no idea then that I should ever use these characters on the stage, but they fascinated me and I used to steal into the Tavern like an alien spy and watch them from a corner seat, and without my being aware of it, they fell into a pocket of my memory. And afterward, when I went on the stage, I used to find them popping up and begging for reincarnation.*

* George Arliss, *Up the Years from Bloomsbury.* Little, Brown, and Company, Boston, 1928. By permission of the Estate of George Arliss, London, England.

In addition to his lifelong observation of people, an actor trains himself to be sensitive to sound and color, to atmospheres and moods and all the other sense impressions which enrich his most ordinary experiences. In watching a play he is conscious of voices, blending or in contrast; he notes the sets, costumes, lighting effects, and color schemes. At the same time he enjoys the story and the play as a whole.

**SENSE IMPRESSIONS** For the next minute listen intently to all the sounds, near and far, that you can hear. Jot them down and compare them with those recorded by fellow students. During a three-minute period in an ordinary classroom as many as forty sounds have been recorded, from the drone of a distant airplane to the rustle of leaves outside the window and the creak of a chair in the room. Can you distinguish and identify all the sounds you hear? The mechanic at the garage can usually tell what is the matter with your car by the sound of the engine. He has trained his sense of hearing to detect what is wrong. A doctor can often diagnose an ailment by observing the color of the patient's skin. The tea taster knows the difference between two kinds of tea and can tell where each was grown. The expert buyer can, by his sense of touch, discover the presence of a foreign substance in so-called 100% wool. Part of the training and work of a Federal Food and Drug inspector is to develop a sense of smell so that he can detect even a slight impurity that might be injurious to health. Each of these people represents an occupation which is an important part of our daily living and in each instance the acuteness of one of the senses is vital to the work.

What was your most vivid sense impression yesterday? Was it the smell of the breakfast bacon, or the sound of the rain on the roof as you awakened, or the luxurious feeling of a hot bath? Or was it the fresh cookies you ate after school, or the sunset on the lake? Not all your sense impressions will be pleasant, by any means, but you should train yourself to be aware of beauty and emphasize those things which will be happy memories. According to Sir James Barrie, the Scottish dramatist, "God gave us memories so we can have roses in December."

Where does any creative artist—the painter, the writer, the musician—get ideas for his work? From the record of his senses, of course. And if he sees or hears more than you do, remember it is because he has trained himself to do so. Have you ever walked in the country with a painter? He sees purple tints in the landscape where you see only green. Have you ever attended a symphony concert with a musician? He detects a lovely passage played by the oboe, where you hear only the total effect of all of the instruments. This does not detract from his enjoyment of the whole, but rather gives him added pleasure.

Much as you love drama at the present time, you may not make the theatre your profession. But if you have taken advantage of all the training which a study of acting affords, you cannot but be a happier, more appreciative individual than you would have been without it. If your gift lies in any of the artistic fields you will profit immeasurably by following the suggestions in this chapter. Even if your vocation is far removed from these, your life will be richer because you have learned to sense more vividly the world about you.

**SENSE IMPRESSION NOTEBOOK** You may find it interesting and profitable to record your impressions in a notebook small enough to carry in your pocket or purse. Whenever something occurs which you wish to retain for your storehouse of memories, make a note of it. If you have not recorded anything earlier, take a few minutes in the evening to review the day's events and select the one that you wish to remember. Not all days are eventful but you will be surprised, as you consciously look for them, how many things will seem worth recording as time goes by. This notebook may later prove to be an excellent source of material for all forms of creative work—for the writing of poetry, stories, scenes, pantomimes, dialogues, or plays, or as a basis for the other arts such as painting, dance, or music.

**TRAINING THE FIVE SENSES** In the following exercises you are given an opportunity to experience and to reproduce impressions of seeing, hearing, smelling, tasting, and touching. In the first group (A) of each set you are reacting to *real* objects. In the second group (B) you are recalling experiences and observations and recreating them in episodes in which you are responding to an *imagined* stimulus. All these exercises are to be done in your own character with no attempt at projection.

### Sight: Exercises to develop observation

A. Experiencing

1. On your next trip to school try to see more than you have ever seen before—scenes, colors, the actions and reactions of people. Be ready to tell about all you saw.
2. Look carefully at the costume of someone. Describe it in great detail.
3. Observe a picture which someone has held up for only a few seconds. Comment on color, design, and subject matter.
4. Examine a single object minutely—a vase, a piece of jewelry, a flower, a late-model automobile. Describe it.
5. Let two members of the group enact a brief scene; then you describe what you saw as though you were on the witness stand. It should be original, but something as simple and definite as the following: (A book and a chair have been strategically placed, unnoticed by the group. "A comes storming in, kicks the chair with his left foot, walks up to B, shakes his right fist, goes back to the chair, pushes it with his right hand, goes back to B, shakes his left fist, snaps his fingers twice, goes over and knocks the book to the floor, then storms out." If a violent argument goes on between the two meanwhile, it will add to the confusion. The sequence of actions must be carefully worked out and the action must be smooth and rapid.) Write a detailed description of what you saw.

B. Recreating

In the preceding exercises your attention was focused on *real* objects. Now you are to observe *imaginary* objects. That is, you are to make dramatic use of the sense impressions which you have collected. An active imagination will be needed to translate them into acting material. Do not try to project. Imagine the setting and several well-defined incidents. For example, watch and react to:

1. a cat playing with a mouse

(You are sitting at your desk reading when you think

you hear a light scratching noise at the door. Squeakily the door opens and you see the family cat coming in slowly with something in her mouth. This proves to be a mouse, which puss deposits on the floor and proceeds to pat with her paw. The mouse starts to move and the cat pounces. This game continues for some minutes as you watch, sometimes amused, perhaps, sometimes disapproving, sometimes on the point of rescuing the poor mouse. Finally the cat picks up the mouse and carries it out of the room.)

2. a table tennis game
3. a friend passing by who does not see you
4. an art gallery—see several different kinds of pictures
5. a fly buzzing around a bald head in church

### Hearing: Exercises to develop the ability to distinguish sounds

A. Experiencing

1. During a given time, hear as many sounds as you can: in the room, just outside, far away. Record them.
2. Close your eyes and listen while someone taps on wood, tin, glass, or any other object. Distinguish them.
3. Listen to the tapped rhythm of a well-known tune, such as *Yankee Doodle.*
4. Listen as five students walk across the room and distinguish the sound patterns of each walk.
5. Listen to the many sounds in a grocery store, or a library, or a barn.

B. Recreating

Listen to the following imagined sounds:

1. an auto crash
2. a piece of music of which you are very fond
3. footsteps on gravel
4. a telephone conversation
5. a boring lecture

### Smell: Exercises to develop an acute sense of smell

A. Experiencing

1. Take a journey through your own home blindfolded, using only your sense of smell as a guide; recognize the kitchen, the laundry, your room, the front hall, the back porch, the living room.

2. Have someone fill several bottles with various liquids such as nail polish, vinegar, vanilla, perfume, coffee, oil of peppermint—then try to identify each by smell.
3. Note the odor of a print shop, of a doctor's office. How does it differ from a dentist's office? The use of what materials accounts for the difference?
4. Note the odors in a beauty parlor or barber shop and identify each.
5. Note the odors in a candy shop.

B. Recreating

Smell the following imagined odors:

1. smoke—a definite kind, such as wood smoke or burning feathers
2. moth balls in clothes
3. fresh paint
4. roses
5. freshly ground coffee

In the second section of the exercises for taste and touch it is necessary for you to handle imaginatively objects which are not present. You will seldom be required to do this in a play, but Thornton Wilder's *Our Town* is an exception. It is vital to an understanding of this play that the audience know exactly what imaginary objects the actors are using. Opening doors and windows, cooking breakfast, making, serving, and eating ice-cream sodas, and shelling peas are only a few of the pantomimic actions required in *Our Town.* In preparing such an assignment you should first use the actual object and analyze what you do, step by step. Eat the real food and note your manner of registering your enjoyment. Watch others doing the same. Then discard the object and go through the action again. Have someone watch you and criticize. Keep repeating the process, with and without objects, until your feeling of weight, size, form, and sequence of actions is firmly established.

**Taste: Exercises to develop an acute sense of taste**

A. Experiencing

1. Make several small packets of different foods which have approximately the same texture—baking powder, powdered

sugar, corn starch, flour, cream of tartar. Close your eyes, or have someone blindfold you, and try to name each one as you taste a small portion.

2. Try to distinguish various common spices and condiments—cloves, cinnamon, allspice, mustard, ginger, nutmeg, mace.
3. Recognize cold coffee, cold tea, grape juice, and any other soft drinks that are not carbonated.
4. Contrast the tastes of sweet oranges and sour lemons.
5. Note the taste of your tooth powder or paste. Describe it.

B. Recreating

Taste the following imagined foods or drinks:

1. ice cream
2. a banana
3. lemonade
4. a highly seasoned tamale
5. green olives

**Touch: Exercises to develop an acute sense of touch and feeling of weight**

A. Experiencing

1. Take samples of different materials—cotton, wool, rayon, linen, silk, velvet, flannel, jersey, organdy—and, blindfolded, try to identify each by feeling it.
2. Take a series of weights and, blindfolded, try to arrange them according to weight. (The Science Department will lend a set.)
3. Close your eyes and have someone give you a number of articles—an engraved box, leather goods, costume jewelry—which you examine by touch and then describe, giving size, texture, weight, use.
4. Dip your hand into ice water.
5. Run sand through your fingers.

B. Recreating

Using imaginary articles, do the following things:

1. Touch a hot stove.
2. Lift wet clothes.
3. Carry a heavy suitcase.
4. Raise a window.
5. Fill a glass with water.

The next time you have an opportunity to watch people in life situations of seeing, hearing, smelling, tasting, and touching, carefully note their reactions and compare them with your own.

**DEVELOPING THE POWER OF ASSOCIATION** In order to recall and recreate imaginatively, you will need also to develop your power of association—the ability to see relationships and similarities in what you experience and observe. One small element may suggest others only distantly related or set off a chain of memories that will give background and reality to your portrayal. Sometimes inanimate objects or even animals will remind you of people. With a little imagination you can incorporate some of their qualities in your characterization.

I. Describe the person to whom each of these articles belonged:

| | |
|---|---|
| an old battered hat | a pipe |
| a handful of jacks and a ball | a shoe |
| a pair of reading glasses | a bicycle |
| a pair of sun glasses | a mitten |
| a sequin evening bag | a tennis racket |

II. Bring to class or recall objects from which you can construct a character. For example—a single white rose on a long stem might suggest a tall, slender, sophisticated, reserved, slightly haughty woman in a white brocaded silk dinner dress.

| | |
|---|---|
| a thin, sleek, leather billfold | a hoe |
| a very ornate picture frame | an oriental vase |
| a piece of Mexican pottery | an Airedale |
| a fishing basket | a bottle of glue |
| a black woolen shawl | a Persian kitten |

**EMOTION** The previous exercises have, no doubt, made you realize the important part that sensory experiences play in everyday life. You have seen, too, how through recreation they can be used dramatically. Undoubtedly you also discovered that sense impressions aroused emotional responses. You were fascinated or annoyed at the fight scene; you liked or disliked the taste of the lemon. You can recall that when you burned your hand on a hot stove you were frightened or angry, or both. One of an actor's essential skills is his ability to make a convincing emotional response to sensory impressions, for emotion is one of the major commodities of the theatre. People come to a play to be entertained or amused or to be emotionally moved to laughter or tears. They will respond unreservedly to the extent that the actor presents apparent truth upon the stage. His ideas of truth will be formed not only from the record of his own senses and emotions but also from a keen understanding and interpretation of the emotional responses of others. These emotional responses are the key to the real or inner character, which is what the actor must first create.

What is emotion? It is the way you feel about something—the way you feel about your family, about the movie you saw last night, about your athletic rival, or about a blazing fire. Emotions are the essence of living; they color the way you look at life. And they are constantly changing according to what is happening. You do not have the same feeling at all times toward any individual or situation. You love your family and home, but sometimes when you are angry you wish you could leave them. Often the way you feel about something is more important than what you think about it, for your emotions are more apt to direct your course of action.

**SENSES AND EMOTIONS IN CHARACTER PORTRAYAL** In your development and dramatic use of sensory and emotional responses, there are three steps.

1. Through **observation** and **experience**, at which time you are dealing with real objects and life situations, you build a storehouse of memories.

2. Using this material, you **recreate** for stage presentation the required situation, character, and responses. Now, however, the stimulus, or spur to action, is not real but make-believe or imagined.

3. By means of voice and body you **project** the character and his responses to an audience, in the dual role of character and actor, using such techniques and departures from reality as artistry requires.

In preparing to play any part, then, you will select from your storehouse of memories an experience similar to the one you are to portray. Fortunately for us, outstanding incidents in our lives are easily recalled. The scent of a gardenia brings a particular dance vividly to mind; certain melodies call up a flood of memories; at the sound of a boat whistle we instantly relive the scurry, dash, and excitement of our first big boat trip; the sight of the collar and leash of a beloved pet revives the grief caused by his loss. These and thousands of other experiences and observations are stored away to be recalled when needed. Even our muscles have memories—we never forget how to ride a bicycle or how to skate, though years may pass without our doing either.

At will you can recall the emotional and muscular reactions you want, provided they have been a part of your living. Sometimes, however, you must substitute an experience that was vital to you, but quite different from the one called for in the play. For example, you are playing a scene in which you must show great shock. You just can't seem to register it. Nothing you have ever experienced seems to create the right mood. Suddenly someone rushes into the room shouting, "Bill, your car has just rolled down the hill and crashed into a telephone pole!" Your beloved jalopy, for which you have just finished paying! Yes, now you can register shock, for you just did. Many times a stimulus which bears no relation to the required situation will create the desired emotional response.

If you are called upon for a response with which you are quite unfamiliar, you will need to rely completely upon imagination. You may find that you can employ an "if" situation to advantage: "*If* this or that were true, what would I do?" Or you may be able to recall the experience of someone else, or one that you learned of by reading, by seeing plays, movies, television, or by listening to the radio. These are called **vicarious** experiences, and they will impress you more strongly if you will enter so thoroughly into the spirit of each situation that you are virtually a part of it. This is what you do when, from the grandstand, you help to push the ball over the goal line for a touchdown. This taking upon yourself the feelings of others, even to the point of giving a muscular response, is known as **empathy.** The ability to make an empathic response is one of your real acting talents.

Having recreated the emotion yourself, the next problem is to make it clear to your audience. It is not sufficient for you to feel the emotion. Through the mediums of voice and body and the use of stage technique you must reveal and project the ideas and emotions so that others will know what you are thinking and feeling.

Now your emotional responses in life come as the result of something that happens to you. For instance, you are confronted by an armed robber and are frightened, or someone makes an unkind remark and you are hurt or angry. In life situations your responses come naturally and spontaneously and you show these feelings in a bodily or vocal response. You may scream and run when you encounter the robber, and cry or make an angry retort to the unkind remark. But on the stage you are dealing with make-believe. The robber is a fellow actor—quite harmless. You know this and so does the audience, but the theatre is a make-believe world and your audience will play the game with you as long as you have the skill to make them want to. Herein lies much of the actor's secret formula for success. For he is constantly dealing with things on the stage that are not real. The gorgeous flowers, which are paper; the warm, glowing fire, which is a colored light bulb; the delicious food, the rich clothing, the luxurious surroundings, all of which are make-believe—these take on reality only as the skilled actor is able to project them as real. As he looks into the wings to describe an airplane landing, what the actor actually sees are dingy stage walls and an array of props and stage hands. His ability to make his audience see the airplane depends upon the accuracy of his own sense impressions plus his expertness in projecting them. It is part of his training and technique to make the audience feel what he wants them to feel, and believe what he wants them to believe.

This brings us to the intangible part of the actor's work. Kipling made one of his characters accomplish something "by instinct and by magic." Surely much of any great artist's skill defies analysis. What makes the playing of one musician more moving than that of another when both are skilled technicians? Too many elements go into the mixture to make a ready answer possible. Part of the alchemy is a personal affair that even the artist himself cannot define. What he takes from each experience he may take by instinct, and surely many of his results seem to be magic. But this we do know—the great artist is a highly sensitive and expressive person.

How deeply does the actor himself feel the emotion he is projecting? This is a debatable question. Perhaps it is safe to say that he feels it in varying degrees, depending upon who he is. At some time he undoubtedly did feel the emotion, or at least was able to imagine it, otherwise he would not have the knowledge necessary for him to project it to others. While acting his role he is, no doubt, partly controlled by the emotions of the character, but just as surely does he know what he is doing. This is the dual role which was mentioned earlier. It has been proved many times that unrestrained emotion on the part of the actor usually does not affect the audience as much as greater restraint does. How deeply the actor feels the emotion is beside the point, since it is the emotional response of the audience that shows his skill. Sometimes the actor is an emotional wreck and the audience is bored, slightly revolted, or highly amused.

While there are some basic rules and techniques that can be learned, in addition you must experiment and discover for yourself what you can do to be effective. The audience is your court of last appeal; if they understand what you are trying to portray, you are right; if they don't, technical excellence is not enough. If your audience is confused or inattentive, or if they laugh in the wrong places, you haven't accomplished what you planned to accomplish, and it is your responsibility to find a remedy. Sometimes you can figure this out for yourself, but usually you will need help. That is why so much emphasis is placed upon the need for good, intelligent, constructive criticism for everything you do.

Learning to create and project the emotional responses of your character is by far your most difficult task as an actor. The rest of this chapter is devoted to exercises planned to aid you in this phase of your training.

**CONCENTRATION EXERCISES** The actor, in the dual role which he must play, is subjectively himself, the actor; objectively he is the character, who is apparently living his own life. Being both himself and a character at the same time is often confusing to the beginning actor. As an intermediate step in preparation the two must be separated, and first you must learn to concentrate—to focus your entire attention on what you are doing or feeling, to the complete exclusion of everything else. Here is a simple exercise.

Take some small article, such as a ring, which will be the sole object of your interest. Everything you do must have a reason or motive. Why did you take the ring from your finger? (The setting seemed loose.) As you examine it, the following ideas may be racing through your mind and will dictate what you do. (Well, I didn't know the setting was loose. I'll have to get it fixed. I wonder if it's safe to keep on wearing it? Needs cleaning too, and here's one prong that is practically worn off. It certainly is wearing thin; you can scarcely see the date engraved inside. Oh, well, maybe I'll get a new one on my next birthday. I'll take a chance and wear it a little longer.) And you return the ring to your finger.

If you are not careful you will find yourself trying to do things that will impress someone. In other words, you will be thinking about what you are doing, instead of thinking only about the ring. So it is better to have no audience at this point in your training, for it frees you of any concern about "getting it over."

Repeat the exercise, using any one of the following objects. Focus your entire attention upon it. You are concerned only with experiencing the sense impression and following a logical line of thought.

| | | |
|---|---|---|
| 1. a key | 5. a jackknife | 9. a pill box |
| 2. a fountain pen | 6. a nail file | 10. an address book |
| 3. an earring | 7. a china figurine | 11. a wrist watch |
| 4. a billfold | 8. a single flower | 12. a bangle bracelet |

When you are developing any character, this complete concentration upon what he is thinking and doing is your first concern. Only after this is well established should there be any thought of projection, for with the effort to project the actor consciously enters the scene in his dual role of directing and at the same time being the character.

The ability to concentrate serves in other ways. During every second in a play the actors are grouped to form a well-designed picture with one center of interest, toward which everyone on the stage directs the eyes and thoughts of the audience. But because the center of interest changes constantly, the actors must quickly, and apparently naturally, keep focusing on the new center of attraction. This may be likened to watching a ball being tossed from one person to another. This same comparison may be used in relation to speeches—one person's remark being picked up and answered by someone who tosses the idea on to a third member of the group, who passes it on to someone else and so "keeps the ball in play." To do this successfully requires mental alertness and good concentration.

**ESSENTIAL ELEMENTS IN A PANTOMIME** Many of the following exercises take the form of pantomimes in which your ability to concentrate will be a factor contributing to success. Pantomime is the bodily expression of an idea or emotion. Without saying a word, an actor should convey to the audience what the character is thinking and feeling. There are three essential ingredients in pantomime: character, situation, and mood. Always work with a definite character, in a definite situation, registering a definite mood. The character may be yourself. The situation should include both setting and incidents; and the mood, which is the result of the emotional response, naturally dictates the physical response.

For example: You (the character) are at your desk (the setting), enjoying a good book (the mood), when the phone rings (the incident). You are annoyed (the emotional response), and slam your book down (the physical response).

In the presentation of detailed pantomimes it is necessary that

1. the character, situation, and mood be clearly established at the outset;
2. the location, size, and kind of furniture that you use be made clear and not change shape or location;
3. the size, weight, shape, and appearance of any object with which you deal be accurate and not change during the pantomime;
4. all movements be clearly defined and complete, with no distracting or unnecessary details;
5. all movements be motivated by thought, or emotion, or both;
6. the series of incidents build to a climax and a well-defined ending —sometimes a surprise finish;
7. accurate timing be developed to give precision;
8. a degree of exaggeration be employed, since it is essential to projection.

You must make your audience see each detail, but avoid a tendency to use an excessive number of gestures. Practice artistic economy! Keep your pantomime as simple as is consistent with being understood.

**DEVELOPING EMOTIONAL RESPONSES** Make experiences which you have had the basis for the recreation of the emotion in the following exercises. Recreate the scene, using the lines given.

1. I can't; I'm scared. (fear)
2. Shh, careful, they might hear. (caution)
3. Stop! I won't listen to any more! (anger)
4. Don't be upset; you couldn't help it. (kindness)
5. I'm so tired. I can't move. (laziness)
6. I'm cold. Isn't there a draft somewhere? (irritation)
7. There, that's the way to do it. (conceit)

8. Please let me go. (pleading)
9. There's been an accident—hurry! (excitement)
10. Of all the grateful people! (sarcasm)

The changing moods of a character help to sustain interest and suspense in a play. As in life, emotions are never static, but vary according to what is happening. Examples will be found in the scenes in Chapter 11. For instance, in *Life With Father* we find that Father's anger increases with every bill he checks; in *Blind Alley* Wilson gradually loses his belligerence as Professor Shelby talks to him, until in the end he is quite subdued; in *Inherit the Wind* Rachel's certainty changes slowly to doubt; in *The School for Scandal* Lady Teazle's sarcasm is prompted by mischief rather than ill humor. To suggest this while railing at Sir Peter requires the kind of subtlety and skill which the following exercises are designed to develop. Build a pantomime of character and situation to illustrate the following mood changes.

A. Through a series of well-established steps *increase* in intensity from
    1. irritation to anger
    2. shock to tears
    3. smiles to laughter
    4. timidity to fright
    5. cockiness to defiance
B. Through a series of well-established steps *decrease* in intensity from
    1. anger to sullenness
    2. grief to sadness
    3. amazement to mild wonder
    4. laughter to chuckles
    5. fear to caution
C. Change from one emotion to another which is the *opposite*
    1. indifference to cordiality
    2. depression to joy
    3. happiness to sadness
    4. courage to fear
    5. boastfulness to humility
D. Experience a *combination* of conflicting emotions
    1. sarcasm and mischief

2. jealousy and admiration
3. fear and defensiveness
4. sulkiness and impatience
5. pride and helplessness

E. Develop and project a story in pantomime in which you show three or more different emotions. Take time to register one mood before changing slowly and gradually to the next. The plot need not be original, but the scene should be complete. You might use one of the scenes which you have memorized previously and present it in pantomime, with emphasis on the changes of mood. The following list of emotions is merely suggestive:

| | | |
|---|---|---|
| indecision | mystery | bitterness |
| cordiality | pain | indifference |
| curiosity | enthusiasm | scorn |
| jealousy | eagerness | arrogance |
| mischief | defiance | sullenness |
| worry | slyness | timidity |
| affection | respect | tenderness |
| impatience | joy | sulkiness |
| sympathy | anger | grief |
| coyness | servility | awe |

### CHAPTER HIGHLIGHTS

- Resources for creating the inner character
  - Life Study
  - Sense impressions
    - Observation
    - Experience
- Senses and emotions in character portrayal
  - Emotional responses
    - Recreation
    - Projection
- Essential elements in a pantomime
- Exercises to develop emotional responses

# THE BODY ☆☆☆

THE CURTAIN OPENS. It is the chamber room of a palace, the Emperor Jones's palace.

"A native negro woman sneaks in cautiously from the entrance on the right. She is very old, dressed in cheap calico, bare-footed, a red bandana handkerchief covering all but a few wisps of white hair . . . She hesitates beside the doorway, peering back as if in extreme dread of being discovered. Then she begins to glide noiselessly, a step at a time, toward the doorway in the rear."

At this moment, "a tall, stoop-shouldered man" appears and watches the woman suspiciously. "His bald head, perched on a long neck with an enormous Adam's apple, looks like an egg . . . A cartridge belt with an automatic revolver is around his waist. He carries a riding whip in his hand."

"Then, making up his mind, he steps quickly on tiptoe into the room . . . he springs forward and grabs her firmly by the shoulder. She struggles to get away, fiercely, but silently."*

As the curtain rises everyone present is caught by the tension in the native woman's movements, and as the cruel-faced man crouches to

* Eugene O'Neill, *The Emperor Jones*. By permission of Random House, Inc. Copyright 1920.

spring at her, the heartbeats of everyone in the audience quicken in response to her danger.

Eugene O'Neill has begun his play *The Emperor Jones* with a dramatic pantomime. Within the first ten seconds of performance a woman who suggests trouble and fear, and a man who conveys ruthlessness, shrewdness, and evil, have swept the audience into the mystery of the play without a word having been spoken. There is conflict, suspense, and dramatic reality in every attitude and movement of their bodies. This is an instance in which the body alone tells a story, when the voice is not needed to convey either the idea or the emotion.

Suppose, however, that the actor playing this scene was so awkward and clumsy that instead of being able to step "quickly on tiptoe" he stumbled as he entered, or that the actress was so stiff and ungainly that she could not "glide noiselessly." Undoubtedly much of the dramatist's message to the audience would be lost.

In order to be an effective instrument of dramatic expression, the actor's body must be strong, flexible, and controlled. With perseverance anyone can accomplish this. Dancing, swimming, fencing, in fact, all the sports are beneficial, but in addition a systematic practice of specially designed exercises is essential to complete development.

The problem of body training is much the same for the actor as for the athlete. Both must be physically fit. Both are working for strength, agility, and economy of movement. The runner wants to go the farthest, the fastest, with the least expenditure of energy. What we call "form" in any sport is simply the best method of accomplishing this, and is largely a matter of coordination, balance of weight, and endurance. The actor, too, needs endurance and a body that moves with the minimum of effort and is capable of responding quickly and accurately to the demands of any situation. Knute Rockne, the great Notre Dame football coach, realized the similarities between football and theatre, as is told by one of his former players in *Knute Rockne, Man Builder*.

The theatre was one of his sources of inspiration . . . He borrowed from the chorus the rhythm and harmony that made so many legs kick

SET: SHE STOOPS TO CONQUER *Beverly Hills High School*

SET: TWELFTH NIGHT *Beverly Hills High School*

ARENA: THE HAPPY JOURNEY *Santa Monica City College*

LECTERN READING: *Forest Park High School, Baltimore*

as one, so many arms swing, and so many heads nod in unison . . . He took in the fact that the audience was bored by a play that dragged, but they flocked to a play that swept along . . . Rockne took back to the practice field all the lessons he had learned from the dancing chorus and the scenery painter, and he began to set his stage for his own show . . . Then Rockne began to develop the shift . . . Every movement had to count for something and no movement could be wasted . . . For the past sixteen years the technique and rhythm of the Notre Dame shift have been something to marvel about.*

Yes, athletics and acting have much in common: not only rhythm, harmony, and teamwork, as Rockne observed, but such simple fundamentals as daily practice and the keeping of training rules. Good health is as essential to the actor as to the athlete. Proper food at regular hours, and sufficient rest as well as exercise, are needed to keep the whole system in condition.

So, like the squad preparing for the games ahead, you are now going into training for the positions and plays in drama. You will be coached in exercises and drills designed to start you on a course of training which will eventually give you a body that is both controlled and expressive.

Have you ever stopped to think just what you bring to the theatre by way of a trained and responsive body? This is a good time to take an inventory. Walk across the stage and ask the director to give you a criticism on your posture and walk, using the following Personal Inventory as a guide. This will indicate what specific defects you need to work on first. Find the exercises in this chapter that will provide correction, as indicated in parentheses, and begin practicing them daily.

**PERSONAL INVENTORY OF POSTURE AND WALK**

1. Head
   - A. forward, leading body (posture and torso)
   - B. held too high, or tipped down, or on one side (posture and head)

* Harry A. Stuhldreher, *Knute Rockne, Man Builder*. By permission of Macrae-Smith Company. Copyright 1931.

2. Shoulders
   A. one higher than the other (mirror exercise)
   B. tense and hunched (relaxation)
   C. one leads (posture and mirror exercise)
   D. both twist—helping a too-long step (walking)
3. Arms
   A. one swings farther than the other (relaxation)
   B. one or both are stiff (relaxation)
4. Hips
   A. rotate up and down—caused by shifting weight with every step (walking)
   B. one higher than the other (mirror exercise)
   C. tipped forward (balance of weight and mirror exercise)
   D. twist forward and back—helping a too-long step (walking)
5. Legs
   A. one step longer than the others; almost a limp (walking)
   B. steps too long—causing hips and shoulders to swing (walking)
   C. steps too short—making a mincing walk (walking)
6. Ankles
   A. tight and stiff—making walk clumsy and stumping (feet)
   B. too loose—making walk ungainly (feet)
7. Feet
   A. weight on heels—making walk heavy; heels scuffing (walking)
   B. toe in, or out, or toes turned up (walking and feet)
8. General walk and posture
   A. weight not well balanced (balance and coordination)
   B. chest not held high (posture)
   C. slumps and plods (posture, balance of weight)
   D. stiff and unnatural (relaxation)
   E. unrhythmic and jerky—bounces (walking)
   F. loose-jointed—rest of body working to make up for inactivity of legs (walking)

## ☆☆☆ TRAINING FOR STRENGTH, FLEXIBILITY, AND CONTROL

**RELAXATION** One of the first things to be learned in relation to any bodily activity is relaxation. The speed and complexity of modern life, causing as they do nervous tensions and even diseases, have made necessary a serious study of ways and means of releasing tensions in order to keep the mind and body functioning normally. No one has greater need of this knowledge than the actor. Constantly under pressure, emotional as well as physical, he must learn to relax at odd moments, or he will not have the strength to go on with his assignment. Long hours of rehearsal, irregular periods of rest, inadequate food, all will deplete his physical energy if he does not know how to combat tension. Many a talented actor has ruined a promising career through ignorance of this one fact. Doctors and trainers of athletes have perfected a number of exercises for releasing tensions, and some of these you must learn. The exercises included here are simple and will provide merely a beginning. Read and practice, and receive professional help if possible, for this is a vital part of your training.

There are two kinds of relaxation, and as an actor you need to know both. The first may be called total relaxation. (Since complete relaxation is impossible to a living person the word is used here relatively.) This is the kind that makes it possible for you to relax mind and body in a few minutes, drop off to sleep instantly, and awaken in about fifteen minutes, refreshed and ready to go on with your work. It is worth more than any stimulant. It may take months to acquire this skill, but it is one which everyone working in the theatre should possess. Notice how many good actors mention relaxation as a factor in their success.

There is another way of releasing tensions which can be used more often in everyday situations. This is what is known as partial or differential relaxation, which means that all muscles that are not necessary for the task at hand are relaxed. Activity of the arms, for instance, is not required when one is sitting in a chair. Yet some people constantly fuss with some object, or fold their arms rigidly on their chests. Letting the hands lie quietly relaxed in the lap, besides being more restful, is infinitely more attractive.

Dr. Edmund Jacobson in his excellent book *You Must Relax* says:

A large variety of instances of differential relaxation can be found in daily life. The speaker with a trained voice does not tire even after prolonged effort if he keeps his throat differentially relaxed. The billiard player spoils the delicate shot if he is generally too tense. The golf or tennis player learns to mingle a certain relaxation in strokes that are successful. The comedian often makes his ludicrous effects depend upon the extreme relaxation of certain parts of his body while others are active or held rigid. The individual who holds himself rigid in these acts fails in his effects. A particular exercise is repeated until grace is attained. This means that those muscles alone are used which are needed for the act and that no excess tension appears in them or in others.*

### Exercises for complete relaxation

In order to relax completely it will be necessary for you to lie down. Therefore these exercises must be done at home, or even in your dressing room at the theatre, as a prelude to the cat nap that you can take while waiting for the stage hands to shift the set.

Lying flat on your back and as relaxed as possible (a very small pillow under your knees will help), raise your right arm as high as you can, stretching to your finger tips. Relax it suddenly and completely. Try not to touch your body, and do not move your arm from the position in which it falls. Keep it entirely limp. Repeat with the left arm.

Raise your right leg at right angles to your body. Shake your foot until it is perfectly relaxed, then let the leg drop limply. Do not move it from the position in which it falls. Repeat with the left foot and leg.

Without disturbing the relaxation of other parts of the body, raise the head, then let it drop back suddenly.

Lie very still for several minutes trying to keep the mind a blank. If tension appears in any part of the body, repeat the entire exercise.

### Exercises for partial or differential relaxation

If you will employ some of the following exercises before beginning, and at intervals during, any period of study, you will find that you not only will accomplish more, but will be able to work longer. If possible, practice them in the fresh air. Even a few minutes of deep

* Dr. Edmund Jacobson, *You Must Relax*. By permission of McGraw-Hill Book Company, Inc. Copyright 1934, 1942.

breathing, stretching, and yawning will provide a most beneficial break in any prolonged period of study or rehearsal. Some of these exercises may be practiced while you are standing in the wings, waiting for your next entrance.

1. Stretch, all the way to your finger tips, yawn, relax. Repeat. Take a deep breath, yawn as you exhale, relax. Repeat.
2. Kneel before an imaginary fireplace in which a cheerful fire is burning. Let your whole body respond to its warmth. Relax and enjoy it. Take a deep breath and smell the wood smoke.
3. Hold the body erect, the arms and hands reaching as high as possible above the head. Slowly relax the arms, dropping them to the sides on a count of five. As they pass the head, let the neck relax and the head drop forward. Relax the shoulders, then the back, with arms leading as the body folds down. Soften the knees, drop to one knee, then to both, then fold the entire body into as small a ball as possible on the floor. The body should now be completely relaxed and the position one of comfort. Hold for a count of ten, then slowly come up into an erect position, reversing the process—first hips, then knees, shoulders, head.
4. Sit in a comfortable chair in a relaxed but dignified position (as you would before an audience) and listen to some beautiful, soothing music from the radio or a record. Do not move any part of the body during the entire selection (usually about three minutes). Change your position slightly and listen again.

**POSTURE** Too much cannot be said about the importance of good posture, not only from the standpoint of appearance and general movement on the stage but for good health as well. Since the actor is seen before he is heard, his posture, his stance, and his bodily attitude give the first hints of his character.

As a matter of training you should first acquire perfect posture—a body properly aligned, with weight well balanced. Acting upon the criticism which the director has given you, try to eliminate any faults which you may have, for perfect posture is what you want for daily living, and for your roles as a leading man or leading lady. When preparing an acting assignment, you will deviate from this in any required direction, but not until you have achieved it are you ready to assume the eccentricities of a character. In fact, some of the bad habits of which you rid yourself may, at a later date, be employed as the mannerisms of a character. But they should be assumed; you should not be saddled with them for life.

Recall from your study of physiology that the spine is made up of a series of vertebrae, one above the other and padded between with

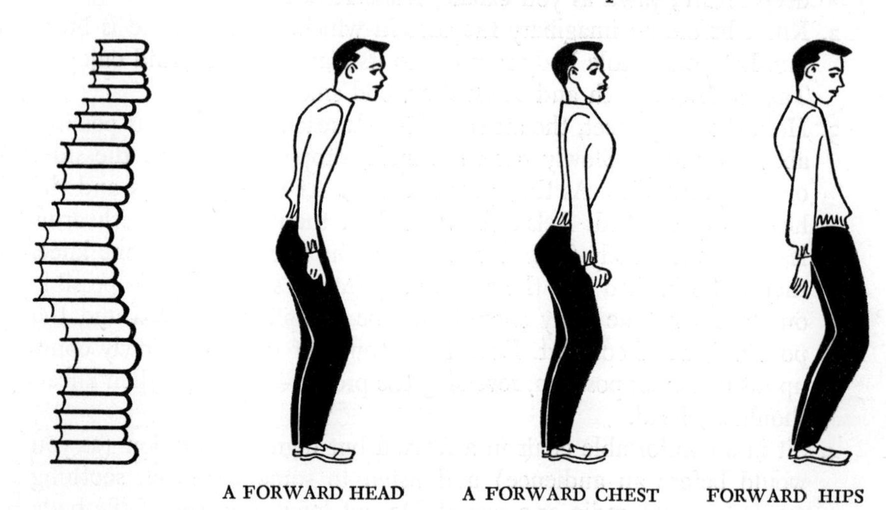

A FORWARD HEAD A FORWARD CHEST FORWARD HIPS

cartilage. Observing what happens to a stack of books if you push some of them out of line, note what happens to your posture when you have a forward head, a forward chest, or forward hips.

The bodily adjustment is much the same as that of the pile of books —some other section moves out of line in compensation. Eventually this posture becomes set and cannot be changed.

Picture yourself as similar to the snowman we make by stacking three balls of snow one above another. In your case the materials are pelvis, torso, and head, which should also be lined up one directly above another. Because the head is very heavy it is frequently thrust forward, thus throwing the whole body out of line.

When your body is properly aligned and balanced it should be possible to hang a plumb line from your ear to your wrist to your ankle bone with half of your weight on either side of the line.

Bad posture is not corrected in a day or a week. First, of course, you must be convinced that good posture is important. Then faithful practice, eternal vigilance, and a strong will can accomplish whatever you set as your goal.

Practice the checks and exercises for improvement which are given here, until you can answer "yes" to each question.

**POSTURE CHECK**

As you stand, are you thinking yourself tall?
Is your chest high but relaxed?
Is your back fairly straight, with the pelvic bones rotated slightly forward, thus tightening the muscles of the abdomen and hips?
Is your weight well balanced on the balls of your feet, a little to the outside?
Can you pass the plumb line test?
*If not ------ then, here's what you can do:*

## Posture exercises

1. Good posture begins with the feet. They should be pointed straight ahead, with the weight well forward on the balls of the feet and slightly toward the outer edge.
2. Stand against the wall, very tall, and flatten the curve in your back a little by tipping the hip bones under and forward. Hold the chest high

but relaxed. Have plenty of room between the ribs. Zip up behind the ears and look up and over without straining.

3. Keeping the body against the wall, reach as far as you can with the toes of your right foot; then transfer your weight to the right foot, at the same moment coming down on the right heel and moving away from the wall. Bring the left foot forward so that both feet are parallel and about three inches apart. (Men take a slightly wider base.) Test your balance of weight by rising on the toes and settling down lightly on the heels. If your weight is properly balanced it will not be necessary to sway forward in order to rise on the toes.
4. Stand before a full-length mirror at home and assume a correct posture. Make sure that your shoulders are level and relaxed, but not slumped. *See* the correct posture, then close your eyes and *feel* it in your muscles so strongly that you will be able to assume it at any time away from the mirror. Walk around the room and return to the mirror. Have you been able to retain the posture with which you started? If not, repeat the process until you can.

### Exercises for balance and coordination

1. Stand with the feet a few inches apart. Starting with the right foot, (1) take one small step forward, reaching with the toe and instantly transferring your weight to the forward foot, letting the other foot rest lightly on the floor; (2) shift the weight to the ball of the back foot; (3) return the forward foot to its original position. Repeat with the left foot. Practice this to a count of three (waltz time) in one continuous gliding rhythmic movement. Don't bounce. Knees and ankles must be flexible. Increase the speed as you become more expert. There should be no stiffness anywhere. Keep the back straight, head up, chest leading. Work for a sense of buoyancy, lightness, and smoothness.
2. Fencing exercise. Stand with your feet two and a half or three feet apart, weight evenly balanced on the balls of both feet. Pivot right, bend right knee directly over right toe, straighten left leg, keeping weight evenly balanced on both legs, and both heels off the floor. Pivot smoothly to the left, bend left knee directly over left toe, straighten right leg, keeping weight evenly balanced on both legs, and both heels off the floor. Practice to a rhythmic count of 1, 2.
3. Beginning with the right foot and with toes pointed straight ahead, walk to a count of one, two, three; stop and keep your weight balanced

on the right leg while you swing the left leg forward and back without touching the toes to the floor for three counts; step forward on the left foot and repeat—step, step, step; swing, swing, swing. Keep the rhythm even and the body erect. Circle formation may be used for groups, with music in 6/8 rhythm—a barcarole.

**WALKING AND TURNING** The secret of a beautiful walk is the ease with which you move your weight in action. A good walk is rhythmic and graceful. The steps are even and not too long for the body. The weight is so well balanced on the balls of the feet that the whole body moves easily with no apparent effort. If the weight is held high there is no obvious shifting of weight on every step. If it is settled in the heels, however, you will drag your feet or scuff your heels and part of the task of walking will, of necessity, be taken over by other parts of the body. Swinging shoulders and arms and shifting hips are all evidences that the legs are not functioning properly.

Turns on the stage must be accomplished with a minimum of movement, which occurs when there is perfect balance and a quick easy transfer of weight.

**WALKING CHECK**

Do you swing from the hips with ease and rhythm?
Do your knee and ankle joints function properly?
Is your body always in perfect balance?
Do your feet point straight ahead?
Is your weight on the balls of your feet?
Does your walk express vitality?
*If not - - - - - here's what you can do:*

### Walking and turning exercises

1. Stand with your back against the wall; flatten the curve in your back a little by rotating the hip bones under and forward. (1) Pull up the right knee. (2) Then reach as far as you can with the toes of the right foot while keeping the back against the wall. (3) Come down on the heel of the right foot, moving away from the wall and at the same time transferring the weight to the ball of the right foot.

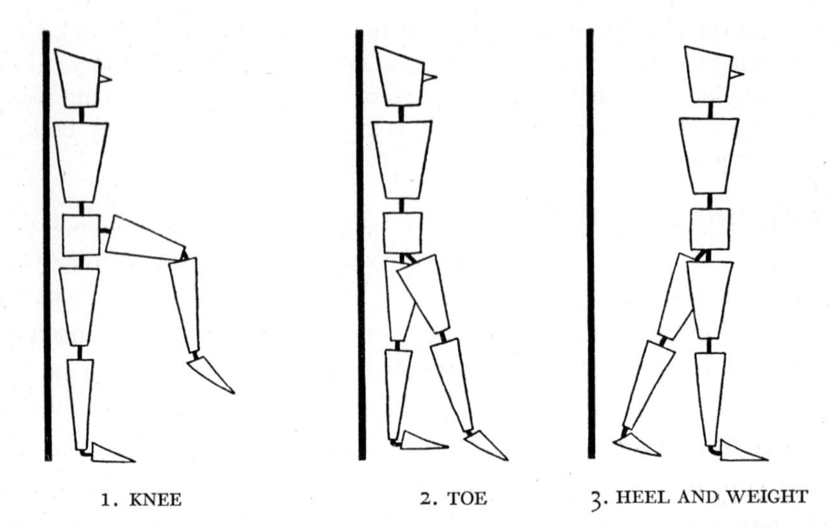

1. KNEE 2. TOE 3. HEEL AND WEIGHT

Have a feeling of pushing forward with the back foot. Without returning to the wall, pull up the left knee and repeat to three counts—(1) knee, (2) toe, (3) heel and weight forward. Repeat. Make all three movements as smooth as though you were riding a bicycle, and transfer to the other foot without a break in rhythm. Keep repeating until you get the feeling of a smooth glide with weight so far forward that unless you keep moving you will fall. Then change to normal walking, that is, with the heel coming down a fraction of a second before the toes, which protects the arch from strain. This exercise is designed to keep you from coming down too heavily on your heels. Alternate the exercise with normal walking until you form the habit of keeping the weight forward on the balls of the feet. Remember your plumb line!

2. Walk backward, swinging from the hips.
3. Advancing the upstage foot first, take five steps, pivot on the balls of both feet, and end with the weight on the downstage foot, thus releasing the upstage foot for the next step. Keep repeating until you can do this automatically and inconspicuously. Rarely should you do a sharp pivot in turning, but using this technique make a soft easy turn with no unnecessary movement.
4. To correct a tendency to make one step shorter than the other, walk on a surface where you can *hear* your steps. Concentrate on making them of equal length and get the muscular feeling of this when it

is right. Sometimes it is helpful to overcompensate by making your habitually short step extra long for a while. Be sure the steps are not too long for your body.

### Exercises for the torso

1. Stand with the feet set firmly but slightly apart. The knees should be kept flexible throughout this exercise, ready to give with the flow of the movement. With the waistline as a pivot, swing the torso in a complete circle, arms hanging limply at sides; start by bending right, then forward as low as possible, left, and up into position. Repeat left. When the body is making the movement with ease and a strong flowing motion, let the arms follow through; right, forward, left, over the head, down, right. The body must continue to lead.
2. Keeping the head erect and chest high, extend the arms forward at shoulder height; swing them to the sides at the same level and as far back as possible, to a rhythmic count of two: (1) swing back, (2) swing forward. Repeat many times. The head must not tip forward or move during the exercise. (Excellent for forward head and round shoulders.)

### Exercises for the legs

1. Placing your left hand on the wall for support, with hips tucked under and weight on the left leg, swing the right leg from the hips: (1) forward, (2) back, (3) forward, then bend knee and kick forward again; swing it (4) back, (5) forward, (6) back, then bend knee and kick back again. Return to position. Reverse and repeat with the left leg.
2. With feet together drop to knees, straighten feet so that the insteps are resting on the floor, settle weight back so you are sitting on your heels, then sway weight forward, return feet to original position, and rise. This is all one smooth, continuous motion and should be accomplished without extra support.

### Exercises for the feet

1. With the weight on the left leg, rotate the right foot at the ankle, then relax it and shake the foot. Repeat left.
2. Take a good standing position with hip bones rotated under, hip

muscles taut, and head erect; rise on toes and walk, keeping arch of foot extended and body erect. This is done more easily without shoes.

#### CHECK FOR ARMS AND HANDS

Do your arms hang relaxed, with elbows slightly away from your sides?
Do your gestures begin at the shoulder and end at the finger tips?
Are your hands alive and energetic?
Are they able to tell a story?
Are they used artistically, with economy of motion?
Are they part of your arm or do they dangle?
*If not - - - - - - - - here's what you can do:*

### Exercises for arms and hands

1. Raise right arm forward, wrist relaxed. Describe a figure 8 horizontally to the side and back to the front, wrist leading. Repeat left. Repeat with both arms together, starting in front.
2. Taking a firm stance, swing the arms limply from left to right like a pendulum, to a rhythmic count of two. Keep swinging until arms and hands are completely relaxed. Keep head up and back straight.
3. Open and close the fists rapidly, five times, stretching the fingers as far apart as possible each time. Relax them by shaking vigorously.
4. Vitalize the finger tips by snapping the thumb against each one; thumb against first finger, against second, third, and fourth—forward and back. Relax by shaking the hands.

### Exercises for the head

1. Hold your head high, with chin level and drawn back slightly. Turn it to the right directly over the shoulder but not tipped toward it. Repeat left.
2. Drop your head forward on your chest; tip it backward. Tip it toward the right shoulder; toward the left shoulder; repeat. Do not turn your head.

### Exercises for the face

1. Let your face light up with glad surprise; change to discouragement.
2. Let it relax in fatigue; change to horror.

### Exercises for the eyes

1. Starting at the right, roll your eyes in circles: right, down, left, up, level. Repeat, starting left.
2. Open your eyes as wide as possible, as though staring in horror; look through half-closed lids, as though concealing something.

### Exercises for the mouth

1. With lips closed, bring the corners up; then pull them down.
2. With lips open a little, bring the corners up in a smile; then pull them down in disgust or loathing. Open your mouth very wide as in hearty laughter.

In order to accomplish results you must be systematic and regular in your practice—*do something every day.* Here is a simple routine requiring but a few minutes of time. For variety, you can substitute other exercises from the chapter for the ones given here. Cover all six items every day.

#### A DAILY ROUTINE OF BODY EXERCISES

Aim to have a body that is free from tension and mannerisms, that is flexible and well coordinated, with weight so balanced that all movement is graceful and effortless.

I. Relaxation

Assume a good standing position. Relax the muscles of the neck, letting the head fall forward. Slowly and smoothly, with head approaching the floor, relax shoulders and chest until body is suspended at the waist as though hung over a clothesline, arms limp and dangling. Come up slowly into an erect position, begin ning at the waist and imagining that one by one the vertebrae are being pulled slowly into line. The head comes into position last. Stretch and yawn.

II. Torso

Clasping the hands, push arms vigorously above the head, palms up. Swing arms to the right, then down, to the left, and up into position, keeping the head between the arms. Repeat to the left.

III. Legs

Assume a good posture; point the toes of the right foot about twelve inches in front of the left foot, tense, and return to position. Repeat with the left foot. Repeat several times. The object is to train the feet to point straight ahead, with legs and feet moving as a unit.

IV. Feet

With the feet parallel to each other, (1) rise on your toes as high as possible; (2) turn the heels out, toes facing each other; (3) down on the heels and you are standing pigeon-toed; (4) up on the toes; (5) turn heels back to original position; (6) down on the heels. Repeat to a rhythmic count of six.

V. Arms

Rotate shoulders up and down, forward and back, with arms hanging limp.

VI. Hands

Clench fists tightly. Unroll them, (1) pushing palms forward with fingers still closed, (2) exposing first joint of fingers only, (3) opening hand wide with fingers spread as far apart as possible and vital to the tips. Four counts—clench, 1, 2, 3. Repeat, increasing speed. Relax fingers by shaking them.

## ☆☆☆ THE BODY AS AN ACTING MEDIUM

So far in this chapter you have been working to develop strength and freedom of movement. Now you are ready to put this training to dramatic use. For a strong, coordinated body is of little value dramatically unless it is also expressive, and so responsive to the actor's will that it is capable of revealing thoughts and emotions as clearly as speech does.

Some people express their feelings quite easily and spontaneously. Others are always being misunderstood because their actions do not indicate what they really think and feel. You can, no doubt, recall seeing someone suddenly clench his fists and stiffen his jaw and you knew that he was very angry. But you have known others equally angry who gave no indication of it except to become very quiet. Such persons are called inarticulate. If they wish to become actors they must learn to give visible and audible evidence of their feelings. They must be able both to reveal and to project them.

**PHYSICAL EXPRESSION OF EMOTIONAL STATES** Recall from your Life Study (or take another trip) the three general types of people that you observed—the extroverts, the introverts, and those who were a little of both and were therefore called normal. In general, when your thoughts and feelings are those of an extrovert all the body lines will tend to radiate from a central body line. When your thoughts and feelings are those of an introvert, all the body lines will tend to draw in toward a central body line. In the normal person, lines are level and balanced.

Many extrovert qualities are most admirable—the vitality, exuberance, fearlessness, and driving power. But when undesirable extrovert traits predominate, the person is likely to be a bully—egocentric, aggressive, and noisy, with little regard for the feelings and rights of others. These are the brash, insensitive people who go through the world brushing others out of their way. Such a character is Wilson in *Blind Alley.*

Many introvert qualities are also attractive—reserve, humility, quiet. But when undesirable introvert qualities predominate, the person is introspective, unresponsive, and pretty much of a failure. Sometimes ill, often filled with self-pity, these are the people who go through the world drawn within themselves, self-conscious and supersensitive. Such a person is Sibyl in *Separate Tables.*

According to some psychologists, by assuming certain physical attitudes you automatically create an inner emotion. Others claim that the inner emotion is responsible for the physical attitude. For purposes of drama, both ideas are valid. As a practical demonstration try the following exercise.

Taking a good stance, with perfect posture and balance, with head and eyes level, say the line, "This is the proudest moment of my life." Doesn't your posture help to give you a feeling about the words, and don't the words make you want to pull yourself up to your most dignified height?

Changing from this ideal attitude, with legs spread apart, hands on hips, chin thrust out, and the general attitude of a bully, defy the world with the words, "So what?" And strangely enough, you feel like a bully.

Go back to a normal stance, and from this position draw yourself in, with shoulders drooping, chest sunken, knees and feet close together, elbows hugging your sides, hands clasped helplessly in front of you, head down. Take up as little room as possible and feel apologetic for occupying that much. Whisper the line, "What's the use, I'm no good." And you feel completely defeated. Mr. Milquetoast, the cartoon character, is an excellent example of an introvert.

Through this simple exercise you are able to experience to some extent how your bodily attitude affects your feelings. It is knowledge that will help you in many situations. If you are applying for a position, you can deliberately assume an attitude of assurance which will disguise your inner insecurity and help to banish your fear. Even with a violent case of stage fright, you can step out onto the stage and convince people of your complete command of the situation, if your bodily expression is right. And that, in turn, will help to give you the confidence you need.

Perhaps the pictures and diagram on the opposite page will help to make these ideas more clear.

Note on the diagram the *degrees* of radiation and contraction from normal. *Belligerence,* for example, is a more pronounced extrovert quality than *enthusiasm,* and *reserve* is only slightly removed from *self-confidence.* Any number of traits could be added, for, generally speaking, practically all characteristics tend to either the extrovert or introvert side. Bodily movements of attraction and repulsion, that is, movements toward or away from objects or people, are also related to these fundamental attitudes.

Sometimes it is a good idea to try to imitate someone exactly, just to increase your skill in making your body follow the dictates of your mind. Try assuming different postures and attitudes in order to determine to what extent the physical pose expresses the personality. Note, also, how it affects your emotional state. Study the excellent and amusing Norman Rockwell painting (facing page 50) which so graphically pictures the two extreme types.

**PANTOMIMES** In the following pantomimes you are really acting. They are in many instances only fragmentary, but your whole pattern of character creation and responses is made up of such fragments. If carefully worked out they may prove valuable in some future characterization.

Reread the pantomime instructions in Chapter 5 (page 77) and keep in mind the basic rules. Watch carefully as different members of the group present their scenes and note the wide range of observation and experience they display.

In these simple exercises of standing, walking, sitting, and rising you will do the first five each time in your own character, trying always to exhibit your best qualities in every situation. In the second five you are to assume a character and present him as you would if this were a scene in a play.

### Simple pantomimes

STANDING: You are (1) waiting for a bus which you see coming, (2) waiting in a long line at the bank, (3) waiting to be introduced to someone at a party, (4) watching a beauty contest, (5) waiting for the class to become quiet so you can announce your play.

The character is (1) a baseball catcher ready to receive the ball, (2) a child having her hair brushed, (3) a short girl trying to see a parade over the heads of the crowd, (4) a bully defying a group, (5) a clerk having nothing to do, waiting for customers.

WALKING: You are (1) strolling beside your best friend on the way home from school, (2) hurrying to get to class before the bell rings, (3) walking nervously to the platform to make a speech, (4) walking beside an elderly person, (5) leaping to answer the telephone.

The character is (1) a traffic policeman walking toward a car to give a ticket, (2) a fat, tired laundress trudging home after a hard day's work, (3) a feeble, old person hobbling about in the garden, (4) a sly shoplifter moving past a counter of merchandise, (5) a noisy teen-ager coming home from school.

SITTING: You are (1) in a dentist's chair, (2) at a baseball game, (3) at home listening to the radio, (4) at a formal party, (5) at a boring lecture.

The character is (1) an old man fishing, (2) a little girl reading, (3) a secretary taking dictation, (4) a fat, middle-aged lady shelling peas, (5) a tired, middle-aged man watching television.

RISING: You are rising (1) to try out new shoes, (2) to go on an errand, (3) to avoid being injured, (4) to go out with friends who are in their car outside, (5) to go to dinner.

The character is (1) a very elderly gentleman rising from

a bench, (2) a woman who uses a cane rising from a deep chair, (3) a scrubwoman rising from cleaning floors, (4) a large, heavy-set man rising from being knighted, (5) a leading man or woman rising to receive an introduction.

### Combination pantomimes

Now, in a situation and character of your own choosing, combine standing, walking, sitting, and rising in one scene. Assume the character off-stage, enter, sit, rise, and leave. Stay in character until you are again in the wings. A single hand mannerism may be added. Your only props will be a straight chair or armchair and, if desired, a table.

### Pantomimes for specific members

These exercises are designed to make you aware of the particular contribution which various parts of the body can make to the total characterization. A screen or curtain may be used to hide from audience view the part of the body which is not the object of the exercise.

EYES:

1. The neighborhood gossip, in looking over a fence, discovers a child burying something which turns out to be a chemistry set.

   (Successive expressions: mild interest, curiosity, suspicion, amazement, understanding, smug satisfaction.)
2. A timid student looks at another's examination paper on the sly and is caught by the teacher.

   (Successive expressions and actions: blank response to the examination question, discovery of fellow-student's paper, fear of detection, concentration on paper, surprise, embarrassment, shame.)

HEAD:

1. A boy is being scolded by his father for disobeying orders to do his homework instead of watching television.

   (Successive expressions: guilt, sullen acceptance of lecture, relief when scolding is over, determination to do better, concentration on studies.)
2. An elderly person is beginning to doze off in the presence of company and tries to keep his head from nodding.

   (Successive expressions and actions: patient listening, drowsiness, gentle bobbing of head, abrupt return to consciousness, struggle to keep awake, slow nodding of head, sleep.)

HANDS: 1. A miserly person finds a large roll of bills of different denominations. He greedily counts them, becoming more and more excited as he discovers several large ones.

(Successive actions: picks up roll of bills, closes fist over them, slowly opens fist, riffles through the roll, increasing in speed; rolls bills up again, puts them in pocket or purse.)

2. A concert pianist is in a doctor's office having the bandages removed from his hands, which have been severely burned. As each hand is unbandaged he tries to move his fingers.

(Successive actions: tries to move each finger on the right hand, but finds it almost impossible to move them, drops hand limply in despair, concentrates on left, painfully moves each finger a little as he would in playing.)

ARMS: 1. A hotel bellboy carries a heavy suitcase for a visitor. His arms become strained and tired.

(Successive actions: picks up suitcase, carries it a few steps, sets it down, picks it up with other hand, carries it a few steps, sets it down, tries to use both hands, gives up and skids it along the floor to the desk.)

2. A woman is starting to rub clothes on a washboard. Her sleeves keep slipping down and her hair gets in her eyes.

(Successive actions: rolls up sleeves, pushes back her hair, starts to rub clothes, stops and pushes up her right sleeve, rubs again, stops and pushes up left sleeve, rubs again, stops and pushes hair out of her eyes, rubs again, stops, dries her hands on her apron, pins sleeves up, fastens hair securely, begins to rub clothes again.)

FEET: 1. A salesperson returns home very tired after being on her feet all day.

(Successive actions: pushes shoes off with each foot, twitches toes, slips into soft slippers, rests feet on footstool, relaxes.)

2. An irritable, flighty person is waiting for a friend who is long overdue.

(Successive actions: walks impatiently up and down, wheels suddenly as she thinks friend has arrived, stamps foot, sits down, crosses legs at ankles, recrosses them, taps right foot in annoyance, rises, again paces impatiently.)

LEGS:

1. A burglar enters a strange house.

   (Successive actions: slides cautiously over window sill, tiptoes stealthily around room, crouches and stops suddenly as he hears someone coming, hurries noiselessly to window, slides quickly over sill.

2. A student starts to rise from his (or her) seat after listening to an assembly program. His legs have been crossed and one leg has gone to sleep.

   (Successive actions: sits with legs crossed, uncrosses them, starts to rise, one leg buckles and he almost falls, puts weight on good leg, shakes leg that is asleep, bounces up and down to restore feeling, steps gingerly, moves off limping.)

### Pantomimes of situation

In the following exercises you are to create a particular situation or environment and respond to it in your own character.

1. Walk through tall underbrush and protect your head from the branches.
2. Wade into the ocean. The water is very cold or warm.
3. Walk through an imaginary door, get something, and walk back.
4. Be a cashier making change. Respond to different customers. Know exactly what money is given to you and what change you are giving.
5. Walk through a dark alley alone at night.
6. Visit a pet shop and select a kitten or puppy.
7. Enter your home very late at night, trying not to awaken anyone.
8. Sit before an open fire. Respond to its warmth and cheerfulness.
9. Walk along a very crowded street with a friend.
10. Step out onto the porch of the ski lodge. Respond to the cold air and to the joy of being there.

### Pantomimes of character and situation

You are now ready to progress to very detailed and complete pantomimes involving both character and situation. Before creating your own pantomimes, see if you can present the one given here. Follow exactly every direction given, making all the ideas clear to the audience without unnecessary movement or any of your own mannerisms.

You are a college girl. You and your older sister are both interested in the same young man. (Boys may revise the pantomime to read, "You and your brother are both interested in the same girl." Substitute shaving lotion for perfume.) She has received a letter which you would like very much to read and which you know she has left in her room. Dinner is over and your sister is playing the piano, so you have come upstairs and now enter her room. Stop and think where the letter might be. Look carefully on top of the dressing table. It isn't there, but your attention is arrested by a perfume bottle which you pick up and open. You smell the perfume, put a little behind your ears, replace the cork, and return the bottle to the exact spot on the dressing table where you found it.

You see a package of candy mints; take one and eat it. You open a drawer in which you find a new cashmere sweater; remove it and admire the texture. You return the sweater and close the drawer.

You start to open the second drawer when you realize to your dismay that the piano playing has stopped. You listen intently as you hear steps coming up the stairs and then down the hall toward the door of this room. You react to this. Just as you expect to be caught, you realize that the person has gone on and you are safe. At that moment, to your great relief, the piano playing starts again. Now you hunt through the drawer and find the letter. Finish the story in your own way.

What is the dominant mood in the scene? What different moods are induced by the various incidents? Note the part that each of the five senses plays in the story. Register them accurately.

Have clearly in mind and project (1) the size and arrangement of the furniture in the room, (2) the size and appearance of the dressing table, (3) the articles on top of the dressing table, (4) the size of the perfume bottle and the odor of the perfume, (5) the flavor of the candy, (6) the color of the sweater, (7) the location of the stairs, (8) who went by the door, (9) the size of the drawer in which you find the letter, (10) the other articles in the drawer, (11) how the envelope was opened, (12) what the letter says.

After you have presented this pantomime create an original one. From the limited information given, develop a well-rounded character and a complete story. Try to incorporate the elements of conflict and suspense and build to a climax. Add as many complications as you like.

The character is

1. a woman at church whose husband goes to sleep.
2. a little old lady in a railway station whose purse has been stolen.
3. a business executive, whose airplane crashed in the desert, waiting for a rescue plane to come. One flies over, doesn't see him, then returns.
4. a jolly, fat woman sitting in a doctor's office trying to talk to different people, including a small child. She is ignored by everyone.
5. a new and inexperienced waiter (or waitress) who keeps spilling food and apologizing.
6. a young stenographer on her first day in a big office. She finds the work difficult and confusing. A girl at a nearby desk is apparently watching her with interest.
7. a very pompous professor who is always lecturing on punctuality and preparedness. He finds that he has forgotten to bring the questions for an examination which the class is expecting to take.
8. a hard-boiled reporter (man or woman) who is sent to get an interview with a gushing, affected movie star in her too-rich and ornate home. There are countless interruptions by servants, tradespeople, telephone calls, and so forth.
9. an old man (or woman) alone and penniless in a big city, walking along a narrow, dirty street. He suddenly sees a wallet lying in the gutter. Someone sees him pick it up.
10. a gum-chewing and aggressive factory girl (or man) who has been scolded by her foreman for overstaying her lunch hour. She suspects a nearby worker of having reported her.
11. a very excitable alumnus at a football game raising his megaphone to shout. It slips from his hand and hits the girl in front of him. Her escort becomes very angry.
12. the postmaster (or postmistress) in a small country postoffice. He tries to explain to a very deaf person that a letter needs more postage.

### Character from a scene

Recreate the character from one of the scenes you have played. Develop a pantomime showing the character in a plausible situation but one not used by the dramatist.

### Group pantomimes

Working in groups of three or more, select a familiar scene from a play and present it in pantomime, thinking the speeches but not mouthing the words. This may be a scene which you have presented before.

Next create an original scene. Develop distinct characterizations and devise a series of incidents which build to a climax. Your story must be completely clear without the use of dialogue.

A more difficult variation of the group pantomime may be given by the addition of music. Listen to records and select one that suggests a story to you. Plan action which not only will synchronize with the music but will also interpret its emotional content. This requires great sensitivity and freedom in emotional response. In addition, this exercise gives excellent training in precise timing.

#### CHAPTER HIGHLIGHTS

- Personal inventory of posture and walk
- Exercises for strength, flexibility, and control
- A Daily Routine of Body Exercises
- Physical types expressing emotional states
    - Extrovert—radiating from central body line
    - Introvert—contracting toward central body line
    - Normal—expressing balance
- Pantomimes

# THE VOICE ☆☆☆

## ☆☆☆ ELIZABETH THE QUEEN

**by Maxwell Anderson**

Act I, Scene 3

SCENE: *An entrance hall before a council chamber in the palace at Whitehall. The doors to the council room have been thrown back, revealing a chair of state for the Queen, and beneath it a table at which her Councilors sit. The Queen's Jester sits cross-legged on a mat.*

ELIZABETH. Lord Burghley,
You shall speak first. What's to be done in Ireland?

BURGHLEY. If my son is right, and I believe him to be,
We can bide our time no longer there.
They have
Some help from Spain, and will have more,
no doubt,

---

Maxwell Anderson, *Elizabeth the Queen*. By permission of Longmans, Green and Company, Inc., and the author. Copyright 1932.

And the central provinces are rising. We must
Stamp out this fire or lose the island.

ELIZABETH. This means
Men, money, ships?

BURGHLEY. Yes, madam.

CECIL. A Lord Protector
Of Ireland who can carry sword and fire
From one end of the bogs to the other, and have English law
On Irish rebels till there are no rebels.
We've governed Ireland with our left hand, so far,
And our hold is slipping. The man who goes there now
Must be one fitted to master any field . . .
The best we have.

ELIZABETH. What man? Name one.

CECIL. We should send,
Unless I am wrong, a proved and able general,
Of no less rank, say, than Lord Howard here,
Lord Essex, Sir Walter Raleigh, Knollys or Mountjoy . . .
This is no slight matter, to keep or lose the island.

ELIZABETH. I grant you that also.

THE FOOL. I also grant you. Be quiet,
Fool!
(*He slaps his mouth.*)

ELIZABETH. I ask you for one and you name a dozen,
Sir Robert.

RALEIGH. Why should one go alone, if it comes
To that? Why not two expeditions, one

To Dublin, one into Ulster, meeting halfway?

ELIZABETH. Are there two who could work together?

CECIL. Knollys and Mountjoy.
They are friends and of one house.

ESSEX. Yes, of my house.

ELIZABETH. Essex, whom would you name?

ESSEX. Why, since Lord Cecil
Feels free to name my followers, I shall
feel free
To name one or two of his . . .

ELIZABETH. In other words,
You would rather Knollys and Mountjoy
did not go?

ESSEX. I would rather they stayed in England, as
Sir Robert knows.
I have need of them here. But I will spare
one of them
If Lord Cecil will let Sir Francis Vere go
with him.

ELIZABETH. Let Vere and Knollys go.

CECIL. Lord Essex names
Sir Francis Vere because he knows full
well
I cannot spare him, my liege.

ELIZABETH. Is this appointment
To wait for all our private bickerings?
Can we send no man of worth to Ireland,
merely
Because to do so would weaken some house
or party
Here at court?

THE FOOL. Your Majesty has said . . .

ELIZABETH. Be quiet . . .

THE FOOL. Fool!
ELIZABETH. Be quiet!
THE FOOL. Fool!
ELIZABETH. Be quiet!
(THE FOOL *forms the word "fool" with his lips, but makes no sound.*)

Just as the scene from *The Emperor Jones* illustrated the dramatic power of movement alone, so does this scene from *Elizabeth the Queen* illustrate the dramatic effect of speech alone. This, too, is an emotional scene, but it is controlled emotion, and the ideas expressed are of great importance. As you listen intently to the lines you sense the veiled hostility of Essex and Cecil and feel the underlying struggle for power that is going on among all present. Through the beauty and power of the spoken word both the meaning and emotions are conveyed to you. You are intrigued; you are believing.

Suppose you were to play the role of Elizabeth in this scene; how would you give the speeches? In an analysis of any speech, two questions must first be answered: What does it mean, and how does the character feel about it? What is Elizabeth's attitude toward this situation? What is her dominant mood? What does she mean to find out or accomplish? What is the conflict in this scene? How does she mean to overcome the obstacles presented?

As queen, Elizabeth is used to commanding. She is in the habit of discussing problems with Lord Burghley, her prime minister, so (crisply and with authority) she directs him to speak first. Burghley's line, "We can bide our time no longer," tells why there is urgency in her question, "What's to be done in Ireland?" As Burghley answers her she is weighing his every word and coming to a decision in, "This means men, money, ships?" Cecil's carefully phrased suggestion that a strong man be sent to govern Ireland evidently meets with her ready approval, for without wasting words she says, "What man? Name one" (fearful that they will name Essex). Lord Cecil, the politician, craftily working against Lord Essex, names him as one of those best suited for the job in "This is no slight matter, to keep or lose the island." To this Elizabeth readily agrees, but a bit impatiently, for her next speech is undoubtedly one of irritation: "I ask for one and you name a dozen." Raleigh's suggestion that two expeditions be sent brings her question (in a skeptical tone) of the possibility of finding two who would be willing to work together. Upon Lord Cecil's naming two, Essex, whose indignation has been growing, bursts into the conversation for the first time (strongly and sarcastically). Elizabeth immediately asks his advice (for, of course, she does love him). Essex's angry retort to Lord Cecil makes her realize the undercurrent of intrigue, and she boldly brings the question out into the open (bluntly and concisely) with "In other words, you would rather Knollys and Mountjoy did not go?" In an attempt to profit by the advice of both she says (very matter-of-factly), "Let Vere and Knollys go." But Lord Cecil, finding himself outmaneuvered, frankly tells why Essex named Vere. Angry by this time at what she knows to be rivals bidding for power, she storms at her courtiers in her next speech. With growing irritation, she takes out her venom on the Fool, each "Be quiet" becoming louder and angrier than the last.

In this brief and sketchy analysis of the scene only the most obvious interpretation has been given. As a competent actor playing any of the roles, you will do a great deal of research and study before even attempting to interpret the lines. You will become familiar with Elizabethan England, its life, manners, politics, and court intrigues. Since all the characters actually lived, you will want to know what history has to say about them. It is of primary importance that all the ideas be clear, not only to you but to the audience. Therefore, you will study all the speeches carefully, those of the other characters as well as your own, weighing each word for possible hidden meanings.

The beauty of the language in *Elizabeth the Queen* makes it imperative that the actors speaking the lines have expressive voices. Of what consequence is it to the pianist that he can read perfectly every note of the Emperor Concerto if he has no instrument on which to play it? Likewise, what does it profit you, the actor, to understand every word of Elizabeth's or Essex's speeches, with all their emotional overtones, if you have a vocal instrument incapable of giving such life and form to this understanding that an audience can share it with you?

That the voice is responsive to training is well known, but that the process takes much time and eternal vigilance, not all young actors realize. From two to three years are required to make a fairly adequate speaking voice, and six years to make an excellent one—six years of daily practice and attention, and the rest of your life to keep it in condition. Chronic colds, sinus afflictions, drinking, and smoking (advertisements to the contrary notwithstanding) all impair the speech mechanism. Since the voice is one of the actor's two mediums of dramatic expression, he cannot afford to neglect or abuse it. For not only must he be heard and understood, but his voice must be capable of reflecting all shades of meaning and emotion. Furthermore, it must be able to stand the strain of long rehearsals and long runs.

What do you bring to the theatre by way of vocal ability? Suppose you start with an inventory. Give a short memorized selection (four to eight lines) and ask the director to criticize it, using the following outline as a guide. Find in this chapter the exercises that will correct the imperfections he lists and practice daily until you have eliminated them.

#### PERSONAL INVENTORY OF VOICE AND SPEECH

1. Enunciation
    - A. tight upper lip (lips)
    - B. lips spread in a smile (lips)
    - C. hissed s's (tongue and jaw)
    - E. nasality (soft palate)
    - F. slurred speech—caused by thick or inactive tongue (tongue)
2. Pronunciation
    - certain sounds mispronounced (43 sounds)
3. Breathing
    - A. uncontrolled breath—makes voice sound breathy (breathing)
    - B. insufficient breath—affects volume and projection (breathing)

4. Placement
   throaty—should bring tones to lips (lips and projection)
5. Quality
   A. hard—lacks resonance (resonance)
   B. flat or thin—lacks color (resonance and tone)
   C. singsong—lacks rhythm (tempo and rhythm)
6. Interpretation (section on interpretation)
   A. phrasing and subordination
   B. inflection
   C. pitch—too high or too low
   D. tempo—too fast or too slow
   E. projection
   F. volume
   G. rhythm
7. Vitality
   A. listless—affects voice quality (body exercises)
   B. bad posture—affects breathing and projection (posture)

## ☆☆☆ TRAINING FOR SPEECH IMPROVEMENT

It would be impossible, of course, to give an adequate treatment of voice training in one small section of a book. There are, however, some fundamentals which you should know, and you will improve by following the suggestions in this chapter. As soon as possible, you should take some lessons from a good speech teacher.

There are three phases in your work for speech improvement. First, you will need to acquire good enunciation, which necessitates the training of the organs of speech in agility and precision. Second, you will need to be able to pronounce correctly all the speech sounds of American English. Third, you will want to improve the quality of your voice so that it will be more pleasant and more expressive than before.

In dealing with voice you are dealing with sound which is produced by vibrations in the air. Speech sounds are formed by air which has been expelled from the lungs, usually by strong action of the muscles controlling the ribs and by the diaphragm, a large flat muscle separating the chest from the abdominal cavity. On its way out the breath is modified by the organs of speech—the vocal cords, the cavities of the upper throat, the mouth, the nose, the tongue, jaw, teeth, lips, cheeks, and the hard and soft palates—and emerges in the form of definite speech sounds. Clear enunciation, correct pronunciation, and resonance depend upon the effective use of these organs of speech. Not all of them can be controlled, but those that can may be trained through the frequent practice of well-planned exercises.

A. Sinus
B. Nasal cavity
C. Hard palate
D. Soft palate
E. Lips
F. Teeth
G. Uvula
H. Tongue
I. Pharynx
J. Epiglottis
K. Vocal cords
L. Windpipe
M. Lungs
N. Diaphragm in repose
O. Diaphragm on inhalation

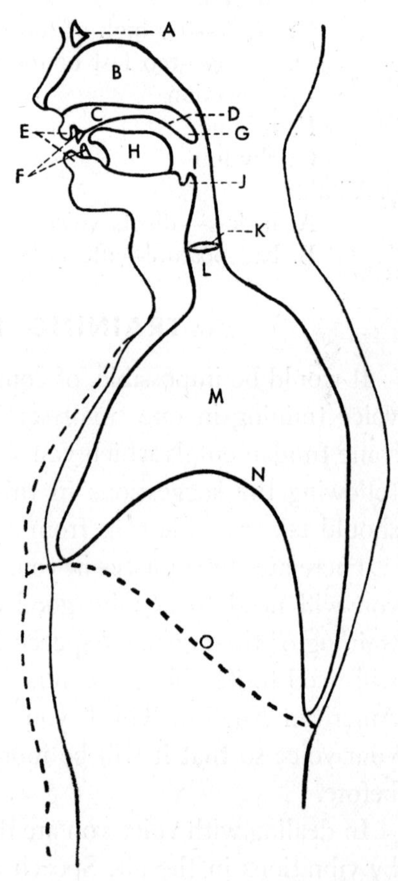


**RELAXATION** Begin all voice work with relaxation exercises. The neck, shoulder, and throat muscles in particular must be relaxed in order to avoid strain on the vocal cords. Review the exercises given in Chapter 6 and add these.

1. Take a deep breath, stretch, yawn, exhale as you relax. Repeat. Whenever your throat feels tense, yawn lazily to relax it—don't cough or try to clear it. Yawn and relax frequently during voice practice to avoid strain.
2. Drop your head forward on your chest, roll it very slowly to the right, to the back, to the left, and forward. Let the mouth open as the head rolls back. Repeat a number of times, then roll it to the left. Keep rolling it around and around until the neck and shoulders are relaxed.
3. Reach as high as you can. Suddenly relax the arms completely, letting them fall limply at the sides.

**POSTURE** Good posture is vital to proper tone production. Take a correct standing position—back fairly straight with pelvic bones rotated slightly forward, weight well balanced on the balls of your feet a little to the outside, chest high but relaxed. Review exercises in Chapter 6 (page 87.)

**BREATHING** Many of your vocal difficulties stem from improper breathing habits. If you were criticized for insufficient or uncontrolled breath you will need to work on these exercises particularly.

1. Place your hands on your sides just above the waist, with the thumbs toward the back and the fingers almost touching in front. Breathe, expanding at the sides so that the fingers are many inches apart. The greater the expansion the farther apart the fingers will be.
2. Place one hand a little above the waist in front and center the strength of the breath there. Inhale to a count of five, hold the breath for five counts, exhale slowly and evenly on five counts. Practice while walking.
3. Inhale. Sustain the breath and count "1, 2, 3, 4, 5." Give a firm, sharp attack. Keep increasing the number until you can count to twenty or thirty on one breath, keeping the tones strong and even.
4. Breathe. Explode the breath, saying "ho." Repeat, saying "ho, ho." Repeat, saying "ho, ho, ho." Repeat, saying "ho, ho, ho, ho." Repeat, saying "ho, ho, ho, ho, ho." Be conscious of the action of the diaphragm. Repeat the entire exercise, saying "ha." At the end, take a deep breath and break into uncontrollable laughter. When that breath is exhausted take another and keep on laughing.

**ENUNCIATION** Active lips, tongue, jaw, and soft palate are necessary if you are to have speech that is clear and a voice quality that is pleasing. All these organs are trainable.

**Exercises for lips, tongue, jaw, and soft palate**

The **lips** should be able to spread in a smile, also to round, and to protrude.

1. Blow out an imaginary candle, focusing the breath at the lips.
2. Spread the lips in a smile for e̅e̅, round and close them for o͞o, e̅e̅-o͞o e̅e̅-o͞o e̅e̅-o͞o. Open the mouth wide with lips round for äh, close them halfway, keeping them round for a̤w, äh-a̤w, äh-a̤w äh-a̤w.

The **tongue** should be active at the tip, at the middle, at the back. It should be able to lengthen and point, or spread and thicken. It should be able to flip agilely at the tip or lie relaxed and troughed in the bottom of the mouth.

1. Point the tongue straight out of the mouth, making it long, thin, and pointed. Pull it back and spread it behind the upper teeth so that it is spread from cheek to cheek. Repeat several times, using a mirror.
2. Relax tongue in the bottom of the mouth; trough it, with sides curling up. If this is impossible at first, hold it down with a pencil. This relaxed, troughed position is correct for making final "r" as in "weather." It will prevent you from overemphasizing the "r."
3. Practice saying the following:
   Tiny Tilly toddled toward the lily pond.
   lällery, lŏllery, lĭllery, lăllery lo͞o (distinguish among the vowels).

The flexibility of the lower **jaw** is necessary for a rich tone quality. Tight jaws have a tendency to harden the tones and to interfere with crisp enunciation.

1. Let your head fall forward on your chest; lift it slowly up and back, letting the jaw remain loose. Repeat slowly.
2. Waggle the jaw from side to side gently.

An active **soft palate** is required in the production of the three nasal sounds—m, n, and ng. You make these sounds by lowering the soft palate and allowing the breath to pass freely into the resonating chambers of mouth, nose, and throat, which act as a sounding board, adding richness to tones. Any obstructions in the nasal passages prevent correct production of these sounds and the voice is said to be nasal (positive nasality). Such obstructions need to be removed. If, however, there is no physical defect, then the nasality is caused by an inactive soft palate which allows the air to escape through the nose and mouth at the same time, thus nasalizing all the sounds (negative nasality). You can correct this lazy habit by practicing the soft palate exercises.

1. Pronounce "ah" strongly, watching in a mirror the action of the soft palate. It should rise against the back wall of the throat. Then relax the soft palate and send the air through the nose by pronouncing "ng." Repeat äh-ng äh-ng äh-ng
2. You can increase resonance by humming.
   Hum softly and musically, then vary the pitch.
   Pronounce m—n (m vibrates at the lips; open the mouth slightly and place the tongue behind the upper teeth for n).
3. Give these sentences, prolonging the nasal sounds:
   A drum! a drum! Macbeth doth come.
   Calm and smooth like music murmuring.

**FORWARD PLACEMENT** Tones that are tipped off the lips will carry better than those that are not, and will cause less strain on the throat and vocal cords. Think of the breath as coming from the region of the diaphragm and flowing through a clear channel to the lips, with no obstructions along the way. Talk *through* the throat, not *with* it. Keep the tones at the lips in these exercises. Assume good posture with weight well forward.

1. Warm weather and warm water will work wonders. (Do not overpronounce the r's. Syllabify water correctly—wä′tẽr.)
2. Thirteen thick thorns and thirty thistles. (The tip of the tongue should be very active. Pronounce ir as ẽ.)
3. The earthworm works early. (The ẽ sound is identical in earth, works, and early.)

### Exercises for voice projection

Imagine that there is a small box on the floor a few feet in front of you. Pronounce "warm," tossing it into the box by holding the vowel and thinking of the tone as describing a circle. Send the tone up and over. Move the box to the back of a small room; repeat "warm," making this larger audience hear. Use more force, hold the vowel longer, make the circle in the voice larger, hold the "m" a little. Move the box to the back of a large theatre, making the entire audience hear. Retain the same rich quality of voice, use still greater diaphragmatic force, hold the vowel longer, and make the inflection still greater as you repeat "warm." Keep a relaxed throat; yawn at intervals if necessary. Be sure that the power comes from the region of the diaphragm and that the tones are centered at the lips.

Repeat, using the word "halt." Enunciate the "t" clearly but do not allow the word to become "halta." A sharp, strong release is required.

In order to accomplish results you must be systematic and regular in speech practice as in body exercises. Here is a simple routine requiring but a few minutes. You can vary it by substituting other exercises from the chapter for the ones given here. A little work every day is better than a longer period once a week. Don't hurry. Let every sound you utter be your best. Add to this routine a daily reading aloud of poetry and well-written prose, working for tone color and expression.

#### A DAILY ROUTINE FOR SPEECH PRACTICE

Aim toward a speech that is neither slovenly nor too precise, that is easily understood and pleasing in tone quality.

I. Relaxation
  - A. Stretch, yawn, relax. Repeat.
  - B. Drop the head on the chest. Roll it lazily around with the jaw relaxed.

II. Posture
  - A. Stand erect and very tall, with plenty of room between the ribs.

B. Feet should be pointed straight in front and about three inches apart.
C. Rise on toes and settle down gently on heels, keeping the weight well forward.

III. Breathing

A. Place the hands on the ribs at the sides just above the waist. Inhale—pushing the hands out. Exhale. Repeat. (Do not raise the chest.)
B. Place the hands at the diaphragm, just above the waist, one in front, one in back.
Push the hands apart by breathing. Inhale, exhale. Repeat.

IV. Exercises for agility of the speech organs

A. Lips.
1. Bite the lips and the tip of the tongue a little to make them sensitive. Blow the breath through the lips, making them vibrate. Bbbbbbb.
2. Vibrate the lips by saying Bumble-bee-mum.
Bumble-bee-mum, bbbb; Bumble-bee-mum, bbbb; Bumble-bee-mum, bbbb. Bbbbbbb.

B. Tongue
1. Separate the lips and teeth an inch.
Flip the tip of the tongue *up* behind the upper teeth, *down* behind the lower teeth, up and down quickly saying lĭ, lĭ, lĭ, lĭ.
2. Trill—prrrrrr.

C. Jaw
1. Pronounce ē̄e with a smiling mouth position.
Drop your jaw and say äh. ē̄e-äh. Repeat.
2. Read any sentence and after every word drop the mouth open so that it is possible to insert two fingers between the teeth. Do not overdo this exercise.

D. Soft palate
1. Pronounce "hung ē̄e." Repeat. (Make two separate syllables.)
2. Pronounce "hum-nome-ring."
Keep repeating until the sound sings through the resonators. Don't force it—let it float.
"Hum-nome-ring; hum-nome-ring; hum-nome-ring."

**PRONUNCIATION** Correct pronunciation depends upon the accurate production of all the speech sounds, the proper division of words into syllables, and the correct placing of accents. Recognition of the different lengths of the vowels is also essential to clarity and rhythm.

Speech sounds are divided into two classes, vowels and consonants. A **vowel** is a voiced sound we make by allowing the breath stream to pass through the mouth unobstructed but modified by the shape of the mouth and the position of the tongue. There are twelve pure vowels, that is, those made with a single mouth and tongue position.

There are six diphthongs. A **diphthong** is a combination of two pure vowels. It is a glide sound, with the tongue starting in the position for one vowel and moving immediately toward another vowel position, which it does not necessarily reach.

The sounds as recorded in the chart opposite are such as occur in accented syllables. When ā and ō occur in unaccented syllables they are pure vowels, since the time for uttering them is too short to allow for the second sound. All other vowels occurring in unaccented syllables change in one of two ways—either they retain approximately the same sound but with the time of pronunciation shortened (the dictionary records this as a suspended bar ⊥), or else the neutral sound ə is substituted for the vowel. For all practical purposes ə is pronounced like ŭ shortened, or like the final ȧ in sofȧ. It is so brief that **it is sometimes** described as a vowel murmur. In some unaccented syllables the vowel is omitted altogether.

Care should be observed not to overpronounce unaccented syllables, since that makes speech stilted and destroys the rhythm. Weak, or unstressed, forms of many words are used in connected speech. *The* is pronounced *thə* before a consonant (thə table), and *thē* before a vowel (thē apple), and for emphasis. A is ə before a consonant (ə table), and ā only for emphasis; before a vowel it becomes *an* (an apple). While slighting unaccented syllables, avoid any slovenliness which might make your speech difficult to understand.

A **consonant** is a sound we make by obstructing the breath stream somewhere in the mouth. It is necessary to know where this interrup-

## AMERICAN SPEECH SOUNDS*

FRONT VOWELS — IPA

1. ē — ēve [i]
2. ĭ — ĭt [ɪ]
3. ĕ — ĕnd [ɛ]
4. ă — ăt [æ]
5. â — âsk [a]

BACK VOWELS

6. ä — äh [ɑ]
7. ŏ — ŏdd [ɒ]
8. a̤ — a̤ll [ɔ]
9. o͝o — fo͝ot [ʊ]
10. o͞o — bo͞ot [u]

MIDDLE VOWELS

11. ẽ — ẽarth [ɝ]
12. ŭ — ŭp [ʌ]

DIPHTHONGS ENDING IN ĭ

13. ā — āte ĕĭ [eɪ]
14. ī — īce ȧĭ [aɪ]
15. oi — oil a̤ĭ [ɔɪ]

DIPHTHONGS ENDING IN o͝o

16. ou — out äo͝o [ɑʊ]
17. ō — ōld ŏo͝o [oʊ]

DIPHTHONG ENDING IN o͞o

18. ū — cūbe ĭo͞o [ɪu]

LIP CONSONANTS

19. p — pat (breath)
20. b — boy (voice)
21. m — mum (nasality)
22. hw — what [ʍ] (breath)
23. w — went (voice)

LIP AND TEETH CONSONANTS

24. f — fan (breath)
25. v — vain (voice)

TEETH CONSONANTS

26. th — think [θ] (breath)
27. t̶h̶ — t̶h̶en [ð] (voice)

TEETH-RIDGE CONSONANTS

28. t — tea (breath)
29. d — did (voice)
30. n — none (nasality)
31. l — lace (clear)
 l — tall (dark) [ɫ]
32. s — sun (breath)
33. z — zone (voice)
34. r — red (voice)

PARTLY TEETH-RIDGE AND PARTLY HARD PALATE CONSONANTS

35. sh — shall [ʃ] (breath)
36. zh — azure [ʒ] (voice)
37. ch — church [tʃ] (breath)
38. j — just [dʒ] (voice)

HARD PALATE CONSONANT

39. y — yet [j] (voice)

SOFT PALATE CONSONANTS

40. k — kite (breath)
41. g — go (voice)
42. ng — king [ŋ] (nasality)

GLOTTIS CONSONANT

43. h — he (breath)

* Grace Barnes, *General American Speech Sounds*. D. C. Heath and Company, 1946.

tion takes place and also the manner in which the breath is released. Most consonants come in pairs, the position of the speech organs being identical for both. One, however, is made with breath only and the other is made with voice, that is, with a vibration of the vocal cords. These pairs are bracketed in the chart on page 121. Consonants are divided into five classes—plosives, nasals, laterals, fricatives, and affricatives—according to how they are made. There are twenty-five consonants.

You should be able to produce all the American speech sounds correctly. If there are any that you do not pronounce properly, drill especially on these. You will need to learn the diacritical markings so that you can use the dictionary easily. Since you will want to study foreign languages later, it would be well to become familiar also with the phonetic symbols of the International Phonetic Alphabet—I.P.A. These will be found in brackets after the key words in the chart. Where no symbol is given it is the same as that of the regular alphabet. The diacritical markings used here are those found in *Webster's Collegiate Dictionary,* Fifth Edition. The International Phonetic Alphabet symbols are those found in *A Pronouncing Dictionary of American English* by Kenyon and Knott.

## ☆☆☆ THE VOICE AS AN ACTING MEDIUM

So far in this chapter you have been concerned with the mechanics of speech; now you are ready to use your voice as an instrument of dramatic expression. A person speaks in order to communicate ideas to someone else. But, speech may be clear and completely understandable and still not always convey the intended meaning. Just as some people are unable to show an emotion by bodily reactions, so others are unable to express vocally what they think and feel. To learn the technique of doing this is your second problem in projection.

**TONE** When you meet and talk with a person for the first time—in applying for a position, for instance—you are very apt to judge him, unconsciously, perhaps, by his tone of voice. You decide that he is kindly, or gruff, or humorous, and you respond accordingly. So expressive of one's personality is the habitual tone of his voice that ideas and feeling will be conveyed even though words are lost.

If you have any doubt as to the power of tone to influence reactions, try the following experiments. Tell your dog in an angry voice that he is the nicest, brightest, most beautiful dog you know and see his tail slink between his legs. Then in your pleasantest tones tell him what an ugly, good-for-nothing creature he is and watch him wag his tail.

People, too, will respond more quickly to the tone of your voice than to actual words. On your next shopping tour, try asking a clerk for something, using polite language but an unfriendly tone. Approach another with the same request, expressed this time in the same words but with a gracious, courteous tone. The reactions of both clerks will not only teach you the importance of your tone of voice, but in addition will give you a valuable lesson in human relations. A smile in the voice works miracles, for people usually respond in kind.

Anger, fatigue, happiness, fear—in fact, all emotions—can be projected more strongly by tone than by words. Such simple exercises as the following will give you practice in registering emotions and moods through tone.

### Exercises for tone quality

*Words*

Work in groups of five. Each group will select one of the following words; each individual in the group will give it a different interpretation according to his character and mood.

| | | |
|---|---|---|
| yes | tomorrow | did you |
| perhaps | don't | so |
| no | scared | I |
| never | please | good |
| ha | sorry | tell me |
| go | clever | guess |
| well | really | I do |
| oh | why | possibly |
| see | come here | help |

*Suggested emotions or moods*

| | | |
|---|---|---|
| kindness | embarrassment | sarcasm |
| pleading | gaiety | amusement |
| bashfulness | sadness | fright |
| coquetry | relief | nonchalance |
| stubbornness | command | irritability |
| questioning | disappointment | helplessness |
| pride | suspicion | resentment |
| laziness | innocence | fatigue |
| hesitation | doubt | remorse |
| amazement | insolence | surprise |

*Characters*

Create characters to whom these emotional states are habitual and give an appropriate sentence in a tone which reveals both the general characteristics and the present mood of each one:

A person who is (1) excited and rather hysterical, (2) shrewish and frequently angry, (3) inclined to laugh uncontrollably, (4) tense, nervous, and tending to talk too much, (5) tired and listless, (6) cheerful and energetic, (7) discouraged and pessimistic, (8) calm and relaxed, (9) frightened and panicky, (10) angry and noisy, (11) mischievous and prankish, (12) suspicious and fearful, (13), romantic and affected, (14) whining and self-pitying, (15) triumphant and boastful.

*Scenes*

Work in groups of three. Each group will select one of the following sentences; each individual in the group will give it a different interpretation according to the character and situation which he has created.

(1) Good morning, are you the piano tuner? (2) I don't believe a word of it. (3) I don't understand. (4) We can't fail—can we? (5) It's raining. (6) I don't blame you. (7) So that's that. (8) Did you say Friday? (9) Who? Me? (10) You call that good? (11) Someone is coming. (12) Do you know to whom you are speaking? (13) He didn't mean to. (14) Where are you going? (15) Which way?

EXAMPLE: (1) Good morning, are you the piano tuner?

(a) A young pianist walks onto the theatre stage where he wishes to rehearse. He is tense and nervous as he says, "Good morning, are you the piano tuner?"

(b) A young girl goes to the door in answer to the bell. She is gay and flirtatious as she asks the question.

(c) A nearsighted old person is seated in his living room, when someone enters. He is cross and fussy.

Your actions should make clear the answers to these questions: Is the person a piano tuner? Does he answer your question? What is his reaction? Why do you react as you do?

*Sound and Color*

An expressive voice takes on the emotional coloring of the words, often reproducing the sounds they describe. The actor augments with tone what the author has suggested with words. Give the following words with tone color.

| | | |
|---|---|---|
| yelp | buzz | plop |
| crunch | squirm | tinkle |
| bang | jog | swish |
| rustle | twist | whir |
| sputter | snip | dull |
| roar | pelt | thin |
| crackle | saunter | harsh |
| whimper | cackle | weird |
| grunt | jerk | flat |
| puff | whine | clammy |
| hum | whinny | wild |
| chug | chuckle | sullen |
| wheeze | coo | limp |

Vocal responses which can be developed to express or intensify a character's mood are: laughs, chuckles, shrieks, screams, gurgles, snickers, sneers, coughs, wheezes, grunts, groans, humming, panting, sobbing, audible breathing.

**PRINCIPLES OF INTERPRETATION** In working for projection through the body, you found that often the emotional impulse was sufficient to create the right bodily response. This is equally true of voice. If you really understand the thought of the passage and are experiencing the emotion it calls forth, your interpretation of the speeches will often be spontaneously right. But, unfortunately, this cannot always be relied upon, so it is necessary for you to learn the underlying principles of interpretation in order to employ them consciously and effectively.

While it is best to try the emotional approach first, since it will give naturalness to your reading of lines, you will always go back and check what you have done, working out those speeches that were faulty by applying proven principles.

### Grouping and Phrasing

Ideas, in order to be understood easily, must be conveyed by speech that is distinctly heard and lines that are intelligently phrased. Words must be grouped to show their proper relation to one another. An entire sentence is a single thought, but within the sentence are smaller units, some more important than others, but all a part of the whole. Sometimes the punctuation will help you to determine relationships, but the only infallible guide is the sense, or meaning.

Do you agree with the phrasing as indicated in this speech from Richard II (v, 2)?

YORK. As in the theatre, the eyes of men, √
After a well-grac'd actor leaves the stage, √
Are idly bent on him that enters next,
Thinking his prattle to be tedious; √
Even so, √ or with much more contempt, men's eyes
Did scowl on gentle Richard: √ no man cried, God save him; √
No joyful tongue gave him his welcome home. √

### Subordination, Coordination, Emphasis

The groups which carry the main idea we usually make prominent by saying them more slowly, more forcefully, and often louder. Those that explain or qualify we make less important, or subordinate, by saying them faster, in a lower tone, and, in some cases, practically "throwing them away." Coordinating ideas, being of equal importance, are given equal vocal prominence. In the above selection the main idea is in the clause, "men's eyes did scowl on gentle Richard." Number the other thought groups in order of importance.

Within each unit there are some words which must be heard and understood if the meaning of the entire passage is not to be lost. These words are brought into prominence by emphasis. Words or phrases may be emphasized in a number of ways: by force, inflection, pause, rate, pitch, or tone color. The author states his new idea; this is important, so it is emphasized. But when it is repeated it is no longer new or important, so it is subordinated, as are those ideas which are implied. The words *and, but, the, a, an,* as well as *on the other hand* and similar words and expressions which convey no real thought, may be slighted.

**ELEMENTS OF VOICE** In common with all sound, voice has four elements—quality, force, rate, and pitch. You will need to know the particular nature of each in order to work intelligently for variety and contrast in interpretation.

You have already dealt with **quality** of tone earlier in this chapter, noting that it best conveys the emotion or mood.

### Force

Force relates to **volume,** to **attack,** and to **intensity**. The relative importance of a person's thoughts can be expressed by the intensity of utterance as well as the amount of tone used. It is possible to change the meaning of a sentence completely by the forceful emphasis of different words. Read this sentence five times, shifting the emphasis each time.

DID John tell you that? (I know you said so, but did he really?)
Did JOHN tell you that? (Or was it someone else?)
Did John TELL you that? (Or did you just infer it?)
Did John tell YOU that? (Or did he tell someone else?)

Did John tell you THAT? (Or something different?)

Increase in volume and intensity gives the effect of vigor and determination, or shows progressively mounting emotion. A gradual decrease in volume gives an impression of weakness or futility.

**Rate**

Rate, or time, relates to rate of speed, to pause, and to quantity. It is an integral element of speech as it is of music, and is one of the revealing forms of emotion.

A rapid **rate** of speech is associated with the go-getter, the salesman, and with youthful or with nervous types. It may express happiness, excitement, anger, or tension. Very slow, deliberate speech is that of serious-minded or slow thinkers. It may show deep thought, reverence, sorrow, or doubt. Nothing more strongly conveys an impression of poise and assurance than carefully timed, even, controlled speech—neither too fast nor too slow. This is the speech to cultivate for your own. It should be slow enough to be clear and understandable, and fast enough to be interesting. Important ideas are given more time; less important ones are spoken more rapidly. Phrasing, grouping, co-ordination, and subordination are all time elements.

**Pause** in speech corresponds to the rest in music, and to space in design. Sometimes a pause will best give prominence to a word or idea. A pause before a word calls attention to it; a pause after a word reinforces it. Suspense and tension can be built up in a scene by an expert use of dramatic pause.

Comedy effects are produced by skillfully timed pauses. Learning to "take laughs" requires experience with many different kinds of audiences and an almost uncanny sense of timing in order for one to resume speaking at exactly the right moment. Properly timed pauses are also a part of good grouping and phrasing.

**Quantity**, the third element of time, means duration, or the length of time required to voice the sound. There are long and short sounds, syllables, and words. Compare the two a's in *arm* and *cat*, the first two syllables in *va ca tion*, and the words *blow* and *flit*. Long vowels are most easily prolonged for projection. Attention should be given to the full pronunciation of accented syllables and the subordination of unaccented ones to preserve the rhythm of speech.

### Pitch

Pitch is closely allied to tone, since both are governed to an extent by emotion. There are three elements in pitch which must be considered: key, step, and inflection. The **key** is the tone level of the voice and is what is usually meant when pitch is mentioned. A high pitch, while in some instances due to physical causes, is more often the result of tension or emotional upset. In dramatic use, high pitch may indicate anger, excitement, or any number of similar emotions. A medium pitch usually indicates poise and control. A low pitch may express pathos, despair, or tragedy. A fairly low pitch and slow tempo are commanding. A change of key, or tone level, is one of the most effective ways of showing a change in mood or idea.

**Step** relates to the range in pitch which a voice may have. A wide range expresses interest, enthusiasm, and vitality; a small range sullenness, sorrow, boredom, or little intelligence. A monotone speaks on one tone level, having no range.

**Inflection** is a slide or glide from one tone level to another. Questions are asked with an upward inflection. A movement downward gives an impression of determination and finality. A combination of the two, which is called a circumflex movement, expresses doubt, sarcasm, or innuendo. Iago's speech, page 138, illustrates the dramatic use of inflection. Pitch is employed effectively for cutting in and topping speeches, both of which require a decisive attack, force, and successively higher tone levels.

**RHYTHM** Throughout nature there is evidence of rhythm—in the beat of the surf, the rise and fall of the tides, the return of the seasons, the beat of your heart, breathing, and countless other natural occurrences. Rhythm is pulse; it is rise and fall, attack and release, and recurrent tensions and relaxations of muscular movement. Rhythm is an inner quality—a pattern, a design—most easily recognized in music and poetry, but inherent in all the arts. Good prose, as well as poetry, is rhythmic. There is a characteristic rhythm to each sport, to many occupations, to different languages. Each individual has a distinct rhythm of his own which is revealed in his actions and his voice, and which is the product of heredity and environment.

Mary Austin, in her book on American rhythms, calls attention to some that are the outgrowth of our living and so are an unconscious part of us.

As the pioneer track made westward-flowing patterns, the rhythm of horse-back riding, of a rise and fall distinctively of the American continent, superseded the foot pace. Now and then one picks it up in the work of Vachel Lindsay and Carl Sandburg, and not only the saddle jog, but the unintermittent cluck and roll of the Overland Flyer. . . . [Lincoln in his Gettysburg Address] fell unconsciously into the stride of one walking a woodland path with an ax on his shoulder,

It is rather for us
To be here dedicated to the great task
Remaining before us;
That from these honored dead we take
Increased devotion to that cause
For which they gave the last full measure of devotion.

Thus the railsplitter arrives at his goal with the upswing and the down-stroke:

That government of the people
By the people
For the people
Shall not perish from the earth!

And the ax comes to rest on the chopping log while a new length is measured.*

Pause is an element in rhythm—pause not only in speech but in bodily movement as well. The perfect integration of speech and movement makes a pleasing rhythmic pattern. One feels the swing of rhythm in walking, running, singing, and dancing.

Don't confuse rhythm with tempo, although the two work in con-

* Mary Austin, *The American Rhythm*. Houghton Mifflin Company. Copyright, 1930.

junction. Tempo is speed—fast or slow. Rhythm deals with the regularity of the recurring beats. If the distance between the beats is short, you will feel that there is greater speed than when the distance is greater.

A walk may be very fast but unrhythmic, because the person is taking uneven steps and never repeating the same pattern. As an actor you will use such a walk to indicate confusion and lack of poise. A controlled, graceful, effortless walk is rhythmic.

**VARIETY AND CONTRAST** To make your character interesting, to reveal the numerous facets of his personality, and to interpret fully the plot of the play, you will need to work constantly for variety in your speeches.

Every character will have his own tone quality, force, tempo, and pitch. Radiating, extrovert persons will tend to have rich, booming tones, vigor and force, deliberate timing, and a low pitch. Introverts may have thin tones, little force, and whining or weak voices. An unrepressed person will display a wider range in all these qualities; one more inhibited will have less range.

Very attractive qualities may become tiresome if unrelieved by occasional contrast with their opposites. In playing a very pleasant person, look for places in the script where he can logically show a bit of temper. When playing a grouchy character, find times when he can be at least reasonably agreeable. Besides heightening suspense and so holding the audience interest, this will make the character more true to life. Unless monotony is the keynote of the character, speech and movement patterns will vary from scene to scene, from speech to speech, and within the speeches themselves. Every phrase has distinct qualities of its own; every new idea causes a change in one of the speech elements. Many of these changes will, and should, occur naturally if you have a thorough understanding of the meaning of the lines and are able to assume the mood of the character. When they do not, you can always work them out by analysis and experimentation.

**DIALECTS** Since all beginning voice work can most profitably be devoted to the improvement of your own voice and speech, no practice in dialects is given. Your first aim is to make your own speech clear, accurate, and pleasant. Not all the characters you play will call for perfect speech, but you should be able to assume peculiarities at will. As a versatile actor you will later wish to learn dialects, but this is advanced work and should not be undertaken until good speech has become habitual.

It is often difficult, after working on a role which requires a dialect or speech eccentricities, to keep from retaining some of the inflections or mispronunciations. As soon as you have finished playing a part which requires such imperfections, make it a point to eliminate every trace of them from your own speech. You may find this harder to do than you imagine, but it is important that you do it.

**IMPROVISATIONS** While apparently acted upon the spur of the moment, improvisations depend for their effectiveness upon the observance of a few definite rules. Each character must have one or two very pronounced traits which will be revealed in his actions and his manner of speaking, as well as in the actual words that he speaks. Movement and business should be created as freely as they are when a role is being developed. A general sequence of incidents and conflicts should be decided upon, all progressing toward a climax which may or may not have been settled in advance. No dialogue should be written.

This is the old Commedia dell' Arte technique as developed by strolling players in the sixteenth century in Italy. Only the outline or "scenario" was traced, the rest being entrusted to the improvisation of the actors. The plots were often taken from stories and plays, but the dialogue was improvised each time by the actors and always included jokes and gossip of local interest. (See page 148.) Because Commedia dell' Arte characters appear in so many plays, you should be familiar with their individual characteristics. The principal characters were Arlecchino, Pantalone, Pulcinella, Scaramuccia, Brighella, Capitano, and Dottore. Many variations were made on each of them.

COMMEDIA DELL' ARTE

*Harlequin* *Pierrot* *Pierrette or Columbine*

Pantalone was portrayed as an old father, niggardly, gullible, and garrulous. Dottore, a verbose, comic doctor, was his frequent companion. Large-nosed Pulcinella, who became Punch in England, was played as a mixture of villainy and stupidity. Capitano was a boastful, cowardly Spanish captain, long-nosed, round-eyed, and grotesque. Scaramuccia, or Scaramouch, was a more romantic captain.

Brighella was villainous, cruel, cynical, witty, and self-seeking. Arlecchino, or Harlequin as he was known in France, was clever, witty, and keen but given to cheating and trickery. Another character, Pagliaccio or Pedrolino, the French Pierrot, was lovelorn and moody, a singer of sad songs, and often a dancer. Still another, Columbine, is really a character from a more modern type of comedy than the Commedia dell' Arte. Through the years, however, she has been more and more included with the latter, possibly through her identification with the character of Pierrette, as a companion for Pierrot in the French version. She is pretty, pert, and flirtatious; usually a servant, sometimes a dancer.

Create characters as definite as these in the following improvisations.

### Reacting to an imagined person or group

Assemble the ideas for a speech of about one paragraph for one of the following characters (or one of your own choice) and give it with an appropriate voice, taking into consideration quality, pitch, rate, volume, and inflection. Do not write the scene, but create the character, visualize the situation, and imagine your fellow actors. Plan the scene so that you build to a definite climax and finish. It may be helpful to prearrange a tag line to which you can build.

Be (1) a gym instructor or dance teacher directing a group in a game, exercises, or a dance, (2) a food demonstrator in a store, (3) a mother giving last-minute advice to a child as he leaves for a party, (4) a movie director giving directions to a group of extras for a definite scene, (5) an auctioneer selling antiques to an indifferent audience.

### Reacting to one person

In these scenes you are to improvise dialogue and business, responding to what your partner does and says. He is, of course, improvising in response to you. Eye contact is important. Take a few minutes to assume the mood of the character and to sense the situation, then keep the scene moving spiritedly to a climax and a conclusion.

EXAMPLE: A hotheaded person, A, is questioned about a check by B, who is calm and poised.

A's gestures and movements are quick, jerky, and numerous, showing that he is excited and angry. B's gestures are few and simple, and he has little body movement, thus registering poise and self-control.

As A becomes increasingly angry his voice becomes more shrill. As B becomes increasingly calm his voice lowers in pitch.

A: I've never been so insulted in my life!
B: I merely asked if you had seen the check.
A: But you implied that I had taken it!
B: I really didn't—I merely asked—
A: You know you did—why deny it?
B: Aren't you being a little hasty? I—
A: Hasty? When you stand there and accuse me of stealing?
B: Oh, take it easy; it's not that important.
A: Important! I'll have you know that I'll not be called a thief! I won't take that from anyone!
(He storms out, or knocks B down, or becomes hysterical, or concludes with any other suitable reaction).

After giving the scene with words, repeat it in pantomime. In like manner create business and dialogue for the following characters, who in each instance should be opposite types.

(1) A stern employer interviews a self-conscious stenographer applying for her first job. (2) A political candidate who has definite ideas about running his campaign discusses them with his manager, who has a completely opposite plan.(3) Two people with opposite ideas of where to go

and what to do plan a trip. (4) A boy or girl, wanting the family car for a very special occasion, tries to get Father, who is out of sorts, to give his consent. (5) A mother and daughter having opposing ideas discuss the way to make the daughter's new dress.

### Reacting to a group of people

After learning to respond to a single character, expand your range to include a group. In each of the following scenes one person is the center of interest, and he is responsible for keeping the scene moving. Every member of the group must show a distinctive, dominant characteristic in speeches, movement, and business. Decide on that characteristic, then devise body attitudes, movements, and gestures that will project it to the audience. Have at least one mannerism, not your own, that will help to make this clear. Decide upon a voice quality and a manner of speaking which will project this same characteristic. In each scene build to a strong, definite climax.

1. A group of art students is being toured through an art gallery by a guide who explains each of the pictures. Most of his information is incorrect, and the students feel the necessity for setting him right.
2. Accompanied by a friend, a mother (or father), whose son has been seriously hurt in an accident, rushes into the reception room of a hospital. The doctor, nurses, and friend try to calm the parent, but permission to see the child is denied. (Build to a strong climax.)
3. Just before show time the manager of a small theatre comes backstage to tell a vaudeville troupe that they are being dismissed after this performance. They try to convince him that they must continue. (Each one reacts to the news in a different way.)
4. A host (or hostess) stands at the door as his guests depart and responds to their words of appreciation for a successful party. Each person will show a different degree of pleasure and expressiveness.
5. The family has just acquired a new station wagon. Father would like to take some of his friends on a fishing trip, but all the children are determined to go camping. They present their arguments, each one having a different method of persuasion. Mother may or may not remain neutral.

**SELECTIONS FOR INTERPRETATION** In the following selections you can employ the voice techniques which you have learned. Although special emphases are indicated, they do not exhaust the interpretive possibilities in the selection.

### Contrast in volume, stage whispers

THE DRAPER. Hello! Master Pierre!

GUILLEMETTE. (*Laying her finger on her lips.*) Oh, sir, if you have anything to say, for mercy's sake speak lower!

THE DRAPER. God keep you, mistress!

GUILLEMETTE. Oh, not so loud!

THE DRAPER. (*Astonished and puzzled.*) Huh? What's the matter?

GUILLEMETTE. (*Feigning amazement.*) Bless my soul!

*Master Pierre Patelin*—ANONYMOUS

### Calling off-stage, sharp changes in volume and pitch

PRUE FORESIGHT *is in her room with the door locked.* THE NURSE *is trying to rouse her.*

NURSE. Miss! Miss! Miss Prue!—mercy on me, marry and amen!—Why what's become of the child? Why, miss? Miss Foresight! —Sure, she has locked herself up in her chamber, and gone to sleep, or to prayers. —Miss! miss! —open the door, miss! Od's my life! I'll come in the back way.

*Love For Love*—WILLIAM CONGREVE

### Fast cues, varied inflection, topping, building to a climax, exit on a line

LADY FANCIFUL *is intent upon leaving* LADY BRUTE *without having the latter follow her.*

LADY FANCIFUL. (*Going.*) Nay, you sha'n't go one step out of the room.

LADY BRUTE. Indeed I'll wait upon you down.

LADY FANCIFUL. No, sweet Lady Brute; you know I swoon at Ceremony.

LADY BRUTE. Pray give me leave.

LADY FANCIFUL. You know I won't.

LADY BRUTE. Indeed I must.

LADY FANCIFUL. Indeed you sha'n't.

LADY BRUTE. Indeed I will.

LADY FANCIFUL. Indeed you sha'n't.

LADY BRUTE. Indeed I will.

LADY FANCIFUL. Indeed you sha'n't. Indeed, Indeed, Indeed you sha'n't.

(*Exit* LADY FANCIFUL *running*. LADY BRUTE *follows*.)

*The Provok'd Wife*—JOHN VANBRUGH

### Insinuation through vocal inflection

IAGO *in his speech plants suspicion in* OTHELLO'S *mind not by his words but by vocal insinuation as his voice takes on inflections filled with villainous intent.*

IAGO. Did Michael Cassio, when you woo'd my lady,
Know of your love?

OTHELLO. He did, from first to last: why dost thou ask?

IAGO. But for the satisfaction of my thought;
No further harm.

OTHELLO. Why of thy thought, Iago?

IAGO. I did not think he had been acquainted with her.

OTHELLO. O! yes; and went between us very oft.

IAGO. Indeed!

OTHELLO. Indeed! ay, indeed; discern'st thou aught in that?
Is he not honest?

IAGO. Honest, my lord?

OTHELLO. Honest! ay, honest.

IAGO. My lord, for aught I know.

OTHELLO. What dost thou think?

IAGO. Think, my lord!

OTHELLO. Think, my lord! By heaven, he echoes me—

*Othello* (III, 3)—WILLIAM SHAKESPEARE

**Vigor, volume, inflection, mood, building to a climax**

DUKE. You are a fool. You niece, provide yourself.
If you outstay the time, upon mine honor,
And in the greatness of my word, you die.
(*Exit.*)

*As You Like It* (I, 3)—WILLIAM SHAKESPEARE

**Positions of equal importance for conversation, eye contact, exact timing, tag line**

COX. Between you and me, I'm rather partial to this house.
BOX. So am I—I begin to feel quite at home in it.
COX. Everything so clean and comfortable—
BOX. And I'm sure the mistress of it, from what I have seen of her, is very anxious to please.
COX. So she is—and I vote, Box, that we stick by her.
BOX. Agreed! There's my hand upon it—join but yours—agree that the house is big enough to hold us both, then Box—
COX. And Cox—
BOTH. Are satisfied.

(*Curtain.*)

*Box and Cox*—JOHN MADDISON MORTON

**CHAPTER HIGHLIGHTS**

Personal inventory of voice and speech
Exercises for speech improvement
  Enunciation
  Pronunciation
  Tone quality
A Daily Routine for Speech Practice
Principles of interpretation
Improvisations
Selections for interpretation

# Eight

## HISTORY AND HORIZONS ☆☆☆

Throughout the history of man the theatre has been a reflection of the life of the people in a particular era. The dramatic history of a country is a record of social, political, economic, and religious events. This is our cultural heritage and the modern theatre is built upon this heritage. A knowledge of those aspects of life will enable you to appreciate more fully productions of literary worth and to form standards of criticism for the diverse theatre media of today: the stage, motion pictures, radio and television.

The following information, although over-simplified, is intended not only to give you names, dates, and facts, but also to show that theatre is actually a study of people in a particular setting. Research topics found later in this chapter suggest areas for continued study which will help to piece together the elaborate and exciting picture of the development of world drama.

# ☆☆☆ HISTORY OF THE THEATRE

**THE BEGINNINGS** Hundreds of years before the first formal theatre productions in Greece, drama was taking shape, as primitive man imitated animals, performed stories of the hunt, magic dances, ancestor worship, and masked pantomimes. These crude ceremonies staged around campfires resembled the theatre of primitive peoples throughout the world today.

While there is no recorded evidence of the stages of development which followed, we do know that in Egypt some five thousand years ago there existed some form of written plays, for texts dealing with the lives and deaths of rulers have been excavated from Egyptian tombs. But just how the glorious theatre of fifth-century Greece evolved is something of a mystery.

**THE GREEK PERIOD: CLASSICAL AGE OF DRAMA** The period between 500 B.C. and 400 B.C., in which all the great tragedies were written, was known as the Golden Age of Greece. During that period contests were initiated and playwright-poets began to compete for annual prizes. Literary principles and conventions in play structure were established. Among these were the unities of Time, Place, and Action and the idea that no acts of violence and murder should occur on stage. These were reported, however, in horrifying detail by messengers or by the chorus.

Because of the close bond between religion and politics, it is not surprising to learn that the first great tragedies were written for religious festivals. It is believed that tragedy originated in the early worship of Dionysus, the god of wine and fertility. At first, groups of revelers celebrating the grape harvest paraded through the city or gathered in "dancing rings" singing choral hymns or dithyrambs in his praise. Later these dithyrambs included the stories of heroes and historical legends. Thespis is credited with first introducing an actor who talked to the chorus and acted out the story. He thus is proclaimed the first actor-dramatist. In his honor actors are called Thespians.

**Aeschylus** (525-456 B.C.) (born ten years after Thespis' innovation) was first of the three great tragic writers. He added the second actor and produced one of the greatest trilogies, *The Oresteia,* which includes the plays *Agamemnon, The Libation-Bearers, The Furies.* **Sophocles** (497-406 B.C.) added the third actor and limited the chorus to fifteen members. This made possible more dramatic action and better balance between the actors' spoken dialogue and the choric songs. Among his great plays are *Antigone, Electra,* and *Oedipus Rex.* **Euripides** (480-406 B.C.), the third great tragic playwright, stirred controversy through his dramas, which reflected the growing skepticism of his age and the questioning of religious ideologies. *The Trojan Women, Medea,* and *Hecuba* are a few of his seventeen extant tragedies. All the dramatists were prolific writers, but unfortunately only forty-four texts have survived.

The plays were staged in large open-air theatres, the most distinguished being the theatre of Dionysus at the foot of the Acropolis. The action of the chorus and actors took place on the circular dancing floor called the *orchestra,* and on the stage, at first unraised, directly behind it. Back of this was a simple portico called the *skene* (from which we derived the word *scene.*) The auditorium was separated from the stage and skene by a wide passageway through which the chorus entered the dancing circle. In later theatres, where the stage was raised, this became a ramp. Three doors in the skene provided the entrances and exits for the actors and represented locales such as the palace or city gates.

Special effects were achieved with the use of the *eccyclema* (a raised platform that was wheeled out revealing a tableau or the bodies of people murdered off-stage), trap doors, thunder machines, the *deus ex machina* (a crane used for lowering and raising characters to and from the stage), *periaktoi* (triangular prisms on which scenes could be painted), and simple altars, statues, rocks, and hand props.

The audience, which started to assemble at dawn, sat on marble or stone seats that were built on the natural slope of the hill and followed the curve of the dancing circle. Since the plays were staged during daylight, they needed no special lighting devices.

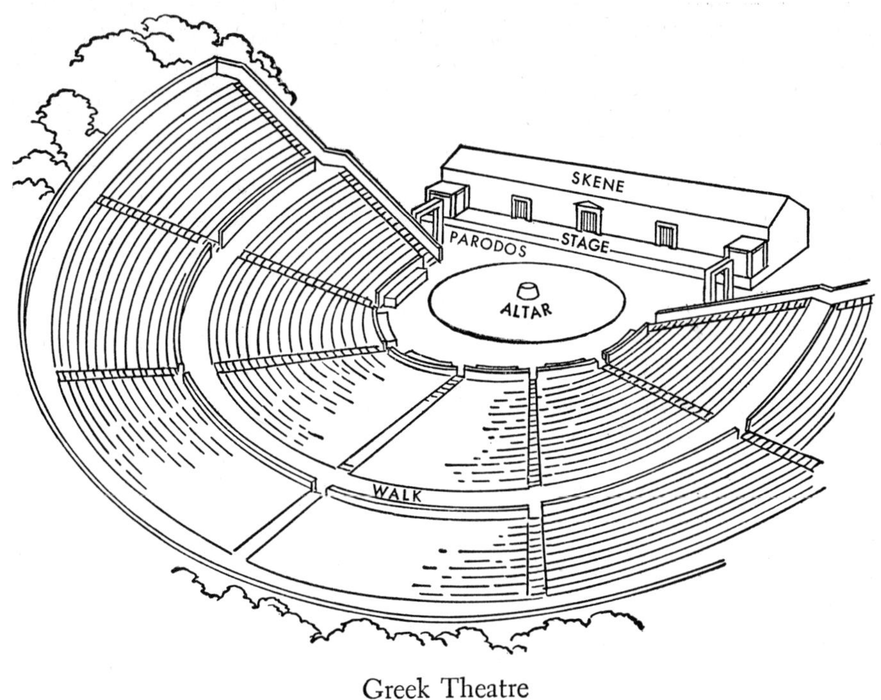


Greek Theatre

The chorus, ranging in number from twelve to fifty, functioned as a link between the audience and actors, giving expression to the emotional suffering of the characters, reacting as citizen groups to the proclamations of a king, interpreting and intensifying the poetic splendor of the drama, and separating scene from scene. Their fluid movement and choric vocal power contrasted vividly with the single actor and orchestrated the entire dramatic action. The actors, always men or boys, wore masks, shoes with built-up soles (called *cothurnus*), headdresses, and padded clothes to increase their size.

Satyr plays and comedies as well as tragedies were presented. All three types used a chorus and masks and were written in verse. Often the satyr plays were vigorous and bawdy burlesques of the legends and heroes presented in the tragedies. Contests in comedies began almost fifty years after those of tragedy. The old comedy dealt with biting, witty satires that lampooned current social figures, politics, and society. **Aristophanes** (450-380 B.C.) was the master playwright of this type. Among his plays are *Lysistrata, The Frogs,* and *The Birds.* In the comedy which followed, stock characters and plots of everyday life were developed. Crystallized by Menander, this form became the model for Roman comedies.

After the Peloponnesian War, when independence was lost, the magnificent theatre of Greece declined and fell into decay.

**THE ROMAN THEATRE** The Romans had little taste for poetic tragedy; they preferred the sensational spectacles of gladiatorial contests, sacrifices of men and beasts in the colossal amphitheatres, and obscene pantomimes and farces. As a result, there was very little creative theatre.

**Seneca** attempted tragedies, probably meant to be read, full of bombast and rhetoric. He is significant mainly because he served as a model for playwrights of the Renaissance. **Plautus** and **Terence** wrote comedies for the popular tastes—neatly turned plots of confusion and love intrigue filled with stock characters, epigrammatic statements and slapstick. They are remembered principally for their influence on later playwrights. Shakespeare borrowed generously both plots and characters from the Roman comedies.

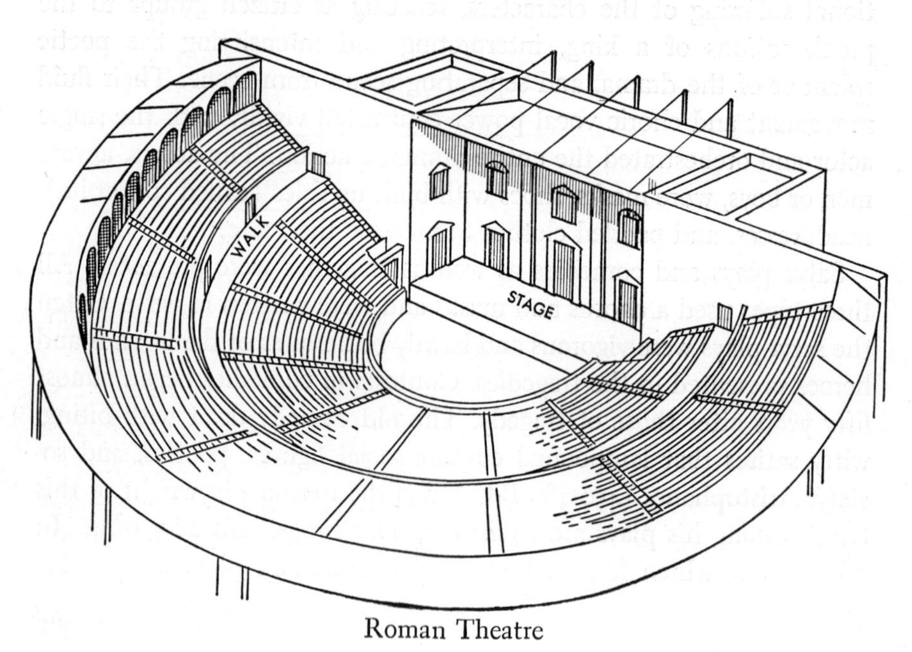


Roman Theatre

Theatres were patterned after the Greek, but somewhat modified. The skene was elaborated and heightened, the dancing circle reduced to a semicircle, and the audience section joined to the stage wall so that the theatre building was a single unit.

As the Empire fell and the Christian Church exerted its power, ostracizing all forms of theatre in the third and fourth centuries A.D., the dramatic forms disappeared, leaving only the Mimes, the little groups of wandering entertainers, and the "jongleurs."

**THE MEDIEVAL THEATRE** For almost seven hundred years there was no real theatre in Europe. When it did appear again, it was rooted in religious ceremony and began almost as though no drama had ever existed before.

Some time in the tenth century, clergymen began to insert in the church services simple tableaux and pantomimes illustrating the stories of the Bible for the instruction of the townspeople, most of whom were illiterate and credulous. This became so popular that soon dramatized stories from both the Old and New Testaments were enacted. As the plays became more elaborate, laymen were added to the acting casts, humor was injected for entertainment, and the scenes were written in the vernacular, since few of the laity knew Latin or could read or write. When the church could no longer accommodate the crowds and numerous cast members, the plays were taken outside onto the church porch. Later they were moved to the market places or public squares, where eventually the entire responsibility of production and performance passed from the church to the trade guilds.

While no plays of literary stature were written, theatrical activity was vigorous and all Europe was alive with pageants, plays, and liturgical drama by the end of the fifteenth century. The specific dates of development and names applied to each dramatic form are not certain, for all the types of plays here described were being performed at different times in different parts of the Continent and England.

1. **Sequences** (tenth century), plays that stood alone from the Mass. *Adam,* written in the twelfth century, is the earliest text in existence. 2. **Miracle Plays** (twelfth century), based on the lives of saints.

3. **Mystery Plays** (twelfth century), Bible stories telling the events from creation to resurrection. 4. **Passion Plays** (twelfth century), scenes depicting the sufferings and resurrection of Christ. The *Valenciennes Passion Play* and *Oberammergau Passion Play* in Bavaria are famous examples. 5. **The Cycles** (fourteenth century), an original type of production developed in England in which each play in a series was produced by a particular guild and staged on a pageant wagon drawn by horses that progressed along the streets or roads stopping at designated places for a performance, then moving on. Thus a crowd gathered at any one corner watched the entire series as the doubledecked wagons passed along the procession route. Only four complete cycle texts remain—*York, Coventry, Chester,* and *Wakefield.* 6. **Morality Plays** (fifteenth and sixteenth centuries), stories of vice conquered by virtue, with characters personifying abstract qualities such as Knowledge, Beauty, Good Deeds, and Death. *Everyman* is still performed today.

The Moralities mark the end of the liturgical drama that instructed medieval man in the lessons of the Church and form the transitional link to Elizabethan drama. As the Church bowed out of dramatic production and the guilds took charge, the Mysteries and Moralities reflected more and more the humorous elements of everyday life. In the fifteenth century the **Interludes** which followed were an offshoot of the Moralities and secular rather than religious.

Medieval man was devout, superstitious, and concerned primarily with life after death, in which he hoped for blessing and feared the punishments of hell. But he also frolicked in costly, imaginative, and spectacular productions, devising ingenious machinery for hell's belching fire and costumes for merry-making demons.

Characteristics peculiar to medieval staging are: 1. the mingling of actors and audience; 2. the graphic representation of Heaven, Hell, and Limbo in structures that sometimes towered several stories high; 3. the use of "mansions" or "stations" (small set units indicating locales such as Pilate's house or the temple of Jerusalem that were arranged between Heaven and Hell); and 4. the use of the space between mansions as acting areas.

GROUPING: STAGE DOOR *University High School, Los Angeles*

GROUPING: THE ROYAL FAMILY *Beverly Hills High School*

GROUPING: IF I WERE KING *University High School, Los Angeles*

MAKE-UP:
*Santa Monica City College*

MAKE-UP:
*Eagle Rock High School,*
*Los Angeles*

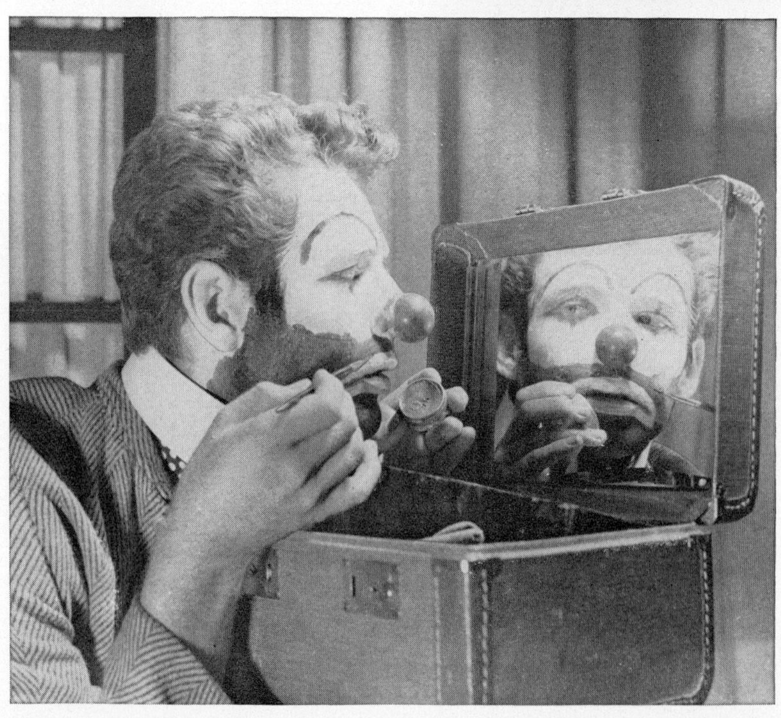

**RENAISSANCE THEATRE IN ITALY** The Renaissance erupted all over Europe during the fourteenth to seventeenth centuries, but reached its greatest flowering first in Italy. This "rebirth" of man's interest in the dignity of the individual and the new age of humanism produced enormous contemporary achievements in philosophy, science, painting, sculpture, and architecture. Universities were established; the masterpieces of Michelangelo, Leonardo da Vinci, Giotto and Brunelleschi were painted; the printing press and gunpowder were invented; and the ancient worlds of Greece and Rome were rediscovered by the scholars. But although there were great poets and writers—Dante, Petrarch, Boccaccio, and Machiavelli—no dramatic literature of lasting merit was written. The Italians did, however, create two new dramatic forms—the pastoral drama (Tasso's *Aminta*, 1573) and opera (Peri's *Daphne*, 1594)—and established rigid theatrical laws for playwriting based on Aristotle's *Poetics.*

As with the other arts, the theatre was supported by the nobles—men of fabulous wealth, despots who vied with each other for power and prestige. Court masques, pageants, pastorals, and classical adaptations were lavishly staged in palaces and gardens.

The archeological findings of earnest scholars of Greek and Roman antiquity led to the construction of permanent playhouses, built on classical models but housed indoors. Of these the first was the Teatro Olimpico (1580) at Vicenza, designed by Palladio. This is, in fact, a small enclosed Roman theatre. Following this, the first permanent proscenium arch was built in the Teatro Farnese at Parma (1618). The master painters of the day developed the art of perspective in drawing and painting and combined its use with inventive three-dimensional constructions that gave an illusion of great depth and space to scenic backdrops.

Subsequent wonders were devised in stage machinery, settings, and lighting effects to produce astonishing spectacles; a raked (slanted) stage to add to the perspective illusion, *periaktoi,* "vistas," sets of revolving prisms for rapid scene changes, sliding wings and "nested wings," cycloramas with slots for manipulating machinery to sail chariots and clouds across painted skies, huge pulleys rotating painted cloth to display running waterfalls, sea monsters, and tossing waves.

At the same time a vigorous and creative professional group of actors were performing for a popular audience in the streets—the Commedia dell' Arte troupes (1550). Their brilliant, improvised comedy was played throughout the Continent and has influenced playwrights from that time to the present day. Two qualities in their acting were unique: their incredible versatility and inventiveness in creating superb comedy, and their set of stock characters, most of whom wore stylized, traditional masks. (See pages 132-134 for descriptions of these characters.)

A typical company composed of seven men and three women, all generously gifted with witty minds and agile bodies, seized upon the inspiration of the moment to perform acrobatics, dances, and songs or deliver impromptu soliloquies of local interest. Playing on portable platforms, these rollicking pranksters improvised dialogue, pantomimed extravagantly, interjected *lazzi* (traditional or stock speeches or bits of business), and deftly embellished the rough plot outline (scenario) posted in the wings, which served as the framework for displaying all their remarkable feats of acting.

**RENAISSANCE THEATRE IN SPAIN** In the "golden age" of Spain (approximately 1550 to 1650) thousands of plays were written, theatres multiplied, and audiences grew. The Spanish dramatists did not follow the literary rules of Italy; instead, they captured the world of romance, chivalry, and "cape and sword" adventure. They invented original plots and characters instead of using the classical legends, and developed dialogue that had an instinctive naturalness.

Three world-famous Spanish playwrights are: **Cervantes,** better known for his novel *Don Quixote* than his plays; **Lope de Vega,** whose almost two thousand plays contained original plots and characters, a high degree of poetic beauty, and a generous supply of dashing action; and **Calderon,** whose plays are noted for their polished grace, spiritual emphasis, and elevated poetry.

**RENAISSANCE THEATRE IN ENGLAND: DRAMA IN THE AGE OF ELIZABETH** Unlike the glittering theatre structures and pseudoclassicism of Italy, England in the Renaissance was able to originate a unique form of playhouse and plays. It was an era of peace after a century of wars. Both time and money were plentiful, and there was a great upsurge of national pride. Religious freedom under Queen Elizabeth permitted open intellectual curiosity.

Elizabeth, a dramatic personality herself, was a patron of the arts and a classical scholar who enjoyed the Greek and Latin plays presented in the original for her pleasure when she visited Oxford and Cambridge. She insured the security of the Burbage Company under license of the Lord Chamberlain's Men, and frequently summoned this same company for command performances at court.

The voyages of discovery which brought back to England material goods, conquests, and tales of fascinating adventures in exotic lands brought also a flood of new wonderful words with which to create vivid imagery. The theatre was, for the English people, their chief source of entertainment, information, and adventure, serving as newspaper, illustrated lecture, moving picture, and travel book.

By the end of Elizabeth's reign there were eighteen theatres in London alone to which apprentices, citizens, and courtiers could go. Not since the Golden Age of Greece had the setting for great dramatic literature and audience appreciation been so perfect.

The transitional links in play performance from the Middle Ages were the Interludes. Interjected with comic relief, they matured into full independent comedies of which *Ralph Roister Doister* (about 1540) by Nicholas Udall, and *Gammer Gurton's Needle* (about 1552) were the earliest. *Gorboduc* (about 1561) by Sackville and Norton, the first tragedy written in English, introduced blank verse, predecessor of the magnificent drama of the Elizabethan playwrights.

The first playhouse, the **Theatre,** was built by James Burbage in 1576. It was designed along the ground plans of the innyards, and influenced the direction playwriting took. Ignoring the classic principles and three unities, the dramatists covered years in one historical drama, introduced horrifying and violent action on the stage, blended poetry and prose, mixed comedy and tragedy in the same play, and frequently ended a scene with a dancing jig.

The **Elizabethan period** extends from 1584 to 1642, includes the reigns of the two Stuart kings as well as Elizabeth, and ends with the closing of the theatres by Puritan law. During this sweep of almost sixty years, there was an abundance of English playwrights. Fortunately for them, Holinshed's historical *Chronicles* had been printed in 1578, and the colorful past of England depicted in it provided abundant material for historical plays. John Lyly, Thomas Kyd, John Webster, Robert Greene, Thomas Dekker, Thomas Heywood, Beaumont and Fletcher and many more penned fine dramas. **Christopher Marlowe,** the first great playwright of the age, who reached poetic heights in his *Tamburlaine* and *Doctor Faustus,* led the way to the glorious, provocative dramas *Hamlet, Macbeth,* and *King Lear.* Shakespeare's closest rival, **Ben Jonson,** was a giant among outstanding dramatists with his plays *Volpone, Bartholomew Fair,* and *The Alchemist.*

During his brief writing span of fifteen years, **Shakespeare** (1564-1616) wrote thirty-seven plays—many among the world's greatest—over one hundred incidental songs, and one hundred fifty-four sonnets. In his plays live the ribaldry, the beauty, and the grandeur of his time. Besides the superb imagery with which he brought every character unforgettably alive, Shakespeare apparently had an uncanny ability to observe and to lay away in the storehouse of his memory intimate details of human nature. As a poet he commanded the entire gamut of poetic experience and could illuminate each character's eccentricities and rhythms in speech and action. He had the unusual combination of a rich sense of humor and great breadth of vision; he was master of every sort of comic effect, and at the same time he created profound dramas on universal themes.

Coupled with Shakespeare's own innate talents as a dramatist was the company of excellent actors who complemented his inspired abilities and for whom Shakespeare created the great tragic characters.

Had Richard Burbage not been eminently capable of playing these roles, or had Kemp not had the agility, quick wit, and singing voice for the clown parts, Shakespeare probably would not have written them. Heminge and Condell, who later edited a First Folio edition of Shakespeare's plays, performed a great variety of roles. The fact that they played women's parts understandingly and well made possible the galaxy of genuine, living women in Shakespeare's plays.

Like the Greek playwrights, Shakespeare had a theatre and stage uncluttered by painted scenes and complex machinery. He painted the scenery and set the mood with words, calling upon the active imagination of the audiences to set the stage as in the Prologue of *Henry V*: "Piece out our imperfections with your thoughts."

Shakespeare took advantage of every possible combination of the seven acting areas of the Globe which allowed the actors to move freely and immediately from one scene to the next without waiting for scenery changes. (See page 42.) There was the large **apron stage** jutting out into the pit, where the elbowing groundlings stood. There were the **study** (a curtained inner room directly behind the apron, which could be set with properties), the **chamber** (a curtained stage directly above the study), the **tarras** (a balcony in front of the chamber), the **music gallery** (a stage for the musicians above the chamber), and two **window stages** (balconies on either side of the chamber). Trap doors in the apron were used for grave scenes. The hut served as a passage to the roof (called the "heavens" or "shadow") where there was machinery for miraculous descents.

When the theatres flew their flags to announce a performance, the citizens thronged across London Bridge and entered one of the "wooden O's," as the theatres were called because they were octagonal in shape and built of wood. Those who could afford seats sat in the tiered galleries, or even on the stage; the others stood in the open pit, or courtyard, under the noses of the players, who could "split the ears of the groundlings" with their zeal. The boisterous mob responded lustily to the dramatic story, the skill of the cast, and the visual splendor of the players, who were often gorgeously arrayed in costumes adapted from the cast-off finery of the court.

The last form of dramatic entertainment to develop in Elizabethan England was the **Masque.** Perfected under the Stuart kings, James I and Charles I, they introduced the scenic display and extravagant spectacles of the Italian Renaissance shows, bringing to the royal palaces pageantry, song, lyric poetry, and dance. Ben Jonson wrote them, and Inigo Jones, who had studied the elaborate scenery and machines in Italy, designed the scenery to ornament them.

**RENAISSANCE THEATRE IN FRANCE** Immediately following the Elizabethan era in England, the greatest period in the French theatre emerged. The Renaissance came late in France (seventeenth century) for two major reasons: like England, France was absorbed in years of foreign and internal wars; and in Paris for over one hundred years theatre productions were monopolized by the favored Confrérie group, who enjoyed the exclusive rights to play productions in the *one* public playhouse. Until unity and prosperity were re-established in the country and the theatre monopoly was broken to allow for competition among acting companies, France had neither a significant theatre nor great playwrights to fill it. Cardinal Richelieu, Prime Minister to Louis XIII, and King Louis XIV were the two powerful figures responsible for France's theatrical greatness in the seventeenth century. This greatness rests chiefly on the neoclassic dramas of **Pierre Corneille** (1606-1689) and **Jean Racine** (1639-1699) and the comedies of **Molière** (Jean-Baptiste Poquelin, 1622-1673).

Corneille, the first great playwright, was not a pure classicist by personal conviction or in spirit. His renowned and successful tragedy, *Le Cid,* displeased the critics because it was romantic in essence and ignored the classic rules in form. As a result he allowed his following works to be dominated by the neoclassic formula. In contrast, Racine's talents fell with natural grace into the rigid form. *Phèdre,* his most acclaimed drama, revealed his skill and brilliant style in handling tragedy according to the French rules.

While Corneille and Racine were reaching glorious heights perfecting the tragic drama, Molière, the comic genius of all French theatre, was training as an amateur actor in a company that toured for thirteen years in the provinces of France. The series of plays which he wrote pictured the foibles and injustices of contemporary society. Although he also wrote farces and comedy-ballets, it is his comedies that make him the greatest playwright of France. Among the most famous ones are *Le Bourgeois Gentilhomme* (*The Would-Be Gentleman*), *L'Ecole des Femmes* (*The School for Wives*), *Tartuffe*, *Le Misanthrope*, and *Le Malade Imaginaire.*

The final contribution that Louis XIV made to drama was the creation of a state-supported theatre. After Molière's death he united the remaining groups in a single company at the Guénégaud theatre, making France the first country to have a **national theatre.** In 1680 the theatre became known as the Comédie Française; its company is still the most important acting group in France.

**RESTORATION AND EIGHTEENTH CENTURY THEATRES IN ENGLAND**

By order of Cromwell, the Puritans closed the theatres in 1642, and for eighteen years they remained closed in England. But performances did exist in London throughout this period in the "private" playhouses, which were exclusive in the sense that they were expensive and clandestine showings at public theatres, inns, and fairs.

When Charles II was restored to the throne in 1660, he ushered in a totally different kind of theatre from the Elizabethan. Nine of his years of banishment were spent in France where he saw the tragedies of Corneille, the tennis-court theatres, and actresses upon the stage. The theatre he licensed on his return to England was strongly influenced by the French, but shaped in a new and distinctly English form.

The former inner stage was enlarged behind a proscenium frame to accommodate scenery—a series of flats or wings, shutters, and backdrops that were painted in perspective and ran in grooves. Set parallel to the curtain line, they were spaced one behind the other in pairs arranged progressively closer together as they approached the rear backdrop. The old platform stage of the Elizabethans became smaller and was called the **apron,** still extending into the audience as an independent acting area where most of the action took place. Doors in front of the proscenium and on either side of the forestage allowed actors to enter and leave the apron while the main curtain was down. Artificial lighting was introduced, candles being placed in meager footlights and chandeliers. Both the stage and auditorium floors were raked for better vision. Benches were provided on the main floor, boxes were located on the stage apron, and galleries extended around the sides and back of the theatre.

To supply the theatres with shows, the playwrights and producers at first altered Shakespeare's plays, revived Beaumont and Fletcher's, translated Molière's, and made an attempt to mix music and drama. A popular triumph, *The Siege of Rhodes,* written by D'Avenant, was the first English opera. Original Restoration tragedies followed, but with few exceptions they were carved to the classical standards and neoclassicism of the French stage. Of the English writers who tried to create heroic tragedy, only three are noteworthy: John Dryden (*All for Love*), Thomas Otway (*Venice Preserved*), and Joseph Addison (*Cato*).

The plays were performed for a sophisticated group of elegant courtiers, fashionably witty, insolent, dissipated creatures who met at the playhouse to see themselves and their "cult of correctness" portrayed. Reflecting the standards of a select and elegantly mannered group, the Restoration playwrights wrote social satires on the artificialities and absurdities of the age. Characters bore such telling titles as Tattle, Crab, Sir Fopling Flutter, Scandal, Heartfree, and Sir Wilful Witwoud. Writers who wittily captured the vices of the rake, the heartless lady, and the decadent morals of the age were Sir George Etherage (*Love in a Tub*), William Wycherley (*The Country Wife*), John Vanbrugh (*The Provok'd Wife*), George Farquhar (*The Beaux' Stratagem*). But the men who brought the comedy of manners to its highest peak of perfection came after the Restoration period (1660-1700)—**William Congreve** (*The Way of the World,* 1700), **Oliver Goldsmith** (*She Stoops to Conquer,* 1773), and **Richard Brinsley Sheridan** (*The Rivals,* 1775, *The School for Scandal,* 1777).

The Restoration period saw the rise of a great actor, Thomas Betterton, and the entrance of engaging actresses who were adored and pampered by nobles and kings—Mrs. Betterton, Mrs. Bracegirdle, and Nell Gwynn. But the eighteenth century, known as the "age of great actors," was enriched with the talents of Colley Cibber, David Garrick, Kitty Clive, Charles Macklin, John Philip Kemble, Nancy Oldfield, Elizabeth Barry, Peg Woffington, and Sarah Kemble Siddons.

**David Garrick**—actor, director, producer, dramatist—influenced the reform in acting from ranting, declamatory delivery to a more natural style and brought about an improvement in lighting techniques.

Under the reign of George III, the character of the audience changed, and the typical comedies of the eighteenth century, though they were inferior plays, reflected the tastes of a dominant middle-class group who demanded reform from the "sinful" theatre fare of the Restoration comedies. To satisfy this demand, *sentimental* comedies were written with proper words and moral standards rigidly upheld. The virtuous heroines were rewarded, the evil characters punished, and edifying sermons were preached to show pity, charity, repentance, and forgiveness as the chief virtues to be exalted. To house the huge audience of merchants and tradesmen, the theatres were enlarged to accommodate over three thousand people.

## MODERN THEATRE: NINETEENTH AND TWENTIETH CENTURIES

The last one hundred and sixty years have brought so many changes—social, political, industrial, and artistic—that the story of the theatre and its developments cannot be neatly dated and pigeonholed.

For the first eighty years of the nineteenth century, playwriting did not achieve impressive heights. Initiated by Goethe and Schiller, **Romanticism** as a movement filled the theatres for over fifty years with plays of sentimental idealism, emotional escape, adventure, and melodrama. In France, romantic tragedy moved to romantic melodrama in the plays of Victor Hugo, the elder Alexandre Dumas, and Guilbert de Pixérécourt and then spread to other European countries.

In addition, the plays of Eugène Scribe and Victorien Sardou, both prolific writers, swelled the repertoires of the theatres of France.

In England, the romantic poets—Swinburne, Tennyson, Byron, Coleridge, Shelley, Matthew Arnold—wrote "closet dramas" (plays better read than acted). Long-run performances were the practice, and touring companies took to the road. However, the significant progress in acting technique was made by the directors, who, in rebellion against bravura display, established *ensemble* acting methods. A few forerunners of Ibsen made important strides toward **realism** and the "slice-of-life" drama, but this type was not prevalent until the last decade of the nineteenth century.

The experiments in France of Antoine and his Théâtre Libre gave great impetus to the realistic movement by promoting the development of European playwrights who wrote about such current problems as social evils, domestic shams, and economic forces which destroy the individual; by demonstrating how to produce realistic plays; and by influencing the status of the theatre in other countries.

In Norway, **Henrik Ibsen,** often referred to as the "father of modern realistic drama," dominated the realistic movement in playwriting not only by his revolutionary themes, but also by his technical skill in play construction and his keen analysis and penetrating understanding of human character. He was followed by other giants on the Continent who rebelled against the superficialities of Romanticism and wrote powerful dramas on the contemporary scene: Björnstjerne Björnson, August Strindberg, Gerhart Hauptmann, Frank Wedekind, Arthur Schnitzler, Hermann Sudermann, Leo Tolstoy, Anton Chekhov, Maxim Gorky, Leonid Andreyev, and John Galsworthy.

The extension of realism was furthered by the founding of other theatre groups dedicated to high standards and experimental production: Otto Brahm's Freie Bühne in Germany, Constantin Stanislavsky and Vladimir Nemirovich-Danchenko's Moscow Art Theatre in Russia, William Butler Yeats and Lady Gregory's Irish National Theatre in Dublin, and J. T. Grein's Independent Theatre in London. A host of literary titans appeared, among them **George Bernard Shaw,** the greatest modern English dramatist.

Besides plays of realism, continental dramatists emerged with poetic fantasies, dramas of mysticism, symbolism, satire, and whimsy. Among the non-realists are: **France**—Edmond Rostand, Jean Giraudoux, Jean Anouilh, Jean-Paul Sartre; **Belgium**—Maurice Maeterlinck; **Hungary**—Ferenc Molnar; **Spain**—García Lorca, Jacinto Benavente; **Italy**—Gabriele D'Annunzio, Luigi Pirandello; **Russia**—Leonid Andreyev; **England**—Oscar Wilde, J. M. Barrie, J. B. Priestley, Christopher Fry, T. S. Eliot; **Ireland**—Lord Dunsany, Sean O'Casey, John Millington Synge.

Famous actors of this early period include: **France**—Rachel, Sarah Bernhardt, Coquelin; **Italy**—Eleonora Duse; **England**—Charles Kemble, Edmund Kean, Ellen Terry, Henry Irving, Johnston Forbes-Robertson.

On the American scene the development of realism and a notable theatre came much later than in Europe. Its slow beginnings, its dependence upon imported English stars, playwrights, and companies, and its absorption with minstrel shows, melodramas, and with unique forms of entertainment in showboats occupy most of the nineteenth century. David Belasco—producer, playwright, actor—first established realism in production and staging methods, and such notable actors as Joseph Jefferson, Edwin Booth, Julia Marlowe, E. H. Sothern, Maude Adams, Richard Mansfield, John Drew created the traditions of the American stage.

In both Europe and America theatres increased in number but shrank in size; the box set replaced wings and backdrops to achieve realistic settings for realistic plays; and advances in lighting devices and equipment expanded production possibilities.

The movement known as "the new stagecraft" was set in motion at the turn of the century by Adolph Appia (Swiss) and Gordon Craig (English)—a revolution in production techniques that not only released theatrical expression from the limiting restraints of realism, but electrified playwrights and artists in every branch of the theatre all over the world. The stage began to unfold beautiful visions through the use of fluid lighting; wagon, elevator, and revolving stages; multiple sets and projected scenery.

The first important progress in developing American playwrights of unusual quality was made by two theatre groups and a professor at Harvard University. The Washington Square Players and the Provincetown Players, both small amateur groups established about 1915 and both dedicated to producing plays of merit, sponsored the dramas of new, promising writers. Under the leadership of George Pierce Baker, Harvard offered classes in playwriting, an example which influenced other universities to establish similar courses. **Eugene O'Neill,** who possessed a brilliant and kaleidoscopic mind, received inspiration from Baker—as did S. N. Behrman, Sidney Howard, Philip Barry, and Robert Sherwood—and encouragement from the Provincetown Players, who first produced his work.

O'Neill was the greatest force in the twentieth century in leading American playwriting away from realism into freer forms. From 1921 on, in such plays as *The Emperor Jones, The Hairy Ape, The Great God Brown, Strange Interlude,* and *Mourning Becomes Electra* he experimented with production devices and play construction to express penetrating psychological truths, using masks, expressionism in thought and staging, and soliloquies.

He has been followed by numbers of gifted writers who, still dealing with thought-provoking social themes, have treated these contemporary problems in a variety of ways: through fantasy, satire, symbolism, humor, and expressionism.

**THEATRE TODAY** The last few years have been a time of great experimentation and change. Rising production costs have impelled stage designers to a greater use of the multiple set, and more and more community theatres have turned to arena or horseshoe staging. The Penthouse Theatre at the University of Washington in Seattle; Royce Hall 170 at U.C.L.A.; the Arena Theatre in Washington, D.C.; the Dallas, Texas, Theatre-in-the-Round; New York's Circle-in-the-Square; and many other off-Broadway theatres attest to the popularity and effectiveness of this type of presentation.

Another innovation is the *reading* of plays—usually with no staging and the use of a lectern, or reading stand—but sometimes in costume and make-up. Recent performers have been Dorothy Stickney—*A Lovely Light* (a biography of Edna St. Vincent Millay); John Gielgud—*The Ages of Man* (readings from Shakespeare); Hal Holbrooke—*Mark Twain Tonight;* Katharine Cornell and Brian Aherne—*Dear Liar* (the letters of Mrs. Patrick Campbell and George Bernard Shaw); Emlyn Williams—*Readings from Charles Dickens;* Charles Laughton and Company—*Don Juan In Hell.*

In the new era of the theatre starting with the 'sixties, some prominent figures of the first half of the century are still active, though many new artists are making their debut. Some current names are:

**Playwrights**—Gore Vidal, Lillian Hellman, William Saroyan, Lindsay and Crouse, Tennessee Wiliams, Robert E. Anderson, Thornton Wilder, William Inge, Samuel Taylor, Arthur Miller, S. N. Behrman, William Gibson, Terence Rattigan, T. S. Eliot, Peter Ustinov, J. B. Priestley, John Osborne, Samuel Beckett, Noel Coward, Jean Anouilh, Eugene Ionesco, Friedrich Duerrenmatt.

**Directors**—Harold Clurman, Joshua Logan, Elia Kazan, George Abbott, Herman Shumlin, Burgess Meredith, Peter Hall, Tony Richardson, Peter Brook.

**Stage Sets and Lighting**—Donald Oenslager, Jo Mielziner, Boris Aronson, Mordecai Gorelik, Oliver Messel, George Jenkins, Peter Larkin, Oliver Smith, Ben Edwards, Jean Rosenthal.

**Costumes**—Irene Sharaff, Lucinda Ballard, Cecil Beaton, Edith Head.

**Actors**—Alfred Lunt, Lynn Fontanne, Katharine Cornell, Helen Hayes, Jessica Tandy, Margaret Leighton, Maureen Stapleton, Laurence Olivier, Cyril Ritchard, Maurice Evans, Alec Guinness, Julie Harris, Anne Bancroft, Anthony Perkins, Siobhan McKenna, Geraldine Page, Kim Stanley, Christopher Plummer, John Kerr, Audrey Hepburn, Cloris Leachman, Barbara Bel Geddes, Pamela Brown, John Neville, Laurence Harvey, Louis Jourdan, Claire Bloom, Joan Plowright, Jason Robards, Jr., Eileen Herlie, Richard Burton.

## ☆☆☆ HORIZONS

"An actor should know something of everything and not too much of anything," said Sir Herbert Beerbohm Tree, the eminent English actor-manager. With a broad general background of knowledge and interests you will, of course, have more to convey to an audience. A certain amount of formal education, most easily acquired in college, is highly recommended. But much of your future training will no doubt depend upon your ability to plan and successfully follow a course of your own devising.

In order to grow in acting skill you must have opportunities to play a variety of roles in different types of plays. Community theatres and college groups or your own acting company, as previously suggested, will provide this. In addition you can study good plays, both modern and classic, and learn scenes from them; become familiar with the works of outstanding authors and poets; continue to collect sense impressions; do daily exercises and voice drills. It is helpful to keep a scrapbook of articles, pictures, play programs, and other items that you collect, as well as some well-organized files. Invaluable, too, is your own library of carefully selected books.

### HISTORY OF THE THEATRE: RESEARCH TOPICS

#### Greek and Roman

1. Select one of the tragedies of Aeschylus, Sophocles, or Euripides and plot or describe the staging of the play in terms of the actors, chorus, and costumes. Portray the audience.
2. Describe and sketch the Greek theatre and staging devices.
3. Explain in detail the forms of Roman entertainment: mimes, pantomimes, *Atellanae, naumachiae,* circus, puppet shows.

#### Medieval

1. Trace the development of the Trade Guilds in England; show how they influenced the life of medieval man and how the cycles for the Whitsuntide and Corpus Christi Day festivals evolved.
2. Read *The Second Shepherd's Play, Abraham and Isaac,* and *Everyman* and find in each the elements of everyday life experiences.

### Renaissance

1. Sketch and describe the Italian scenic devices: perspective vistas, sliding wings, prisms, stage arrangement, cyclorama and machinery, and lighting effects.
2. Give the distinctive characteristics of each of the Commedia dell' Arte figures and sketch or describe their costumes.

### Elizabethan Period

1. Recreate a day in the life of Christopher Marlowe.
2. Study the life of Ben Jonson and the types of plays he wrote.
3. Build a model of the Globe theatre and describe how each playing area was used in the staging of a play.

### Restoration Period in England

1. Show how a famous character from a Restoration play reflected the contemporary manners, evils, or affectations.
2. Compare John Dryden's *All for Love* and Shakespeare's *Antony and Cleopatra*—in plot, language, and dramatic effects.

### Eighteenth Century

1. Prepare a biography of one of the following: (a) David Garrick; (b) one of the other great actors or actresses of England; (c) Richard Brinsley Sheridan (discuss his comedies: *The Rivals, The School for Scandal, The Duenna, The Critic*).
2. Describe the beginnings of theatre in America: Puritan censorship, imported English actors, Hallam's acting company, William Dunlap and his first history of the American theatre, the first theatre buildings and audiences.

### Modern Theatre: Nineteenth and Twentieth Centuries

1. Types of plays: comedy, tragedy, farce, fantasy, melodrama, mystery, musicals, pageants.
2. Finest motion pictures of the past year.
3. Acting groups: Duke of Saxe-Meiningen (Germany), André Antoine's Théâtre Libre (France), Otto Brahm's Freie Bühne (Germany), Moscow Art Theatre, Gate and Abbey (Dublin), New York Theatre Guild.
4. Movements: "New Stagecraft," Little Theatres, Federal Theatre Project, Community Theatres, Children's Theatre.
5. Great names in the theatre during the period—actors, directors, dramatists, scene designers. American and foreign.
6. Present dramatic offerings on television.

# Nine

## TECHNIQUE ☆☆☆

There are certain mechanics, conventions, and rules in any art which have been developed through the years as the result of the experimentation of experienced craftsmen. These are the ABC's which every young artist must learn first. They are the tangibles, the concrete things which anyone can master if he really wants to and will do the amount of work that is required. The painter learns to handle his brushes and oils, the violinist to hold his violin and bow, the football player to carry the ball, the dancer to execute basic steps and arm positions. This so-called **technique** is simply the most skillful, effective, and economical method of accomplishing something.

Being able to use acting techniques automatically will help to make you that boon to directors—a good craftsman. Few have the God-given gift of genius, but everyone can be a good craftsman. Renoir, the French artist, counseled his students, "First of all be a good craftsman. This will not keep you from being a genius." Well-grounded technique will often triumph over undisciplined genius, for great gifts must be channeled, controlled, and directed. Ability coupled with hard work makes the superior artist.

This Technique chapter is your handbook of mechanics; refer to these pages often and eventually know everything contained here. Add material of your own when you see clever business or observe effective technique, for this is the recording place of **How to Do.** You will wish to obtain a complete mastery of techniques of moving onto and around the stage; executing common business such as eating, crying, fainting, using the telephone, and understanding and using stage terminology and expressions. Practice until you do not have to think about using your upstage foot first, covering another person, descending stairs without looking at the steps, keeping your head and eyes up on entrances and exits. When you have drilled sufficiently on such mechanics, your muscular memory will take care of them and you can concentrate on creating mood and interpreting your character. Use technique deliberately and effectively, but make it appear so natural that it does not project as technique.

After years of experience you may find other ways of accomplishing desired results, but always conform to established usage unless you can offer something better. Not "always," but "in general," these are the techniques which are employed in the theatre.

## ☆☆☆ ACTING TECHNIQUE

Your first problem is to become acquainted with the **stage areas** and learn how to move in them. The acting stage is divided into fifteen main areas on a large stage, or nine on a small one. Downstage is nearest the audience, while upstage refers to the section farthest away from the audience. In early days the stage floor slanted up toward the rear wall, which accounts for these terms. Taken from the standpoint of the actor there is stage (R) Right, (C) Center, and (L) Left. 1, 2, and 3 refer to the entrances from the wings as well as the section of the stage. "Playing in 1," which is an old vaudeville expression, means using only the front third of the stage.

**MOVEMENT AND BUSINESS** So that the entire stage will be clearly visible to all members of the audience, sets are designed with the side walls slanting upstage center.

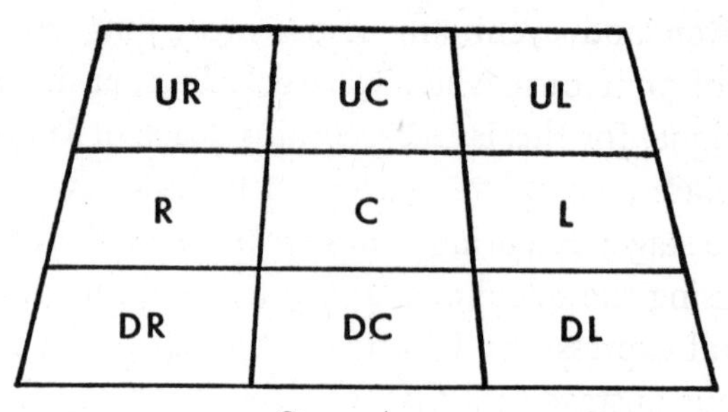

Stage Areas

The actor, too, in order to be seen to advantage, must learn to "open" toward the audience by using a one-quarter position; that is, standing at a 45-degree angle toward the audience. In this position, he shares the scene with another actor, as in conversation. When he stands on stage right, his weight should be on the right foot, which is turned toward the audience while the left foot is parallel with the footlights. In addition, he leads toward center stage slightly with his left shoulder. The reverse position is used when the actor stands on stage left. The profile position is used for brief direct action or for comedy effects. The actor may face directly front, especially when delivering important lines. He will rarely, but may if necessary, stand with his back to the audience. If he takes a three-quarter position, that is, turns away from the audience so that only one quarter of his face is seen, he "gives the stage" to the other actor. (See diagram.)

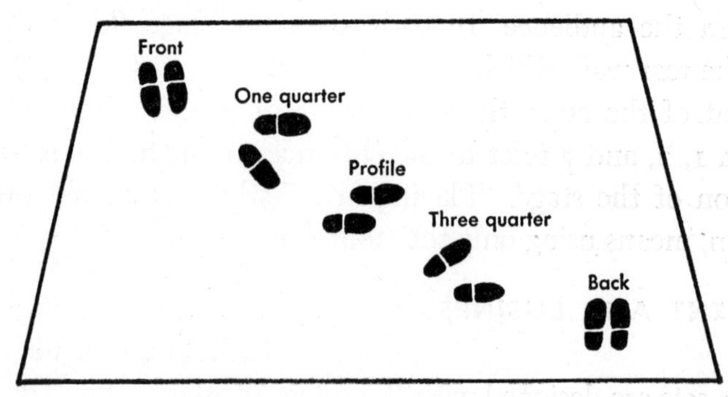

Positions of Feet and Body

In moving on stage, begin your **crosses** with the upstage foot. This technique, besides being more graceful, keeps the body turned toward the audience. Gestures should be made with the upstage hand to avoid "covering" the face or body. Turns are nearly always made toward the audience, in order to let the face be seen as much as possible. Crosses are of several kinds, depending upon the motivation. Direct crosses are made on a straight line and suggest strength and determination. Curved crosses may swing downstage or upstage, giving the effect of casualness, indecision, or ease. The double curved cross, which consists in making an "S" pattern, is frequently used in costume plays to give grace, a flowing movement to the action, and to display the costume.

**Countering** is the process of adjusting to another actor's cross. For example, two actors are in conversation.

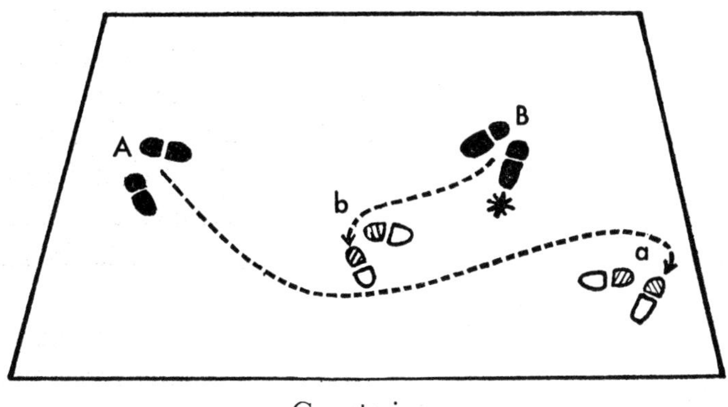


Countering

A, the speaker, crosses left in front of and beyond B, who will counter. B does not move until A is directly in front of him. This is called "easing the cross." He then takes a step or two right. Both finish the movement in a one-quarter position, the reverse of their first one. B may, on his next speech, drop down so that he is level with A.

When an actor is **covering,** that is, standing in front of another actor so that he cannot be seen by the audience, it is the responsibility of the upstage actor to move sufficiently to be uncovered. Such movements should be made so casually that they will not be observed by the audience. Usually a slight shifting of weight will accomplish the desired result. Never back into a better position, or slide, or shuffle, for this will be far more noticeable than a step or two.

Effective **entrances** and **exits** require a keen sense of timing. Start an entrance in character at least six feet back in the wings in order to acquire the rhythm of the character's walk. Come from a definite place and enter for a specific purpose. You should make the entrance with head and eyes up and come well onto the acting area. The same technique applies to exits. Keep in character until you have completed the exit at least six feet into the wings and be going to a definite place for a specific purpose.

Learning how to **walk up and down stairs** silently and gracefully is important, since stairs have such dramatic possibilities for actors. Reach for each step with the toes and come down on the heel afterward. The weight must be kept on the balls of the feet and transferred quickly. If possible, point the feet straight ahead to avoid an unseemly angle of knees projecting out at the sides. Before walking down a long flight of stairs, pause an instant and then descend on a curve, which is more graceful than coming down on a direct line. All movements should be smooth, rhythmical, and perfectly balanced. (See exercises on page 91.)

On the stage the simple action of **sitting in and rising from a chair** can be an awkward affair unless properly rehearsed. When approaching a chair don't focus your gaze upon it, but, with head and eyes up, cross casually to it, turn toward the front, and feel the crosspiece of the chair with the calf of the upstage leg. With your weight on this leg, lower your body to the chair, keeping the spine straight and letting your hands fall easily into your lap. Once seated, avoid fussing with your clothes or rearranging your position. Your costume should have been checked before you left your dressing room and then given no further attention. Boys may pull up their trousers slightly, but girls should not scoop their skirts under them. Girls should be certain that knees are together and legs parallel, or an ugly line of the leg will result. Never sit far into the corner of a deep couch, for you not only will appear at a disadvantage but will have difficulty in rising. A board placed under the pillows is often necessary to keep the couch firm. If someone is to sit on the couch with you, be sure to leave enough room so that you will not have to slide over. The person with the most speeches should sit upstage. When two or more people sit together on a couch or bench, they do not assume the same position, unless this is planned for comedy effect.

In **rising** from a sitting position, place your feet so that you can push with the upstage leg, keeping the spine straight; then transfer the weight to the forward leg, thus releasing the upstage leg for the first step. Never push yourself forward with the hands unless you wish to appear middle-aged or older. If, however, you have been sitting in a deep chair, it may be necessary for you to make a previous adjustment forward in order to put yourself in a position to rise gracefully. In this case, anticipate the need, and make the adjustment on an early speech.

When **stooping** to pick up an object from the floor, face the audience at a 45-degree angle, place the upstage foot slightly in front of the other, and keep the body erect as you settle down over the heel of the downstage foot.

In **kneeling,** you must keep the back straight and the action smooth. With the weight on the upstage leg, drop to the floor on the downstage knee, at the same time pushing back a little, for the upstage leg must be bent at right angles. From this position, the upstage leg may be brought into a kneeling position also.

The **American bow** is a modest bend from the waist with the body relaxed, whereas the **European bow** requires a deeper bend from the waist, with the legs stiff and hips tucked under. An aid in learning to execute the latter properly is to stand with your back and heels against the wall and then bend at the waist, keeping the lower spine touching the wall.

For the common **curtsy** begin with both feet quite close together; then swing one foot slightly behind the other at a 45-degree angle and bend the knees a little; then return to the original position. The result is a quick bob. This is the curtsy of maidservants.

For the deep, low curtsy of the gentlewoman, place the weight on the left leg; slide the right foot, with the instep pressing the floor, well behind and slightly to the left of the left leg. The weight is gradually shifted to the right leg as you sink to the ground, finally sitting on the bent right leg. Keep your back straight and your head up.

The **Shakespearean bow** for men was called "making a leg." Swing the left leg about two feet behind the right, with the left foot pointed out at a 45-degree angle. Bend the left knee directly over the left foot and settle the weight on the left leg, leaving the right leg pointing directly in front with the knee straight. Be sure to settle the weight on the back leg, practically sit on it, and keep the front leg free but touching the floor.

Bring the right arm across the front of the body a little above the waist; extend the left arm back paralleling the torso, or rest the hand lightly on the sword hilt. Keep the back straight and bend slightly at the waist.

**Stage slaps** must be executed with care and precision so that they are convincing but not harmful. With a cupped hand strike the person at least two inches from the ear on the jawbone or on the chin. Never slap on the neck. The cupped hand will give a more resounding smack and will not leave finger marks on the face.

For a **stage embrace,** the boy stands firmly with feet some distance apart; the girl's upstage foot is placed between the boy's feet and her downstage foot is used as a balance, with the heel lifted slightly to give grace to her stance. The boy's downstage arm slips under the girl's downstage arm and just above her waist. The boy's upstage arm goes over the girl's upstage arm. The girl's downstage arm either swings over the boy's arm and up to his shoulder, or rests on his chest. The girl's upstage arm rests on the boy's chest. The boy turns the girl slightly so that the audience sees the back of the girl's hair during the kiss, and the break from the kiss is made so that the girl's face opens toward the audience.

For effecting a **stage fall,** which may be the result of fainting, stabbing, shooting, and so forth, hold your weight on the opposite leg from the side on which you will fall. Start straight down at first, then relax completely, buckling from the knees and breaking your fall with the knee, hip, and shoulder, which strike the floor successively. The leg which does not hold the weight should slide back under the other leg. The arm may slip forward and thus protect the face and head. Feet must not flip up after the fall.

**Shooting** must be timed accurately in order to be convincing. The reaction must be neither too fast nor too slow. When a man is shot, no matter in what position, he tenses immediately and inhales; usually, there is a slow doubling up toward the wound. If he is shot in the stomach or the front of his body, the hands should draw to that spot; if, however, the wound is in the back, he usually wrenches backward and falls more stiffly, either to the side or to the front.

In **fighting,** whether it is to be a wrestling bout, a fist fight, or a fencing duel, the series of clinches and attacks must be so well planned and rehearsed that they seem unpremeditated. The sequence of blows must be as definite as a dance routine. Practiced in slow motion at first, they are speeded to the proper tempo only after the sequence is well established.

To create the illusion of **dying,** the actor must analyze the cause of the death and know what would occur in real life. Dying from a heart attack and death from a prolonged illness are quite different. It is best to gain accurate knowledge from a doctor and then select the action and vocal responses that will be dramatically effective. Timing is extremely important, or the result will be humorous instead of tragic.

**Doors** on stage are usually hinged on the upstage side and open toward the backstage area. The actor must open and close the doors in the most efficient manner so that he is "open" toward the audience during both processes, whether he is entering or leaving the set. With the hand nearest the hinges open the door, keeping control of it as you cross over the doorsill, turn toward the audience, and close the door with the other hand. (On a fast entrance it is advisable to have someone offstage close the door while the actor pretends to.)

**Curtains** are sometimes used for dramatic entrances; at other times they must be opened or closed by hand to suit the action of the script. When curtains or drapes hung on rings are to be opened, the draperies are grasped at shoulder level with both hands and pushed up and out with both arms, in one continuous motion. When an actor or announcer must speak before the main curtain, he holds the front flap with the downstage hand and the back flap with the upstage hand. As he steps forward he crosses his hands behind his back and so brings the curtains together again. The object, of course, is to keep the set covered as one moves between the curtains.

The **telephone** is a much-used stage prop. Hold the phone receiver with the upstage hand and below the chin so that the face is not covered. In addition, listen to what the other person says by creating conversation for the supposed speaker; then cut that conversation 50 per cent and the timing will be about right.

When food or drinks are served in a play they should be kinds that the actors will enjoy. In **eating** foods on stage, however, avoid any that make speech difficult, such as crackers, nuts, and milk. Fruit juices, especially lemon, which is excellent for clearing the throat, are better than carbonated drinks. Grape juice looks like coffee from the audience and is easier to drink. Substitute foods may be used when a menu is awkward to provide; for example, vanilla ice cream or white sherbet will serve for potatoes, and chocolate ice cream simulates meat. Actors should have ample rehearsals in using real food, for the problems involved in the combination of eating and speaking are obvious.

Dancing, playing a musical instrument, singing, playing games, and countless other activities are called for in plays. Whatever the need, the conscientious actor will find someone to teach him and will then practice until he is proficient in any skill demanded of him.

**SPEECH** In addition to developing the voice as an instrument of characterization, you will also need to learn a number of speech conventions of the stage. As an experienced actor you should know that important scenes are usually played downstage, because they can be heard more easily; that when two characters enter the scene in conversation, the speaker enters last; and that you walk on your own speech, not the speech of another actor. You always need to have a good position on the stage for important speeches, and a speech is stronger and more effective if you give it standing. An exit speech should carry you off the acting area with exact timing and crescendo, as you "toss it off" over the downstage shoulder and disappear from sight on the last word.

When speaking with another actor on stage establish **eye contact**; that is, look at the eyes and face of the one with whom you are conversing. This does not mean to stare at the person continuously, but rather to look at him often enough so that the audience knows to whom you are directing a speech.

When two actors are on the stage in **conversation,** both should stand in one-quarter position, and at about the same distance from the footlights. The space between the two speakers should be greater when the stage is large. (*Box and Cox,* page 139.)

A **cue** is a signal for action or speech. Your cues are usually the last few words of the actor's speech which precedes yours. Sometimes, however, action or some sound effect, such as a doorbell, may be a cue for dialogue or movement. You will "pick up your cue" on time if you take a breath just before the other character has finished speaking, so that you are ready to speak, with an attack that is strong and decisive, as soon as he stops.

In **topping** a speech you come in stronger, faster, and with a higher pitch than the previous speech. A series of topped speeches will build a ladder of sound, but in building to a climax it is important for you to start low enough to allow for a steady build to the very last word. (*The Provok'd Wife,* pages 137-138, *As You Like It,* page 139.)

When **cutting in** on the speech of another character, you must make the attack sharp, definite, and timed to a split second. The first man must always be prepared to finish his sentence and go right on in case the cue is picked up late.

In **overlapping speeches** precise and accurate timing is again the keynote. Decide how many words of the other character's speech you can cover with your own without destroying the sense of what he is saying, then practice until you can come in on the beat as accurately as the drummer in the orchestra does. This is a technique often used when a crowd is talking, but key speeches must be heard above a general effect of group conversation.

A **tag line** is the last line in an act or the play. It is usually a "punch" line in a modern play and must be said very distinctly and with a bit of a flourish. Sometimes a slight pause preceding it will make it stand out. It may have been previously "planted" or it may come as a shock. In either case it must be heard and understood. This requires accurate timing, rhythm, and volume. (*Box and Cox*, page 139.)

**Asides** are lines delivered to the audience which other characters on stage presumably do not hear, and may be considered as thinking aloud. The aside is a convention that was frequently used in nineteenth-century melodrama, in Restoration comedies, and in Shakespearean plays.

As a preliminary to projecting **stage whispers**, try unvoicing sentences. All the unvoiced consonants are good for this exercise—p, t, k, hw, f, th, s, sh, ch, h. Use breath only and a strong diaphragmatic action.

"Fetch fresh fish." "Patches of poppies." "Thrust through the thickets." When stage whispers are given, however, a little voice is required, and a lower pitch will aid projection. (*Master Pierre Patelin*, page 137.)

**Calling off stage** requires that the actor adjust mentally to the idea of distance and then increase volume, intensity, and pitch. A slower tempo and a degree of inflection will aid the carrying power. (*Love for Love*, page 137.)

The words **ad lib** are taken from the Latin ad libitum, meaning "at pleasure," "as one wishes," and refer to lines not in the script but originated by the actors. There are two uses for ad lib. The first and most frequent use is to cover an accident of some sort. If an actor forgets his lines his fellow players must keep the scene moving by making up lines on the spur of the moment, in which case the ideas can be given if not the exact words. If an actor is unable to carry on even though he is prompted (which should always be done by the prompter, not another actor) his partner can sometimes take the speech, revamp it, making it his own, and so hold the stage until the actor can get back to his lines. If there is a late entrance and one actor is left on the stage alone for some minutes, he can hold the scene by recounting some of the events that have already occurred and commenting on them. He must be careful, however, not to tell any of the plot which is still to come. All such ad libs should be given with full voice and assurance as if they were memorized lines of the script.

The second use of ad lib is planned to aid in the effectiveness of the action. Crowds may need to ad lib speeches with their pantomime to make a situation seem more natural, especially when entering a scene.

To project the illusion of **crying,** inhale in little gasping sobs, building to the physical and audible manifestations of sobbing. The spoken words should be shaken out on a gasping breath between sobs. Do not cry on the actual words or you will not be understood. For convulsive crying use the abdominal muscles to make the sobs more violent.

**Laughing**, while apparently spontaneous, must be regulated and done on cue. The technique is just the opposite of that employed in sobbing, though both are the outcome of controlled breathing. In laughter the air is expelled explosively by strong diaphragmatic action. (See exercise on page 115.)

To incite laughter in an audience you must deliver humorous and telling lines clearly and put them right over the footlights, but without seeming to do so. The ability to "take laughs" properly depends upon great sensitivity to audience response and an excellent sense of timing, and will be acquired only with experience. When the laughter has reached its peak and subsided a little, give your next line with extra volume and intensity, which you will lessen when the audience is once more attentive. This is a form of topping. Never wait for a laugh. It is better to come in with your line too soon than to have an awkward pause. Learn to hold your reactions and character during the laughter without appearing to "freeze."

**Exercises in stage mechanics**

A. The following groups of exercises will give you an opportunity to practice the stage techniques and conventions explained in the previous pages.
   1. Go to the stage area, taking a position center stage. Then, make a series of crosses to other areas on the stage which the rest of the group must identify, such as UL, DR, LC, URC, and so forth. Be sure that you use your upstage foot first each time you begin a cross.
   2. With a partner take the one-quarter position on stage as if you were in conversation. Then make a downstage cross to the opposite side of the stage while the other actor counters to a position where he is again facing you for conversation.
   3. Join two other students in an exercise to illustrate countering for the entrance of a new actor.

B. The techniques of sitting and rising from chairs, walking up and down stairs, and stooping and bending for objects may be demonstrated by individuals or by a group working in unison.

C. In a group of two, three, or more, improvise a short scene to incorporate the following sets of stage mechanics. Plan a situation, establish a setting, and then create spontaneous dialogue as you enact the scene. Repeat in pantomime.
   1. Answering a phone, rising from a chair, sitting, eating, falling on stage.
   2. Stooping, laughing, opening drapes, whispering, serving tea.
   3. Overlapping speeches, crying, fighting, making an entrance, countering.
   4. Asides, stage slap, dying, kneeling, topping.
   5. Calling off stage, cutting in, stage embrace, shooting, making a curtsy.

## ☆☆☆ PRODUCTION TECHNIQUE

**DIRECTING** The director's job is to bring to life on the stage the author's ideas as expressed in print. Aside from his supervision of the entire production, his special problem is to develop the action so that both story and characters are made clear to the audience. The manipulation of action on the stage involves a knowledge of art principles, a musical sense, and an instinct for what is dramatically effective.

**Movement** helps to keep a play alive, but it must be motivated by a purpose consistent with characters and plot. Walking across stage, lifting a book, raising an eyebrow, though they may be called action, business, pantomime, or gesture, are all forms of movement. Stage pictures are arrested movement.

What a character does depends upon the actor's conception of him. He may chew gum, or fidget; he may pick up a magazine and read; he may jam his hands into his pockets. Whatever the business, it must serve the play and never be done because the actor has no speeches for a time or is self-conscious and ill at ease.

*How* a person moves is determined by his personal characteristics. He may habitually walk with a limp; he may stump along rapidly; he may move slowly and gracefully. *Why* he moves is determined by the way he reacts to other people and situations. He may move toward someone to show affection or defiance, away from him to show disgust or fear. He will rise to his fullest height in pride or determination; he will sink in illness or defeat.

Mood can be created by movement. In *Rosalind* the Dame rocks slowly and contentedly, establishing the peace of the place. In *The Royal Family* the maid flies around answering doorbell and phone, setting an atmosphere of confusion.

**Stage groupings** are problems of design of which both the settings and the actors are a part. They must conform to art principles of mass, line, and color. They must have balance, coordination, proportion, emphasis and subordination, rhythm, unity, variety, and contrast. Every second on the stage should be a picture with the

Focus on Center of Interest

center of interest, to which all lines converge, constantly shifting as different characters "take the stage." Ways of obtaining focus of attention are many. Perhaps the most dramatic is for the character to stand on a higher level—a step at the entrance to the room, a stairway leading up to rooms off stage, or a balcony.

The use of space is also an effective way of emphasizing the center of interest. When an actor is set apart from the group he immediately achieves prominence if the attention of the crowd is focused upon him. If, however, the crowd turns away from him or is dispersed in a variety of positions, his importance is weakened.

The center of interest may also be pointed up through the use of contrasting elements. If one character alone remains standing while everyone else is seated, he is emphasized. If all the other characters are dressed in subdued colors and his costume is brilliant, he will stand out from the group. This is true also if the material of his costume is more rich in texture than that of the others.

If one character stands in a brilliantly lighted spot on the stage while the others are in a dimmer light, or if he occupies a stronger stage position, such as any of the downstage areas, or stage center, he can dominate the scene.

Other characters on stage can also help to give focus in a number of ways. Besides looking toward the center of interest, a character can direct the attention of the audience by the tilt of his head, the angle of his shoulder, the slant of his whole body, or the position of his arms, hands, legs, and feet.

Groupings should at all times show the relationships of the characters and their moods. They must be psychologically right; antagonists, for example, would not sit together. It is best to avoid even spacing and even heights, except in stylized plays. People should not stand in a straight line, or in huddled groups, or in a semicircle. Visual interest will be maintained through variations in the bodily positions of each character composing the group.

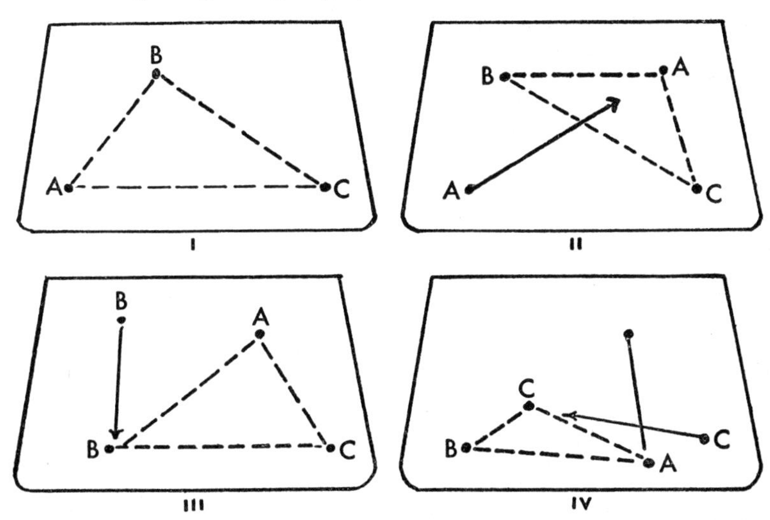


I. *B* is the center of interest. II. A moves up onto a level with *B*. III. *B* drops downstage, making A the center of interest. IV. C crosses to center stage, becoming the center of interest, while A drops downstage left.

Of the various art forms, the triangle in all its varieties is the one most used for stage pictures. Every movement of the characters causes a change in the shape of the triangle, as may be noted above.

Although the character at the apex of the triangle has the strongest position, he is the center of interest only when the other characters direct their attention to him.

One way to learn design for stage grouping is to study good paintings for both composition and color.

Here are a few general suggestions on directing. Do sufficient desk work—that is, study and planning—so that you know what you want and how to get it. After settling the interpretation of the play and of the individual characters, take care of the mechanical details: essential blocking, general movement, entrances, exits, and ensemble groupings. Then work for fine points in interpretation and for projection. In case an actor needs help, be ready to suggest appropriate business and mannerisms to bring out the distinctive quality of his character. Make actors aware of points of conflict and of climaxes. As rehearsals progress develop contrast and variety, mood, rhythm, and speed. Watch to see that actors do not play behind furniture or too far upstage, or turn their backs to the audience. See that the speaker crosses in front of others, that he gives his strong speeches standing and in a good position on the stage, and that he times his entrances and exits well and executes them with head and eyes up. Insist that the actors, at least part of the time, look at the people to whom they are speaking, and, above all, that they do not look at the floor.

**STAGING** The primary purpose of the set is to serve the play; that is, to provide an environment and atmosphere that will bring out the values which have been agreed upon as being of prime importance. Suitability to type, truth to period, and correctness of furnishings and color all point up the theme and help to make it clear. An actor plays *in* a setting, not *against* it, and everything about the scene should help, not create hazards for him. A good set should suggest action and business to an alert actor.

One constructs a set on the principles of good design, and employs the fundamentals of architecture and painting in its construction and decoration. At the same time he is capable of modifying any theory to make the set theatrically more effective.

As soon as the set has been designed and approved, a ground plan, or stage plot, is made to scale, showing the position of all the furniture. The scale may be one-half, three-eighths, or one inch to a foot.

In addition to the stage plot a miniature set may be made. This

GROUPING: THE TEAHOUSE OF THE AUGUST MOON
*Roosevelt High School, Des Moines*

GROUPING: PEG O' MY HEART
*Portland High School, Portland, Maine*

GROUPING: THE LARK *Forest Park High School, Baltimore*

GROUPING: SUNDAY COSTS FIVE PESOS
*Roosevelt High School, Seattle*

will help the actors to visualize the setting and will assist the crew in construction and lighting problems.

A good set provides a number of acting areas so that no two scenes need to be played in the same place or with an identical arrangement of actors. Different levels make possible the arrangement of interesting groups for final pictures.

**Entrances** should be planned for easy entrance and exit, not blocked by furniture on the stage or stage braces in the wings. Upstage center is the best entrance, but a door at the side makes a better exit. A raised entrance is very effective. A single entrance makes a play seem static. Usually it is advisable to have a number of entrances so placed that actors must cross the stage. This gives a sweeping action and movement to the play.

Seldom, if ever, place a large piece of furniture in the center of the stage, since that is the best acting area. Employ artistic economy, remembering that everything on the set must be used. The position of furniture usually indicates its importance, so don't make a piece of furniture conspicuous if its principal function is to dress the set. Place groups of furniture or large pieces, such as couches, so that actors can move around them easily.

Small props and all the **furnishings** of the set should provide the proper atmosphere for the play. Color schemes should produce the desired emotional response in the audience. Warm colors—reds, yellows, browns—express joy and lightness and are used for comedy. The cold colors—blues, grays, greens—express sadness and tragedy.

There is a technique of **shifting a set.** This involves flymen, who work the ropes that send sections of scenery up into the fly gallery; grips, who shift the scenery on stage; prop men who handle the large props, such as furniture; prop men, or girls, who take care of the small props that dress the set; and electricians. As the curtain goes down, all these technicians are in their places in the wings, ready to go onto the set the minute the stage manager says "Strike." (It is important that they wait for this direction from the stage manager, especially if there are curtain calls, since only he knows when the curtain is down for the last time.) All work simultaneously. The prop girls collect the small props in baskets while the flymen fly any scenery which can be flied; the grips strike the back wall as the electricians break the electrical connections, and the prop men move all furniture to the front of the stage near the footlights. Then the grips take sections of the back wall into the wings and return with pieces of the new set; likewise, the electricians take the old electrical equipment into the wings and return with the new pieces; the prop men carry the furniture into the wings and bring in the new pieces, which they place at the front of the stage. Meanwhile the grips are fastening the new scenery in place and the electricians are making the new electrical connections. When all that is finished the prop men move the furniture into proper position on the set, and the prop girls place the small props. Each member of the crew must know exactly what equipment he is to handle, where he is to get it, and where in the wings he will place what he takes off.

Stage **lighting** has two main functions: to give visibility, and to create mood or atmosphere. It is important that the actor be seen, not equally well at all times, but highlighted at crucial moments. Straight, even lighting which illuminates all parts of the stage equally well is unreal and tiring.

In general, observe these suggestions:

Highlight entrances.

Highlight important playing spaces with spots from the borders or from light trees placed just behind the proscenium.

Keep light off the walls, to prevent glare as well as to conceal imperfections.

Kill shadows by using some footlights.

To make a strong light on some object appear logical, plan an apparent light source, such as a lantern, or a table lamp, or light from a fireplace, in which a spot has been placed.

Put all equipment on dimmers so that light can be controlled.

Raise lights gradually, never snap them on. This applies to house lights also.

The use of **sound** is one of the most telling ways of creating or heightening emotional responses. Besides the common sound effects which are realistic in their purpose, there are sounds which are designed primarily to create mood and atmosphere, as the sound of the storm in *King Lear,* of the drum in *The Emperor Jones,* of the click of the milk bottles in *Our Town.*

Since nearly every play requires some sound effects, it is practical to have on hand equipment for making the common ones: doorbells, telephone bells, slamming and opening doors, airplanes, trains, horses' hoofs, wind, rain, thunder, cars starting and stopping, and crashes. Staging books give thorough instructions for constructing or assembling them. A bell box for doorbell and telephone can be made easily with dry cell batteries, or an electrical connection, and two bells with different tones, or a bell and buzzer. Sound records of all kinds can be purchased.

The selection of **music** which will best serve the play requires considerable research and musical knowledge. Offstage mood music should not consist of selections with which the audience is familiar, unless this is desirable for specific reasons. Otherwise people are apt to be conscious of what is being played instead of being emotionally moved.

Intermission music should serve as an emotional transition to the next scene or act. When the school orchestra is not available, recorded music can be successfully used. This is especially true of a period play such as *The Rivals,* where a great number of acts need to be tied together and the mood sustained. Records of musical instruments of the period, such as the clavichord, add much to the flavor of the play.

When a script calls for an actor to play an instrument, it is obviously desirable to cast in the part someone who can do so. However, when this is not feasible, the instrument can be played in the wings as close as possible to the onstage actor, who then fakes the movements of the musician. This can be completely convincing if it is well executed.

All sound and music must be carefully rehearsed, and split-second timing is imperative. When there is much equipment to manage, sound and music technicians can profitably work in twos, with one person holding a script, giving the cues, and the other one executing the business.

**Costumes** are a distinct part of the characterization, for they tell many things about the individual—his tastes, habits, temperament, and station in life. Costumes for the stage must be designed for the character, not only in style but in color and in importance relative to others on the stage. Color merits particular consideration, for not only must all the costumes on the stage at one time be harmonious with each other and with the setting, but they must have pyschological significance also.

The quality and texture of the material must also be considered for both pictorial and psychological influence; flowing materials produce a different emotional effect than stiff ones do. At all times the costuming must emphasize the meaning and purpose of the play and contribute to the constantly changing picture.

An essential requisite of good costuming is that it be an aid to the actor, not a hindrance. Costumes should be easy to put on and take off, should fasten well and easily, and should be easy to manage in movement. They should, moreover, be strong enough to withstand considerable strain and hard usage.

The period costume demands substantial research. Although complete faithfulness to period is not so important as suggestion of the period, there are many details that must be considered. In working with period shows, it is especially important for actors to know what limitations and adjustments they will have to make in walk and carriage. Hoops, trains, bustles, unusual shoes, and other unfamiliar apparel require a great deal of practice and rehearsal if they are to be handled convincingly. Actors should approximate these costume peculiarities at all rehearsals by improvising some substitute, so that they can learn to move with ease and freedom.

For classroom productions, very effective period costumes can be contrived from clothes that are found in everyone's wardrobe. For example, here is what you can improvise for your Shakespearean Scene:

For the man's costume, a boy may wear blue jeans or slacks and pin the legs tightly in back. If one of the girls will donate a separate collar which she wears with sweaters, he will have a ruff, or one may be made from a paper doily. On a sports coat which is worn backwards a leather belt can be buckled low, just above the hip bone. For a cape use a bathrobe, preferably woolen, and cinch it at the waist with the sash. Pull the sleeves inside, hide them in the back, and draw the collar of the robe up to the sash. For a bonnet, use a man's old hat, covered with a bright solid-colored blouse with all the edges and sleeves tucked inside the hat. With a feather, a brooch, or an ornament added, the effect will be a Milan hat.

A girl may wear a long-sleeved blouse and a long formal skirt to give the illusion of a courtly Elizabethan robe. Over this put a jumper dress, for the bodice effect, and draw the skirt of the jumper to the waist in front and back with pins or ribbons to give an over-skirt effect around the hips. If hoops are available, use them; however, two large bath towels wrapped into a sausage shape and fastened about the waist can serve as the farthingale. Wire coat hangers can also be shaped into hoops, or a pair of football shoulder pads may be used. If long skirts are not available, draperies can be fashioned into a skirt, giving a rich brocaded effect. There is no limit to the masterpieces that can be improvised with a little ingenuity, and their effect on the actor is amazing.

**Period movement,** while determined to a great extent by the costumes that were worn, also reflected the manners and customs of the age. As you learn about the history of drama you will want to include a detailed knowledge of costumes and the techniques of movement for each period. The realistic handling of hats, canes, fans, handkerchiefs, snuff boxes, and costume skirts will be part of your future training.

The primary function of **make-up** is to aid in the projection of the character. Due consideration must be given to the effect of stage lights and distance. Much or little make-up will be required according to the size of the theatre. Because there will be greater realism without it, most classroom productions will require no make-up.

Every actor should know how to apply his own make-up, but this is something to be learned over a period of time through study and practice. Two or three students of similar coloring might pool resources, purchase some basic supplies and a good make-up book, and experiment. (Note Max Factor booklets, page 353.)

### Central and Flexible Staging

Acting and production techniques described in this chapter have referred to the traditional stage, a proscenium-framed area where the audience is seated on one side of the theatre, viewing the play as through a picture frame. In recent years there has been increasing interest in experimental types of staging. Among these are central or arena staging, in which the acting area is a circle surrounded by the audience; and horseshoe staging, in which the audience sits on three sides of the action. Popular with both actors and audience, they have been called circle theatre, circus theatre, penthouse, and theatre-in-the-round. Whether the acting area is round, square, rectangular, or fluidly shaped, the experiments have been aimed at bringing the audience and actors into closer relationship.

While central and flexible staging have assumed a place of importance in the modern theatre by breaking from the conventional staging pattern, various seating arrangements of the audience have existed in theatres of past centuries. Primitive man probably acted his pantomimes for fellow tribesmen in the round; the Greeks performed in theatres constructed in a semicircle; and Shakespeare's actors played on an extended platform, surrounded on three sides by the groundlings, who stood on the ground below.

Many schools and community and professional groups are enthusiastic about flexible staging not only because the audience is brought into more direct participation with the action of the play, but also because productions can be staged more economically and presented in gymnasiums, barns, stores, or any room large enough to provide the desired seating capacity and an adequate acting space. And since many classrooms do not have stages on which the students can produce their scenes and one-act plays, central or flexible staging can be used to provide a creative performance opportunity. Because of the wide interest in and many possibilities for using central staging methods in the classroom, the following simplified techniques for presenting scenes and one-act plays requiring not more than two entrances are given. For more detailed instruction on production methods refer to the bibliography on page 352.

In the transition from acting on the traditional proscenium stage to acting in central staging there is no basic difference in creating the character. The difference lies in the **technical adjustments** which the actor makes to the smaller playing space and to the audience, seated beside and around him. The closeness of the audience makes even greater demands on the actor to develop a detailed, sincere characterization and to maintain complete concentration on the dialogue and action of the play. You will find that you must give the utmost attention to the center of interest, if you are not to be distracted. Listening and response are of paramount importance. Any superficial movement, false emotion, or technical flaw is quickly detected.

The well-trained actor who is secure in his characterization and concentration will make the transition from proscenium to central staging with ease. The same principles of logically motivated movement, play development, and variety in stage pictures apply to both. The technical adjustments to be made are largely problems of movement and blocking. However, there are no rigid rules to be followed. Imagination and resourcefulness, coupled with a knowledge of the following points of technique, will enable you to explore the challenge in flexible staging.

### ACTING

1. Develop a complete and well-rounded characterization.
2. Modify your physical movements and attitudes to those that are natural in daily life; since the audience can see every muscle of the face, even a raised eyebrow is meaningful.
3. Keep all responses subtle, selective, and controlled.
4. Modify your vocal projection to the size of the performing area, which is undoubtedly smaller than that of a conventional theatre, but speak with perfect clarity.
5. Memorize your lines to perfection, since there is no possibility of a prompter giving lines from off stage.
6. Sustain intense concentration on the scene in progress, for you are always in direct sight of some part of the audience.
7. Establish direct eye contact with the actor to whom you are speaking when more than two actors are on stage.

### STAGING

1. Depending upon the shape and size of the available acting space, decide upon a circle, square, or horseshoe for the stage.
2. Design the ground plan with unobstructed aisle entrances or exits, using no more than two in beginning experiments.
3. Arrange the set pieces within the space to provide opportunities for movement, good balance within the area, and freedom to motivate crosses around stage furniture.
4. Select essential pieces of furniture that are low enough not to interfere with the spectator's sight—no higher than the shoulder level of the seated actor is the general rule.
5. Plan to suggest the placement of windows and doors by pantomimic action.
6. Select properties to dress the room that will establish the locale, the period, and appropriate decor, but make certain that they do not obstruct sight lines.
7. Choose authentic hand and small props, since they are under close observation by the audience.

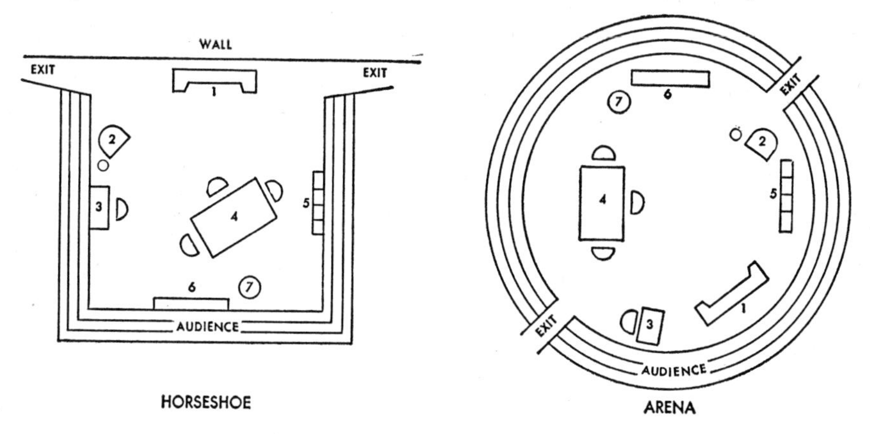


1. Couch 2. Easy chair and small table 3. Desk and chair 4. Dining table and three straight chairs 5. Window 6. Bookcase 7. Rocking chair

### BLOCKING

1. Designate on the floor plan a key for the entrances such as A and B, and use numbers 1, 2, 3, 4, etc., to indicate the furniture to which actors make crosses. (See diagrams above.)
2. Select either the points of the compass or hours of the clock to direct general movement and crosses.
3. Consider the exact center of the acting area as the strongest position, with the less important areas closest to the audience.
4. Consider the spaces in front of the aisle openings weaker positions for placing less important characters in a scene.
5. Whenever possible, seat minor characters so that the focus is centered on those standing.
6. Avoid static positions for any length of time since some part of the audience is observing the back of an actor's head; but motivate logically every movement from within the lines, emotion, character, or thought of the play.
7. Use variations of the triangle for grouping and moving three or more characters, for then every audience member is seeing one actor's full face, and the partial face or profiles of the others.

## THEATRE VOCABULARY

*Acting*

**antagonist:** character who most actively opposes the protagonist.
**artistic economy:** the precise amount of anything needed to serve the actor or the play.
**atmosphere:** expression of mood, usually applied to the set.
**blocking:** the plotting of action by the director.
**center of interest:** point of focus at any given time.
**climax:** the high point of action in the play, which is the turning point in the plot.
**concentration:** focused attention.
**conflict:** dramatic opposition of the protagonist (a) with himself, (b) with his fellow man, or (c) with society or fate.
**contrast:** differences emphasized by the presence of the opposite.
**cover:** obscuring an actor from sight of the audience either by furniture or by another actor.
**critiques:** evaluations wherein both strengths and deficiencies are noted.
**cue:** a signal for an actor's speech or action, usually the last three words of another actor's speech.
**cut:** take out; or stop action.
**downstage:** toward the footlights, so called because stages formerly slanted.
**drama:** a composition in prose or verse portraying life and character by means of dialogue and action; a play, a story presenting the conflict of two opposing forces, designed to be presented by actors before an audience.
**esprit de corps:** the common spirit pervading the members of a group. It implies enthusiasm, devotion, and jealous regard for the honor of the group.
**expressionism:** an objective representation of the subjective—i.e., of thoughts and emotions.
**farce:** a play in which the comedy is based on exaggerated or absurd situations.
**high comedy:** a play based on wit.
**impressionism:** the projection of a sense impression without adherence to reality or factual detail.
**ingenue:** the young girl character in the play.
**juvenile:** the young man character in the play.
**low comedy:** a play based on broad physical humor.
**memorization:** the learning of lines so that they can be reproduced verbatim.

**mood:** an emotional state, usually the result of a combination of emotions.
**motivate:** have a reason for doing or saying something.
**motivating force:** the impelling desire which causes one to act fairly consistently in all situations.
**naturalism:** an extreme form of realism.
**nemesis:** forces set in motion by the character which cause his destruction.
**pace:** the over-all movement of the play; a combination of tempo and rhythm.
**pantomime:** the bodily expression of an idea or emotion.
**personal magnetism:** power to attract.
**places:** the call for actors and technicians to take their places for the opening of an act.
**plot:** (a) the contrived sequence of events in a play;
(b) the production form used in stage arrangement.
**protagonist:** the pivotal character; the center of the conflict.
**realism:** a presentation of life—external reality—in acting and staging.
**romanticism:** a representation of the chivalrous, the adventurous.
**royalty:** money paid for permission to present a certain play.
**rhythm:** the pulse or beat.
**showmanship:** a sense of what is theatrically effective.
**sides:** a page of the actor's lines and cues; a half page of typing paper.
**simplicity:** "the exact medium between too little and too much."
**sincerity:** honesty of mind and action.
**spontaneity:** freshness; as of the first time.
**stage left:** the stage to the left of the actor as he faces the audience.
**stage picture:** the grouping of actors at any given time in the play.
**stage right:** the stage to the right of the actor as he faces the audience.
**suspense:** expectancy, uncertainty.
**tag line:** an actor's speech at the close of an act, or of the play.
**tempo:** time, rate of speed.
**theme:** the major premise on which the play is based; the proposition to be proved.
**timing:** the art of regulating the execution of a line or movement to occur at the exact psychological moment.
**tragedy:** a play in which the protagonist, a noble character, is defeated by forces beyond his control.
**upstage:** away from the footlights toward the back wall of the stage.
**variety:** diversity, difference, lack of monotony.
**vitality:** vigor, life.
**warn:** notification that a cue is coming.

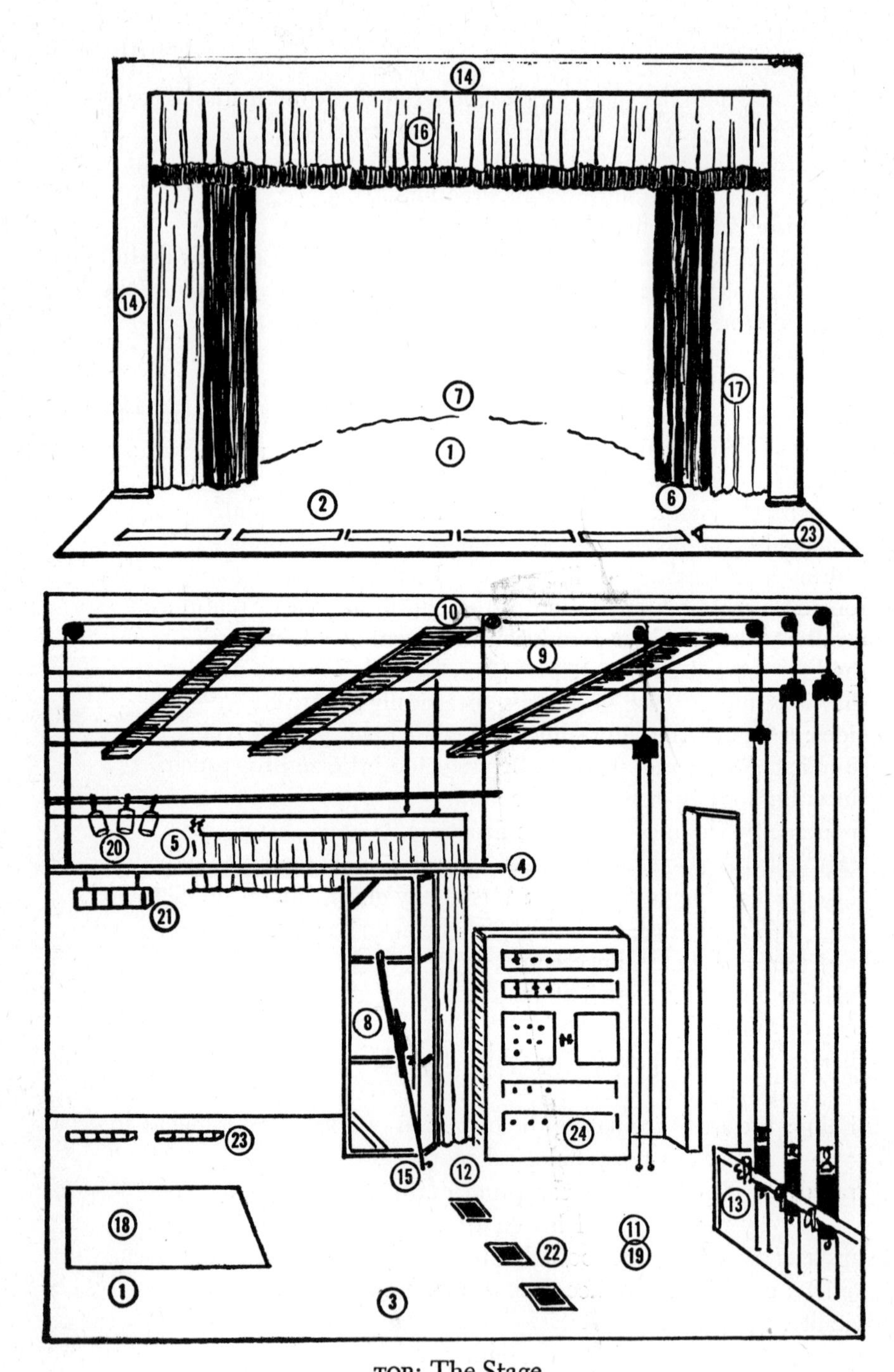


TOP: The Stage
BOTTOM: Backstage Rigging—Right Half of Stage

*Staging (see diagram for location of numbered items)*

**acting area** (1): the space on stage where the actors perform.
**apron** (2): the floor of the stage extending beyond the front curtain line.
**back stage** (3): area behind the curtain line.
**battens** (4): horizontal supporting bars of wood or pipe from which curtains and scenery are suspended.
**border strips** (5): short overhead curtains masking border lights.
**box set:** a room set, three walls and a ceiling.
**ceiling:** a canvas-covered frame which closes the top of a box set.
**curtain line** (6): a line on the stage where the main curtain falls.
**cyclorama** (7): a three-sided sky curtain hung from a U-shaped frame around the back and sides of the set.
**drapes:** curtains with fullness, usually velour.
**drops:** painted curtains without fullness.
**flats** (8): sections of scenery.
**flies** (9): space above the acting area where curtains and scenery are stored.
**fourth wall:** an imaginary wall at the footlights, completing a box set.
**Green Room:** a special room where actors in costume and make-up may meet their friends.
**gridiron** (10): overhead structure supporting curtains, rigging, drops.
**ground cloth:** a canvas floor covering to absorb sound.
**ground row:** a flat profile of ground foliage or scenery which stands alone.
**mask or backing:** flats used behind doors and windows.
**off stage** (11): off the acting area.
**"OP":** opposite side from the prompt side.
**"P"** (12): prompt side.
**parallel:** a frame which supports a stage platform and is collapsible; sometimes called a riser.
**pin rail** (13): the control railing for rigging.
**practical:** usable, as a window that can be raised.
**properties:** (a) stage, articles used to dress the set;
(b) hand, articles used by the actors.
**proscenium** (14): picture-frame opening through which the play is viewed.
**ramp:** a sloping platform from the floor to a higher level.
**stage brace** (15): an adjustable brace for supporting flats.
**strike:** the signal to change the set; usually given by the stage manager.
**teaser** (16): a short overhead curtain masking the first row of border lights; the first border strip.
**tormentors** (17): the first side curtains mounted on flats, usually matching the teaser.

**trap** (18): a trap door in floor of stage.
**traveller:** slotted track to hang draw curtains; often the curtain itself.
**wagon:** a rolling platform on which sets or pieces can be mounted to change scenes quickly.
**wing flats:** two or three flats hinged together so that they fold like a screen; used for masking.
**wings** (19): offstage spaces on the right and left of the acting area.

*Lighting*

**baby spot** (20): a small focusing light (400 watts).
**blackout:** an instantaneous cutting off of all light.
**borders** (21): rows of overhead lights.
**cable:** a heavy electric light cord.
**color mediums:** glass, silk, or gelatin slides used to color lights.
**floodlight:** light without lens, used to diffuse light and give general lighting.
**floor pocket** (22): an outlet in the floor where lights may be plugged in.
**footlights** (23): row of lights in the apron of the stage.
**highlight:** an intense light on a particular spot.
**house lights:** lights in the auditorium.
**rheostats:** dimmers on switchboard to control the amount of light.
**spotlights:** focusing lights.
**strip lights:** long troughlike reflectors.
**switchboard** (24): control board for lights.

#### CHAPTER HIGHLIGHTS

- Acting technique
  - Movement and business
  - Speech
  - Exercises in stage mechanics
- Production technique
  - Directing
  - Staging
    - Traditional stage
    - Central and Flexible stage
- Theatre vocabulary

# Ten

## PLAY PRODUCTION ☆☆☆

The following three-act play production outline is simply an enlargement of the form you have already successfully followed for your one-act play. Regardless of the size of the production, these are the three main divisions of work. If you are to be the student director or the manager of any section, you will need to know much that is included in this chapter. However, the knowledge needed in order to produce plays is so great that no single chapter in a book such as this could possibly give all the necessary information. Many excellent books covering all phases of the subject are available and should be consulted. (Pages 351-352.)

The explanations are given here in terms of a regular auditorium stage in a secondary school where the director is aided by other teachers. In a school where the drama teacher is responsible for all phases of production, students will take over the various departments under the supervision of the director. In the situation where advanced students are directing their own plays, without adult supervision, they will first select (from their own group) a director whose final decisions they will honor.

See page 390 for Work Assignment Chart.

## THREE-ACT PLAY PRODUCTION OUTLINE

| DIRECTOR | STAGE MANAGER (TECHNICAL & ART DIRECTOR) | BUSINESS MANAGER (HOUSE MANAGER) |
|---|---|---|
| *is responsible for:* | *is responsible for:* | *is responsible for:* |
| selection of play | all plots, charts, cue sheets | outline of business management |
| of quality | sets | budget |
| suitable to cast | design | checks it |
| suitable to audience | construction | pays bills |
| making the budget | painting | publicity |
| supervision of other directors | props | writing |
| holds discussion | stage | printing |
| assigns duties | set (furniture) | distribution |
| compilation of prompt book | small (decorations) | tickets |
| interpretation of play | hand (for actors) | printing |
| style of production | electrical effects | sale |
| rehearsal schedule | equipment | programs |
| movement and business | placement | printing |
| scene plots | operation | distribution |
| prop lists | sound effects | ushers |
| light plots | equipment | flowers for foyer |
| sound plot | operation | arrangements for play pictures |
| costume plots | sound | mailing list or guest book |
| make-up charts | music | |
| cue sheets | recorded | |
| sound | live (on set) | |
| lights | orchestra (during show) | |
| curtains | costumes | |
| outline of business management | design | |
| names, addresses, phone numbers of cast | construction | |
| selection of cast | assembling | |
| rehearsal of cast | pressing, storage, upkeep | |
| checking all phases of production | make-up | |
| assembling material for program | creation | |
| | purchase of materials | |
| | application | |
| | cleanup crews | |
| | for stage | |
| | for dressing rooms | |

| DIRECTOR | STAGE MANAGER (TECHNICAL & ART DIRECTOR) | OTHER DIRECTORS |
|---|---|---|
| submitting ideas for publicity | *supervision while running the show* | Dance director |
| supervision of cast pictures | grips (scenery) | Music director |
| | flymen (curtains) | orchestra |
| | prop men (furniture) | vocal numbers |
| | prop girls (small props) | Social director |
| | electricians | picnic supper |
| | sound men | cast party |
| | make-up artists | |
| | wardrobe managers | |
| | dressers (for actors) | |
| | call boys | |
| | prompters | |

Although the director cannot be an expert in all branches of theatre work, he must know enough about each to be able to organize and allocate the duties of the other specialists and be able to supervise to the extent of bringing all phases into a unified whole.

## ☆☆☆ PREPARATION

**SELECTION OF THE PLAY** The production begins with the selection of the play. There are three major points to consider: (1) quality, (2) suitability to cast, and (3) suitability to audience.

In order to have educational value for the cast as well as for the audience, it is important that the play be of sufficient worth to justify the time spent on it. Therefore, plays should be chosen which are wholesome, which are written in literate English, and which present a theme within the comprehension and interest of young actors. The importance of working with well-written plays and finely drawn characters cannot be emphasized too strongly.

As a rule, participating students should have a voice in the play selection, but since they have not read widely the director should have two or three ready to suggest and read. No play which in any way contradicts the principles of good taste and character building, with which education is chiefly concerned, should ever be proposed or performed.

If the play is to be cast from a drama class, the talents of the available actors are known, but if it is to be a play for which anyone in school may try out the problem is more difficult. Usually some much-needed information may be gained if all who are interested are asked to attend a pre-tryout meeting, at which time those attending can discuss the kind of play they would like and can also sign up for tryouts. Even the finest plays will not survive poor casting, so unless there are adequate actors for most of the parts, it is better to choose a simpler play which is within the range of the acting abilities of the average student.

Plays are an experience shared between the artists on the stage and the people in the auditorium. No matter how artistically a play is staged or how excellent the acting is, if the audience is bored, offended, or unprepared to receive the play, the production cannot be considered successful. Over a period of time it is often possible to educate an audience to accept different kinds of plays. This can be done gradually as their confidence and respect are won through good productions and honest publicity.

In the selection of a play for production in a secondary school, two types of audience must be considered. First, there is the student body, composed of people the age of the actors. Usually a play that interests the actors will please their fellow students. Then there are the adults—parents of the actors and friends of the school. In order to be of interest to them the play must have elements that appeal to mature minds. Since adults are familiar with adolescent behavior and the problems of family relationships, situations that present a true picture of family life are apt to meet with their approval. That is why the so-called "family play" is so successful in the average secondary school. Obviously a school cannot repeatedly present plays of this sort but must alternate them with those having a more advanced or serious theme, and should frequently present costume plays that give a complete release to another period of history. The latter also afford opportunities for school-wide study and cooperation, but they take far more planning and better publicity than ordinary plays do.

A definite dramatic policy in the planning of a series of plays will provide not only entertainment but also dramatic education for both actors and audience. Many different types of plays should be presented, and there should be sufficient variety so that no comparison of consecutive plays is possible. A light comedy followed by a more serious play, then a comedy of a different kind followed by a costume play, will make a good sequence. For example: (1) *Time Out For Ginger* or *Ever Since Eve,* (2) *Our Town* or *Stage Door,* (3) *Our Hearts Were Young and Gay* or *The Teahouse of the August Moon,* (4) *If I Were King, Twelfth Night,* or *The Rivals.* Shakespearean plays, because of the size of the casts and the difficulties of costuming, cannot be presented often. However, the educational value to the entire school cannot be overestimated, and by long-range planning a Shakespearean play can be made a dramatic event of major importance in the school's history. The director's own enthusiasm is usually sufficient to inspire cast and faculty to the greater effort required for such a production.

**THE DIRECTOR'S PRELIMINARY PLANNING** When the play has been selected, the director must do a great deal of preliminary planning before he meets the other production heads. He first analyzes the play until he is completely familiar with the ideas and intentions of the playwright. He visualizes the production as it will be staged, lighted, and costumed, so that he can plan constructively with the technical directors. He has ideas for publicity and sales promotion.

**PLANNING WITH THE OTHER DIRECTORS** The first conference with the production heads is usually a round-table discussion. Included in this group will be the technical and art director, and, at his discretion, his department heads; the music and dance directors, and the business manager. Each has been provided with a copy of the play, which he has read before the meeting. The director brings his outline of the desired goals. In this early planning, the values to be emphasized and the atmosphere to be created must be established, with each department head making his contribution. Although it is to be expected that new ideas will develop which will call for further meetings and consultations, time will be saved and misunderstandings among members of the group will be eliminated if this first meeting is well managed. This is the responsibility of the director, who sets the working atmosphere which will prevail throughout rehearsals and production. There must be a give-and-take attitude on the part of everyone, for it is of the utmost importance that each member be saying in his own medium what the author intended, and that there be complete and harmonious agreement on the subject. Then, each department head should be left to make his own translation under the supervision of the director, whose duty it is from this time on to make a unified whole of the production.

At this first meeting the director will go down his list and assign all the responsibilities, reserving for himself those for which he has no adequate worker. Student managers may recruit their own crews. In order that there may be no misunderstandings, the list of assignments, with deadline dates for the completion of each task, should be posted at once, and either the director or his student director should check at intervals on progress. This makes it possible for the director to give extra help where there are difficulties.

Assuming that there are regular classes in stage arts, the stagecraft teacher becomes the art and technical director, who takes charge of the design and construction of settings, costumes, and lighting. He works closely with the director at all times. The first designs to be settled are the scene plots or ground plans for each act, for unless the drama director knows the location of doors, windows, furniture, and important props, he cannot block the movement of the actors.

Working under the direction of the stage teacher is the student stage manager, who supervises the making and assembling of everything on the stage. The crew working under him consists of the stage carpenter who, with his crew, constructs and paints the set; the property men, who assemble and often make furniture and props; the electricians, who work out the lighting and set electrical equipment; and the sound men, who are responsible for collecting and placing sound equipment. During rehearsals and the run of the play these crews are enlarged by the grips, who move the flats; by flymen, who fly curtains and scenery; by the wardrobe managers, who take charge of mending, pressing, storing, and checking costumes in and out for rehearsals and performances; by make-up artists, dressers, call boys or girls, a prompter, and often by a special man for the main curtain.

With a total time allotment of ten weeks to select, cast, prepare, and present the three-act production, it is feasible to spend one week in selecting the play, one week for casting, seven weeks for rehearsal, and one week for dress rehearsals and playing. This allows eight weeks for staging, since work on the set can begin as soon as the play is selected. The set should be completed at the end of the ninth week, ready for final rehearsals and production the tenth week.

Costume plays with large casts will require at least three additional weeks of rehearsal if the regular routine of classes is to be preserved without interruptions for extra, unscheduled rehearsals.

**PREPARATION OF THE MASTER PROMPT BOOK** The organization of this entire venture is included in the master prompt book, which the director begins alone and gradually builds up as others contribute their working drawings and plans. Eventually it will contain all movement and business; all plots, charts, and cue sheets; an outline of the business management; the rehearsal schedule, and the names, addresses, and phone numbers of cast members. It will, in fact, be a complete working record of everything connected with the show.

This is a general outline of the prompt book:

A. The **interpretation of the play** includes a statement of the theme, an outline of the plot by development, a description of the major conflicts, the suspense elements to be heightened, a statement of the climax, and a decision as to the style which will best project the play. The general atmosphere to be attained, and the mood and tempo with which the show will be developed, should also be specified.

B. The **rehearsal schedule** of the play should be planned and mimeographed copies of it made as soon as the production date is set. (See page 391). Everyone connected with the show should have one. In planning it the director will take into consideration the availability of the rehearsal stage, the other activities of the school and community which might conflict, and the commitments of the actors to their studies and to other activities. Every effort should be made to conserve the time and energy of the students. Time should be allotted for visits to the costumer and the beauty shop. The director will have a definite objective for each rehearsal as well as a breakdown of the episodes and acts. In conference with the technical director, a time will be arranged for the technical rehearsal. So far as possible, everything that might happen should be anticipated, so that no changes in the rehearsal schedule will be necessary.

C. Some **movement and business** will be planned by the director ahead of time; the rest will be put into the prompt book as it is developed.

D. **Plots** of scenes, props, lights, and sound will be prepared by the technicians in charge and submitted to the director for approval.

E. **Costume** and **make-up charts** will be prepared by the artists responsible for them.

F. The **business management** should be outlined, including a campaign for promotion and publicity.

**CASTING** Much of the success of any play depends upon good casting. Parts are assigned through **tryouts.** It is most satisfactory to have the entire play read to the candidates, but if that is impossible the story should be told, some of the most effective scenes read, and a brief analysis of each character given. Tryout parts may be half a typewritten page in length and for two characters only. If a role calls for two violently contrasting moods in a character, two tryout parts must be used to be sure that the actor can interpret both moods satisfactorily. It is best not to use the climax of the play or a scene that reveals too much of the plot, for much repetition will tend to make it sound trite, and in later rehearsals it may be difficult to play the scene with spontaneity.

One or two days should be allowed for memorization. Tryouts may be held in any number of ways; in all cases they should be businesslike but at the same time sufficiently informal to relieve the actor of undue tension and allow him to show his real ability. Time permitting, actors should be given an opportunity to try out for more than one role, having indicated their first and second choices ahead of time. There are actors who give a striking first reading but are unable to grow beyond that, while others make a poor showing in a tryout but have a great capacity for growth. The director must be on the alert to detect signs of both of these qualities, which through experience he will learn to recognize more readily.

In educational dramatics, where the development of the actor as an individual is of first importance, a number of reasons may motivate the director in his selection of a cast.

1. **Dependability** should be first on the list of requisites, for the damage to the morale of the cast is too great when a talented actor is irresponsible or uncooperative. No one who is unreliable or is not a good citizen should ever be assigned a role, for no one is indispensable, and acting ability must be coupled with integrity to be of greatest value.

2. **Ability** is the second consideration for casting, because the drama group has the responsibility for giving the public the best performance possible. While any student may enroll in and receive the benefits of the drama class, only those who are sufficiently

talented to make a show interesting to an audience should be cast in the major plays.

3. The **size and appearance of actors** must be considered in order to make the characters convincing and the ensembles pleasing. Groupings in various scenes must be visualized or tested on the stage. Obviously a very tall girl cannot play opposite a short man. As a rule, strong contrasts are used for comedy only.

4. Other factors which may enter into decisions on casting, especially of the smaller roles, are recognition of a student's contribution to other school activities, or his need to learn teamwork or social adjustment.

**Double casting** has long been a practice in amateur groups. Each part may be assigned to two people, and two complete casts formed, even to the smallest roles or walk-on parts. It is essential, of course, that two shows be scheduled so that each cast has an opportunity to play before an audience. Double casting has many advantages for both the actor and the director, and good student directors can assist with the extra work entailed.

It gives more actors a chance to develop.

It gives more actors training for future shows by giving them the experience of being in a big production, even though in a small part.

It gives each actor the benefit of another person's thinking in the creation of the same character.

It creates a helpful attitude and provides good-natured cast rivalry which is wholesome and social.

It gives an opportunity for alternate casts to watch a complete show from the audience and so learn much that could not be learned otherwise, both about acting and about audience reaction.

It protects rehearsals and performances in case of illness or accident.

It prevents actors from feeling too important and keeps discipline problems at a minimum, since the director can dismiss an uncooperative member and thus uphold proper standards of conduct.

It creates greater audience interest among students because they like to judge and compare the work of individual actors. By so doing they unconsciously develop in drama appreciation.

It stimulates more community interest in the play because more students are involved.

Since the cast is responsible for delivering a show that is worthy of the attention of the audience, it should be understood that casting is always tentative, and that any actor who does not develop to the point of giving an acceptable performance will be dropped from the cast. This is what happens on athletic teams, and actors should be as sportsmanlike in their acceptance of such a decision as athletes are.

**REHEARSALS** All rehearsals should be carefully planned. Steady progress and growth in the production are possible only when adequate preparation for each rehearsal period is made by both director and cast. A businesslike working atmosphere must be maintained at all times.

**The reading rehearsal (A)** When the casting is completed, the director calls the cast together for their first reading rehearsal. Seated informally, often around a large table, they read through the play. At this time the director discusses the interpretation and characterizations, following the outline in his prompt book. Each actor should bring a pencil to all early rehearsals and should insert in his script extra sheets of paper on which to record suggestions. These notes he may later use for reference and study, for he should expect to create his role with only a limited amount of further help from the director. (Review Understanding the Part, page 7.)

**Blocking rehearsals (B)—movement and business** In the first blocking rehearsal the director starts the actors in their positions for the opening of the curtain. Scripts in hand, they walk through the play much as they do in their own first walk-through rehearsals. Now, however, they must modify their actions and movements to conform to an over-all pattern which the director visualizes and which, together with the actors, he develops. While allowing the actor much leeway for the creation of business, the director, as a rule, plans most of the large movement, the positions of the actors at the opening, and groupings for entrances, exits, curtains, and all ensemble effects.

At this first rehearsal the actors should have in their books a sketch of the stage plan showing the furniture arrangement. A makeshift set with accurate dimensions should be improvised. Sometimes the outline can be chalked or painted on the floor and chairs used to indicate entrances. Furniture of some sort, properly placed, should be used. As the actors move through the action of the play they will record on their scripts all directions as to movement and interpretation.

Working with amateurs, the director usually goes straight through the entire play, blocking the scenes in sequence, with just sufficient rehearsal after blocking each section to set the business and movement reasonably well before going on. This method has the advantage of giving the actors a better understanding of the play as a whole and bringing to their attention the scenes which are crucial to the plot, as well as giving guidance for their self-rehearsals. It also prevents too much time being spent on the first part of the play at the expense of the last part. Rehearsal time should be carefully allotted, with extra time for the more difficult sections. Large ensemble scenes involving actors not appearing in other scenes may be rehearsed separately. In his zeal to perfect the play's action, the director must guard against so involving the actors in mechanical details that they lose sight of the fact that the creation of a character is their most important work. Movement and business are the outgrowth of the character's development and must never seem to be something that is superimposed by the director. Even in blocking rehearsals the actors should be in character and should give their lines with full interpretation as soon as the mechanical details have been mastered.

**Developing rehearsals (C)** As rehearsals progress, new business is added, changes and adjustments are made, and the play begins to take shape. Gradually movement and business will be set, lines learned, and characterizations clarified, although there will be growth up to the time of dress rehearsal. Actors should plan additional outside rehearsals for themselves, following the routine established in

Chapter 1. By working in groups of two or three, they can accomplish much that will aid the big rehearsals.

Scripts should be discarded as soon as possible. The first act ought to be fairly well memorized at the end of the first week, and the whole show letter-perfect two weeks before the performance date.

Costumes should be selected early and, even though modern, should be used before the dress rehearsal. Shoes are particularly important. Period costumes require extra rehearsal in order to be handled effectively.

When the show is double cast, it is good experience and training for an actor to rehearse with both groups so that, in case he must substitute for his alternate, he will be able to adjust more readily to the other actors. But after the personnel of the two casts is permanently settled, that is, from the time of the first run-through, he rehearses only with his own cast.

**Run-through rehearsals (D)** Two weeks before the date of production, when the play is completely memorized and casts are settled, two complete run-through rehearsals should be given. One cast may go through the play in the afternoon; then, with time out for a picnic supper, the other cast may repeat it in the evening. Each cast should watch the other, and feel a responsibility for helping to perfect the show. During these rehearsals the director takes notes on every phase of the performance. The strong and weak spots in characterization and play development will be most evident at this time; insecure passages of interpretation and staging snares will loom large. With the casts gathered together after the run-through, the director and actors will discuss critically and constructively the problems to be solved, and note with confidence the sections which were well done. A run-through so early provides an additional impetus to the cast to smooth out difficulties before dress rehearsal. Unless memorization is completed at this time, there will be little opportunity to work out the tempos and rhythm which put the finishing touches on a performance.

**Polishing rehearsals (E)** The run-throughs bring to light the parts of the play that need extra rehearsal. Without regard to sequence, these should be worked upon until perfected, and then followed by a run-through of the act in which they occur.

**Technical rehearsals (F)** Several days before the dress rehearsals, a technical rehearsal should be given. This is a rehearsal for the staging group. At it they work out all the technical problems involving the actors, who should be prepared to repeat any speeches or business as many times as may be necessary to perfect the mechanics. The entire show will not be rehearsed but only those sections designated by the technical director. This is the time for testing sound and lighting cues, the timing and speed of the final curtains, and other mechanical details.

If there are to be changes of scenery, these should be rehearsed by the stage crew alone at a special technical rehearsal when actors are not present. Speed, accuracy, and quiet are the goals. To insure a harmonious blending of costumes by acts, they should be checked under stage lighting either at the technical or at a separate rehearsal. This is particularly important in a modern show where clothes are being provided by the actors.

Adequate technical rehearsals insure an excellent dress rehearsal which, despite superstition to the contrary, is vital to a finished performance.

**Dress rehearsals (G)** At least one day before the first dress rehearsal the mimeographed Instruction Sheet should be given to all members of the production cast and crew. It should contain full instructions about the show: time of dress rehearsals, time of performances, time to report for make-up, information about care of costumes, props, and stage equipment, and anything else about which there could be the slightest doubt. This saves a great deal of time, repetitious questions, and misunderstandings. Actors might again read Theatre Conventions (page 215).

Two complete dress rehearsals are necessary when parts are double cast, and more than two for a costume play. Anything which is to occur during a performance must be rehearsed. For instance, if there are to be curtain calls they must be not only planned for but practiced. Many drama teachers feel, and in this the authors agree, that curtain calls, by giving undue prominence to the actors, defeat the whole idea of cooperative effort upon which the production is built. Some schools have found that an excellent substitute, which gives a more satisfying feeling of achievement to all concerned, is to invite the audience to come onto the stage after the performance and meet everyone connected with the production.

There are other customs of the professional theatre which many educators feel are not sufficiently democratic to be followed in a school situation. Such is the practice of presenting flowers to the actors. Since only those taking the leading roles are, as a rule, given flowers, this nullifies the philosophy that there are no small parts, and that every actor and every technician is equally important to the production. Flowers and gifts which are sent could go to the dressing rooms and be presented inconspicuously after the performance, but not over the footlights or on the stage proper. Students should be informed ahead of time of the school's policy or tradition on all such matters.

When all instructions have been given, the dress rehearsal should commence and be run as nearly like a performance as is humanly possible. The only exception to this rule is that it is not always necessary to use perishables such as flowers. Substitutes can be used for the latter when they are needed for business. Prop tables should be placed in each wing, with all the small props and hand props arranged by acts; a crew member should be in charge of them. Food which is to be eaten in the play should be provided.

There should be no stops during the dress rehearsals. All scenery shifts should be made quietly and speedily. This is the time when actors who are not engaged, members of the crew who are not working on a particular scene, and sometimes members of the orchestra who will be playing for the show, may watch from the auditorium. An audience gives the actors an added spur, tends to put them on their mettle, and gives them an insight into the reactions that they can expect on opening night. However, no one not a part of the show should ever be allowed at any rehearsal.

Although costumes have been tested previously, the first dress rehearsal, in which all are playing together in costumes for the first time, presents problems. Both actors and directors must expect this and be prepared to keep poised in emergencies.

The director again takes notes and times the show, which should now be running with accurate speed. Afterward he gives a talk to the assembled cast, pointing out details that can be improved. He gives individual criticisms to cast members and expresses his confidence that the show will run smoothly if everyone does his best.

No long last-minute rehearsals should be necessary. Proper rest and food during the entire rehearsal period will help to insure a cast that will play the third act with as much vigor as they play the first. In order to play a superior show, the actors must go into it knowing that they are well prepared and that all mechanical details are taken care of. They should feel relaxed and confident. There is little danger of their being overconfident for, even with the best-laid plans, enough things go wrong in any dress rehearsal to put them on guard during the show.

## ☆☆☆ PERFORMANCE

**PLAYING THE SHOW** This is the actors' contribution to the performance. On the evening of the show the atmosphere backstage is one of quiet, organized activity. Actors will report for make-up at the time designated on the Instruction Sheet—usually an hour or more before curtain time. They check props and costumes carefully, are ready on time, and then wait in their dressing rooms until called, a few minutes before an entrance. While waiting for their first cues they should get into character and stay in it until the play is over. At the time of performance the actor represents the work of the entire theatre organization, and because this is so he has a tremendous responsibility to play the best show of which he is capable.

One last word about the **audience**. On the whole, most audiences are generous and honest in their appraisals of a play. In all fairness, however, it must be admitted that the actor is not always at fault when there is an unfavorable criticism. For what anyone receives from a play or from an experience depends not only upon what is presented, but also upon what he himself brings to the situation by way of past experience, intelligence, and open-mindedness. A child, for instance, would not understand Ibsen's "Ghosts," even though Eleanora Duse, that greatest of Italian actresses, played the leading role. Theatre audiences in remote towns fail to grasp the humor in a play which depends upon a knowledge of current New York shows. Whenever a play has little or nothing in common with the background and interests of the audience, its failure is inevitable, and the responsibility rests with those who selected it and not upon the actors who perform it. This is also true of inferior plays which no amount of good acting can salvage.

Another exception arises from the unfortunate fact that some people bring to the theatre prejudices and preconceived judgments which keep them from forming honest opinions of true worth. When this occurs you should, as an actor of integrity, evaluate all the criticisms fairly and refuse to be affected by any that are unjust or founded on ignorance.

Above all, be warned against letting audience taste influence you to lower your acting ideals. Keep your standards high; never present a cheap, tawdry play, no matter what a popular success it might be. Always try to give plays that have both appeal and merit so that at the final curtain you can feel a thrill of pride over a good job well done.

**RUNNING THE SHOW** This is the technicians' contribution to the performance. A smooth-running show depends upon the knowledge, skill, adequate preparation, and coolheadedness of a great number of people. It is never a one-man job, but one incompetent person may do infinite damage. True, only the actors appear before the audience and as a result receive most of the praise. But people wise in the ways of the theatre know that the manner in which a curtain is raised or lowered, or the way a light dimmer is handled, may make a great difference in the effectiveness of the actor's work. When the final curtain goes down, congratulations should be in order for everyone connected with the show.

**Stage crew** The stage crew handle the scenery, lights, props, and sound. The stage should be completely set at least an hour before the show to give adequate time for checking lights and placement of props. The wings should be clean, with all furniture and props neatly arranged there in proper sequence for quick changes. The time element is of great importance in the theatre. Not only must the play itself move with spirit and rapid tempo, but the intermissions must be timed accurately also, for if they are too long the audience loses the mood and trend of the story. Set changes should have been rehearsed until they can be completed in a minimum amount of time. (See Technique of Shifting, page 179.) Five minutes for the first intermission and seven for the second make good timing.

Plays should begin on time. The orchestra should enter the pit five minutes before starting time, and the Overture should begin exactly at the time it was advertised that the show would start. As the applause for the orchestral number dies down the house lights begin to dim, and the curtain goes up the second that the house is dark. House dimming and curtain raising need to be rehearsed until a definite rhythm is established.

Besides the stage crew members, there are other important groups of back-stage technicians: the make-up artists, the wardrobe managers, the dressers, the call boys, and the prompters.

**Make-up artists** Make-up procedures vary according to whether actors can apply their own make-up or not. Generally, amateurs are not sufficiently skillful to do it well, and a make-up crew of art students can be more easily trained to take over the responsibility. It is preferable to provide a separate room for this purpose. Neatness is essential, since make-up materials can easily ruin a costume. Because speed, as well as artistry, is important, make-up routine should

CHARACTER: STAGE DOOR *University High School, Los Angeles*

CHARACTERS: I REMEMBER MAMA *University High School, Los Angeles*

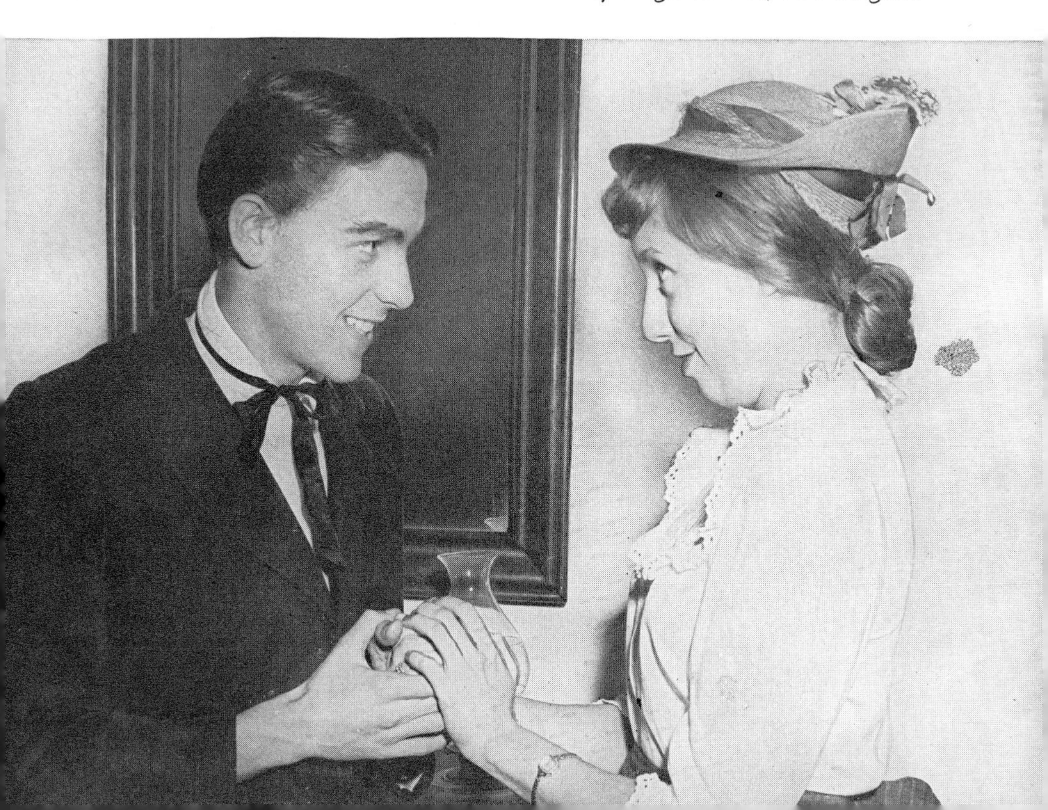

CHARACTER:
QUEENS OF FRANCE
*Sutro School, Los Angeles*

CHARACTERS: JUNE MAD *University High School, Los Angeles*

be carefully organized and rehearsed. A time schedule for make-up appointments, posted ahead of time and rigidly followed, insures a sufficient amount of time for each actor. Character make-ups require more time than straight make-ups. Leads should come in about the middle of the schedule.

**Wardrobe managers** A well-organized dressing room will facilitate costume changes and make-up work. Dressing rooms should be assigned and each actor should paste on his mirror a list of his costumes and props by acts. Wardrobe managers or costume assistants should take charge of costumes for dress rehearsals and performances, and should see that they are pressed, mended, and properly hung. Costumes should be pressed before *every* performance. Each actor should hang his costumes in act sequence, with the accessories for each act placed in separate suit boxes which are well labeled as to owner and act. Street clothes should be hung in a separate part of the dressing room so that nothing which is not a part of the play takes up valuable space.

For costume plays with large casts, when costumes have been rented or made, more assistants are needed. Costumes should then be hung alphabetically according to the name of the actor, with the letters of the alphabet separating them. Wardrobe managers will keep an accurate check on all costumes issued and returned, and each actor should be most careful to see that every article is returned in good condition as soon as he has finished using it.

**Dressers** If a quick costume change is necessary, screens may provide a portable dressing room on stage. Dressers to assist in all quick changes should be trained to work with the actor.

**Call boys** For large casts particularly, it is advisable to have a call boy or girl for each side of the stage. They should have their play books marked with the entrances and exits of each actor. They should stand in the wings following the script until it is time to go to the dressing room to call the actors on stage. Plenty of time should be given for each actor to come up, usually a warning of about three minutes, but he should not be called too early, as there is a tendency for him to become tense when waiting too long for an entrance.

**Prompters** Present at every rehearsal is the person who holds the prompt book. As movement and business are developed, he records it in his book. This he transfers later to the master prompt book. In order to have room for his notes he must either insert blank pages between the leaves of the book, or mount the pages on large pieces of paper from which the centers have been cut.

Because the prompter has rehearsed constantly with the cast, he knows the pauses which different actors take and so is able to prompt only when needed. Of course, prompting should be unnecessary in a properly rehearsed show and should occur only in an emergency, which might arise at any time with any group.

When a play is double cast, each cast will have its own prompter. On a big stage there should be a prompter in each wing, so both prompters work on all shows. Often the student director acts as prompter.

**MANAGING THE SHOW** This is the business staff's contribution to the performance. Usually the business management of a production is under the direction of the financial head of the school. It will differ in various situations. Many good books have been written explaining a number of methods. You should find or develop a way of handling the finances of your organization and of publicizing your productions so that they will be financially successful.

**Budget** A budget is vital to any organization which must support itself. This is especially true of theatre productions in schools where shows not only must clear expenses but should provide a small profit to be used for stage equipment and future productions.

In preparation of the budget the estimated expenditures for all phases of the production are set down: royalties, sets, lighting, costumes, make-up, publicity, tickets, programs, and so forth. It is always wise to have some leeway, labeled miscellaneous, for unexpected emergencies. The budget is made by the director with the aid of the business manager, and sometimes of the stage director.

**Publicity** The publicity for a play should progress according to a carefully planned sequence, and should begin a week or two after the casting. There should be established at the outset definite dates when certain sections of the campaign will be launched. In a school where there is a weekly paper, a series of articles could cover the general information about the play, the cast, the sets, the costumes, music, and any other phases of the production. Credit should be given to everyone making a contribution to the show. A feature story based on amusing incidents occurring during rehearsal, or some other topic suggested by the actors, might be written by a clever journalist. The week of the show a review of the first performance can sometimes be written in advance by a person attending the first dress rehearsal, if he has sufficient imagination to know what will be added by audience participation.

Accompanied by a picture or two, articles following this same general scheme can be published in the local papers. Other devices for publicizing the production are:

Colored cardboard posters that will stand up in store windows or can be tacked up anywhere.
Dodgers that can be folded and mailed to other schools and organizations and then posted on a bulletin board.
The essential information printed on two-cent postal cards or on slips of paper the same size to be mailed in bank statements (the bank willing) or given out with merchandise or bills at any local store.
Slides made especially for the local movie or for the school projection machine.
Signs for automobile bumpers.
Stickers for car windshields (for which you must secure police regulations on size and position).
Banners across the street (for which you must secure city permission).
Large signs on the front of the auditorium.
Actors' pictures displayed in enclosed cases in the main hall.
Daily bulletin notices for the last two weeks before the show.
A short scene from the play, given in an all-school assembly.

Skits presented during the noon hour.
Sandwich boards carried by someone, or hung on a large dog, and paraded around the campus during lunch hour to the accompaniment of a drum or other band instrument.
Talks in classes by actors or members of the public speaking class.

Always be honest in your publicity. Aim to stimulate interest and also to prepare your audience for the kind of entertainment which you are presenting.

**Tickets** Have the tickets printed in plenty of time and accurately numbered to facilitate checking on sales. You may devise many clever ways of selling tickets—by organizations, by clubs, by classes —but the main thing is to sell them. Having competitions between classes is an excellent way of creating interest and sales. The winning class could be admitted to the matinee free. The admission charges must be well considered, and should conform to prevailing prices in the community.

**Programs** A well-designed program containing the names of all persons working on the show is the generally accepted standard. Program covers may be designed and block-printed by the art department, or simply printed in the school print shop. Or they may be made from gay wallpaper, for which a local store might donate a book of samples. Many ingenious ideas will occur to a resourceful group. If your budget is limited, a single mimeographed page is adequate.

**Ushers** Students of the beginning drama classes may usher, and thus be enabled to see all the performances. The Junior or Senior class or some other campus organization may wish the privilege. Some responsible person, preferably a teacher, should be in charge of training the group to see that they are familiar with the seating arrangements of the auditorium, that they are suitably dressed, and that they know how to meet the public graciously. This is an important community contact. A play is a festive occasion which calls for good clothes and good manners.

**Pictures** Pictures of the show, which will provide a permanent record for the actors, for the school yearbook, and for the community papers, should be taken after the first performance. These should be planned by the director to be sure that the story is covered and that every actor appears at least once. One picture of each complete cast, and a few close-up shots of small groups on different parts of the stage, will make a good record.

**Mailing list** An active and accurate file of the names and addresses of people who wish to be informed about future plays has box-office value. It is to these people that the postal cards announcing the show are sent. During the last intermission, ushers may pass pencils and cards to obtain these names and addresses. Names may also be secured by means of a guest book which may be signed before and after the show and at intermissions.

## ☆☆☆ AFTER THE SHOW

**CAST PARTY** Because play production is a social activity, it is a custom with many drama groups to have a cast party after the last performance. This can usually be arranged by a student committee to take place in the home of a cast member. After the long weeks of rehearsal this provides a memorable occasion when the entire group can enjoy the results of their work together. It has been called a time to "gather up your compliments," and is a fitting finale to a most happy experience.

**CLEANUP CREW** After "the tumult and the shouting dies" and the production is only a memory, although a recent one, the set must be struck and all props and costumes returned to their proper places. This is the last job for the stage crew or for a specially organized cleanup crew.

### THEATRE CONVENTIONS

These rules, or theatre conventions, the experienced, well-trained, and considerate actor observes, for they constitute good stage etiquette.

He is enthusiastic about the show.
He always accepts criticism graciously and is never anything but kind and courteous.

He is not impatient at reasonable delays during rehearsals, but adjusts cheerfully to situations.
He does not discuss mistakes during the show.
He is prompt for rehearsals and is always businesslike.
He is quiet in the wings; he does not talk, but gets into character and awaits his entrances.
He does not handle props on the prop table.
He does not sit on stage furniture except during the show.
He does not stumble over cables and props in the wings, or in any other way hamper the work of the stage crew.
He gives no directions to the stage crew.
He goes at once to his dressing room as soon as the curtain is down, leaving the stage to the stage crew.
He never appears anywhere in costume or make-up except backstage.
He never looks through the main curtain at the audience.
He never looks at the prompter when needing a prompt.
He never breaks up and laughs or gets out of character during a show, no matter what happens.
He is a poised, self-disciplined, agreeable person at all times.

#### CHAPTER HIGHLIGHTS

- Outline of three main divisions of work
- Preparation
  - Selection of play
  - Planning with other directors
  - Preparation of Master Prompt Book
  - Casting
  - Rehearsals
- Performance
  - Playing the show (actors)
  - Running the show (technicians)
  - Managing the show (business office)
- After the show
- Theatre Conventions

# Part 3

# ACTING MATERIALS

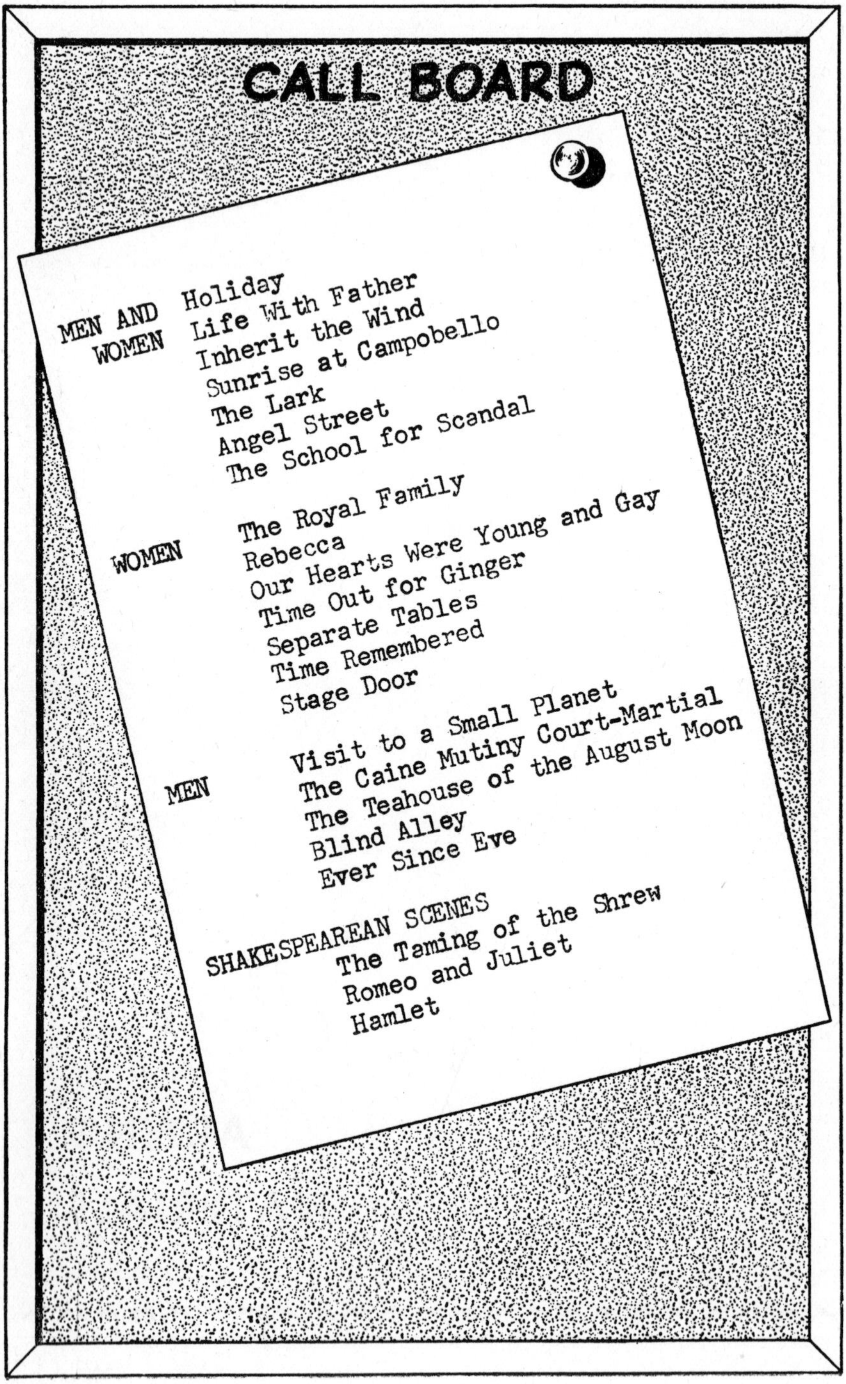

# CALL BOARD

MEN AND WOMEN
- Holiday
- Life With Father
- Inherit the Wind
- Sunrise at Campobello
- The Lark
- Angel Street
- The School for Scandal

WOMEN
- The Royal Family
- Rebecca
- Our Hearts Were Young and Gay
- Time Out for Ginger
- Separate Tables
- Time Remembered
- Stage Door

MEN
- Visit to a Small Planet
- The Caine Mutiny Court-Martial
- The Teahouse of the August Moon
- Blind Alley
- Ever Since Eve

SHAKESPEAREAN SCENES
- The Taming of the Shrew
- Romeo and Juliet
- Hamlet

# Eleven

## SCENES ☆☆☆

### ☆☆☆ HOLIDAY

**by Philip Barry**

ACT I

SCENE: *The third floor sitting-room of Edward Seton's house in New York. It is a comfortable room very richly furnished. The time is about twelve o'clock on a bright, cold Sunday in mid-December.*

CHARACTERS: JULIA SETON
JOHNNY CASE
LINDA SETON

NOTE: Virtually all the detailed movement and business in this scene from *Holiday* have been added by the authors to give you a model to follow in the creation of business for any scene you may use. For stage plot, see page 388.)

(JULIA *is seated on* R *end of couch;* JOHNNY *is seated at her left with his arm around her shoulders.* LINDA *enters wearing hat and coat. She is pulling off her hat and speaking as she enters, but stops short as she sees* JOHNNY CASE, *whom she does not know.*)

LINDA. I must say, that of all the boring—(*Stops, in mild astonishment.*)—why, Julia. Is this a way to spend Sunday morning? Who's your pardner? Anyone I know? (*Puts hat and purse on table.* JOHNNY CASE *rises.*)

JULIA. It's—This is Mr. Case—my sister Linda.

JOHNNY. (*Standing* C.) How do you do?

LINDA. (*Taking off gloves and placing them on bookcase.*) Well, thanks,—And you?

JOHNNY. I couldn't be better.

LINDA. Good.

JULIA. *Johnny* Case, his name is. I'm going to marry him.

LINDA. That makes it all right then. (*Comes down to table.*) Who's coming to lunch? Nick and Susan didn't telephone, did they?

JULIA. In just about one month I'm going to marry him.

LINDA. Stand over there in the light will you, Case. (*Smiling, he takes one step.*) But I've never even seen you before.

JULIA. Neither had I until ten days ago at Placid.

LINDA. (*Pretending to be horrified.*) You aren't a guide, are you?

JOHNNY. (*Laughing.*) No, I'm a lawyer.

LINDA. Wouldn't you know it?

JULIA. I want you to be maid-of-honor, Linda. (LINDA *moves down to chair* L.)

LINDA. I accept. (*Sits.*) What'll we wear? Listen, (*Turns to* JULIA.) is this what came over Father in church?

JULIA. I imagine so. (JOHNNY *sits in center of couch.*)

LINDA. Then you've told him already.

JULIA. Yes.

LINDA. Tsch—tsch, this modern generation. (*Gives a gesture of hopelessness.*) Well, young man (*To* JOHNNY.), I hope you realize what you're getting in for.

JULIA. (*A bit annoyed.*) That's pleasant.

LINDA. I don't mean you. You're divine. I mean Father—and Cousin Seton Cram and Laura and the rest of the outlying Setons (*She gives a broad gesture.*)—and the general atmosphere of plenty, with the top riveted down on the cornucopia. (*She pantomimes it.*)

JULIA. Johnny will try to bear up, won't you, Johnny? (*She smiles at him.*)

JOHNNY. I'll do my best. ( *He smiles at her lovingly.*)

LINDA. But how *did* you two happen to get together? (*She moves quickly to* L *end of couch and sits beside* JOHNNY.) Tell Linda everything.

JULIA. Well, I was walking along the road with Miss Talcott, one morning on the way to the rink and who should I see but—

LINDA. (*Pretending to correct her.*) *Whom* should I see but—

JULIA. And who should I see but this man coming along carrying skis. (*She and* JOHNNY *look at each other and smile.*)

LINDA. Fancy that. A downright romance. Go on, dear—

JULIA. Do you really want to know?

LINDA. I'm hungry for romance, Sister. If you knew the way my little heart is beating against its bars right this minute. (*She indicates her beating heart.* JULIA *smiles,* JOHNNY *laughs.*)

JULIA. He had a queer look on his face. (*She looks at him teasingly.*)

LINDA. I can believe that. ( *She raises her eyebrows.*) His eyes must have been burning.

JULIA. As a matter of fact, the trouble was with his nose. So I stopped him and said: (*Very matter-of-factly.*) "I suppose you don't realize it, but your nose is frozen." And he said: (*Dazed.*) "Thanks, I hadn't realized it." And I said: "Well, it is." And he said: (*Hopefully.*) "I don't suppose there's anything you personally could do about it."

LINDA. Fresh.

JULIA. I thought so too.

JOHNNY. She was fresh to mention it. It looked to me like an out-and-out pick-up.

LINDA. Obviously.

JULIA. (*Looking at him admiringly.*) I know a good thing when I see it.

LINDA. (*Gesturing.*) So you swept her right off her snowshoes?

JOHNNY. It was touch-and-go with us.

LINDA. I think I like this man.

JULIA. (*Beaming.*) I was sure you would.

LINDA. (*Rising and starting to leave.*) Well, my dears, take your happiness while you may.

JOHNNY. Watch us.

JULIA. (*AS* LINDA *disappears.*) No—*don't* watch us! (*She looks up at* JOHNNY *who puts his arm around her again as the curtain falls.*)

## ☆☆☆ LIFE WITH FATHER

### by Howard Lindsay and Russel Crouse

ACT II, SCENE 1

SCENE: *The Morning Room of the Day home at 420 Madison Avenue. In the custom of the Victorian period, this was the room where the family gathered for breakfast, and because it was often the most comfortable room in the house, it served also as a living-room for the family and their intimates.*

---

CHARACTERS: FATHER
VINNIE

(*Father rises and holds the bill in question between thumb and forefinger as though it were too repulsive to touch.*)

VINNIE. What's the matter, Clare? What's wrong?

FATHER. I will *not* send this person a check!
(VINNIE *looks at it.*)

VINNIE. Why, Clare, that's the only hat I've bought since March and it was reduced from forty dollars.

FATHER. I don't question your buying the hat or what you paid for it, but the person from whom you bought it—this Mademoiselle Mimi—isn't fit to be in the hat business or any other.

VINNIE. I never went there before, but it's a very nice place and I don't see why you object to it.

FATHER. (*Exasperated.*) I object to it because this confounded person doesn't put her name on her bills! Mimi what? Mimi O'Brien? Mimi Jones? Mimi Weinstein?

VINNIE. How do I know? It's just Mimi.

FATHER. It isn't just Mimi. She must have some other name, damn it! Now, I wouldn't make out a check payable to Charley or to Jimmy, and I won't make out a check payable to Mimi. Find out what her last name is, and I'll pay her the money.

VINNIE. All right. All right. (*She starts out.*)

FATHER. Just a minute, Vinnie, that isn't all.

VINNIE. But Cora will be leaving any minute, Clare, and it isn't polite for me—

FATHER. Never mind Cora. Sit down.
(VINNIE *reluctantly sits down opposite* FATHER *at the table.*)
Vinnie, you know I like to live well, and I want my family to live well. But this house must be run on a business basis. I must know how much money I'm spending and what for. For instance, if you recall, two weeks ago I gave you six dollars to buy a new coffee pot—

VINNIE. Yes, because you broke the old one. You threw it right on the floor.

FATHER. I'm not talking about that. I'm simply endeavoring—

VINNIE. But it was so silly to break that nice coffee pot, Clare, and there was nothing the matter with the coffee that morning. It was made just the same as always.

FATHER. It was not! It was made in a damned barbaric manner!

VINNIE. I couldn't get another imported one. That little shop has stopped selling them. They said the tariff wouldn't let them. And that's your fault, Clare, because you're always voting to raise the tariff.

FATHER. The tariff protects America against cheap foreign labor. (*He sounds as though he is quoting.*) Now I find that—

VINNIE. The tariff does nothing but put up the prices and that's hard on everybody, especially the farmer. (*She sounds as though she is quoting back.*)

FATHER. (*Annoyed.*) I wish to God you wouldn't talk about matters you don't know a damn thing about!

VINNIE. I do too know about them. Miss Gulick says every intelligent woman should have some opinion—

FATHER. Who, may I ask, is Miss Gulick?

VINNIE. Why, she's that current-events woman I told you about and the tickets are a dollar every Tuesday.

FATHER. Do you mean to tell me that a pack of idle-minded females pay a dollar apiece to hear another female gabble about the events of the day? Listen to me if you want to know anything about the events of the day!

VINNIE. But you get so excited, Clare, and besides, Miss Gulick says that our President, whom you're always belittling, prays to God for guidance and—

FATHER. (*Having had enough of Miss Gulick.*) Vinnie, what happened to that six dollars?

VINNIE. What six dollars?

FATHER. I gave you six dollars to buy a new coffee pot and now I find that you apparently got one at Lewis & Conger's and charged it. Here's their bill: "One coffee pot—five dollars."

VINNIE. So you owe me a dollar and you can hand it right over. (*She holds out her hand for it.*)

FATHER. I'll do nothing of the kind! What did you do with that six dollars?

VINNIE. Why Clare, I can't tell you now, dear. Why didn't you ask me at the time?

FATHER. Oh, my God!

VINNIE. Wait a moment! I spent four dollars and a half for that new umbrella I told you I wanted and you said I didn't need, but I did, very much.

(FATHER *takes his pencil and writes in the account book.*)

FATHER. Now we're getting somewhere. One umbrella—four dollars and a half.

VINNIE. And that must have have been the week I paid Mrs. Tobin for two extra days' washing.

FATHER. (*Entering the item.*) Mrs. Tobin.

VINNIE. So that was two dollars more.

FATHER. Two dollars.

VINNIE. That makes six dollars and fifty cents. And that's another fifty cents you owe me.

FATHER. I don't owe you anything. (*Stung by* VINNIE'S *tactics into a determination to pin her butterfly mind down.*) What you owe me is an explanation of where my money's gone! We're going over this account book item by item. (*Starts to sort the bills for the purposes of cross-examination, but the butterfly takes wing again.*)

VINNIE. I do the very best I can to keep down expenses. And you know yourself that Cousin Phoebe spends twice as much as we do.

FATHER. Damn Cousin Phoebe! I don't wish to be told how she throws her money around.

VINNIE. Oh, Clare, how can you? And I thought you were so fond of Cousin Phoebe.

FATHER. All right, I am fond of Cousin Phoebe, but I can get along without hearing so much about her.

VINNIE. You talk about your own relatives enough.

FATHER. (*Hurt.*) That's not fair, Vinnie. When I talk about my relatives I criticize them.

VINNIE. If I can't even speak of Cousin Phoebe—

FATHER. You can speak of her all you want to—but I won't have Cousin Phoebe or anyone else dictating to me how to run my house. Now this month's total—

VINNIE. (*Righteously.*) I didn't say a word about her dictating, Clare—she isn't that kind!

FATHER. (*Dazed.*) I don't know what you said, now. You never stick to the point. I endeavor to show you how to run this house on a business basis and you wind up by jibbering and jabbering about everything else under the sun. If you'll just explain to me—

(*Finally cornered,* VINNIE *realizes the time has come for tears. Quietly she turns them on.*)

VINNIE. I don't know what you expect of me. I tire myself out chasing up and down those stairs all day long—trying to look after your comfort—to bring up our children—I do the mending and the marketing and as if that isn't enough, you want me to be an expert bookkeeper, too.

FATHER. (*Touched where* VINNIE *has hoped to touch him.*) Vinnie, I want to be reasonable; but can't you understand?—I'm doing all this for your own good.

(VINNIE *rises with a moan.* FATHER *sighs with resignation.*) I suppose I'll have to go ahead just paying the bills and hoping I've got money enough in the bank to meet them. But it's all very discouraging.

VINNIE. I'll try to do better, Clare.

(FATHER *looks up into her tearful face and melts.*)

FATHER. That's all I'm asking.

*(She goes to him and puts her arm around his shoulder.)*

I'll go down and make out the checks and sign them.

## ☆☆☆INHERIT THE WIND

### by Jerome Lawrence and Robert E. Lee

ACT I, SCENE 2

SCENE: *The Courtroom in a small town.*

CHARACTERS: RACHEL BROWN, BERTRAM CATES, HENRY DRUMMOND, MEEKER (x)

RACHEL. Mr. Drummond. You've got to call the whole thing off. It's not too late. Bert knows he did wrong. He didn't mean to. And he's sorry. Now why can't he just stand up and say to everybody: "I did wrong. I broke a law. I admit it. I won't do it again." Then they'd stop all this fuss, and—everything would be like it was.

(DRUMMOND *looks at* RACHEL, *not unkindly.*)

DRUMMOND. Who are you?

RACHEL. I'm—a friend of Bert's.

(DRUMMOND *turns to* CATES.)

DRUMMOND. How about it, boy? Getting cold feet?

CATES. I never thought it would be like this. Like Barnum and Bailey coming to town.

DRUMMOND. (*Easily.*) We can call it off. You want to quit?

RACHEL. (*Coming to* BERT's *side.*) Yes!

CATES. People look at me as if I was a murderer. Worse than a murderer. That fella from Minnesota who killed his wife—

---

remember, Rachel—half the town turned out to see 'em put him on the train. They just looked at him as if he was a curiosity—not like they *hated* him! Not like he'd done anything really wrong! Just different!

DRUMMOND. (*Laughs a little to himself.*) There's nothing very original about murdering your wife.

CATES. People I thought were my friends look at me now as if I had horns growing out of my head.

DRUMMOND. You murder a wife, it isn't nearly as bad as murdering an old wives' tale. Kill one of their fairy-tale notions, and they call down the wrath of God, Brady, and the state legislature.

RACHEL. You make a joke out of everything. You seem to think it's so funny.

DRUMMOND. Lady, when you lose your power to laugh, you lose your power to think straight.

CATES. Mr. Drummond, I can't laugh. I'm scared.

DRUMMOND. Good. You'd be a damned fool if you weren't.

RACHEL. (*Bitterly.*) You're supposed to help Bert; but every time you swear you make it worse for him.

DRUMMOND. (*Honestly.*) I'm sorry if I offend you. (*He smiles.*) But I don't swear just for the hell of it. (*He fingers his galluses.*) You see, I figure language is a poor enough means of communication as it is. So we ought to use all the words we've got. Besides, there are damned few words that everybody understands.

RACHEL. You don't care anything about Bert! You just want a chance to make speeches against the Bible!

DRUMMOND. I care a great deal about Bert. I care a great deal about what Bert thinks.

RACHEL. Well, I care about what the people in this town think of *him.*

DRUMMOND. (*Quietly.*) Can you buy back his respectability by making him a coward? (*He spades his hands in his hip pockets.*) I understand what Bert's going through. It's the loneliest feeling in the world—to find yourself standing up when everybody else is sitting down. To have everybody look at you and say, "What's the matter with him?" I know. I know what it feels like. Walking down an empty street, listening to the sound of your own footsteps. Shutters closed, blinds drawn, doors locked against you. And you aren't sure whether you're walking toward something, or if you're just walking away. (*He takes a deep breath, then turns abruptly.*) Cates, I'll change your plea and we'll call off the whole business—on one condition. If you honestly believe you committed a criminal act against the citizens of this state and the minds of their children. If you honestly believe that you're wrong and the law's right. Then the hell with it. I'll pack my grip and go back to Chicago, where it's a cool hundred in the shade.

RACHEL. (*Eagerly.*) Bert knows he's wrong. Don't you, Bert?

DRUMMOND. Don't prompt the witness.

CATES. (*Indecisive.*) What do you think, Mr. Drummond?

DRUMMOND. I'm here. That tells you what I think. (*He looks squarely at* CATES.) Well, what's the verdict, Bert? You want to find yourself guilty before the jury does?

CATES. (*Quietly, with determination.*) No, sir. I'm not gonna quit.

RACHEL. (*Protesting.*) Bert!

CATES. It wouldn't do any good now, anyhow. (*He turns to* RACHEL.) If you'll stick by me, Rache—well, we can fight it out. (*He smiles at her wanly. All the others have gone now except* MEEKER and DRUMMOND. RACHEL *shakes her head, bewildered, tears forming in her eyes.*)

RACHEL. I don't know what to do; I don't know what to do.

CATES (*Frowning.*) What's the matter, Rache?

RACHEL. I don't want to do it, Bert; but Mr. Brady says—

DRUMMOND. What does Brady say?

RACHEL. (*Looking down.*) They want me to testify against Bert.

CATES. (*Stunned.*) You can't!

MEEKER. I don't mean to rush you, Bert; but we gotta close up the shop. (CATES *is genuinely panicked.*)

CATES. Rache, some of the things I've talked to you about are things you just say to your own heart. (*He starts to go with* MEEKER, *then turns back.*) If you get up on the stand and say those things out loud—(*He shakes his head.*) Don't you understand? The words I've said to you—softly, in the dark—just trying to figure out what the stars are for, or what might be on the back side of the moon—

MEEKER. Bert—

CATES. They were questions, Rache. I was just asking questions. If you repeat those things on the witness stand, Brady'll make 'em sound like answers. And they'll crucify me!

(CATES *and* MEEKER *go off. The lights are slowly dimming.* DRUMMOND *puts on his coat, sizing up* RACHEL *as he does so.* RACHEL, *torn, is almost unconscious of his presence or of her surroundings.*)

DRUMMOND. (*Kindly, quietly.*) What's your name? Rachel what?

RACHEL. Rachel Brown. Can they make me testify?

DRUMMOND. I'm afraid so. It would be nice if nobody ever had to *make* anybody do anything. But—(*He takes his brief case.*) Don't let Brady scare you. He only *seems* to be bigger than the law.

RACHEL. It's not Mr. Brady. It's my father.

DRUMMOND. Who's your father?

RACHEL. The Reverend Jeremiah Brown. (DRUMMOND *whistles softly through his teeth.*) I remember feeling this way when I was a little girl. I would wake up at night, terrified of the dark. I'd think sometimes that my bed was on the ceiling, and the whole house was upside down; and if I didn't hang onto the mattress, I might fall outward into the stars. (*She shivers a little, remembering.*) I wanted to run to my father, and have him tell me I was safe, that everything was all right. But I was always more frightened of him than I was of falling. It's the same way now.

DRUMMOND. (*Softly.*) Is your mother dead?

RACHEL. I never knew my mother. (*Distraught.*) Is it true? *Is* Bert wicked?

DRUMMOND. (*With simple conviction.*) Bert Cates is a good man. Maybe even a great one. And it takes strength for a woman to love such a man. Especially when he's a pariah in the community.

RACHEL. I'm only confusing Bert. And he's confused enough as it is.

DRUMMOND. The man who has everything figured out is probably a fool. College examinations notwithstanding, it takes a very smart fella to say "I don't know the answer!"

(DRUMMOND *puts on his hat, touches the brim of it as a gesture of good-bye and goes slowly off.*)

## ☆☆☆ SUNRISE AT CAMPOBELLO

### by Dore Schary

ACT II, SCENE 2

SCENE: *The living room of the Franklin D. Roosevelt home in New York, May, 1922.*

CHARACTERS: FRANKLIN (F.D.R.)
SARA, his mother

SARA. Oh, Franklin, I'm getting some men at Hyde Park to determine how we can electrify the lift. It is, after all, only a large-size dumbwaiter and I—

F.D.R. (*Quickly.*) No.! (*Perhaps he's been too sharp.*) I mean, please don't. The exercise of pulling those ropes is helpful to me. I need it for my arms and shoulders. So, if you're thinking of me—please don't change the dumbwaiter.

SARA. I feel you're doing too much, physically.

F.D.R. I wish I could do more. Ma*ma*—it's only my legs that are temporarily bothered. The rest of me is as healthy as ever.

---

SARA. I know that. I know that. I talk to the doctors. They tell me. But sometimes I think that Eleanor, certainly only with motives of deep love, and that ugly little man, push you too rapidly.

F.D.R. I don't think so. Dr. Draper doesn't think so. And please, Ma*ma*, don't refer to Louie Howe any longer with that unpleasant phrase. I've endured it too long as it is.

SARA. (*Walking about, genuinely disturbed.*) Franklin, your tone of voice is very disturbing to me.

F.D.R. Ma*ma*, if possible, I should like to have a quiet talk with you. I should like not to quarrel. Now, Ma*ma*. I know how upset you've been. This is a real wrench for you. But I'm going to get over this—and—if I don't—a big *if*—I shall have to become accustomed to braces and canes and wheel chairs. And so will you.

SARA. Oh, Franklin—

F.D.R. Please, let me finish. Louie Howe—(SARA *makes an involuntary grimace.*) Ma*ma*, stop that. Louie Howe told me, while I was in the hospital after Campobello, that I had one of two choices. I could lie on my back, be a country squire and write books—*or*—get up and become President of the United States. *Now*—I believe Louie's dreams are far too bright—but I've no intention of retiring to Hyde Park and rusticating.

SARA. (*Quietly.*) Franklin, when you were a little boy, your dear father took you for a visit to the White House to see President Cleveland.

F.D.R. (*Fidgets.*) Ma*ma*, I know.

SARA. (*Firmly.*) Let me finish. And President Cleveland said, "I make a strange wish for you. It is that you may never be President of the United States."

F.D.R. Well, he was playing the odds in wishing that.

SARA. Your Cousin Teddy died because of ambitious people around him. Died because he didn't know when to stop—didn't know that you can't make it the same world for all people.

F.D.R. Maybe we can't. But it seems to me that every human has an obligation in his own way to make some little stab at trying.

SARA. It's not such a bad world, Franklin—not at all.

F.D.R. I have no personal complaints. I'm lucky. I had rich parents.

SARA. Don't be self-conscious about that, Franklin. Advantages of birth should be worn like clothes, with grace and comfort.

F.D.R. (*A familiar tale—and he knows it.*) Yes—yes. *Noblesse oblige.* The poor will always be with us. We went through that when I sold the mining stock.

SARA. On reflection—you must admit that was a childish gesture.

F.D.R. (*The heat is on.*) I would not hang onto stock bringing me an income over the tortured bodies of miners who lived as though they were in the Middle Ages. These are different times. The attitude of *noblesse oblige* is archaic.

SARA. Franklin!

F.D.R. It's another name for indifference.

SARA. How dare you! You are talking to your mother. Even if I were to agree with your romantic political ideas, it would be absurd for you to consider running for public office. The traveling and the speeches would be an enormous strain for you.

F.D.R. At the moment I'm not running for anything—and I won't until I can get around and stand up on my two feet—but that doesn't mean I have to go into hiding.

SARA. (*Icily.*) I'm not asking you to do that. I'm asking you to be sensible—to take up a permanent residence in Hyde Park where you could be comfortable—where you could use the time for resting and regain your strength.

F.D.R. I love Hyde Park. But I want to use it—not let it bury me.

SARA. That's a terrible thing to say.

F.D.R. You know what I mean.

SARA. No, Franklin, I do not know what you mean. I only know that your stubbornness is not only your strength but your weakness. And you needn't—

F.D.R. (*Getting angry.*) I needn't do a damn thing! I am not going to let myself go down a drain. A bad beating either breaks the stick or the student—Well, I'm not broken. I'm not settling for the life of an ailing invalid. And I will no longer abide implications, innuendos or insinuations that I do so.

SARA. I don't want you getting angry. It's not good for you.

F.D.R. (*Heatedly.*) It's damn good. For me.

SARA. Franklin, I wonder if you truly know what is good for you. You come by your Dutch stubbornness by birth. And, Franklin, some of that Dutch stubbornness is mine—from long association. (*She now becomes firm and dominant.*) Franklin, many many years ago, when I was a little girl, I sailed to China with my father on a clipper ship. As we rounded Cape Horn, we headed into a fearful storm. My father, eager and headstrong, urged the Captain to head into the sea—to fight through the storm. But fortunately the Captain of the ship was a better sailor than my father. He wanted to save his ship. He trimmed sails, gave orders to "heave to," rode out the storm safely, and then, when the heavy weather was gone, we were able to sail ahead and nothing was lost—nothing. Be wise, Franklin—ride out the storm. (*A pause.* SARA, *emotionally wrought-up by now, strikes hotter.*) Son, let me ask you—what do you believe I want for you—obscurity? Invalidism? Do you believe that this is my ambition for you? Having been a mother for over forty years, do you think this is what I want? Any dream you ever had or could have, I have. All pain you have felt, I have felt. (*By now she is sharp and hard.*) I don't want to see you hurt.

F.D.R. That's enough. There'll be no more talking—no more.

## ☆☆☆ THE LARK

### by Jean Anouilh

ACT I

SCENE: *The Dauphin's Court*

CHARACTERS: CHARLES
JOAN

CHARLES. Do you know how to play at cards?

JOAN. I don't know what it is.

CHARLES. It is a nice game invented to amuse my Papa when he was ill. I'll teach you. (*He begins to hunt for the cards.*) I hope they haven't stolen them. They steal everything from me around here and cards are expensive. Only the wealthiest princes can have them. I got mine from Papa. I'll never have the price of another pack. If those pigs have stolen them—No. Here they are. (*He finds them in his pocket.*) My Papa was crazy. Went crazy young—in his thirties. Did you know that? Sometimes I'm glad I am a bastard. At least I don't have to be so frightened of going crazy. Then sometimes I wish I were his son and knew that I was meant to be a king. It's confusing.

JOAN. Of the two, which would you prefer?

CHARLES. Well, on the days when I have a little courage, I'd risk going crazy. But on the days when I haven't any courage—that's from Sunday to Saturday—I would rather let everything go to hell and live in peace in some foreign land on whatever little money I have left.

JOAN. Today, Charles, is this one of the days when you have courage?

CHARLES. Today? (*He thinks a minute.*) Yes, it seems to me I have a little bit today.

---

JOAN. You will have courage every day. Beginning now.

CHARLES. You have a charm in a bottle or a basket?

JOAN. I have a charm.

CHARLES. You are a witch? You can tell me, you know, because I don't care. I swear to you that I won't repeat it. I have a horror of people being tortured. A long time ago, they made me witness the burning of a heretic at the stake. I vomited all night long.

JOAN. I am not a witch. But I have a charm.

CHARLES. Sell it to me without telling the others.

JOAN. I will give it to you, Charles. For nothing.

CHARLES. Then I don't want it. What you get free costs too much. (*He shuffles the cards.*) I act like a fool so that people will let me alone. But don't think you can catch me too easily. I know a little about the world.

JOAN. You know too much. You are too smart.

CHARLES. Yes. Because I must defend myself against these cut-throats. They've got large bones, I've got puny sticks. But my head's harder than theirs and I've clung to my throne by using it.

JOAN. (*Gently.*) I would like to defend you against them, Charles. I would give my life to do it.

CHARLES. Do you mean that?

JOAN. Yes. And I'm not afraid of anything.

CHARLES. You're lucky. Or you're a liar. Sit down and I'll teach you to play.

JOAN. All right. You teach me this game and I'll teach you another game.

CHARLES. What game do you know?

JOAN. How not to be too smart. (*Softly.*) And how not to be afraid.

CHARLES. (*Laughs.*) You'll be here a lifetime, my girl. Now. See these cards? They have pictures painted on them. Kings, queens and knaves, just as in real life. Now which would you say was the most powerful, which one could take all the rest?

JOAN. The king.

CHARLES. Well, you're wrong. This large heart can take the king. It can put him to rout, break his heart, win all his money. This card is called—

JOAN. I know. It is called God. Because God is more powerful than kings.

CHARLES. Oh, leave God alone for a minute. It's called the ace. Are you running this game? God this and God that. You talk as if you dined with Him last night. Didn't anybody tell you that the English also say their prayers to God? Every man thinks God is on his side. The rich and powerful know He is. But we're not rich and powerful, you and I—and France.

JOAN. That isn't what God cares about. He is angry with us because we have no courage left. God doesn't like frightened people.

CHARLES. Then He certainly doesn't like me. And if He doesn't like me, why should I like Him? He could have given me courage. I wanted it.

JOAN. (*Sharply.*) Is God your nurse? Couldn't you have tried to do a little better? Even with those legs.

CHARLES. I am sorry to know that my legs have already come to your attention. It's because of my legs that Agnes can never really love me. That's sad, isn't it?

JOAN. No.

CHARLES. Why not?

JOAN. Because your head is ugly, too, and you can't be sad about everything. But what's inside your head isn't ugly, because God gave you sense. And what do you do with it? Play cards. Bounce a ball in the air. Play baby tricks with the Archbishop and act the fool for all to see. You have a son. But what have you made for him? Nothing. And when he's grown he, too, will have a right to say, "God didn't like me, so why should I like Him?" But when he says God he will mean you because every son thinks his father is God. And when he's old enough to know that, he will hate you for what you didn't give him.

CHARLES. Give him? What can I give him? I'm glad to be alive. I've told you the truth: I am afraid. I've always been and I always will be.

JOAN. And now I'll tell you the truth: I am also afraid. (*With force.*) And why not? Only the stupid are not afraid. What is the matter with you? Don't you understand that it was far more dangerous for me to get here than it is for you to build a kingdom? I've been in danger every minute of the way, and every minute of the way I was frightened. I don't want to be beaten, I don't want pain, I don't want to die. I am scared.

CHARLES. (*Softly.*) What do you do when you get scared?

JOAN. Act as if I wasn't. It's that simple. Try it. Say to yourself, yes, I am afraid. But it's nobody else's business, so go on, go on. And you do go on.

CHARLES. (*Softly.*) Where do you go?

JOAN. (*Slowly, carefully.*) To the English, outside Orléans. And when you get there and see the cannon and the archers, and you know you are outnumbered, you will say to yourself, all right, they are stronger than I am, and that frightens me, as well it should. But I'll march right through because I had sense enough to get frightened first.

CHARLES. March through a stronger army? That can't be done.

JOAN. Yes, it can. If you have sense and courage. Do you want to know what happened in my village last year? They tell the story as a miracle now but it wasn't. The Bouchon boy went hunting. He's the best poacher in our village, and this day he was poaching on the master's grounds. The master kept a famous dog, trained to kill, and the dog found the Bouchon boy. The boy was caught and death faced him. So he threw a stone and the dog turned his head. That was sense. And while the dog turned his head the boy decided the only way was to stand and fight. That was courage. He strangled the dog. That was victory. See?

CHARLES. Didn't the dog bite him?

JOAN. (*As if to a stupid child.*) You're like the old people in the village—you really believe in miracles. Of course the dog bit him. But I told you the boy had sense, and sense saved his life. God gave man an inside to his head, and He naturally doesn't want to see it wasted. (*Smiles.*) See? That's my secret. The witches' secret. What will you pay me for it now?

CHARLES. What do you want?

JOAN. The army of France. Believe in God and give me the army.

CHARLES. (*Moves away from her.*) Tomorrow. I'll have time to get ready—

JOAN. (*Moves after him.*) No, right now. You are ready. Come on, Charlie.

CHARLES. Perhaps I am. Perhaps I've been waiting for you and didn't know—(*Laughs nervously.*) Shall we send for the Archbishop and La Tremouille and tell them that I have decided to give the army to you? It would be fun to see their faces.

JOAN. Call them.

CHARLES. (*In a panic.*) No, I'm frightened.

JOAN. Are you as afraid as you ever can be, ever were or will be, then, now and in the future? Are you sick?

CHARLES. (*Holding his stomach.*) I think so.

JOAN. Good. Good. Then the worst is over. By the time they get scared, you'll be all over yours. Now, if you're as sick as you can get, I'll call them. (*She runs upstage and calls out.*) Monseigneur the Archbishop. Monseigneur de la Tremouille. Please come to the Dauphin.

CHARLES. (*Almost happy.*) I am very sick.

JOAN. (*Moves him gently to the throne and arranges his hands and feet.*) God is smiling. He is saying to Himself, "Look at that little Charles. He is sicker than he's ever been in his life. But he has called in his enemies and will face them. My, such a thing is wonderful." (*With great force.*) Hang on, Charles. We'll be in Orléans. We'll march right up.

## ☆☆☆ ANGEL STREET
### by Patrick Hamilton

ACT I

SCENE: *Living room of a house on Angel Street, London, 1880.*
CHARACTERS: MR. MANNINGHAM ELIZABETH (x)
MRS. MANNINGHAM NANCY (x)

MRS. MANNINGHAM. What is it? What's the matter? What is it now?

MR. MANNINGHAM. (*Walking over to firelace in front of settee, and speaking with his back to her.*) I have no desire to upset you, Bella, but I have just observed something very much amiss. Will you please rectify it at once, while I am not looking, and we will assume that it has not happened.

MRS. MANNINGHAM. Amiss? What's amiss? For God's sake don't turn your back on me. What has happened?

MR. MANNINGHAM. You know perfectly well what has happened, Bella, and if you will rectify it at once I will say no more about it.

MRS. MANNINGHAM. I don't know. I don't know. You have left your tea. Tell me what is it. Tell me.

MR. MANNINGHAM. Are you trying to make a fool of me, Bella? What I refer to is on the wall behind you. If you will put it back, I will say no more about it.

---

MRS. MANNINGHAM. The wall behind me? What? (*Turns.*) Oh—yes—The picture has been taken down—Yes—The picture—Who has taken it down? Why has it been taken down?

MR. MANNINGHAM. Yes. Why has it been taken down? Why, indeed. You alone can answer that, Bella. Why was it taken down before? Will you please take it from wherever you have hidden it, and put it back on the wall again?

MRS. MANNINGHAM. But I haven't hidden it, Jack. (*Rises.*) I didn't do it. Oh, for God's sake look at me. I didn't do it. I don't know where it is. Someone else must have done it.

MR. MANNINGHAM. Someone else? (*Turning to her.*) Are you suggesting perhaps that I should play such a fantastic and wicked trick?

MRS. MANNINGHAM. No, dear, no! But someone else. (*Going to him.*) Before God, I didn't do it! Someone else, dear, someone else.

MR. MANNINGHAM. (*Shaking her off.*) Will you please leave go of me. (*Walking over to bell.*) We will see about "someone else."

MRS. MANNINGHAM. (*Crossing to front of settee.*) Oh, Jack—don't ring the bell. Don't ring it. Don't call the servants to witness my shame. It's not my shame for I haven't done it—but *don't* call the servants! Tell them not to come. (*He has rung the bell. She goes to him.*) Let's talk of this between ourselves! Don't call that girl in. Please!

MR. MANNINGHAM. (*Shaking her off violently.*) Will you please leave go of me and sit down there! (*She sits in chair above the desk. He goes to fireplace.*) Someone else, eh? Well—we shall see. (MRS. MANNINGHAM *in chair, sobs.*) You had better pull yourself together, hadn't you?—(*There is a* KNOCK *at the door.*) Come in. (*Enter* ELIZABETH LC *and leaves the doors open.*) Ah, Elizabeth. Come in please, Elizabeth—Shut the door—(*Pause as she does so.*) Well, come in, come into the room—(*Pause as* ELIZABETH *crosses to the back of the chair* L *of the table.*) Now, Elizabeth, do you notice anything amiss in this room?—Look carefully around the walls, and see if you notice anything amiss—(*Pause as* ELIZABETH *looks around the room and when she sees the space of the missing picture she stands still.*) Well, Elizabeth, what do you notice?

ELIZABETH. Nothing, sir—Except the picture's been taken down.

MR. MANNINGHAM. Exactly. The picture has been taken down. You noticed it at once. Now was that picture in its place when you dusted the room this morning?

ELIZABETH. Yes, sir. It was, sir. I don't understand, sir.

MR. MANNINGHAM. Neither do I, Elizabeth, neither do I. And now, before you go, just one question. Was it you who removed that picture, Elizabeth?

ELIZABETH. No, sir. Of course I ain't, sir.

MR. MANNINGHAM. You did not. And have you ever, at any time, removed that picture from its proper place?

ELIZABETH. No sir. Never, sir. Why should I, sir?

MR. MANNINGHAM. Indeed, why should you?—And now please, Elizabeth, will you kiss that Bible, will you as a token of your truthfulness—fetch that Bible from my desk? (*Pause.* ELIZABETH *hesitates. Then she does so.*) Very well, you may go. (*She starts to the desk with Bible and* MANNINGHAM *motions to her to put it on* Center *table.*) And please send Nancy in here at once.

ELIZABETH. Yes sir. (*Opens doors, goes out, closes doors, looking at both.*)

MRS. MANNINGHAM. (*Going to him.*) Jack—spare me that girl. Don't call her in. I'll say anything. I'll say that I did it. I did it, Jack, I did it. Don't have that girl in. Don't!

MR. MANNINGHAM. Will you have the goodness to contain yourself? (*There is a* KNOCK *at the* LC *door.* MRS. MANNINGHAM *sits in chair below fire-place.*) Come in.

NANCY. (*Opens doors, enters and leaves doors open. Crossing to settee.*) Yes, sir. Did you want me?

MR. MANNINGHAM. Yes, I do want you, Nancy.—If you will look at the wall behind you, you will see that the picture has gone.

CHARACTERS: LIFE WITH FATHER *Santa Monica City College*

CHARACTERS: MACBETH
*Evanston Township High School, Evanston, Illinois*

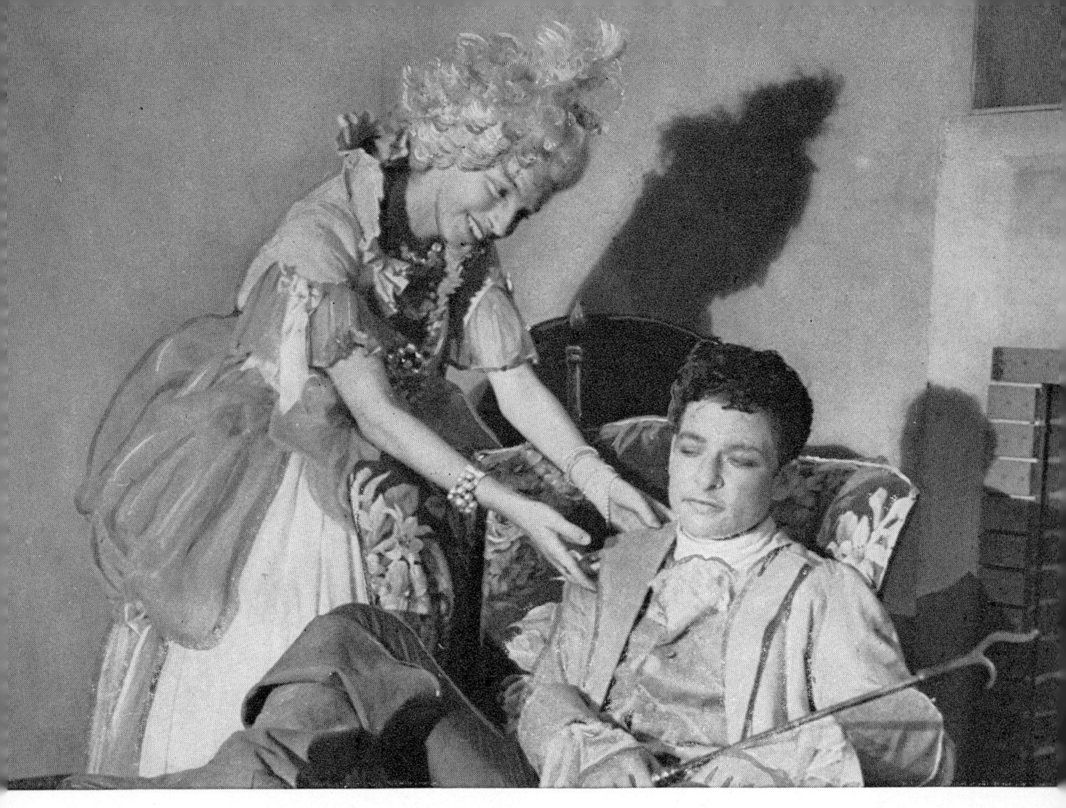

CHARACTERS: SHE STOOPS TO CONQUER *University High School, Los Angeles*

CHARACTERS: THE BARRETTS OF WIMPOLE STREET
*University High School, Los Angeles*

NANCY. (*Going upstage.*) Why. My word. So it has. (*Turns.*) What a rum go! (*Turns to* MANNINGHAM.)

MR. MANNINGHAM. I did not ask for any comment on your part, Nancy. Kindly be less insolent and answer what I ask you. Did *you* take that picture down, or did you not?

NANCY. Me? Of course I didn't. (*Comes to him slyly.*) What should I want to move it for, sir?

MR. MANNINGHAM. Very good. Now will you kiss that Bible lying there, please, as a solemn oath that you did not—and you may go.

NANCY. Willingly, sir. (*She does so, and places Bible on* Center *table again with a little smile.*) If I'd done it I'd've—

MR. MANNINGHAM. That is all, Nancy. You may go. (NANCY *goes out and closes doors. Going to Bible as if to replace it on the desk.*) There! (*As he crosses down* Left *and faces* MRS. MANNINGHAM.) I think we may now be said to have demonstrated conclusively—

MRS. MANNINGHAM. (*Rises; crossing* Left *to him.*) Give me that Bible! Give it to me! Let me kiss it, too! (*Snatches it from him.*) There! (*Kisses it.*) There! Do you see? (*Kisses it.*) There! Do you see that I kiss it?

MR. MANNINGHAM. (*As he puts out his hand for the Bible.*) For God's sake be careful what you do. Do you desire to commit sacrilege above all else?

MRS. MANNINGHAM. It is no sacrilege, Jack. Someone else has committed sacrilege. Now see—I swear before God Almighty that I never touched that picture. (*Kisses it.*) There! (*She comes close to him.*)

MR. MANNINGHAM. (*He grabs Bible.*) Then, by God, you are mad, and you don't know what you do. You unhappy wretch—you're stark gibbering mad—like your wretched mother before you.

MRS. MANNINGHAM. Jack—you promised you would never say that again.

MR. MANNINGHAM. (*Crosses* R. *Pause.*) The time has come to face facts, Bella. (*Half turns to her.*) If this progresses you will not be much longer under *my* protection.

MRS. MANNINGHAM. (*Crossing to him.*) Jack—I'm going to make a last appeal to you. I'm going to make a last appeal. I'm desperate, Jack. Can't you see that I'm desperate? If you can't, you must have a heart of stone.

MR. MANNINGHAM. (*Turns to her.*) Go on. What do you wish to say?

MRS. MANNINGHAM. Jack, (*Crosses to front of settee.*) I may be going mad, like my poor mother—but if I am mad, you have got to treat me gently. Jack—before God—I never lie to you knowingly. If I have taken down that picture from its place I have not known it. *I have not known it.* If I took it down on those other occasions I did not know it, either. (*Turns and crosses to* Center.) Jack, if I steal your things—your rings—your keys—your pencils and your handkerchiefs, and you find them later at the bottom of my box, as indeed you do, then I do not know that I have done it—Jack, if I commit these fantastic, meaningless mischiefs—so meaningless—(*A step toward him.*) why should I take a picture down from its place? (*Pause.*) If I do all these things, then I am certainly going off my head, and must be treated kindly and gently so that I may get well. (*Crosses to him.*) You must *bear* with me, Jack, *bear* with me—not storm and rage. God knows I'm trying, Jack, I'm trying! Oh, for God's sake believe me that I'm trying and be kind to me!

MR. MANNINGHAM. Bella, my dear—have you any idea where that picture is now?

MRS. MANNINGHAM. Yes, yes, I suppose it's behind the cupboard.

MR. MANNINGHAM. Will you please go and see?

MRS. MANNINGHAM. (*Vaguely.*) Yes—yes— (*Crosses below him, goes* Right *to upper end of secretary and produces it.*) Yes, it's here.

MR. MANNINGHAM. (*Reproachfully. As he crosses to the desk, places the Bible on it and crosses up* L.) Then you did know where it was, Bella. (*Turns to her.*) You did know where it was.

MRS. MANNINGHAM. (*As she starts toward him.*) No! No! I only *supposed* it was! I only supposed it was because it was found there before! It was found there twice before. Don't you see? I *didn't* know—I didn't!

## ☆☆☆ THE SCHOOL FOR SCANDAL

**by Richard Brinsley Sheridan**

ACT II, SCENE 1

SCENE: *A room in Sir Peter Teazle's house.*

CHARACTERS: SIR PETER TEAZLE
LADY TEAZLE

SIR PETER. Lady Teazle, Lady Teazle, I'll not bear it!

LADY TEAZLE. Sir Peter, Sir Peter, you may bear it or not, as you please; but I ought to have my own way in everything . . . and what's more I will, too. What! though I was educated in the country, I know very well that women of fashion in London are accountable to nobody after they are married.

SIR PETER. Very well, ma'am, very well; so a husband is to have no influence, no authority?

LADY TEAZLE. Authority! No, to be sure. If you wanted authority over me, you should have adopted me, and not married me; I am sure you were old enough.

SIR PETER. Old enough! . . aye, there it is. Well, well, Lady Teazle, though my life may be made unhappy by your temper, I'll not be ruined by your extravagance.

LADY TEAZLE. My extravagance! I'm sure I'm not more extravagant than a woman of fashion ought to be.

SIR PETER. No, no, madam, you shall throw away no more sums on such unmeaning luxury, 'Slife! To spend as much to furnish your dressing room with flowers in winter as would suffice to turn the Pantheon into a greenhouse, and give a fête champêtre at Christmas.

LADY TEAZLE. And am I to blame, Sir Peter, because flowers are dear in cold weather? You should find fault with the climate, and not with me. For my part, I'm sure I wish it was spring all the year round and that roses grew under our feet.

SIR PETER. Oons! Madam . . . If you had been born to this, I shouldn't wonder at your talking thus; but you forget what your situation was when I married you.

LADY TEAZLE. No, no, I don't; 'twas a very disagreeable one, or I should never have married you.

SIR PETER. Yes, yes, madam, you were then in somewhat a humbler style . . . the daughter of a plain country squire. Recollect, Lady Teazle, when I saw you first sitting at your tambour, in a pretty figured linen gown, with a bunch of keys at your side, your hair combed smooth over a roll, and your apartment hung round with fruits in worsted of your own working.

LADY TEAZLE. Oh, yes! I remember it very well, and a curious life I led . . . my daily occupation to inspect the dairy, superintend the poultry, make extracts from the family receipt book, and comb my aunt Deborah's lapdog.

SIR PETER. Yes, yes, ma'am, 'twas so indeed.

LADY TEAZLE. And then, you know, my evening amusements! . . . To draw patterns for ruffles, which I had not materials to make up; to play Pope Joan with the curate; to read a sermon to my aunt; or to be stuck down to an old spinet to strum my father to sleep after a fox chase.

SIR PETER. I am glad you have so good a memory. Yes, madam, these were the recreations I took you from; but now you must have your coach . . . vis-à-vis . . . and three powdered footmen before your chair; and in the summer a pair of white cats to draw you to Kensington Gardens. No recollection, I suppose, when you were content to ride double, behind the butler, on a docked coach horse.

LADY TEAZLE. No . . . I swear I never did that. I deny the butler and the coach horse.

SIR PETER. This, madam, was your situation; and what have I done for you? I have made you a woman of fashion, of fortune, of rank . . . in short, I have made you my wife.

LADY TEAZLE. Well, then, and there is but one thing more you can make me to add to the obligation, and that is . . .

SIR PETER. My widow, I suppose.

LADY TEAZLE. Hem! hem!

SIR PETER. I thank you, madam . . . but don't flatter yourself; for, though your ill conduct may disturb my peace, it shall never break my heart, I promise you; however, I am equally obliged to you for the hint.

LADY TEAZLE. Then why will you endeavor to make yourself so disagreeable to me and thwart me in every little elegant expense?

SIR PETER. 'Slife, madam, I say, had you any of these little elegant expenses when you married me?

LADY TEAZLE. Lud, Sir Peter! Would you have me be out of the fashion?

SIR PETER. The fashion, indeed! What had you to do with the fashion before you married me?

LADY TEAZLE. For my part, I should think you would like to have your wife thought a woman of taste.

SIR PETER. Aye . . . there again . . . taste! Zounds! madam, you had no taste when you married me!

LADY TEAZLE. That's very true, indeed, Sir Peter, and, after having married you, I should never pretend to taste again, I allow. But now, Sir Peter, if we have finished our daily jangle, I presume I may go to my engagement at Lady Sneerwell's.

SIR PETER. Aye, there's another precious circumstance . . . charming set of acquaintances you have made there!

LADY TEAZLE. Nay, Sir Peter, they are all people of rank and fortune, and remarkably tenacious of reputation.

SIR PETER. Yes, egad, they are tenacious of reputation with a vengeance, for they don't choose anybody should have a character but themselves! Such a crew! Ah! Many a wretch has rid on a hurdle who has done less mischief than these utterers of forged tales, coiners of scandal, and clippers of reputation.

LADY TEAZLE. What, would you restrain the freedom of speech?

SIR PETER. Ah! They have made you just as bad as any one of the society!

LADY TEAZLE. Why, I believe I do bear a part with a tolerable grace. But I vow, I bear no malice against the people I abuse; when I say an ill-natured thing, 'tis out of pure good humor, and I take it for granted they deal exactly in the same manner with me. But, Sir Peter, you know you promised to come to Lady Sneerwell's too.

SIR PETER. Well, well, I'll call in, just to look after my own character.

LADY TEAZLE. Then, indeed, you must make haste after me, or you'll be too late. So good-bye to ye. (*Exit* LADY TEAZLE.)

SIR PETER. So . . . I have gained much by my intended expostulation! Yet with what a charming air she contradicts everything I say, and how pleasingly she shows her contempt for my authority! Well, though I can't make her love me, there is great satisfaction in quarreling with her, and I think she never appears to such advantage as when she is doing everything in her power to plague me.

## ☆☆☆ OUR TOWN

### by Thornton Wilder

ACT II

SCENE: *Bare stage. Board placed across two chair-backs,* R, *to serve as a soda-fountain. Two stools behind board.*

CHARACTERS: GEORGE
EMILY
STAGE MANAGER

(EMILY, *carrying an armful of imaginary school-books, comes along Main Street from the left.*)

EMILY. I can't Louise. I've got to get home. Good-by. Oh Ernestine! Ernestine! Can you come over tonight and do algebra? I did the first and third in Study Hall . . . No, they're not hard. But, Ernestine, that Caesar's awful hard. I don't see why we have to do a thing like that. Come over about seven. Tell your mother you *have* to. G'by. G'by. G'by, Helen. G'by, Fred.

(GEORGE, *also carrying books, catches up with her.*)

GEORGE. Can I carry your books home for you, Emily?

EMILY. (*Coldly.*) Thank you. (*She gives them to him.*)

GEORGE. Excuse me a minute, Emily . . . Say Bob, get everything ready. I'll be there in a quarter of an hour. If I'm a little late start practice anyway. And give Herb some long high ones. His eye needs a lot of practice. Seeya later.

EMILY. Good-by Lizzy.

GEORGE. Good-by Lizzy . . . I'm awfully glad you were elected too, Emily.

EMILY. Thank you.

(*They have been standing on Main Street, almost against the*

---

*back wall.* GEORGE *is about to take the first steps toward the audience when he stops again and says:)*

GEORGE. Emily, why are you mad at me?

EMILY. I'm not mad at you.

GEORGE. You . . . treat me so funny.

EMILY. Well, I might as well say it right out, George. I don't like the whole change that's come over you in the last year. I'm sorry if that hurts your feelings, but I've just got to tell the truth and shame the devil.

GEORGE. I'm awfully sorry, Emily. Wha-a-what do you mean?

EMILY. Well, up to a year ago I used to like you a lot. And I used to watch you as you did everything . . . because we'd been friends so long . . . and then you began spending all your time at baseball . . . and you never even spoke to anybody any more . . . not even to your own family you didn't, and George, it's a fact, you've got awful conceited and stuckup, and all the girls say so. They may not say so to your face, but that's what they say about you behind your back, and it hurts me to hear them say it, but I've got to agree with them a little. I'm sorry if it hurts your feelings . . . but I can't be sorry I said it.

GEORGE. I . . . I'm glad you said it, Emily. I never thought that such a thing was happening to me. I guess it's hard for a fella not to have faults creep into his character.

(*They take a step or two in silence then stand still in misery.*)

EMILY. I always expect a man to be perfect and I think he should be.

GEORGE. Oh . . . I don't think it's possible to be perfect, Emily.

EMILY. Well, my father is, and as far as I can see, your father is. There's no reason on earth why you shouldn't be, too.

GEORGE. Well, Emily . . . I feel it's the other way around. That men aren't naturally good, but girls are. Like you and your mother and my mother.

EMILY. Well, you might as well know right now that I'm not perfect. It's not as easy for a girl to be perfect as a man, because we girls are more nervous. Now I'm sorry I said all that about you. I don't know what made me say it.

GEORGE. No, no . . . I guess if it's the truth you ought to say it. You stick to it, Emily.

EMILY. I don't know if it's the truth or not. And I suddenly feel that it isn't important at all.

GEORGE. Emily, would you like an ice-cream soda, or something, before you go home?

EMILY. Well, thank you, I would.

(*They seat themselves on the stools.*)

STAGE MANAGER. (*As* MR. MORGAN.) Hello George. Hello, Emily. What'll you have? Why Emily Webb, what've you been crying about?

GEORGE. (*He gropes for an explanation.*) She . . . she just got an awful scare, Mr. Morgan. She almost got run over by that hardware store wagon. Everybody always says that Tom Huckins drives like a crazy man.

STAGE MANAGER. Here, take a drink of water, Emily. You look all shook up. There! Now what'll you have?

EMILY. I'll have a strawberry phosphate, thank you, Mr. Morgan.

GEORGE. No, no. You go and have an ice-cream soda with me, Emily. Two Strawberry sodas, Mr. Morgan.

STAGE MANAGER. (*Working the faucets.*) Yes, sir, I tell you, you've got to look both ways before you cross Main Street these days. Gets worse every year. There are a hundred and twenty-five horses in Grover's Corners this minute I'm talking to you. State Inspector was in here yesterday. And now, they're bringing in these auto-mo-biles, the best thing to do is just stay home. Why I remember the time when a dog could lie down all day in the middle of Main Street and nothing would come to disturb him—Yes, Miss Ellis, be with you in a minute. Here are your sodas; Enjoy 'em. (*He goes off.*)

EMILY. They're so expensive.

GEORGE. No, no—don't think of that. We're celebrating. First, we're celebrating our election. And do you know what else I'm celebrating?

EMILY. No.

GEORGE. I'm celebrating because I've got a friend who tells me all the things that ought to be told me.

EMILY. George, *please* don't think of that. I don't know why I said it. It's not true. You're . . .

GEORGE. No, you stick to it, Emily. I'm glad you spoke to me like you did. But you'll see, I'm going to change so quick . . . you bet I'm going to change. And, Emily, I want to ask you a favor.

EMILY. What?

GEORGE. Emily, if I go away to Agriculture College next year, will you write me a letter once in a while?

EMILY. I certainly will. I certainly will, George . . . (*Pause.*) It certainly seems like being away three years you'd get out of touch with things.

GEORGE. No, I mustn't do that. You see I'm not going to be just a farmer. After a while maybe I'll run for something to get elected. So your letters'll be very important to me; you know, telling me what's going on here and everything . . .

EMILY. Just the same, three years is a long time. Maybe letters from Grover's Corners wouldn't be interesting after a while. Grover's Corners isn't a very important place when you think of all New Hampshire, but I think it's a very nice town.

GEORGE. The day wouldn't come when I wouldn't want to know everything that's happening here. I know *that's* true, Emily.

EMILY. Well, I'll try to make my letters interesting. (*Pause.*)

GEORGE. Y'know, Emily, whenever I meet a farmer I ask him if he thinks it's important to go to Agriculture School to be a good farmer.

EMILY. Why, George . . .

GEORGE. Yeah, and some of them say that it's even a waste of time. You can get all of those things out of pamphlets the government sends out. And Uncle Luke's getting old, . . . he's about ready for me to start in taking over his farm tomorrow, if I could.

EMILY. My!

GEORGE. And, like you say, being gone all the time . . . in other places and meeting other people . . . if anything like that can happen I don't want to go away. I guess new people aren't any better than old ones. I'll bet they almost never are. Emily . . . I feel that you are as good a friend as I've got. I don't need to go and meet the people in other towns.

EMILY. But George, maybe it's important for you to go and learn all about cattle-judging and soils and things. And if you're going into politics, maybe you ought to meet people from other parts of the State . . . of course, I don't know.

GEORGE. (*After a pause.*) Emily, I'm going to make up my mind right now. I won't go. I'll tell Pa about it tonight.

EMILY. Why, George I don't see why you have to decide right now. It's a whole year away.

GEORGE. Emily, I'm glad you spoke to me about that . . . that fault in my character. And what you said was right; but there was one thing wrong in it, and that was when you said that for a year I wasn't noticing people, and . . . you, for instance. Listen, Emily, you say you were watching me when I did everything . . . Why, I was doing the same about you all the time. Why, sure I always thought about you as one of the chief people I thought about. I always made sure where you were sitting on the bleachers, and who you were with. And we've always had lots of talks . . . and joking in the halls, and they always meant a lot to me. Of course, they weren't as good as the talk we're having now. Lately I'd been noticing that you'd been acting kind of funny to me, and for three days I've been trying to walk home with you, but something's always got in the way. Yesterday I was standing over against the wall waiting for you, and you walked home with Miss Corcoran.

EMILY. George! . . . Life's awful funny! How could I have known that? Why, I thought . . .

GEORGE. Listen, Emily, I'm going to tell you why I'm not going to Agriculture School. I think that once you've found a person that you're very fond of . . . I mean a person who's fond of you too . . . at least enough to be interested in your character . . . well, I think that's as important as college is, and even more so. That's what I think.

EMILY. I think it's awfully important, too.

GEORGE. Emily. . .

EMILY. Yes, George.

GEORGE. Emily, if I improve and make a big change . . . would you be . . . I mean, *could* you be . . .

EMILY. I . . . I am now. I always have been.

GEORGE. (*Pause.*) So I guess this is an important talk we've been having.

EMILY. Yes.

GEORGE. (*Takes a deep breath and straightens his back.*) Wait just a minute and I'll take you home. (*He rises and goes to the* STAGE MANAGER, *who appears and comes towards him.*) Mr. Morgan, I'll have to go home and get the money to pay you for this. I'll only take a minute.

STAGE MANAGER. What's that? George Gibbs, do you mean to tell me . . !

GEORGE. Yes, but I had reasons, Mr. Morgan . . . Look, here's my gold watch to keep until I come back with the money.

STAGE MANAGER. That's all right. Keep your watch. I'll trust you.

GEORGE. I'll be back in five minutes.

STAGE MANAGER. I'll trust you ten years, George . . . not a day more. Get all over your shock Emily?

EMILY. Yes, thank you, Mr. Morgan. It was nothing.

GEORGE. (*Taking up the books from the counter.*) I'm ready.

(*They walk in grave silence down the stage, turn, and pass through the trellis at the Webbs' back door and disappear.*)

## ☆☆☆ THE ROYAL FAMILY

### by George S. Kaufman and Edna Ferber

ACT II

SCENE: *The duplex apartment of the Cavendishes, in the East Fifties, New York.*

CHARACTERS: JULIE
GWEN
FANNY

JULIE. Do you want to sit here, dear? Or shall we go in by the fire?

GWEN. (*Sits.*) Oh, this is all right. (*Glances up with a rather wan smile.*) I don't mean to act like a prima donna. I just feel horrible, that's all.

JULIE. (*Standing over her.*) I know how you do, dear. I hate to see you unhappy like this. (*Leans over and kisses the top of her head lightly.*) But you have so little sense.

GWEN. (*Her lip quivering. Very low.*) He didn't even telephone. He might at least have telephoned.

FANNY. How do you know he didn't? Tony had the receiver off most of the day.

JULIE. (*Puts receiver back on hook.*) Yes.

GWEN. (*Eagerly.*) Do you think so? He might have, mightn't he? Oh! (*A little whimper of dismay. She even weeps, weakly.*)

JULIE. (*Pats her shoulder tenderly.*) Now, Gwen.

GWEN. Oh, Mother, I love him so.

---

JULIE. There's nothing to cry about. *(A hand on her shoulder, patting her into calm.)* There! *(A moment's pause while* GWEN *grows quieter.)*

FANNY. You can love him and marry him, too, can't you?

JULIE. Of course you can marry him, Gwen, and live happy ever after.

FANNY. Only why you think you have to quit the stage to do it is more than I can figure out.

JULIE. It's hard for us to realize that you wouldn't want to keep on, Gwen.

FANNY. Your mother and I both got married. But we didn't drop more important things to do it.

GWEN. There isn't anything more important.

FANNY. Fiddlesticks! Marriage isn't a career. It's an incident! Aubrey Cavendish and I were married in the Church of St. Mary Redcliffe, in Bristol, England, just before the matinee. The wedding supper was served on the stage of the Theatre Royale between the matinee and night performance—we played "She Stoops to Conquer" in the afternoon, and "A Scrap of Paper" was the night bill. They sent the supper in from the George and Lion next door, and very nice it was, too, but I remember they'd gone and put nutmeg in the gooseberry tarts, and Aubrey never could abide nutmeg. It must have been that that upset him, for he gave the only bad performance that night that I ever saw him give.

GWEN. I know, Grandma, but that's got nothing to do with me. You married an actor, and—*(Turning to her mother, swiftly.)* —so did you. You lived the same sort of lives.

JULIE. Oh, I knew some rather nice men who weren't actors—didn't I, Fanny? *(A gesture from* FANNY *of utter dismissal of this subject as being too vast and agonizing to go into.)* There were lots of times when I thought that being a wife and mother was all that mattered in the world. And then each time I'd learn all over again that that wasn't enough for me.

FANNY. I should say not.

JULIE. Earthquakes, and cyclones, and fire and flood, and somehow you still give the show. I know it says in the contract that you stop for "acts of God," but I can't remember that I ever did. (*Rises.*)

FANNY. Nor I. Nor your grandfather. Nobody ever knew what a sick man Aubrey Cavendish was, those last months. But he played a full season of thirty-five weeks. Dropped dead on the stage of Macauley's in Louisville two minutes after the curtain fell on Saturday night, the week we closed. Not only that, but he waited to take four calls.

GWEN. I know, I know. (*Rises, goes right.*) But—I'm not like that, that's all. (*Sits near window.*)

JULIE. (*Rises, crosses to* GWEN.) You think you're not, but you are! Marry him if you love him, Gwen, but don't give up everything to do it! The day might come when you'd hate him for it.

GWEN. Hate Perry. (*A little bitter, scornful laugh.*) You just don't know what you're talking about.

JULIE. Gwen, do you think it's going to be any fun for me to have them see you step out—acting with me in my play, and, for all I know, walking away with it! You'll be so fresh, and such a surprise. And it'll be your night. I'll be very proud and happy, of course. (*A very little pause, and then, almost as though to convince herself.*) . . . of course. They'll say, "That's her daughter." But ten years from now it'll be, "That's her mother."

GWEN. I'll never be half the actress you are.

JULIE. Gwen, if I could only make you realize that the thrill you get out of doing your work is bigger than any other single thing in the world! (*A little gesture of protest from* GWEN.) Oh, I know! There's love. But you can be the most fortunate person in the world, Gwen. You can have both. But for Heaven's sake don't make the mistake of giving up one for the other.

FANNY. No, child.

GWEN. Work! Acting isn't everything. What's acting compared to—

FANNY. It's everything. It's work and play and meat and drink. They'll tell you it isn't—your fancy friends—but it's a lie. They'd give their ears to be in your place. Don't make any mistake about that.

JULIE. There'll be plenty of things that you'll have to give up—gay things and amusing things—I've missed dinners—and parties and rides and walks and—

FANNY. Yes, you've got to leave, and go down to a stuffy dressing room and smear paint on your face and go out on the stage and speak a lot of fool lines, and you love it. You love it! You couldn't live without it! Do you suppose I could have stood these two years, hobbling around with this thing—(*Brandishing her cane.*)—if I hadn't known I was going back to it!

JULIE. Long as I've been on the stage there isn't a night when I stand in the wings waiting for my cue that I don't get that sick feeling at the pit of my stomach. And my hands are cold and my cheeks are hot, and you'd think I'd never been on the stage before.

FANNY. Yes, yes! that's it! Every night when I'm sitting here alone I'm really down there at the theatre. Seven-thirty, and they're going in the stage door. Good evening to the door-man. Taking down their keys and looking in the mail rack. Eight o'clock. The stage hands are setting up. (*Raps with her cane.*) Half hour, Miss Cavendish. Grease paint, rouge, mascara. Fifteen minutes, Miss Cavendish! My costume . . . More rouge . . . Where's the rabbit's foot! . . . Overture! . . . Good evening, everybody . . . How's the house to-night? . . . The curtain's up! . . . Props! . . . Cue . . . Enter. (*Rises.*) That's all that's kept me alive these two years. If you weren't down there for me, I wouldn't want to live . . . I couldn't live. You . . . down there . . . for me . . . going on . . . going on . . . going on . . . (*The excitement and strain are too much for her. Suddenly*

*She goes limp, topples, crumples.* JULIE *and* GWEN, *standing near her, catch her as she is about to fall, and place her in the chair from which she has risen. She is briefly unconscious.*)

JULIE. Mother! Mother, what's the matter!

GWEN. Grandma! Grandma!

JULIE. Jo! Tony! Della! Quick!

## ☆☆☆ REBECCA

### by Daphne du Maurier

ACT II, SCENE 2

SCENE: *The Hall, or living-room, at Manderley, the home of Maxim de Winter, in England. The room is spacious and comfortable and suggests wealth and culture. Upstage left is a balcony. Leading down from the balcony is a stairway.*

CHARACTERS: MRS. DE WINTER
MRS. DANVERS

MRS. DE WINTER. I don't want him to love me. I don't mind about that any more. I only want him to be happy.

(*She breaks down and sits on staircase. Goes on sitting on stairs crying, tearing at a shred of handkerchief in her hands.* MRS. DANVERS *comes to head of stairs.* MRS. DE WINTER *hears her move. She looks up. They stare at one another.*)

You've done what you wanted. You meant this to happen, didn't you? Why do you hate me? What have I done to you that you should hate me?

MRS. DANVERS. You tried to take *my* Mrs. de Winter's place.

---

MRS. DE WINTER. I love him; you don't seem to realize that. Haven't we as much right to be happy as anyone else?

MRS. DANVERS. Mr. de Winter isn't happy, any fool can see that.

MRS. DE WINTER. He was happy when we were in France together, he was younger, much younger, and happy and gay.

MRS. DANVERS. Well, he's a man, isn't he? (*She laughs, shrugs her shoulders, begins to go.*)

MRS. DE WINTER. How dare you speak to me like that? How dare you! (*Goes up to* MRS. DANVERS *and grabs her by the arm.*) You made me wear that dress, you did it because you wanted to hurt him. Hadn't he suffered enough without your playing that hideous trick on him?

MRS. DANVERS. What do I care for his suffering? He's never cared about mine. How does he think I've felt, watching you sit in her place, touching her things? What does he think it's meant to me knowing that you wrote at her desk in the morning-room, using the very pen she used? How does he think I've liked hearing Frith and Robert and the rest of the servants talking about you as Mrs. de Winter? And all the while my lady, with her smile and her lovely face and her brave ways, lying cold and forgotten in the church crypt. If he suffers he deserves to suffer, marrying a girl like you not twelve months afterwards. Well, he's paying for it now, isn't he? I've seen his face. He knows she sees him. He knows she comes by night and watches him. And she doesn't come kindly, not she, not my lady. She never was one to stand by and be wronged. "I'll see them in hell first, Danny," she'd say. She did what she liked, she lived as she liked. She cared for nothing and for no one.

MRS. DE WINTER. Stop!

MRS. DANVERS. Stop, eh? And what then? You'll go running to Mr. de Winter about me, as you did about Mr. Favell this morning.

MRS. DE WINTER. I never said a word about your Mr. Favell.

MRS. DANVERS. That's a lie. Why shouldn't I see Mr. Jack here at

Manderley? He is the one link I have left now with my lady. He's not forgotten to be jealous, has he?

MRS. DE WINTER. Jealous?

MRS. DANVERS. Yes.

MRS. DE WINTER. What do you mean?

MRS. DANVERS. He was jealous while she lived, and he's jealous now she's dead. Of course he was jealous. So was I. So was everyone who knew her. A man had only to look at her once and be mad about her.

MRS. DE WINTER. (*Puts hands over her ears.*) I don't want to know. I don't want to hear.

MRS. DANVERS. She's still mistress here, even if she is dead. It's you that's the shadow and the ghost. It's you that's unwanted and forgotten and pushed aside. Well, why don't you leave Manderley to her, why don't you go? (MRS. DANVERS *goes up to* MRS. DE WINTER, *who slowly backs against rail of stairs.*) He doesn't want you. He wants to be alone in the house again, with her. (*Pushes her closer and closer to rail.*) What's the use of your staying here at Manderley? You're not happy. He doesn't love you. There's not much for you to live for, is there? (MRS. DE WINTER *is right back against the low rail, bent over it.* MRS. DANVERS *holds her arm.*) Why don't you fall? Why don't you let yourself go?

(*Suddenly phone starts ringing, a shrill, compelling summons.* MRS. DANVERS *relaxes her grip on* MRS. DE WINTER'S *arm. Waits. The phone continues. Then* MRS. DANVERS *lets* MRS. DE WINTER *go.* MRS. DE WINTER *leans against rail half sobbing, bewildered and shaken. There is a sound of footsteps running along the terrace.* MRS. DANVERS *looks over her shoulder and exits along passage.*)

## ☆☆☆ OUR HEARTS WERE YOUNG AND GAY

**by Jean Kerr**

*based upon the book by Cornelia Otis Skinner and Emily Kimbrough*

ACT I

SCENE: *The interior of a cabin, aboard ship. The year, 1923. The entrance from the corridor is upstage center.*

CHARACTERS: CORNELIA
EMILY

(*There is a sudden sound of light, rapid footsteps racing down the stairs.* CORNELIA *starts, and turns toward the door, breathless. A few more footsteps are heard in the corridor, and then* EMILY *slips in, up center closing the door tightly behind her, wide-eyed.*)

CORNELIA. Emily!

EMILY. (*Desperately, leaning on the door, breathing hard.*) Sh-h-h! Quiet!

CORNELIA. (*Going to* EMILY.) Emily, you gave me such a fright! When I heard all that shouting and screaming, I was sure it was you!

EMILY. (*Feverishly.*) How did you know?

CORNELIA. How did I know what?

EMILY. (*Panting, terrified.*) That it *was* me.

CORNELIA. Then it *was* you?

EMILY. Yes, Cornelia, I did it.

CORNELIA. But you couldn't have fallen overboard! You're not even wet!

EMILY. Oh, Cornelia, it's much worse than that. Cornelia—

CORNELIA. (*Breathless now, too.*) Yes?

EMILY. I killed a man.

CORNELIA. (*Gasping, and stepping back.*) Who? What man?

EMILY. The man that fell overboard.

CORNELIA. Emily! You didn't *push* him?

EMILY. (*Between breaths, reliving the whole horrible sequence.*) I was on deck. All of a sudden there was a splash and a lot of commotion. Somebody shouted "Man overboard!" So I ran to the rail like everybody else. And there he was! I could see him down in that dark water, splashing and swimming. Oh, he looked so pathetic—clawing the water and kicking his stockinged feet. Then I remembered what they told us in lifesaving class. Throw a buoyant object to the person who is drowning. But I couldn't find a buoyant object. All I could find was a deck chair.

CORNELIA. (*Realizing the full horror.*) Emily! You didn't throw the deck chair?

EMILY. I did. And, Cornelia. It hit him. Right on the head.

CORNELIA. I don't believe it! Your aim was never that good! How do you know it hit him?

EMILY. Just at that moment—they turned on the searchlights! And everybody could see it crash!

CORNELIA. (*Turning away, her hands to her head.*) Oh, good heavens!

EMILY. It was horrible. You should have heard the crack when it landed on his head. And then there was just the chair, wobbling all around by itself—and no man. (*She begins to cry.*)

CORNELIA. (*A sudden hope!*) Emily! Did anybody see you throw the chair?

EMILY. No, I was in the dark.

CORNELIA. Then, don't worry. We'll keep you under cover. No one need ever know.

EMILY. (*Biting her lip.*) No, Cornelia. I know what it is I must do. Give myself up!

CORNELIA. Oh, no, Emily!

EMILY. Yes, it would haunt me all my days.

CORNELIA. But, Emily, you don't *know* what they'll do to you!

EMILY. It doesn't make any difference. I have to confess. I couldn't live with my conscience. Cornelia, you must go and tell the Captain.

CORNELIA. Oh, Emily, I couldn't! I'd be an informer.

EMILY. (*Nobly.*) Please, Cornelia. Don't refuse me this. My knees are shaking so much I could never walk up the steps.

CORNELIA. Emily! (*She breaks.*) All right. If you really want me to.

EMILY. I'll be grateful as long as I live. Mercy! How long do you think they'll *let* me live!

CORNELIA. Don't say things like that!

EMILY. Cornelia, maybe there'll be an inquest. My goodness! Will they have it here on the ship or wait until we get to France? Cornelia, that would be terrible! I couldn't possibly testify in French. (EMILY *is about to sink onto the bunk. She screams and jumps up.*)

CORNELIA. Emily! What now?

EMILY. (*Pointing, horrified, at the shoes.*) The shoes! The shoes!

CORNELIA. Oh, we've got worse things to think about than that!

EMILY. They're his! They must be! The man I killed! A dead man's shoes!

CORNELIA. But—how could they be?

EMILY. I don't know, but he didn't have any shoes on!

CORNELIA. I'll hide them.

EMILY. But why? When I'm going to confess! Oh, Cornelia, go—go, now! While I can still stand.

CORNELIA. (*Running to the door, finally, obediently.*) I'll bring him right down.

EMILY. (*Sinking onto the chaise longue.*) Thank you. Thank you, Cornelia. (CORNELIA *runs out, up center, and closes the door.* EMILY *moans, staring front for a moment; then her chin steadies. She rises, and we realize she is preparing her speech for the Captain.*)

EMILY. Captain . . . Captain. I'm ready to go. (*She puts her hands forward as though to be manacled.*) I won't make any trouble. If you could only keep it out of the papers, so my mother won't know. Let me just disappear, quietly.

## ☆☆☆ TIME OUT FOR GINGER

### by Ronald Alexander

ACT II, SCENE 2

SCENE: *The living-room of the home of Mr. and Mrs. Howard Carol.*

CHARACTERS: JOAN
AGNES, her mother

JOAN. (*Off.*) Oh, thank you. (*Front door slams.*)

AGNES. (*In kitchen.*) Who was it, Joan?

JOAN. (*Off.*) More mail. (*Enters, dragging two mail sacks.*)

AGNES. (*Off.*) How many sacks?

JOAN. Two.

AGNES. (*Off.*) Well, you can handle that.

JOAN. (DR *of phone table.*) Where shall I put them?

AGNES. (*Off.*) Where do they look best, dear? (JOAN *stacks mail sacks one on top of the other sack in front of phone table.*)

JOAN. (*Crossing* U *to get bundle of laundry.*) House work. (*Crosses* L *to kitchen.*) You'd think Lizzie would clean on Friday, being she insists on going to the football game every Saturday. (*Exits into kitchen.*)

AGNES. (*Enters from kitchen.*) Sure. (*Crosses to drum table.*)

JOAN. (*Enters from kitchen. Crossing* R *to foot of stairs.*) Why isn't Jeannie helping today?

AGNES. (*Crossing* R *to sofa.*) She is an actress. Her play opens tonight and she's resting. Shall we try to do something about this fan mail?

JOAN. I don't understand why everybody in America sends Ginger letters.

---

AGNES. Maybe because Yale named her First Lady of the Gridiron.

JOAN. (*Crossing* L *to drum table, picks up mail. Crossing* L *to* DL *corner.*) You'd think Daddy would stay home on Saturday to help us. (*Starts putting mail on bench in* DL *corner.*)

AGNES. (*Putting mail into shopping bag. Leaves two packets on table.*) How do you figure that, dear?

JOAN. If he'd kept Ginger off the squad, he and Lizzie wouldn't be at the football game today, and I would.

AGNES. I see.

JOAN. And I think he might at least assume some responsibility for changing my whole life.

AGNES. I'll tell him when he comes in.

JOAN. (*Crossing* R *below armchair to* C.) Another thing I don't understand about Daddy . . .

AGNES. Joan, please relax. It's four o'clock in the afternoon. (*Crosses up behind sofa, sets shopping bag down.*) What's the matter with you, anyway? (*Joan sits* C *of sofa.*)

JOAN. I've got a big problem.

AGNES. (*Crossing down to sofa.*) What is it?

JOAN. Well, ever since Ginger got on the football team, I've been having a lot of trouble with Eddie, every Saturday night.

AGNES. What sort of trouble? (*Sits on* L *of sofa. Picks up two packets of mail from the coffee table.*)

JOAN. Well, it used to be we'd have a date, go to a movie or a dance, have a soda, talk awhile, and then he'd kiss me good night.

AGNES. And now?

JOAN. Now he wants to start kissing me good night as soon as we get out.

AGNES. Well, believe me when I tell you that has nothing to do with Ginger playing football. (AGNES AND JOAN LAUGH.)

JOAN. What am I going to do?

AGNES. Well, there are several things you can do. First, I'd suggest you develop a kind of attitude and not allow yourself to get into compromising situations.

JOAN. Have you ever been in the front seat of a car with a man?

AGNES. Yes, with your father.

JOAN. What did you do?

AGNES. I managed to fend him off with dignity and the illusion of superiority.

JOAN. It's kind of hard to be more superior than Eddie.

AGNES. I'm sure.—I'll tell you a little secret. I think you're going to have to bend his ego a little. Once you get the upper hand with a kid like Eddie, it's downhill all the way.

JOAN. Suppose Eddie gets the upper hand with me?

AGNES. Oh. That's what you're really worried about, isn't it? (JOAN *nods.*) Well, I know that you're intelligent enough to realize the difference between what's good and real for you, and what isn't, because if you didn't, you wouldn't be sitting here telling me your troubles.

JOAN. I guess that's right.

AGNES. There are times when that choice may be rather difficult, Joan, but speaking as a woman who knows you very well, I have absolute confidence in your judgment.

JOAN. (*Embracing* AGNES.) Thanks, Mom.

AGNES. Don't worry, Joanie, everything will work out fine. (*Laughs.*) And it better.

JOAN. I hope it works out like you and Daddy.

AGNES. So do I. (*Looks at bundles of mail in her hand.*)

JOAN. Mom, how did you meet Daddy?

AGNES. Oh, he picked me up on the street one day.

JOAN. Mom!

AGNES. Yeah. I heard a whistle, and I turned and there was this guy. I said, "Did you whistle at me?" He nodded, and I said, "What for?"

JOAN. What did he say?

AGNES. He didn't say anything. He just put out his hand. He was holding two black jellybeans. That's how it started. He was seven and I was five.

JOAN. And you've loved him ever since?

AGNES. (*Rises. Crossing up to sideboard.*) Ever since and always will.

## ☆☆☆ SEPARATE TABLES
### by Terence Rattigan

ACT II, SCENE 1

SCENE: *Lounge of the Beauregard Hotel, Bournemouth, after tea.*

CHARACTERS: MRS. RAILTON-BELL
SIBYL

MRS. RAILTON-BELL. (*Gently.*) Sibyl, my dearest, do you mind awfully if your tactless old mother whispers something in your ear?

SIBYL. (*Resigned.*) No.

MRS. RAILTON-BELL. I didn't think it was *terribly* wise of you to lay yourself open to that snub just now.

SIBYL. It wasn't a snub, Mummy. I'm sure he really *was* going to see a friend—(MRS. RAILTON-BELL *smiles understandingly and sympathetically, shaking her head ever so slightly.*) Well, I often do go for walks with the Major.

MRS. RAILTON-BELL. I know you do, dear. What is more, quite a lot of people have noticed it. (*Pause.* SIBYL *stares at her mother.*)

SIBYL. (*At length.*) You don't mean—you can't mean—(*She jumps up and holds her cheeks with a sudden gesture.*) Oh, no. How can people be so awful!

MRS. RAILTON-BELL. It's not being particularly awful when an unattached girl is noticed constantly seeking the company of an attractive older man.

SIBYL. (*Still holding her cheeks.*) They think I chase him. Is that it? They think I run after him, they think I want—they think—no, it *is* awful. It *is*. It *is*. It *is*.

---

MRS. RAILTON-BELL. (*Sharply.*) Quieten yourself, my dear. Don't get into one of your *states*, now.

SIBYL. It's all right, Mummy. I'm not in a state. It's just—well—it's just so dreadful that people should believe such a thing is even possible. I hate that side of life. I hate it.

MRS. RAILTON-BELL. (*Soothingly.*) I know you do, dear. But it exists, all the same, and one has to be very careful in this world not to give people the wrong impression. Quieter now?

SIBYL. Yes, Mummy.

MRS. RAILTON-BELL. Good. You must try not to let these things upset you so much, dear.

SIBYL. I only go for walks with the Major because I like hearing him talk. I like all his stories about London and the war and the regiment—and—well—he's seen so much of life and I haven't—

MRS. RAILTON-BELL. I don't know what you mean by that, dear, I'm sure.

SIBYL. I only meant—(*She checks herself.*) I'm sorry.

MRS. RAILTON-BELL. (*Relentlessly pursuing her prey.*) Of course I realize that you must occasionally miss some of the gaieties of life—the balls and the cocktail parties and things—that a few other lucky young people can enjoy. I can assure you, dearest, if I could possibly afford it, you'd have them. But I *do* do my best, you know.

SIBYL. I know you do, Mummy.

MRS. RAILTON-BELL. There was Rome last year, and our Scandinavian cruise the year before—

SIBYL. I know, Mummy. I know. Don't think I'm not grateful. Please. It's only—(*She stops.*)

MRS. RAILTON-BELL. (*Gently prompting.*) Only what, dear?

SIBYL. If only I could *do* something. After all, I'm thirty-three—

MRS. RAILTON-BELL. Now, my dear. We've been over this so often. Dearest child, you'd never stand a job for more than a few weeks. Remember Jones & Jones?

SIBYL. But that was because I had to work in a basement, and I used to feel stifled and faint. But there must be something else.

MRS. RAILTON-BELL. (*Gently patting her hand.*) You're not a very strong child, dear. You must get that into your head. Your nervous system isn't nearly as sound as it should be.

SIBYL. You mean my *states?* But I haven't had one of those for a long time—

MRS. RAILTON-BELL. No, dear—you've been doing very well. Very well, indeed. But there's quite a big difference between not having hysterical fits and being strong enough to take on a job. (*Concluding the topic decisively.*) Hand me that newspaper, would you, dear?

SIBYL. Which one?

MRS. RAILTON-BELL. The *West Hampshire Weekly News.* I want to see what the Major was so interested in. (SIBYL *hands her the paper.* MRS. RAILTON-BELL *fumbles in her pockets.*) Oh, dear me, what a silly billy! I've gone and left my glasses and my book in the shelter at the end of Ragusa Road. Oh, dear, I do hope they're not stolen. I expect they're bound to be. Now—doesn't that show how dependent I am on you, my dear. If you hadn't had that headache you'd have been with me this afternoon, and then you'd never have allowed me to—

SIBYL. I'll go and look for them.

MRS. RAILTON-BELL. Oh, would you, dear? That really is so kind of you. I hate you to fetch and carry for me, as you know—but my old legs are just a wee bit tired—It was the far end of the shelter, facing the sea.

SIBYL. Where we usually sit? I know. (*She goes out.*)

## ☆☆☆ TIME REMEMBERED

### by Jean Anouilh

ACT I, SCENE 1

SCENE: *A Study in the Chateau of the Duchess of Pont-au-Bronc.*

CHARACTERS: DUCHESS
AMANDA

(AMANDA, *left alone, throws her case down on the ground and stamps her foot in fury.*)

AMANDA. Crud! Crud! Crud!

DUCHESS. (*Coming in by another door.*) What a hideously inelegant word! Say "merde," my dear, it's so much more explicit. Crud is not only ugly, it is inexact. (*She addresses* AMANDA *in a sophisticated drawl.*) I must apologize, my dear, for keeping you shut up in this room so long—but the fact is that there is a certain person whom I am particularly anxious should not see you, and he is due back from his walk at any moment. (*She looks out into the garden, suddenly serious.*) It might jeopardize all my plans should you meet him just now.

AMANDA. (*Using this excuse to finish the interview.*) Well, I'd rather tell you straight out, madame, that if the vacancy is for a housemaid, or even a lady's maid . . . I . . . well, I'm a skilled milliner, madame, and I'm determined to carry on with my profession.

DUCHESS. You were quite right, Gaston. The girl has spirit. (*She goes to the door, saying to* AMANDA *as she passes.*) A good point!

---

AMANDA. (*Stopping the* DUCHESS.) No, madame! This time I'm not going to let you go!

DUCHESS. Not let me go? Did you hear that, Gaston? We are to be prisoners in our own home—just as we were under Francis the First.

AMANDA. (*A little taken aback.*) Francis the First?

DUCHESS. Yes, in 1520 we were confined to our estates after an abortive attempt to seize power. Apparently we died of boredom. (*She sits at a desk in front of the bookcase.*)

AMANDA. I promise you, madame, I have no intention of keeping you prisoner. But I arrived here on the 2.17 train from Paris, and it's nearly five o'clock now, and the last train back to Paris tonight is the 6.19. If I'm not going to be of any use to you here, I really must catch it.

DUCHESS. No, child, you will not travel by that train.

AMANDA. Why not, madame?

DUCHESS. Because it is not running.

AMANDA. But I looked it up in the timetable!

DUCHESS. I have no doubt that it appears in the timetable. Nevertheless, it is not running—as from yesterday.

AMANDA. (*To whom anything seems possible by now.*) You stopped it running so that I couldn't get away, didn't you?

DUCHESS. A hundred and fifty years ago, my dear, I would most certainly have done so. Unfortunately, since 1789 my family has lost much of its influence over the Administration. No, it was not I who cancelled the train. (*Darkly.*) It was the Freemasons. They realized that the train enabled the good people of the neighboring towns to come and visit our basilica. We've opened it to the public, you know. Twice a week, ten till six, fifty francs admission. (*She hands* AMANDA *a brochure.*) And very nicely we were doing—I had started a line of souvenirs—medals, rosaries, small blessed candles. (*She indicates stacks of them in the bookcase.*) Oh yes, I move with the times. I realize the value of publicity. And then—out of a blue sky, before I could lift a finger—(*She snaps her fingers.*)—they cancelled my train. Just like that. Ah, but I'm too clever for them. Do you know what I'm going to do? (*In a confidential whisper.*) Motor coaches! What do you think of that?

(*On this triumphant note, she gets up to go.* AMANDA, *at the end of her tether, follows her tearfully.*)

AMANDA. But I don't understand, madame. I don't know what you're talking about—basilicas and trains and Freemasons. I've been waiting for over two hours and I didn't even have time for any lunch before I left home—

DUCHESS. No lunch? No lunch? What can have happened to that egg? I will go and investigate.

(*She makes as if to go again.* AMANDA *raises her voice in a wail of desperation.*)

AMANDA. Oh, madame, please, please don't go away again without explaining things to me, or I'll go mad!

(*The* DUCHESS *stops.*)

DUCHESS. (*Serious.*) You are cleverer than you look, child. I will make a confession to you. I am not sixty. I am sixty-seven. I have survived the birth of the aeroplane, the death of the corset, short hair and World Wars. So if I say that I'm an old woman who has seen many bizarre and exciting things in her time, you believe me, won't you?

AMANDA. (*At a loss.*) Yes, madame . . .

DUCHESS. Well, then, you must take my word for it that the reason I have been popping in and out of this room like a jack-in-the-box for the last ten minutes is simply that I cannot summon up the courage to tell you the truth of why I made you come here.

(*She goes out, leaving* AMANDA *more dumbfounded than ever.* AMANDA *picks up her case, half tearful, half angry, and announces almost hysterically to the empty room.*)

AMANDA. Mad! They're all stark staring mad! I'll . . . I'll *walk* back to Paris!

(*She opens the french window, looks round anxiously to see if she is observed, and then runs out into the garden.*)

## ☆☆☆ STAGE DOOR

### by Edna Ferber and George S. Kaufman

ACT I, SCENE 2

SCENE: *The Footlights Club. A club for girls of the stage. The room we see is the common living room. It is comfortably furnished with unrelated but good pieces, enlivened by a bit of chintz.*

CHARACTERS: TERRY
JEAN

(TERRY *is asleep at the desk. There is a moment of silence, then* JEAN *comes in, bringing with her a quiver of excitement. She flings her evening wrap on the couch, rushes to* TERRY *and shakes her.*)

JEAN. Terry! Wake up!

TERRY. What's the matter!

JEAN. We're in the movies!

TERRY. What?

JEAN. Both of us! We're in the movies! They just heard from the Coast.

TERRY. Jean! How do you know? What happened?

JEAN. Mr. Kingsley just got the telegram. They liked the tests, and we're to go to the office tomorrow to sign our contracts. We leave for the Coast next week! Terry! Can you believe it?

TERRY. (*Bewildered.*) Yes. Yes! You mean—right away?

JEAN. Of course we'll only get little parts in the beginning. But there's that beautiful check every week, whether you work or not. And the swimming and the sunshine and those little ermine jackets up to here. No more running around to offices

COSTUME: LIFE WITH FATHER *Santa Monica City College*

COSTUME: SHE STOOPS TO CONQUER *University High School, Los Angeles*

COSTUME: THE CHINESE CHALK CIRCLE
*Forest Park High School, Baltimore*

and having them spit in your eye. And a salary raise every six months if they like us. So at the end of three years it begins to get pretty good, and after five years it's wonderful, and at the end of seven years it's more money than you ever heard of.

TERRY. Seven years! What do you mean—seven years!

JEAN. Yes, it's a seven-year contract—that is, if they take up the options.

TERRY. But what about the stage? Suppose I wanted to act?

JEAN. Well, what do you think this is—juggling? Motion picture acting is just as much of an art as stage acting, only it's cut up more. You only have to learn about a line at a time, and they just keep taking it until you get it right.

TERRY. *(Staring at* JEAN. *A stricken pause. Then she shakes her head slowly. Her decision is made.)* Oh, no.

JEAN. What?

TERRY. I couldn't.

JEAN. Couldn't what?

TERRY. That isn't acting, that's piece-work. You're not a human being, you're a thing in a vacuum. Noise shut out, human response shut out. But in the theatre, when you hear that lovely sound out there, then you know you're right. It's as though they'd turned on an electric current that hit you here. And that's how you learn to act.

JEAN. You can learn to act in pictures. You have to do it till it's right.

TERRY. Yes, and then they put it in a tin can, like Campbell's Soup. And if you die the next day it doesn't matter a bit. You don't even have to be alive to be in pictures.

JEAN. I suppose you call *this* being alive! Sleeping three in a room in this rotten dump. It builds you up, eh?

TERRY. I'm not going to stay here all my life. This is only the beginning.

JEAN. Don't kid yourself. You've been here three years, and then it's three years more, and then another three—and where are you?

You can't play ingenues forever. Pretty soon you're a character woman, and then you're running a boarding house like old Orcutt. *That'll* be nice, won't it?

TERRY. I don't know. You make me sound like a fool, but I know I'm not. All I know is I want to stay on the *stage.* I just don't want to *be* in pictures. An actress in the theatre, that's what I've wanted to be my whole life. It isn't just a career, it's a feeling. The theatre is something that's gone on for hundreds and hundreds of years. It's . . . I don't know . . . it's part of civilization.

JEAN. All right, you stay here with your civilization, eating those stews and tapiocas they shove at us, toeing the mark in this female seminary, buying your clothes at Klein's. That's what you like, eh?

TERRY. *Yes,* I like it!

JEAN. And I suppose you like this insane racket going on all night! *(She throws open window—street noises start.)*

TERRY. *(Yelling above noise.)* Yes I *do*!

JEAN. And that Cadillac car sign going on and off like a damned lighthouse! *(She turns off light. Again we see the flash of electric sign, off, on, off, on, full up and flashing faster.)* I suppose you've got to have that to be an actress!

TERRY. Yes! Yes! Yes! Yes! Yes!

JEAN. *(Not stopping for her.)* Well, not for me. I'm going out where there's sunshine and money and fun and . . .

TERRY. *(Shouting above her.)* And little ermine swimming pools up to here! *(The street noise, the flashing light, and their angry shouts are still going on as curtain descends.)*

JEAN. *(As the curtain falls.)* I'm going to make something out of my life. I'm not going to stay in this lousy dump.

## ☆☆☆ VISIT TO A SMALL PLANET

### by Gore Vidal

ACT II, SCENE 1

SCENE: *Livingroom of Roger Spelding's house near Manassas, Virginia*

CHARACTERS: KRETON
GENERAL TOM POWERS
ROGER SPELDING

POWERS. Well, Mr. Kreton, they have won . . . again.

KRETON. Who won what?

POWERS. I put it up to you, Mr. Kreton, as an impartial observer. I assume you're impartial . . . why should I be the one who has to carry the ball on this project: Operation Kreton? Not that I haven't enjoyed knowing you—I mean, that's one of the great things about army life; you get to meet all kinds of people, from different places, or, in this case, different *planets* —but after all, Interserv-Strat-Tac's mission is a larger one, covering, as you know, saddle-making, dry-cleaning, hygiene and, of course, laundry. So why, I asked the Chief of Staff, why don't you toss this right back to Com Air Int where it belongs? I've held the fort, and so far I haven't goofed. Well, to make a long story short, I lost. So until the civilians make up their minds what to do with you, I remain in charge. And why? Because I am the innocent victim of conspiracy and intrigue. Ever since Korea, Claypoole has been trying to get my corner office with the three windows and the big waiting room, and I tell you he'll stop at nothing. But I don't want to bore you with my problems. (*Takes a cigar from the coffee table.* KRETON *lights it for him.*)

KRETON. But I love having you bore me. You do it so beautifully.

---

POWERS. Well, thank you, sir.

KRETON. And may I say you have already earned an undying place in the roster of your country's military statesmen.

POWERS. (*Beaming.*) Only my duty.

KRETON. Nonsense; men have become President for less.

POWERS. You can say that again.

KRETON. (*Thoughtfully.*) No, I think once is enough.

POWERS. Anyway, the big thing is you're here and, as of now at least, you're mine. And I know you will understand my position and cooperate to the fullest.

KRETON. Gladly.

(POWERS, *relieved, begins to assert himself.*)

POWERS. Now, right off the bat, you can forget this taking-charge-of-the-world business. That's out. Not even the civilians would sit still for that. So just put it out of your mind. All right? All right. Now, ordinarily with a new weapon like yourself . . .

KRETON. Me? A new weapon?

POWERS. Oh, sure, sure. Forgot to tell you: You've been classified as a weapon. Later on we'll probably be able to figure out some peacetime uses for you, but right now I want to tell you that Central Intelligence was tickled pink when they heard you could read minds. And that force-field thing you do—well, that just about puts radar out of business. Now, ordinarily we'd ship you down to the proving ground at Aberdeen—run you through some tests—but out of respect for your status as alleged mammal, we'll skip that phase. But we *will* expect you to provide us with a comprehensive list of your various unusual powers—we'll need sixteen copies for immediate distribution. You can get on that right away. All right? All right. We'll want to announce your arrival ourselves. Want to see you get the best possible break, publicity-wise. Roger will be very helpful in that area.

KRETON. No, no, I'm sorry. I couldn't allow that. No one must know I'm here. It would spoil everything. I can't allow you to print one single word.

POWERS. (*Forgetting himself.*) Mr. Kreton, just how do you think you're going to stop us? (KRETON *starts to make his magic gestures.* POWERS *ricochets toward the bar.*) All right. All right. Just as you say. You're probably right, too. (*Desperate rationalization.*) We announce we have you, then the damned Russians claim they've got one too . . . only better . . . They haven't got one, have they?

KRETON. No, I'm the only one down here, I'm happy to say.

POWERS. Well, good. Good. And don't you ever forget, Mr. Kreton, that you are a discovery of the United States. And I don't mind saying, right to your face, that in my opinion you—just you alone—are worth all the H-bombs in the world combined.

KRETON. Ah, but I make so much less noise!

POWERS. Well, that's true.

KRETON. What a nice General you are! I'm so glad I got you instead of Lt. General Son-of-a-bitch Claypoole!

POWERS. (*Pleased.*) Yes, well, now, let's get started on that old list, eh? (ROGER *runs in from the porch, wearing his hat, carrying a briefcase.*)

ROGER. Powers! (*Comes down* R.)

POWERS. Hey, now! Wait a minute, Roger; this is a top level security meeting. No unauthorized personnel . . . either military or civilian.

ROGER. (*Desperately.*) Powers! Will you listen to me? The Russians have discovered antigravity!

POWERS. Antigravity?

ROGER. At eleven twenty-six this morning every rifle in the free world was raised fifteen feet in the air for thirty seconds and then lowered again. It's the Russians, obviously.

POWERS. (*Aghast.*) Who else? (*Crosses, sits* DR.)

KRETON. (*Curiously.*) Are you quite sure only *your* rifles were raised?

ROGER. Apparently. There's been a complete news blackout east of the Rhine. Tom, this is it: tactical exercise preparatory to invasion.

(POWERS *has begun to die with terror.*)

KRETON. Oh, General, how wonderful this must be for you! Now you'll have your chance to fight them with hydrogen bombs, with poison gas, with broken beer bottles if necessary . . . to fight them in the alleys, to fight them on the beaches . . .

POWERS. (*Unamused by this reprise.*) Yes, yes, well, yes . . . Rog, you say they raised *all* the rifles?

ROGER. Every last one of them, Tom.

POWERS. (*The mind slowly improvises. He rises.*) I suppose, Mr. Kreton, that if they could raise rifles, there's no *practical* reason why they couldn't successfully raise heavier ordnance, too? I mean machine guns, tanks, battleships—I don't suppose it would affect aircraft, of course, I mean if they're up there already . . . which they would be. (*The enormity of it all is too much for him. He sits heavily on the sofa.*)

KRETON. Of course antigravity is all a matter of concentration, really. Quite simple once you get the hang of it.

ROGER. (*Sudden idea.*) Mr. Kreton! I'm doing my broadcast here at home tonight. And I think it might be a very inspiring thing for Mother and Father America if you'd come on as my special guest and . . .

KRETON. Oh, no, I'm afraid I couldn't do *that!* But why don't you interview General Powers? He'd make a splendid guest.

POWERS. (*Brightens at the thought.*) Well, sure, Rog, be happy to go on with you, help out in any way I can. Don't hesitate to call on me.

ROGER. (*Stricken.*) Well, possibly . . . possibly . . . I'll have to call New York, see if I can get network clearance . . . (*Goes out the hall door.*)

POWERS. (*Puzzled.*) Clearance? Well, that's old Rog for you. . . Now, Mr. Kreton, we've got a lot of work to do—don't want to waste any time—so let's get started, shall we? Now, the desk is in the library. Remember? And the library is right in there. (*Briefcase in hand, he leads* KRETON *into the study.*) Sit right down here. (KRETON *sits at desk.*) Now, if you would be so good as to start drawing up that list we agreed on . . . looks like we'll be using you sooner than we thought, eh? (POWERS *had given* KRETON *a pen which he holds in the air like a wand.*) You do know how to write, don't you?

KRETON. Oh, I love writing. (*Makes elaborate circles and loops to* POWERS' *bewilderment.*)

POWERS. (*Uneasily.*) Good. Try to be as brief and concise as possible. Now, while you're scribbling away, I'll be up with Rog, planning the big broadcast for tonight. (*Opens briefcase.*) Here's some more carbons. (*Stacks the carbon paper on the desk.*)

KRETON. Thank you.

POWER. (*Suddenly.*) Say, you're not worried about this antigravity thing, are you?

KRETON. Oh, dear, no!

POWERS. Glad to hear it. We'll give 'em the old (*Imitates* KRETON'S *gesture.*) eh? (KRETON *giggles.* POWERS *laughs happily and goes.* KRETON *makes more circles with the pen. Then* ROSEMARY *calls to him from the window. He crosses to her, picks her up.*)

KRETON. *There* you are, Rosemary! Were you listening all the time? Oh, you are wicked! But isn't it thrilling? One incident and the whole world is now aquiver! You found a mouse? Oh, how luscious. (*He walks into livingroom, cat in hand.*) Well, you have your hobby and I have mine . . . Oh, I know you don't like people, but then, I don't like mice. *Chacun à son goût.* I simply dote on people . . . Why? Because of their primitive addiction to violence, because they seethe with emotions which I find bracing and intoxicating. For countless ages I have studied them and now I'm here to experience them first hand, to wallow shamelessly in their steaming emotions . . . and to have fun, fun, fun! . . . How? You *were* listening, weren't you? Well, I do believe I have started a war. At least, I hope so. After all, that's what I came down here to see! I mean, it's the one thing they do really well. Oh, I can't think what will happen next. (*He crosses to a globe of the world. He ponders it thoughtfully.*) Rosemary, advise me. Do I dare? Yes? Oh, well, then why not go whole hog? Metaphor! (*He gestures, and the globe explodes. He looks at it in wild alarm.*) Oh, dear! That was a bit much . . . But very pretty! (*Laughing delightedly, he accomplishes a small jig.*)

CURTAIN

## ☆☆☆ THE CAINE MUTINY COURT-MARTIAL

**by Herman Wouk**

ACT II

SCENE: *The General Court-Martial Room of the Twelfth Naval District, San Francisco. The time is February 1945.*

CHARACTERS: LT. COM. PHILIP FRANCIS QUEEG
CAPTAIN BLAKELY
LT. BARNEY GREENWALD
STENOGRAPHER (x)
LT. COM. JOHN CHALLEE (x)

STENOGRAPHER. (*Reads.*) "Commander Queeg, during the period when the *Caine* was towing targets at Pearl Harbor did you ever steam over your own towline and cut it?"

QUEEG. (*Promptly.*) Kay, now—here's the story on that particular slander. I started to make a turn, when I noticed some antiaircraft bursts close aboard to starboard. I was gravely concerned that my ship might be within range of somebody's firing. We were in a gunnery area. I was watching the bursts. This same sailor Stilwell, a very dreamy and unreliable man, was at the helm. He failed to warn me that we were coming around the full 360 degrees. I saw what was happening, finally, and instantly reversed course, and I avoided passing over the towline, to the best of my knowledge. However, the line parted during the turn.

GREENWALD. You say you were distracted by AA bursts. Did anything else distract you?

QUEEG. Not that I recall.

GREENWALD. Were you engaged in reprimanding a signalman named Urban at length for having his shirttail out, while your ship was turning 360 degrees?

QUEEG. Who says that—Keith again?

GREENWALD. Will you answer the question, Commander?

QUEEG. It's a malicious lie, of course.

GREENWALD. Was Urban on the bridge at the time?

QUEEG. Yes.

GREENWALD. Was his shirttail out?

QUEEG. Yes, and I reprimanded him. That took me about two seconds. I'm not in the habit of dwelling on those things. Then there were those AA bursts, and that was what distracted me.

GREENWALD. Did you point out these AA bursts to the officer of the deck or the exec?

QUEEG. I may have. I don't recall. I didn't run weeping to my OOD on every occasion. I may very well have kept my own counsel. And since this shirttail thing has been brought up—I'd like to say that Ensign Keith as morale officer was in charge of enforcing uniform regulations and completely soldiered on the job. When I took over the ship it was like the Chinese Navy. And I bore down on Keith to watch those shirttails and for all I know that's another reason he hated me and circulated all this about my cutting the towline.

GREENWALD. Did you drop a yellow dye marker off Jacob Island on the first morning of the invasion of Kwajalein?

QUEEG. I may have. I don't recall.

GREENWALD. Do you remember what your first mission was during the invasion?

QUEEG. Yes. To lead a group of attack boats to the line of departure for Jacob Island.

GREENWALD. Did you fulfill that mission?

QUEEG. Yes.

GREENWALD. Why did you drop the dye marker?

QUEEG. I don't know for sure that I did drop one. Maybe I dropped one to mark the line of departure plainly.

GREENWALD. How far was the line of departure from the beach?

QUEEG. As I recall, a thousand yards.

GREENWALD. Commander, didn't you run a mile ahead of the attack boats, drop your dye marker more than half a mile short, and retire at high speed, leaving the boats to grope their way to the line of departure as best they could?

CHALLEE. (*Rises.*) The question is abusive and flagrantly leading.

GREENWALD. (*Wearily.*) I am willing to withdraw the question, in view of the commander's dim memory, and proceed to more recent events.

BLAKELY. Court desires to question the witness.

(GREENWALD *crosses to his desk.*)

Commander Queeg, in view of the implications in this line of testimony, I urge you to search your memory for correct answers.

QUEEG. I am certainly trying to do that, sir. But these are very small points. I've been through several campaigns since Kwaljalein and the typhoon and now all this business—

BLAKELY. I appreciate that. It will facilitate justice if you can remember enough to give a few definite answers on points of fact. First of all, were those boats on the line of departure when you turned away from the beach?

QUEEG. As near as I could calculate, yes.

BLAKELY. In that case, Commander, if they were already on the line, what purpose did the dye marker serve?

QUEEG. (*Hesitates.*) Well, you might say a safety factor. Just another added mark. Now—maybe I erred in being over-cautious and making sure they knew where they were but then again, sir, I've always believed you can't err on the side of safety.

BLAKELY. (*Slight acrid impatience.*) Did you have the conn?

QUEEG. (*Pauses.*) As I recall now Lieutenant Maryk had the conn, and I now recall I had to caution him for opening the gap too wide between us and the boats.

BLAKELY. How wide?

QUEEG. I can't say, but at one point there was definitely too much open water and I called him aside and I admonished him not to run away from the boats.

BLAKELY. Didn't you direct him to slow down when you saw the gap widening?

QUEEG. Well, but it was all happening very fast and I may have been watching the beach for a few seconds and then I saw we were running away. And so that's why I dropped the marker, to compensate for Maryk's running away from the boats.

BLAKELY. (*Pauses, face grave.*) These are your factual recollections, Commander?

QUEEG. Those are the facts, sir.

BLAKELY. (*To* GREENWALD.) Resume your examination.

GREENWALD. (*Speaks at once.*) Commander Queeg, did you make it a practice, during invasions, to station yourself on the side of the bridge that was sheltered from the beach?

QUEEG. (*Angrily.*) That's an insulting question, and the answer is no, I had to be on all sides of the bridge at once, constantly moving from one side to the other because Maryk was navigator and Keith was my OOD at general quarters and both of them were invariably scurrying to the safe side of the bridge so I was captain and navigator and OOD all rolled in one and that's why I had to move constantly from one side of the bridge to the other. And that's the truth, whatever lies may have been said about me in this court.

(QUEEG *takes two steel balls out of his pocket.*)

BLAKELY. (*Rings bell.*) The court will question the witness.

## ☆☆☆ THE TEAHOUSE OF THE AUGUST MOON
### by John Patrick

ACT II, SCENE 2

SCENE: *Colonel Purdy's office.*

| CHARACTERS: | COLONEL PURDY | SERGEANT GREGOVICH (x) |
|---|---|---|
| | CAPTAIN FISBY | LOTUS BLOSSOM (x) |

(*The right panel is lifted. A light picks up* COLONEL PURDY. *He sits at his desk fuming over a report. The rest of the stage remains dark. He calls* GREGOVICH *on his office inter-com.*)

PURDY. Gregovich!

GREGOVICH'S VOICE. Yes, sir?

PURDY. Get me Captain Fisby at Tobiki.

GREGOVICH. Yes, sir.

(*The extreme left panel rises, leaving the intervening panels lowered.* FISBY *sits with his feet propped up on his desk. He is wearing his bathrobe "kimono."* LOTUS BLOSSOM *stands at his side fanning him. Over the scene, the sound of hammering and sawing can be heard. Over this the phone can be heard to ring,* FISBY *lifts the receiver.*)

FISBY. Captain Fisby.

PURDY. Colonel Purdy.

FISBY. (*Over noise.*) Who?

---

PURDY. Colonel Purdy.

FISBY. I can't hear you. Hold on a minute. (*He turns to* LOTUS BLOSSOM.) See if you can stop that hammering on the teahouse for a minute. (He *goes through the motions.* LOTUS BLOSSOM *nods understandingly and goes out.*)

PURDY. What's going on down there, Fisby?

FISBY. (*As the noises cease.*) Now, who is it?

PURDY. Colonel Purdy.

FISBY. (*Wraps his robe about his legs quickly.*) Oh, good afternoon, Colonel.

PURDY. I want to talk to you about your Progress Report.

FISBY. I sent it in.

PURDY. I have it. I have it right in front of me. I've read it twice. Now, suppose *you* tell *me* what it says.

FISBY. What would you like to have me explain, sir?

PURDY. I'd like you to explain why there's nothing in here about the schoolhouse. Didn't you get the lumber?

FISBY. (*Uneasily.*) Yes, sir . . . it's being used right now. But we'll need some more, I'm afraid.

PURDY. I sent ample according to specifications. How big a structure are you building?

FISBY. Well . . . we ought to consider expansion. Populations increase.

PURDY. We don't need to consider expansion. Our troops will be out of here by the next generation. Which brings me to another point. (*He refers to the report.*) What's this about six kids being born last week?

FISBY. Well, there wasn't much else to fill the Progress Report, sir.

PURDY. Then you've failed at your indoctrination. Don't you know yet that births are entered under "Population Increases"? They are not considered progress.

FISBY. But they weren't children, sir. They were kids . . . goats.

PURDY. There must be something wrong with this connection. It sounded just as if you said "goats."

FISBY. I did, sir. Kids . . . goats. You see, we're trying to increase the livestock herd down here. I thought . . .

PURDY. Goats! I don't care what you thought. Look here, Fisby, suppose some congressman flew in to inspect our team. How would I explain such a report?

FISBY. Well, goats will breed, sir. Congress can't stop that. And I've been concerned with . . .

PURDY. The population of civilians alone concerns us. I want to know exactly what progress you've made as outlined in Plan B.

FISBY. Well . . . I'm getting along fine with the people.

PURDY. In other words, nothing. Listen to me. Do you realize what Major McEvoy has accomplished in his village?

FISBY. No, sir.

PURDY. Well, I'll tell you. His fourth-graders know the alphabet through "M" and his whole village can sing "God Bless America" in English.

FISBY. Yes, sir. That's real progress, sir. I wish I could say the same.

PURDY. See that you do. I don't want any rotten apples in my barrel. Now . . . I want to know exactly what you have accomplished in the five weeks you've been down there.

FISBY. Well, sir . . . I've started an industry. I'm sending our first shipment out for sale this week.

PURDY. What are you making?

FISBY. (*Looks down at his feet.*) Oh, getas and . . .

PURDY. Wait a minute . . . what in God's name is a *geta?*

FISBY. Not "a" geta . . . *getas* . . . you have to have two.

PURDY. Are you breeding some *other* kind of animal?

FISBY. You wear them on your feet, sir. Excellent for strengthening the metatarsal muscles. Then . . . I have a group busy building cricket cages . . .

PURDY. Captain Fisby!

FISBY. Yes, sir.

PURDY. What kind of cages did you say?

FISBY. Cricket. Like in cricket on the hearth. I think we'll find a great market for them. Of course, we don't supply the crickets.

PURDY. Naturally not. Captain Fisby . . . have you been taking your salt pills?

FISBY. Yes, sir . . . I take them at cha ya . . . with my tea.

PURDY. Have you been going out in the sun without your helmet?

FISBY. I wear a kasa, sir . . . it's more practical . . . wind can blow through the straw.

PURDY. I see. I see. That will be all, Captain. (*He hangs up quickly.*)

FISBY. Hello . . . hello . . .

(*He hangs up and sits looking at the phone rather puzzled. The lights go down in his office and the panel descends.* COLONEL PURDY *also sits looking at the phone in his office. He calls* SERGEANT GREGOVICH *on the inter-com.*)

PURDY. Sergeant! What is the name of that psychiatrist over at Awasi?

GREGOVICH. Captain McLean?

PURDY. Get him on the phone. My man at Tobiki has gone completely off his rocker!

## ☆☆☆ BLIND ALLEY

### by James Warwick

ACT II

SCENE: *The home of William Anthony Shelby, a professor of psychology. The action takes place in the comfortably furnished living room.*

CHARACTERS: WILSON
SHELBY

*(Wilson crosses and punches* SHELBY *in the face, then crosses to upstage of chair left center.)*

SHELBY. *You had to do that, I suppose.*

WILSON. It ain't nothin' to what the dame got.

SHELBY. And you had to do it to her too.

WILSON. That should be a lesson to the lot of yer.

SHELBY. Why don't you put the blame where the blame belongs?

WILSON. (*Turns.*) What? I know where the blame belongs, Mister.

SHELBY. You mean me, of course, but it's not true. You fell down on your job.

WILSON. Aw, you. . . .

SHELBY. If you'd left one of your men in here and he'd let that happen, what would you have done?

WILSON. I'd a plugged him.

SHELBY. Exactly.

WILSON. Sure, nobody . . . (*Pause.*) This was different. I was . . . (*Pause.*) I never let nothing like that happen a-fore and I'll take good care it never happens again, Mister.

SHELBY. You think so?

WILSON. Too right I do.

SHELBY. It must happen again and again . . . unless you find out what causes these rages that suddenly blot everything from your mind. You're scared, Wilson.

WILSON. Scared! I ain't never bin scared of nothin' in my life, an' I ain't gonner start now.

SHELBY. That isn't true for a start.

WILSON. (*Steps toward Shelby.*) Don't call me a liar . . . I don't take that from no one.

SHELBY. I'm sorry. I didn't. . . .

WILSON. Shut up—and listen ter me. I'm gonner take what I want . . . as long as I can get away with it. There ain't no other way I can get by now an' live. Where do you cut inter that picture? (WILSON *crosses to chair left center then right to end of couch.*)

SHELBY. (*Losing his calm for a moment.*) You forced me into it. I didn't ask you to come here . . . to shoot that boy, beat that girl until she was almost dead . . . But that's beside the point. You accused me of calling you a liar. Let's stay with that. You made a flat statement that you were not afraid of anything—and I contradicted you.

WILSON. I ain't.

SHELBY. Then tell me something. What are you trying to escape from?

WILSON. What d' yer mean?

WILSON. You're like a man running down a blind alley in the dark.

WILSON. So what!

SHELBY. What are you going to do when you reach the end? The place where you cannot go any farther?

WILSON. (*Comes down left.*) I'm gonner shoot—an' keep on shootin'! Like I always done. A guy's only got ter get it once—but I won't be alone, don't worry. I'll have lots of company.

SHELBY. You're on the run now. You can't stop to think, can you? You're not going to finish in any blaze of guns and glory. You're going to crack up. You've been on the verge of it for a long time.

WILSON. Crack up? (*Sits on chair at desk* L.)

SHELBY. Yes—(*Pause.*) I'll tell you something about yourself. (*Pause.*) You go along quite calmly as a rule, don't you? See things more or less as they are. (*Pause.*) We'll say, for instance, you're driving a car. There's the road—the different objects you pass,—trees,—automobiles, houses. And then—(*Pause—he leans forward a little.*)—then sometimes you become aware of another thing, don't you? Something you can't see, but can feel. It drives you into going faster and faster, it follows you. You can't shake it off, can you? Your eyes are open, but you can't get rid of it. It's always just behind. And presently nothing matters anymore—only that thing you feel is there, and you go on and on until—

WILSON. (*Leaping to his feet—knocking chair over.*) It's a lie! Who told you that! (*Pause. Threateningly, as he comes closer and stands above* SHELBY.) Who's bin talkin' about me? It's a lie, I tell yer!

SHELBY. What's a lie? If it's a lie why bother about it? Sit down and don't get excited. It's bad for you.

WILSON. Then yer takes it back?—Say yer was lyin'—go on—say it.

SHELBY. All right, I was lying then.

WILSON. (*Crosses back and picks up chair: places it by desk.*) Whatter yer want ter pull them kinda capers for? That kinda junk don't get yer no place with me. (*Crosses to back of chair left center.*)

SHELBY. No . . . perhaps not.

WILSON. Say, Doc, tell me something. How did you know that about me?

SHELBY. It's true, isn't it?

WILSON. Yea, some. Not the way you got it, but near enough.

## ☆☆☆ EVER SINCE EVE

### by Florence Ryerson and Colin Clements

ACT I

SCENE: *Johnny Clover's office. This is a rather misleading room, since, to the casual eye, it does not resemble an office. In point of fact, it was originally the Clover nursery; then for a number of years a storeroom, and has only recently been redecorated and turned over to Johnny. It is a pleasant place, with painted walls and simple furniture . . . a business-like desk, desk chair, and a bookcase . . . couch, and a low table . . . center rear, wide Dutch door . . .*

CHARACTERS: SPUD
JOHNNY

SPUD. (*He crosses left to couch.*) Jeepers what a day! Trying to get ads in this darn town is like pulling teeth, and now this Susan business . . .

JOHNNY. We're sure in a crisis!

SPUD. (*Sitting on couch.*) *You* said it, J.C. What're we going to do?

JOHNNY. (*Bringing his hand down sharply on desk and rising.*) We're going to be firm, that's what! We're not going to stand for it.

SPUD. Um. If Susan tries to butt in, we'll throw her out.

JOHNNY. You can't go throwing a girl out, Spud. It'd hurt her feelings, and besides . . . (*He brings out the truth.*) . . . she'd go straight to Miss Willard.

SPUD. (*Thinking it over.*) I guess you're right, at that.

JOHNNY. You bet I'm right. We've got to use tact.

SPUD. . . . The iron hand in the velvet glove.

JOHNNY. (Crossing to SPUD.) That's it. (*Admiringly.*) You certainly know how to handle women, fellow.

SPUD. Me? Oh, I get by, J. C., get by. (*With a deprecating laugh.*) I wouldn't want to brag, but there just seems to be something about me the fems fall for.

JOHNNY. Gender appeal.

SPUD. Um . . . I guess that's it. You know, sometimes I almost scare myself . . . the power I seem to have. Now take that little jasmine blossom from Tennessee . . .

JOHNNY. I been hearing about her . . .

SPUD. M-m-*m!* Boy, what a honey! Every guy in the class trying to get her wave length. But will she tune in? Not little Miss Mason-and-Dixon. Then mama's baby boy comes along and . . . Well, she's dropping in here this afternoon.

JOHNNY. She is! (SPUD *nods.*) Listen, Spud, you want to watch out.

Someday this woman-business is going to get a grip on you.

SPUD. Oh, we can take 'em, or leave 'em alone.

JOHNNY. You can *now*. But I've watched other fellows. Why, look at Buzz Sawyer . . . best backfield P.H.S. ever had . . . all set for the State Varsity and what happens?

SPUD. (*Disgustedly.*) He meets a sweet dish . . . and zowie!

JOHNNY. Yeah. Starts sitting around writing *poetry*! Doesn't even make the freshman team.

SPUD. I know. (*Sobered.*) It gets lots of good men that way, but it won't get me. No, sir!

JOHNNY. I got my life all planned out.

SPUD. Same here. Of course someday I expect to get married . . . my family always has.

JOHNNY. Oh, sure, I plan to get married, too. But not until I'm middle-aged . . . thirty or thirty-one.

SPUD. I guess that's a good time. By then your life's kind of over, and you might as well settle down.

JOHNNY. . . . But in the meantime, no woman's going to interfere with *me*.

SPUD. Me, neither.

(*They rise, shake hands solemnly. There is a tinny rattle and a crash outside, a loud banging on the door, a voice calling:*)

SUSAN. (*Off stage.*) Hello . . .

(*Instantly the boys spring to attention.*)

JOHNNY. Susan!

SPUD. Yeah!

JOHNNY. Remember . . . the iron hand in the velvet glove.

SUSAN. (*Off stage.*) Hey . . . let me in.

SPUD. Maybe it'd be better if we locked the door and pretended we're not here. (JOHNNY *dashes across the room, slips the bolt in the lock, then returns to* SPUD *at the desk. In the meantime, there is a pounding on the door and* SUSAN'*s voice continues calling:* "What's the matter? Where are you? Let me in". . . .)

## ☆☆☆ THE TAMING OF THE SHREW

### by William Shakespeare

ACT II, SCENE 1

SCENE: *Padua. A room in Baptista's house.*

CHARACTERS: KATHARINA
PETRUCHIO

PETRUCHIO. Good-morrow, Kate; for that's your name, I hear.

KATHARINA. Well have you heard, but something hard of hearing.
They call me Katharine that do talk of me.

PETRUCHIO. You lie, in faith; for you are call'd plain Kate,
And bonny Kate, and sometimes Kate the curst;
But, Kate, the prettiest Kate in Christendom,
Kate of Kate-Hall, my super-dainty Kate,
For dainties are all Kates; and therefore, Kate,
Take this of me, Kate, of my consolation;—
Hearing thy mildness prais'd in every town,
Thy virtues spoke of, and thy beauty sounded,—
Yet not so deeply as to thee belongs,—
Myself am mov'd to woo thee for my wife.

KATHARINA. Mov'd! In good time: let him that mov'd you hither
Remove you hence: I knew you at the first
You were a movable.

PETRUCHIO. Why, what's a movable?

KATHARINA. A join'd-stool.

PETRUCHIO. Thou hast hit it; come, sit on me.

KATHARINA. Asses are made to bear, and so are you.

PETRUCHIO. Women are made to bear, and so are you.

KATHARINA. No such jade as you, if me you mean.

PETRUCHIO. Alas, good Kate, I will not burden thee!
For knowing thee to be but young and light,—

KATHARINA. Too light for such a swain as you to catch;
And yet as heavy as my weight should be.

PETRUCHIO. Should be! Should buzz.
KATHARINA. Well ta'en, and like a buzzard.
PETRUCHIO. O, slow-wing'd turtle! shall a buzzard take thee?
KATHARINA. Ay, for a turtle,—as he takes a buzzard.
PETRUCHIO. Come, come, you wasp; i' faith, you are too angry.
KATHARINA. If I be waspish, best beware my sting.
PETRUCHIO. My remedy is then, to pluck it out.
KATHARINA. Ay, if the fool could find it where it lies.
PETRUCHIO. Who knows not where a wasp doth wear his sting?
In his tail.
KATHARINA. In his tongue.
PETRUCHIO. Whose tongue?
KATHARINA. Yours, if you talk of tails; and so farewell.
PETRUCHIO. Good Kate; I am a gentleman.
KATHARINA. That I'll try. (*Striking him.*)
PETRUCHIO. I swear I'll cuff you, if you strike again.
KATHARINA. So may you lose your arms:
If you strike me, you are no gentleman:
And if no gentleman, why then no arms.
PETRUCHIO. A herald, Kate? O, put me in thy books!
KATHARINA. What is your crest? A coxcomb?
PETRUCHIO. A combless cock, so Kate will be my hen.
KATHARINA. No cock of mine; you crow too like a craven.
PETRUCHIO. Nay, come, Kate, come; you must not look so sour.
KATHARINA. It is my fashion, when I see a crab.
PETRUCHIO. Why, here's no crab; and therefore look not sour.
KATHARINA. There is, there is.
PETRUCHIO. Then show it me.
KATHARINA. Had I a glass I would.
PETRUCHIO. What, you mean my face?
KATHARINA. Well aim'd of such a young one.
PETRUCHIO. Now, by Saint George, I am too young for you.
KATHARINA. Yet, you are wither'd.
PETRUCHIO. 'Tis with cares.
KATHARINA. I care not.

PETRUCHIO. Nay, hear you, Kate; in sooth, you 'scape not so.
KATHARINA. I chafe you, if I tarry; let me go.
PETRUCHIO. No, not a whit; I find you passing gentle.
'Twas told me you were rough, and coy, and sullen,
And now I find report a very liar;
For thou art pleasant, gamesome, passing courteous;
But slow in speech, yet sweet as spring-time flowers;
Thou canst not frown, thou canst not look askance,
Nor bite the lip, as angry wenches will;
Nor hast thou pleasure to be cross in talk;
But thou with mildness entertain'st thy wooers,
With gentle conference, soft and affable.
Why does the world report that Kate doth limp?
O slanderous world! Kate, like the hazel-twig,
Is straight and slender, and as brown in hue
As hazel-nuts, and sweeter than the kernels.
O, let me see thee walk: thou dost not halt.
KATHARINA. Go, fool, and whom thou keep'st command.
PETRUCHIO. Did ever Dian so become a grove
As Kate this chamber with her princely gait?
O, be thou Dian, and let her be Kate;
And then let Kate be chaste, and Dian sportful!
KATHARINA. Where did you study all this goodly speech?
PETRUCHIO. It is extempore, from my mother-wit.
KATHARINA. A witty mother! witless else her son.
PETRUCHIO. Am I not wise?
KATHARINA. Yes, keep you warm.
PETRUCHIO. Marry, so I mean, sweet Katharine, in thy bed;
And therefore, setting all this chat aside,
Thus in plain terms:—Your father hath consented.
That you shall be my wife; your dowry 'greed on;
And, will you, nill you, I will marry you.
Now, Kate, I am a husband for your turn;
For, by this light, whereby I see thy beauty,
Thy beauty that doth make me like thee well,

Thou must be married to no man but me;
For I am he am born to tame you, Kate,
And bring you from a wild Kate to a Kate
Conformable as other household Kates.
Here comes your father; never make denial;
I must and will have Katharine to my wife.

## ☆☆☆ ROMEO AND JULIET

### by William Shakespeare

ACT II, SCENE 5

SCENE: *Capulet's garden.*

CHARACTERS: JULIET
NURSE

(*Enter* JULIET.)

JULIET. The clock struck nine when I did send the nurse;
In half an hour she promis'd to return.
Perchance she cannot meet him: that's not so;
O, she is lame! love's heralds should be thoughts,
Which ten times faster glide than the sun's beams,
Driving back shadows over louring hills:
Therefore do nimble-pinion'd doves draw love,
And therefore hath the wind-swift Cupid wings.
Now is the sun upon the highmost hill
Of this day's journey, and from nine till twelve
Is three long hours, yet she is not come.
Had she affections and warm youthful blood,
She would be as swift in motion as a ball;
My words would bandy her to my sweet love,
And his to me:
But old folks, many feign as they were dead;
Unwieldy, slow, heavy and pale as lead.
O God, she comes!

(*Enter* NURSE *and* PETER.)

O honey nurse, what news?
Hast thou met with him? Send thy man away.

NURSE. Peter, stay at the gate. (*Exit* PETER.)

JULIET. Now, good sweet nurse,—O Lord, why look'st thou sad?
Though news be sad, yet tell them merrily;
If good, thou sham'st the music of sweet news
By playing it to me with so sour a face.

NURSE. I am a-weary, give me leave awhile:
Fie, how my bones ache! what a jaunt have I had!

JULIET. I would thou hadst my bones, and I thy news.
Nay, come, I pray thee, speak; good, good nurse, speak.

NURSE. Jesu, what haste? can you not stay awhile?
Do you not see that I am out of breath?

JULIET. How art thou out of breath, when thou hast breath
To say to me that thou art out of breath?
The excuse that thou dost make in this delay
Is longer than the tale thou dost excuse.
Is thy news good or bad? answer to that;
Say either, and I'll stay the circumstance:
Let me be satisfied, is't good or bad?

NURSE. Well, you have made a simple choice; you know not how to choose a man: Romeo! no, not he, though his face be better than any man's, yet his leg excels all men's; and for a hand, and a foot, and a body, though they be not to be talk'd on, yet they are past compare: he is not the flower of courtesy, but, I'll warrant him, as gentle as a lamb. Go thy ways, wench; serve God. What, have you din'd at home?

JULIET. No, no: but all this did I know before.
What says he of our marriage? what of that?

NURSE. Lord, how my head aches! what a head have I!
It beats as it would fall in twenty pieces.
My back o't other side,—O, my back! my back!
Beshrew your heart for sending me about,
To catch my death with jaunting up and down!

JULIET. I' faith, I am sorry that thou art not well.
Sweet, sweet, sweet nurse, tell me, what says my love?

NURSE. Your love says, like an honest gentleman, and a courteous, and a kind, and a handsome, and, I warrant, a virtuous, —Where is your mother?

JULIET. Where is my mother! why, she is within;
Where should she be? How oddly thou repliest!
'Your love says, like an honest gentleman,
Where is your mother?'

NURSE. O God's lady dear!
Are you so hot? marry, come up, I trow;
Is this the poultice for my aching bones?
Henceforward do your messages yourself.

JULIET. Here's such a coil! come, what says Romeo?

NURSE. Have you got leave to go to shrift to-day?

JULIET. I have.

NURSE. Then hie you hence to Friar Laurence' cell;
There stays a husband to make you a wife:
Now comes the wanton blood up in your cheeks,
They'll be in scarlet straight at any news.
Hie you to church; I must another way,
To fetch a ladder, by the which your love
Must climb a bird's nest soon when it is dark:
I am the drudge and toil in your delight,
But you shall bear the burden soon at night.
Go; I'll to dinner; hie you to the cell.

JULIET. Hie to high fortune! Honest nurse, farewell.

(*Exeunt.*)

## ☆☆☆ HAMLET

### by William Shakespeare

ACT V, SCENE 1

SCENE: *A Churchyard.*

CHARACTERS: FIRST CLOWN, SECOND CLOWN (Gravediggers)

(*Enter two* CLOWNS, *with Spades.*)

1ST CLOWN. Is she to be buried in Christian burial, that wilfully seeks her own salvation?

2ND CLOWN. I tell thee, she is; and therefore make her grave straight: the crowner hath sat on her, and finds it Christian burial.

1ST CLOWN. How can that be, unless she drowned herself in her own defence?

2ND CLOWN. Why, 'tis found so.

1ST CLOWN. It must be 'se offendendo'; it cannot be else. For here lies the point: if I drown myself wittingly, it argues an act; and an act hath three branches; it is, to act, to do, and to perform: argal, she drowned herself wittingly.

2ND CLOWN. Nay, but hear you, goodman delver.

1ST CLOWN. Give me leave. Here lies the water; good: here stands the man; good: if the man go to this water, and drown himself, it is, will he, nill he, he goes,—mark you that; but if the water come to him and drown him, he drowns not himself: argal, he that is not guilty of his own death shortens not his own life.

2ND CLOWN. But is this law?

1ST CLOWN. Ay, marry, is't; crowner's quest law.

2ND CLOWN. Will you ha' the truth on't? If this had not been a gentlewoman, she would have been buried out of Christian burial.

1ST CLOWN. Why, there thou say'st; and the more pity that great folk should have countenance in this world to drown or hang themselves, more than their even Christian. Come, my spade. There is no ancient gentlemen but gardeners, ditchers, and grave-makers; they hold up Adam's profession.

2ND CLOWN. Was he a gentleman?

1ST CLOWN. He was the first that ever bore arms.

2ND CLOWN. Why, he had none.

1ST CLOWN. What, art a heathen? How dost thou understand the Scripture? The Scripture says, 'Adam digged': could he dig without arms? I'll put another question to thee: if thou answerest me not to the purpose, confess thyself—

2ND CLOWN. Go to.

1ST CLOWN. What is he that builds stronger than either the mason, the shipwright, or the carpenter?

2ND CLOWN. The gallows-maker; for that frame outlives a thousand tenants.

1ST CLOWN. I like thy wit well, in good faith: the gallows does well; but how does it well? it does well to those that do ill: now, thou dost ill to say the gallows is built stronger than the church: argal, the gallows may do well to thee. To't again; come.

2ND CLOWN. 'Who builds stronger than a mason, a shipwright, or a carpenter?'

1ST CLOWN. Ay, tell me that, and unyoke.

2ND CLOWN. Marry, now I can tell.

1ST CLOWN. To't.

2ND CLOWN. Mass, I cannot tell.

1ST CLOWN. Cudgel thy brains no more about it, for your dull ass will not mend his pace with beating; and, when you are asked this question next, say, 'a grave-maker': the houses that he makes last till doomsday. Go, get thee to Yaughan; fetch me a stoop of liquor.

(*Exit* 2ND CLOWN.)

(1ST CLOWN *digs, and sings.*)

In youth, when I did love, did love,
Methought it was very sweet,
To contract, O! the time, for, ah! my behove,
O! methought, there was nothing meet.

# Twelve

## ONE-ACT PLAY ☆☆☆

### ☆☆☆ THE TEA-POT ON THE ROCKS

**by John Kirkpatrick**

CHARACTERS: MAY LOVELACE, DAISY ANDERSON, MRS. CARSTAIRS, ROY WILLIAMS, WILLIE, ALEC

TIME: *Five o'clock. An afternoon in spring.*

PLACE: *The "Brass Kettle" Tea-Room.*

SCENE: *The "Brass Kettle" is one of those tea-shops—there must be a million throughout the country—that goes in rather*

---

*heavily for red candle sticks, blue hand-painted modernistic furniture, green paper doilies, and yellow salt-cellars in the shape of kewpies, elephants, etc. It's the sort of place a woman might think was "cosy" and the sort of place a man wouldn't enter even to escape a blizzard.*

*The scene really represents the "back room" of the establishment—the front room is through a door at the left. However, to take care of the "overflow"—alas, there isn't any!—this rear room also has been provided with two or three small tables—and chairs—and in order that the guests who are forced to take refuge in this second room may be spared somewhat that degrading feeling of "eating in the kitchen" two small screens have been placed up center to mask the gas-stove, the sink, etc.*

*At right, upstage, is a curtained window—and below this a door leading into the backyard and alley-way.*

AT RISE: *The stage is held by* MISS DAISY ANDERSON *who is stretched out in an armchair—the only comfortable chair in the entire place. She has her feet propped up in another chair and is taking life decidedly easy as she makes a somewhat elaborate meal off the end of a loaf of bread, the remains of a jar of marmalade—and a cup of tea in which she pours an amazing amount of cream. It is plain to be seen that she is enjoying herself—she eats with relish.*

DAISY *is about twenty-three—large, plump, blonde, pretty—but hopelessly averse to any form of physical activity. She is wearing a gay-colored smock in keeping with her surroundings.*

*A bell is heard—one of those silly little jingles. The bell is over the door left and is used to announce to the occupants of the back room that someone has just entered the front door of the shop.* DAISY, *however, is not perturbed—or hardly so. With as little motion as possible she manages to turn her head to gaze at door left—then subsides in comfort as* MAY LOVELACE *enters.*

*MAY is the direct antithesis of her friend; she is small, dark, vivacious, alert—although at the moment she wears a somewhat sad, woe-begone expression as she comes in and tosses her hat across the room. And the sight of* DAISY *so completely "at her ease" doesn't add to her gaiety at the moment.*

MAY. Well, *you* certainly look happy.

DAISY. (*Her mouth rather full.*) Uh—huh.

MAY. Didn't the bell ring when I came in?

DAISY. (*Managing to nod.*) Uh—huh.

MAY. Well, why didn't you come out to see if it was a customer?

DAISY. Customer?

MAY. Yes, customer.

DAISY. We—we never have had a customer. (*She takes another bite.*)

MAY. Well, that's no sign we never will have one.

DAISY. (*Makes some unintelligible sounds.*)

MAY. What? Daisy, I wish you wouldn't—you know you're eating up all the profits.

DAISY. We haven't got any profits.

MAY. Well, you're not helping the losses any.

DAISY. (*With a sigh.*) Oh, May,—we've already got so many losses the few little mouthfuls I eat won't—

MAY. *Few* little mouthfuls—? Every afternoon you hold yourself a regular banquet!

DAISY. I don't.

MAY. You do, Daisy—and it's *awful.*

DAISY. Oh, May! Just this little dab of—

MAY. *Yes.* Just that little "dab." Four slices of toast—butter—marmalade—tea—sugar—*cream*— Daisy, you didn't use up *all* that cream?

DAISY. Well, suppose I did! It won't keep and there's nobody else to drink it. Besides, I—heavens, I get tired of sitting around here all day with nothing to do.

MAY. And so you eat.

DAISY. Yes—and so I eat. (*A pause.*) Did you see your family?

MAY. (*Between her teeth.*) I saw Father—if that's what you mean.

DAISY. Nothing doing, eh?

MAY. Not a thing.

DAISY. What'd he say?

MAY. (*Impatiently.*) Same old thing. (*Giving an imitation of a very brusque, business man.*) "Daughter"—whenever Father wants to be thoroughly unpleasant he calls me "Daughter"— (*She starts again.*) "Daughter, whenever you get ready to give up this tom-fool idea of running a tea-room and come home to lead a nice, sensible, girlish life"—(*Interrupting to ask* DAISY.) Just what is a "girlish life," will you please tell me?

DAISY. "Girlish life"? Like a girl, I guess.

MAY. (*Contemptuously.*) I thought so. (*Continuing.*) "I'll pay your bills and I'll do anything for you—within reason. But I will not contribute one penny to your support as long as you continue to operate that second-rate jerkwater, hot-dog, ham-and-egg joint!"

DAISY. He called this a "ham-and-egg joint"?

MAY. Those were his very words!

DAISY. *May!* What did you do?

MAY. *Do?* I blew up! That's what I did! "Father," I said—and believe me I put just as much into "Father" as he put into "Daughter." "Father," I said, "I didn't come here to your office to impinge on your paternal generosity—

DAISY. Whew! "Impinge"—that's awful. What does it mean?

MAY. I don't know—but that's the way I put it. I said "I'm here to give you a chance to invest twenty-five dollars in the Brass Kettle Tea-Room Incorporated. The Brass Kettle Tea-Room does *not* sell ham and eggs—it has the most exclusive clientele in town—or will have as soon as we get some customers—and far from being a "joint" it is a much, *much* more important institution than the Gibraltar Life Insurance Company of which you call yourself the agent.

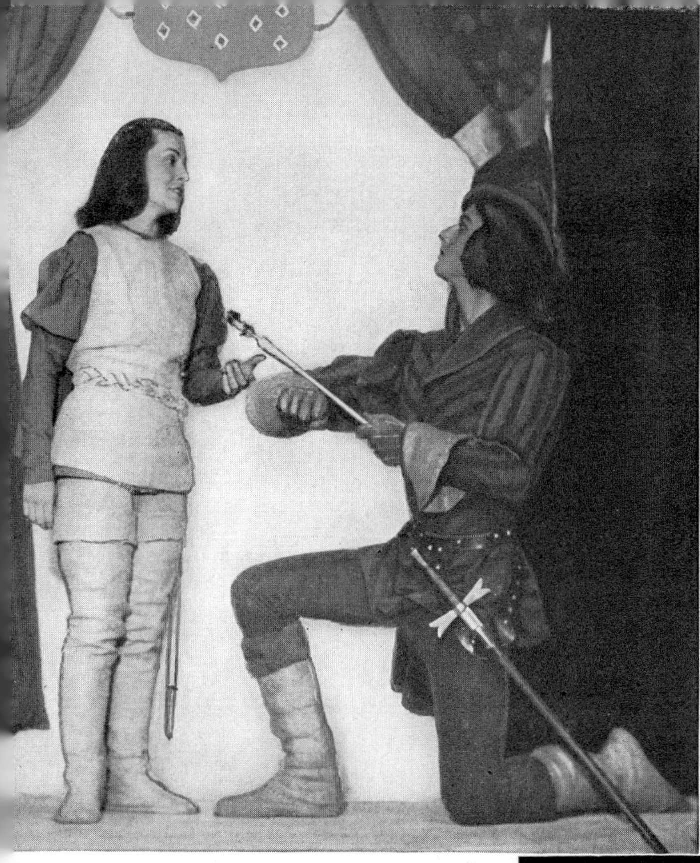

COSTUME: SAINT JOAN
*University of California, Los Angeles*

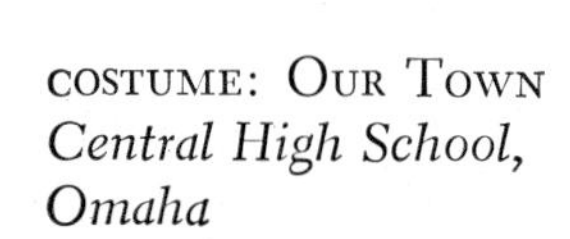

COSTUME: OUR TOWN
*Central High School, Omaha*

LIGHTING: THE TEAHOUSE OF THE AUGUST MOON
*Evanston Township High School, Evanston, Illinois*

LIGHTING: THE DEVIL'S DISCIPLE *Santa Monica City College*

DAISY. What'd he do?

MAY. Then *he* blew up! Fortunately his stenographer came in and separated us. And that's that! (*She pours herself a cup of tea.*)

DAISY. (*Rises and stretches.*) Gosh, parents are stubborn—sometimes I wish I could go back to believing that I was brought here by a stork. (*A slight pause—then.*) Well, old dear—since *my* father won't come across—and *your* father won't, I guess we're sunk.

MAY. What?

DAISY. Yep. S-u-n-k—*sunk*.

MAY. We're not—any such thing!

DAISY. Oh, yes, we are—we might as well admit it. It was a nice little venture while it lasted but it's all over now.

MAY. (*Indignantly.*) Daisy Anderson, do you mean to tell me you've got cold feet?

DAISY. Darling, my feet are *frozen*—they've been frozen for weeks. When you keep a place open for three months and nobody rings the bell but people selling subscriptions to magazines, well—it's time to quit.

MAY. I'm ashamed of you, Daisy.

DAISY. (*Shrugs.*) Can't help it. I've put up all the money I have and you've put up all you have—so what are we going to do?

MAY. Oh, something'll happen—something's *obliged* to.

DAISY. No, it's not. Some people live all their lives and nothing ever happens.

MAY. Maybe—maybe if we advertised—

DAISY. What'll we use for money? I've got twenty cents—how much have you got?

MAY. Fifteen.

DAISY. Besides we *have* advertised. We've put notices in both papers. "Come to tea—come to tea!" People who read it in the morning paper forget about it by afternoon—and by the time the evening paper comes out, it's too late.

MAY. I know, Daisy, but—

DAISY. And look at the big sign we've got out front. What's that but advertising?

MAY. Oh, people just don't notice it.

DAISY. No, and the only way to get 'em to notice it is to cut the ropes and let it fall on somebody's head. May, do you realize that we owe another month's rent?

MAY. Not 'till the thirtieth.

DAISY. Today's the twenty-ninth. And there's the grocery bill.

MAY. You know I think I accidentally tore up that grocery bill.

DAISY. That's no help. Every time you tear up a grocery bill a bigger and better grocery bill comes along to take its place.

MAY. Oh, everybody owes a grocery bill these days and times.

DAISY. *And the gas!*

MAY. The gas?

DAISY. Yes, the *gas!* We've kept that front room in there nice and warm since the first day of February and nobody's even *sat* in it.

MAY. Well, we—we just have to forget about the gas for the moment.

DAISY. I wish I could forget about it! You know last night when I was asleep I dreamt something was after me. I couldn't make out exactly what it was so I yelled out "Who is that?" and then this terrible voice came back, "It's the gas company!"

MAY. They—they can't turn it off, can they?

DAISY. They not only can turn it off—they *will* turn it off! Why, they keep a man—and pay him a big salary—who doesn't do anything else but walk around town disconnecting pipes.

MAY. Oh, Daisy, suppose—suppose he came in here to turn off ours when we had—customers.

DAISY. (*Impatiently.*) There you go again—"customers." What do we know about "customers"? If one accidentally walked in here we wouldn't know what to do with it. (*She sinks in chair.*) No, I give up. I'm going to write Harry tonight and tell him if he still wants to take me for better and worse and all that, why, I'll marry him.

MAY. Oh, Daisy. And give up your career?

DAISY. (*Nodding.*) Uh—huh. Such as it is. Oh, I know. I was like you. I was crazy to be a "tea-room hostess"—but you can't be a tea-room hostess without a little co-operation from the public. (*She looks over at* MAY.) And if you'll take my advice you'll tell Roy just what I'm telling Harry.

MAY. (*Rising.*) I—I won't marry Roy.

DAISY. Why not? You're in love with him.

MAY. I'm not. Oh, I might have been once but not after the way he's acted about *this* thing.

DAISY. Hm. He's acted better than Harry. Roy at least comes around every day—Harry won't stick his toe inside the place.

MAY. (*Vehemently.*) Yes, and what does Roy come for? Daisy, Roy actually *wants* this place to fail—he thinks as soon as I'm out of here I'll marry him—so he sits about and *waits* for it to fail. He—he's like a—like a death angel hanging around for the corpse. I wouldn't marry him for anything on earth!

DAISY. Hm. Better make up your mind then to lead a "girlish life" with "Papa."

MAY. And I won't do that either. I'm not *going* to fail. All we need is a break. Daisy—just one good break. Going to a tea-room is a habit,—just like—like smoking cigarettes. People like a place and tell their friends. Suppose—suppose just for one day, now, we could get just a *few* people.

DAISY. (*Wearily.*) I know—I've been "supposing" since February.

MAY. I know, but wait! Suppose—suppose we got people in here for one day—the right people—like—like Mrs. Alexander—or Mrs. St. John—or Mrs. Carstairs or—

DAISY. Carstairs? Don't be funny. She doesn't even know we're alive.

MAY. But she might just stumble in here one day—and just think of it. Wherever Mrs. Carstairs goes *everybody* goes. Why, we'd make a *fortune!*

DAISY. I don't want a fortune. I want Harry.

(*The bell jingles.*)

MAY. Oh, there's somebody now. Where's my smock?

DAISY. Don't get excited. It's probably just somebody else working his way through college.

(MAY *goes hurriedly over to door left.* ROY *appears.*)

ROY. Hello.

MAY. (*Wearily.*) Oh, it's you. Hello, Roy.

ROY. You sound a little disappointed.

DAISY. Oh, no—not a bit. We weren't really expecting anybody but the Fuller-Brush man.

(ROY *comes in. He's an attractive, good-looking young man of twenty-seven.*)

ROY. Well, how's everything at "Ye Olde Brass Tea-Pot" today?

DAISY. Hm.

MAY. (*Trying to carry it off.*) Oh, fine—everything's fine, thank you.

ROY. (*With a twinkle.*) Packing 'em in as usual, I see. (*He makes himself thoroughly at home.*)

MAY. Oh, yes, I mean—well, not right this minute. You see it—it's sort of an off-hour right now.

ROY. Hm, off-hour. (*Looking at watch.*) Funny. Of course I'm not very well up in such matters but I thought this was the very time when the tea-hounds did their heaviest guzzling.

MAY. (*With dignity.*) I really don't know what a "tea-hound" is—and certainly we don't allow "guzzling," as you call it, around here.

ROY. Oh, my mistake. Sorry.

DAISY. (*Ironically.*) You didn't come in to *order* anything, did you, Roy?

ROY. No, I can't afford but *three* meals a day. Besides if it ever got back to the office that I was seen juggling teacups I'd have to leave town.

MAY. Well, I'd be ashamed to admit it. I'll have you know Americans—women *and* men—are going in for tea in a big way.

ROY. Yes, I can tell that by the crowds. (MAY *gives him a withering look.*) No, Daisy, I just came in for a nice, sociable chat. That is, if I'm not in the way. Of course if I am—

DAISY. Oh, no, keep your seat. It's nice to have *somebody* come in even if it's just for a chat.

ROY. Oh, that bad, is it?

DAISY. Yep—just that bad.

MAY. (*Reprovingly.*) Daisy.

DAISY. Oh, what's the use. Roy knows. No, Roy—there's nobody here today—but there'll be somebody in tomorrow.

ROY. Yeah? Who's that?

DAISY. The landlord.

ROY. Gosh. That's a shame. I'm sorry.

MAY. (*Turning on him furiously.*) You're not—you're not sorry! You just come around here so you can—can gloat over us!

ROY. Oh, don't say that, May.

MAY. It's the truth—and you know it!

DAISY. Oh, stop it—you two! I'm worn out.

MAY. Worn out?

DAISY. Yes. From sitting down. I'm used to being busy. I always was—before I went to work.

ROY. I—I guess spring is a bad time for this sort of business—if it's nice weather people want to stay outside—and if it rains they don't go out at all.

(MAY *gives him another look—and crosses to other side of room.* DAISY *leans back in her chair—a smile comes over her face as her thoughts evidently stray to something pleasant.*)

DAISY. (*Softly.*) Oh, Roy.

ROY. Yeah.

DAISY. Have you still got that engagement ring you had in your pocket the other day?

ROY. (*Slightly puzzled.*) Sure.

MAY. *Daisy.* What on earth are you—

DAISY. I just want to see it, that's all. You don't mind, do you darling?

MAY. I? Why should I?

DAISY. You've been carrying this around some time, haven't you?

ROY. (*With a look at* MAY.) Yeah. I bought it just before you and May opened up this dive.

MAY. Dive????

ROY. Sorry. You know what I mean.

DAISY. (*As* ROY *gives her ring.*) Thanks. Mind if I try it on? (*He shakes his head.* DAISY *slips it on—then holds her hand out to admire it.*) Oh, it's beautiful!

ROY. Oh, it's a cheap one—turning green with the spring. But I couldn't afford a—

DAISY. That's all right—it takes your mind right off the rent—and the grocery bills—and the *gas company!* (*She stretches out her hand to* MAY.) Look, May—isn't it beautiful?

MAY. Hm, some people like them—and some people don't. (*She jerks her chair around and sits with her back to* ROY *and* DAISY.)

DAISY. (*Purring.*) Oh, it's beautiful! (*Suddenly she gets to her feet with decision.*) Yep—I'm going to do it! Here, Roy. (*Handing him ring.*) I'm going to do it right this minute! We've got pen and ink. Where are they, May?

MAY. (*Rising.*) In the front room. But surely, Daisy, you're not going to be such a fool as to—

DAISY. Yes, I am! I'm going to write him this very minute!

ROY. (*Puzzled.*) What's that you're going to do?

DAISY. Hm. You'd be surprised. (*Going to door left, she turns.*) You know my size deceives people—it even deceives myself. I look husky—but at heart I believe I'm just a little clinging vine. (*She goes out, closing door after her.*)

ROY. What's she talking about?

MAY. I—I haven't the remotest idea.

ROY. Er—say, May—er—wouldn't *you* like to try on this—this—(*He holds out ring.*)

MAY. No—much obliged.

ROY. (*Going to her.*) Why, May? Why won't you marry me?

MAY. Oh, do we have to go into all that again?

ROY. (*Indicating room.*) Is it just on account of this joint?

MAY. (*Stamping her foot.*) *Don't call this place a* "joint"! Father called this place a "joint" and—and—

ROY. Well, what about him?

MAY. I don't know what about him *now*—but when I left him he was headed for a bad case of apoplexy.

ROY. But, May dear—you can't succeed here—it's a flop.

MAY. You say that because you want it to be a flop.

ROY. No, I don't. I—

MAY. Yes, you do, Roy—I *know*. You think when I shut up the "Brass Kettle" I'll go galloping right into your arms. Well, let me tell you something. I'm not going to do anything of the kind.

ROY. What do you mean?

MAY. Just what I say. Even if this place is a "flop" and I have to close it up, I'll never marry you, Roy.

ROY. May, don't say—

MAY. I mean it. *Never.*

ROY. (*Looks at her—and sees she means it. There is a pause—then.*) So that's that, eh? (*He picks up his hat.*)

MAY. Oh, you needn't rush off, you know.

ROY. (*A little sullenly.*) Hm. Might as well.

MAY. You're a bad loser, Roy!

ROY. (*Turning around suddenly.*) What?

MAY. You're a bad loser—a bad sport. That's why I'd never marry you!

ROY. (*Furiously—throwing his hat on table.*) You can't say that to me!

MAY. (*Right in his face.*) Well, I *do* say it!

ROY. All right—say it! (*A second's pause—while they glare at each other.*) But the place *is* a "joint"—and it *is* a "flop"! You've had it open three *months* and nobody's walked in the door—and if you keep open three *years* I bet nobody'll walk in!

(*A terrific jingling of the little bell. Almost immediately after the door left bursts open and* DAISY *precipitates herself into the room, slamming the door after her.*)

DAISY. (*In a mild state of panic.*) Customers!

MAY. W—what?

DAISY. *Customers!*

MAY. Y—y—you don't m-m-mean it!

DAISY. But it's true, I tell you—it's true!

MAY. (*Clutching her.*) Oh, Daisy! How did it happen?

DAISY. I don't know—I don't know—I was just sitting there—and the door just opened—and they just *walked in!*

MAY. (*Breathlessly.*) I—I can't believe it! What did you do?

DAISY. I just knocked over the bottle of ink and ran. Look at me. (*She extends her ink-stained hands.*)

MAY. (*She has caught* DAISY's *panic.*) Oh, customers—*customers!* Daisy, what on earth will we do about them?

DAISY. I don't know—I don't know!

ROY. (*With sarcasm—as he sits down.*) One thing you might do is to go wait on them.

MAY. Of course—I never thought of that, Daisy—you go right in and take the order.

DAISY. Oh, May—I don't know how to take an order.

MAY. Yes, you do! You've practised it—you've practised it for *weeks!*

DAISY. I know but—practice is one thing—to actually do it's different. Besides look at me! (*Again she extends her hands.*)

MAY. Oh, then I'll do it! But where's my smock—I had a smock here! Daisy, where's my smock?

DAISY. Oh, I sent it to the laundry.

MAY. Laundry. Oh, Daisy, what for? I'd only worn it once.

DAISY. Well, I can't help it, May. The laundry man kept coming around here—and asking for things. I never have anything to give him because we've never *used* anything. So I gave him the smock.

MAY. Oh, Daisy. Then give me yours.

DAISY. What? wait'll I wash my hands.

MAY. No—no—never mind your hands—give me your smock—quick!

(DAISY *extends her hands and leans over.* MAY *grabs the smock and pulls it over* DAISY'S *head. At this moment the door left is thrown open and* MRS. CARSTAIRS *enters.*)

MRS. CARSTAIRS. Well, is it possible to get a little service around here? (MRS. CARSTAIRS *is a tall woman of about forty with a deep booming voice and an imperial manner that admits of no nonsense.*)

MAY. (*Humbly.*) Why, yes, ma'am, I—I was just—er—

MRS. CARSTAIRS. Well, we can't wait all day, you know. There was a young woman in there when we first walked in but all she did was look at us and run. (*She returns to front room.*)

MAY. Daisy—it's *Mrs. Carstairs!*

DAISY. (*Struggling to get out of the smock.*) What?

MAY. It's Mrs. Carstairs!

DAISY. Well, I can't help it. Get me out of here—I'm suffocating. (MAY *gives it a yank.*)

MAY. (*Excitedly—as she puts on smock.*) Oh, Daisy—our fortune's made! Hurry, Daisy, light the stove and put some water in the kettle.

DAISY. (*Starting for screen.*) All right.

MAY. Where Mrs. Carstairs goes everybody goes. Daisy—Daisy!

DAISY. (*Running back.*) Yes.

MAY. Get out some cups and saucers. (DAISY *starts for cupboard left.*) I wonder how she happened to come in here. Oh, Daisy, *Daisy.* (DAISY *comes trotting back.*) There's butter in the ice-box. (DAISY *starts again—this time for refrigerator down right.*) And *Daisy*—cut some bread.

DAISY. (*Wearily.*) All right. (*She is now running around in circles.*)

MAY. No, no—not there, it's over there, and Daisy—*Daisy*—open up the jar of marmalade. No—no it's in the ice-box. (MAY *goes to door left.*) I knew we'd get our chance—I knew it! Daisy—*Daisy*—light the oven for toast—pour some lemon in the little silver pitcher and slice some milk! (*She goes inside.*)

DAISY. (*Running behind screen.*) Well, I don't know *what* to do!

(*There is a terrific clatter behind screen.*)

ROY. (*He's still on his grouch.*) What's the matter? Break something?

DAISY. I don't know whether I did or not. The idea of those people walking in on us this way.

ROY. You didn't expect them to send you a written notice in advance, did you?

DAISY. I didn't expect them to come in at all. Oh, I don't know whether I turned on the oven or not. You can't tell with this stove.

ROY. That's easy. Just strike a match. If we all get blown up—that means you turned it on.

DAISY. Everything was so nice and quiet here—and they had to come in.

ROY. Don't worry—they probably won't come back.

DAISY. (*Coming from behind screen.*) I hope they don't. I wish they hadn't come at all.

ROY. Hm.

DAISY. Well, I can't help it. I can't *stand* to do things in a hurry. I don't know what it is—my nerves—or my heart—or something, but— (*Suddenly.*) Oh, *heavens!!*

ROY. What's the matter now?

DAISY. (*Coming back.*) Those people in there—I bet they'll want tea!

ROY. Well, this is a tea-room, isn't it?

DAISY. I know but—there *isn't* any tea!

ROY. (*Uninterested.*) Funny, I thought the one thing they'd have in a tea-room would be tea.

DAISY. But I used the last of it this afternoon! And the cream, too —and there's no marmalade. Oh, what'll I do (*She goes to door left and calls.*) May—*May!* Come here quick!

ROY. Oh, I wouldn't get excited. Maybe they'll be satisfied with just a glass of water and a toothpick.

DAISY. Serve them right. There were lots of other places they could go without disturbing us.

MAY. (*Coming in.*) What in the world's the matter, Daisy? I was just taking their order and—

DAISY. Wait! We haven't got any *tea!*

MAY. What? Oh, Daisy—we've got to have tea!

DAISY. But there *isn't* any. And there's no cream—and no marmalade —and no bread.

MAY. You mean you ate it all up!

DAISY. Well, who'd ever have thought we'd have a customer?

MAY. (*Kicking the door shut.*) Sh—h! Don't talk that way—they'll think we never had one before.

DAISY. Well, we haven't.

MAY. Oh, Daisy, this is awful—here, we've got our chance—our big chance—and—

DAISY. Tell 'em to come back tomorrow.

MAY. You can't do that, Daisy—

DAISY. We could give 'em lemonade—if we had any lemons.

MAY. Wait—wait! Let me think.

DAISY. I wish I could.

MAY. (*Suddenly.*) Oh, telephone—telephone!

DAISY. Telephone?

MAY. Yes, the grocer's! Mr. Sampson's just around the corner—tell him what you want—and make him send his little boy Willie over the back way!

DAISY. What's the number? 8621?

MAY. No, 8261.

DAISY. No, it's not—it's—

MAY. Yes it is, Daisy. I *know* it's—

MRS. CARSTAIRS. (*Coming in.*) Young woman, are you going to finish taking our order or not?

MAY. (*Meekly.*) Yes, ma'am.

MRS. CARSTAIRS. Then you'd better hurry up and do so. We want some ice-water right away. (*She returns to front room.*)

MAY. Yes, ma'am. (*To* DAISY.) Ice-water, Daisy—ice-water, quick.

DAISY. (*Crossing.*) Oh, I've got to *telephone!*

MAY. Then, telephone, Daisy—but be sure and get everything—and a lot of it—get everything we haven't got. (*She goes out door left.*)

DAISY. (*At 'phone.*) We haven't got *anything!* (*Into 'phone.*) Hello, 8261. Yes.

ROY. Hm. If you haven't got *anything* I should think you'd save time by sending the customers right around to Mr. Sampson's.

DAISY. You keep quiet. I've got enough on my mind without— (*Into 'phone.*) Hello. Is this Sampson's Grocery?— Well this is the Brass Kettle speaking— I say this is the Brass Kettle speaking and—

ROY. Kettles don't speak—they sing.

DAISY. (*Into 'phone.*) Oh, Mr. Sampson, quick—I want some tea— Oh, I want a lot of tea—what? Oh yes, at least two pounds— What? All right make it three pounds.

ROY. What are you going to do—drown somebody?

DAISY. Keep quiet! (*Into 'phone.*) And I want some cream—yes, a lot of cream and some—some butter—

ROY. (*Mocking her.*) Oh, a lot of butter!

DAISY. And some bread, Mr. Sampson—and some marmalade—and some—some lemons—and some sugar—and some cinnamon —and some—some—

ROY. Spinach?

DAISY. *No!* And oh, Mr. Sampson—your little boy, Willie—

ROY. Tch! Tch! You going to eat little Willie?

DAISY. Will you send him over the back way with it, *at once?* Thank you! (*She hangs up.*)

ROY. Think Willie'll get here with it before morning?

DAISY. I don't care whether he does or not. Listen, Roy—(*She goes over to him.*) It's awful—those people coming here today.

ROY. What do you mean?

DAISY. I was just getting ready to talk May into giving up the place. Now if she thinks she can make a go of it, she'll want to keep it open another three months.

ROY. Well, get out.

DAISY. I can't ditch May like that. Making a success of this thing means an awful lot to May.

ROY. (*Bitterly.*) Yeah—it seems to mean more to her than I do.

DAISY. Oh, no, it doesn't but—well, you see their coming here makes it bad for you, too.

ROY. I don't see how I figure in it—one way or the other.

DAISY. Yes, you do. Don't you see? If it goes under—if we get out—May'll marry you.

ROY. No, she won't. I've got my walking papers.

DAISY. What are you talking about?

ROY. Yep—this afternoon. She said I was a "bad loser"—a "bad sport."

DAISY. Oh, she didn't mean that.

ROY. Yes, she did. I'll show her whether I'm a "bad sport" or not.

DAISY. Oh, Roy, don't be silly. It's just that she cares so much about making a go of this.

ROY. Well, let her make a go of it—if she can.

DAISY. If she can, yes—but she can't—so we might as well give up now.

ROY. What are you driving at, Daisy—you mean you want this place to fail?

DAISY. Yes, I'm sick of it. I want it to fail—and I want it to fail right now. It would be the best thing in the world for all of us if something would happen—if Willie got here too late—or those people in there got sore about something and walked out. May'd realize then that we haven't a chance—and she'd give up—right now.

ROY. (*Softly.*) Be—be awfully tough on her, wouldn't it?

DAISY. Of course it would but—well, she'd get over it in a few weeks —and forget about it. Then she'd marry you—and— See what I mean?

ROY. I see what you mean, but—

MAY. (*Coming in excitedly.*) Daisy—*Daisy*—where on earth is the ice-water?

DAISY. The what?

MAY. The *ice-water*. Mrs. Carstairs is in an absolute rage.

DAISY. Well, I hope she chokes. (*She sits down.*)

MAY. What? What's the matter with you? Oh, Daisy, you're not going to lay down on the job this way, are you?

DAISY. I'm not laying down, May—but I don't see why we have to work ourselves to death just because Mrs. Carstairs wants a cup of tea.

MAY. But it isn't just Mrs. Carstairs, Daisy—it's Mrs. Alexander and Mrs. St. John—the very people we wanted.

DAISY. Well, they ought to've come sooner. They ought to've come three months ago when I was—was young and enthusiastic.

MAY. But it's not too late, Daisy—it's never too late. Oh, Daisy, please don't act like this. We—we're partners, you know, and I can't do it all by myself. If, if you don't help me, why, I—I—

DAISY. (*Rising reluctantly.*) All right—all right—what do you want me to do?

MAY. Crack the ice. That's a good girl, Daisy. Did you light the stove?

DAISY. Yes, but there's nothing to cook on it.

MAY. Didn't you telephone? Isn't Willie coming?

DAISY. (*Finding the ice-pick.*) I expect Willie's around the corner in a crap game.

MAY. (*Behind screen.*) Oh, Daisy, don't let *down* so easy! Keep up your spirits—keep up your—

DAISY. (*Who has opened refrigerator.*) There's no ice.

MAY. (*Coming down to her.*) Oh, Daisy, what are you talking about? Didn't the ice-man come this afternoon while I was out?

DAISY. No, that is unless he came while I was asleep.

MAY. Asleep? Oh, Daisy! I leave you for an hour to take care of the place—you go to sleep and miss the ice-man and when you *do* wake up you eat up all the food!

DAISY. (*Throwing down ice-pick.*) You stop bawling me out, May—I won't have it!

MAY. Oh, Daisy, darling. I'm sorry. I didn't mean to bawl you out. There, there—you know we've always got along beautifully together.

DAISY. We did till a lot of—lot of outsiders—absolute *strangers*—walk in—and then the whole place goes upside down.

MAY. But that's business, Daisy, business.

DAISY. Well, I don't think I'm really cut out for business. I think I'm just a—just a "home-body" gone wrong!

MAY. Oh, don't say that, Daisy. Go on, like a good girl, fill some glasses—quick. If the water's a little warm, maybe they won't notice it. *Willie!* (*She gives* DAISY *a slight shove toward screen.*)

WILLIE. (*Coming in door right.*) *Sampson's Grocery!* (WILLIE *is sixteen—coatless and hatless—and carries a large package.*)

MAY. Willie, you darling! You angel! (*She runs towards him to take package.*)

WILLIE. (*Holding on to it.*) Whoa, ma'am, whoa. Papa says it's C. O. D. three dollars and eighty-seven cents!

MAY. Oh—er—just charge it.

WILLIE. No, ma'am, papa says it's C. O. D. three dollars and eighty-seven cents.

MAY. But, I—er—Willie, I don't believe I have three dollars and eighty-seven cents. Er—have you, Daisy?

DAISY. I haven't had it in years. (*She sets a tray of glasses on table.*)

MAY. You see, Willie, we—er—haven't it right now—so if you'll just leave the package we—

WILLIE. (*Like a refrain.*) Papa says it's C. O. D. three dollars and eighty-seven cents!

MAY. But wait, Willie—wait! I—I haven't—er— (*Timidly.*) Er—Roy—you haven't—er—

DAISY. (*Quickly.*) Roy hasn't any money!

MAY. W—what.

DAISY. I—er—just asked him—a little while ago. (*She shoots* ROY *a quick look.* ROY *looks away.*)

MAY. Oh.

DAISY. (*Going to her.*) So you see, May—it's no use. Let him take it back—your father and mine'll pay all the bills—and we'll just go in there and tell those women that the place is closed. What do you say, old dear?

MAY. (*Pathetically.*) But this is—this is awful. Here's our chance—our big chance and—oh, Willie, couldn't you help us, please? Couldn't you leave the package and—

WILLIE. Papa says it's C. O. D. three dollars and—

ROY. (*Suddenly rising.*) Oh, shut up! (*He walks over to* WILLIE.) Here.

DAISY. What are you going to do?

ROY. I'm going to pay him three dollars and eighty-seven cents.

DAISY. You—you can't do that.

ROY. Can't I? Here you are, Willie. Four dollars. Keep the change. Now beat it!

(WILLIE *goes out. A slight pause.*)

MAY. Oh, thank you, Roy.

DAISY. (*Going to* ROY.) I don't see why you have to butt in on our affairs like this!

MAY. Wait, Daisy—he's helping us.

DAISY. Well, he's not helping himself any.

(*The door left is opened and* MRS. CARSTAIRS *marches in—like a battleship under full steam.*)

MRS. CARSTAIRS. (*Angrily.*) Where's the proprietor of this place?

MAY. Ma'am.

MRS. CARSTAIRS. I want to know what's the matter with the service? If it takes fifteen minutes to get a glass of ice-water it'll probably take two or three days to get a cup of tea. I'm about ready to go. Where's the proprietor?

ROY. (*Going to her.*) I'm the proprietor. What can I do for you?

MRS. CARSTAIRS. (*In surprise.*) You?

ROY. Yes. What can I do for you? (*He smiles at her.*)

MRS. CARSTAIRS. (*Somewhat taken aback.*) Hm. I thought it was one of those young women there.

ROY. No, Mrs. Carstairs. I'm the proprietor. They're just—just servants.

DAISY. (*Flabbergasted.*) Well, I like that!

ROY. (*Turning on her.*) Keep quiet—you! (*Back to* MRS. CARSTAIRS *with his most engaging manner.*) You were saying, Mrs. Carstairs?

MRS. CARSTAIRS. Hm. You know I never heard of a man running a tea-room before.

ROY. Well, to tell the truth I really never expected to run one myself.

MRS. CARSTAIRS. But after all, why not? Women certainly don't know how to run them.

ROY. (*With meaning.*) They certainly do not.

(MAY *and* DAISY *are looking on in open-eyed wonder.*)

MRS. CARSTAIRS. You know, Mr.—er—

ROY. Williams.

MRS. CARSTAIRS. Thank you. You know, Mr. Williams, there's something so authoritative about a man's personality—even in his voice. For instance just then the way you spoke to the maid there.

DAISY. The *what?*

(MAY *claps her hand over* DAISY'S *mouth.*)

MRS. CARSTAIRS. Don't misunderstand me, Mr. Williams. I'm a woman, of course, and—

ROY. (*Smiling at her.*) Oh, but you're different, Mrs. Carstairs. You're one woman in a million.

MRS. CARSTAIRS. (*Beaming modestly.*) Oh, I—er—I wouldn't say that, Mr. Williams. I—er—

ROY. But it's true. Oh, I read of your activities—president of all the clubs—charitable organizations—how efficient you are—

MRS. CARSTAIRS. Why—I—er—it's very kind of you to say that. Very kind, indeed. (*A slight pause.*) I must run along back to my friends. (*She goes toward door left.*)

ROY. (*Following her.*) But you had some complaint to make, Mrs. Carstairs, something that—

MRS. CARSTAIRS. Oh, no. No, nothing at all, really. Awfully nice place you have here, Mr. Williams, awfully nice. (*She passes inside.*)

ROY. Yes, but I have a lot of trouble with the help. (*He closes door after her.*)

MAY. Oh, Roy.

4TH BRAKE

DAISY. (*Furiously.*) Well, I like that! (*She crosses to him.*) What do you think you are—and what do you think you're doing?

MAY. Wait, Daisy!

ROY. I'm a "bad loser"—and a "bad sport"—and I'm trying to help this—this dump.

MAY. (*Meekly.*) Oh, don't call it a "dump."

DAISY. Well, you *can't* help it. It's too late—and if you knew what side your bread was buttered on you'd take my advice and wouldn't try!

ALEC. (*A man in overalls comes in door right and announces loudly.*) *Gas Company!*

ROY. What's that?

ALEC. Gas Company.

DAISY. Well, come right in—I'm delighted to see you.

ROY. (*Going over.*) What do you mean—"Gas Company"? Are you from the Gas Company?

ALEC. Sure am, buddy. Got a little bill for you—(*He grins.*) Just thirty-two dollars.

MAY. Oh.

ROY. Thirty-two dollars????

DAISY. There now, Mr. Smarty! I told you to let things alone. Ha! Trying to prove you're a "good sport." You may have three eighty-seven for the grocer but I know you haven't got—

ROY. Wait a minute. Wait a minute. (*To* ALEC.) I—I haven't got any thirty-two dollars.

ALEC. Well, that's just too bad, buddy—because if you ain't got it, I'll have to shut it off.

MAY. (*Sinking in chair.*) And the toast isn't cooked and the water hasn't boiled.

ROY. Listen friend—be reasonable. People don't walk around the town with thirty-two dollars in their pocket. Come back—come back tomorrow, can't you?

ALEC. Nope—can't do it, Mister. I got a long list of *other* places I got to go to tomorrow.

MAY. But, please, sir we have customers—the only ones we ever had—and if you turn off the gas now—

ROY. Wait! (*To* ALEC.) Come outside with me! (*To* DAISY *and* MAY.) And you two—Go ahead and get things ready! Don't stand there like dummies!! Get a wiggle on! (*He pushes* ALEC *out and follows.*)

MAY. (*Excitedly—as she hurriedly seizes the package of groceries and opens it.*) Come on, Daisy. Get a wiggle on! Didn't you hear what he said?

DAISY. (*Not budging.*) Hm. Yes, I heard.

MAY. Then why don't you—

DAISY. Because it's no use. Roy hasn't got any thirty-two dollars—and you know it.

MAY. But—but Roy'll talk to the man.

DAISY. You can't fool me. A Gas Company has *no soul!*

MAY. (*Pleading.*) But Roy'll fix it—someway—somehow— (*Going to her.*) Oh, Daisy—please help me.

DAISY. Oh, what's the use, May?

MAY. (*Solemnly.*) Daisy, listen! If you'll get busy—and help serve those people in there—so that they'll walk out of here happy and satisfied I—I—

DAISY. Well?

MAY. I'll shut up the tea-room tomorrow.

DAISY. You—you mean that?

MAY. We'll shut it up—and never even think of "The Brass Kettle" again.

DAISY. (*Delirious with joy.*) Oh, May—you *darling!* (*She throws her arms around her. Then—*) But May,—why wouldn't you do it before?

MAY. Because if we'd shut it up before it would have been a failure. Now when we do it—it'll be a success. I wanted to *succeed*—make a *go of it!* Don't you understand?

DAISY. You bet I do! Lord, I'm so happy—I'm so happy! What was I getting ready to do?

MAY. The water—the water!

DAISY. Oh, yes—the water—the water! (*She seizes tray of glasses and starts for door left chattering gaily.*) Gangway, everybody —gangway, please, for Mrs. Gunga Din! (*She stops at door.*) You know, May—I don't think I'll write Harry. I think I'll send him a telegram! (*She goes inside.*)

(*May turns as* ROY *appears at door right.*)

MAY. (*Anxiously.*) Is—is it all right, Roy?

ROY. All set. (*Crossing over.*) I don't imagine you'll have any more trouble. You ought to be able to make out all right now. (*He picks up hat.*)

MAY. Wait, Roy—please. (*He stops. She goes to him.*) Thank you for all you've done, Roy.

ROY. (*Without looking at her.*) Oh, that's all right.

MAY. And I—I'm sorry I said you were a—a "bad sport." (*He doesn't answer.*) Roy, we're closing up the tea-room tomorrow.

ROY. (*Turning around.*) Closing it up? When it's just getting going? Just getting on its feet?

MAY. That's why I'm closing it up.

ROY. That doesn't make sense to me.

MAY. Maybe it doesn't but—well, anyway, Daisy's going to get married and I thought maybe that I—that I—

ROY. Well?

MAY. (*Looking at him.*) Well, that I—that you—oh, don't you understand?

ROY. (*Catching on.*) You mean—?

MAY. (*Nodding.*) Uh—huh. The ring, dear—couldn't I have the ring now?

ROY. Gosh, I—I'm afraid you can't—not now.

MAY. (*In alarm.*) Why? Why?

ROY. Well, you see, I had to give it to the gas man.

MAY. Oh, Roy! (*She throws her arms around him and kisses him as*

THE CURTAIN FALLS

# Thirteen

## LISTS☆☆☆

NOTE: It is possible to use for classroom work scenes from plays that would not be suitable for public production in a school. Doing so affords a greater variety in acting material and allows for much greater growth in the actor than would otherwise be possible. Good taste will always suggest modifications in language and situations that will make material suitable for student use. In some cases it may be necessary to contrive an ending which will give the scene a dramatic finish.

### Key to Abbreviations

B — beginning of scene    E — end of scene
Type: S — serious; C — comedy; Fa — fantasy; My — Mystery
W — women; M — men; x — extra characters with no or few lines
Dr — dramatized by; Ad — adapted by
App — royalty upon application

### Play Publishers

Samuel French (Fr.) 25 West 45 Street, New York 36, New York
7623 Sunset Boulevard, Hollywood 46, California
Baker's Plays (B.) 100 Summer Street, Boston 10, Massachusetts
Dramatists Play Service (D.P.S.) 14 East 38 Street, New York 16, New York
Longmans, Green and Company (L.G) 119 West 40 Street, New York 18, New York
Row, Peterson and Company (R.P.) 1911 Ridge Avenue, Evanston, Illinois
104 So. Lexington Ave., White Plains, New York

Dramatic Publishing Company (D.P.C.) 179 North Michigan Avenue, Chicago 1, Illinois
Drama Book Shop 51 West 52 Street, New York 19, New York (play anthologies and other theatre books)

## ☆☆☆SCENES FOR MEN AND WOMEN

| | TYPE | M | W |
|---|---|---|---|
| JOAN OF LORRAINE—Maxwell Anderson D.P.S. | S | 2 | 1 |

SCENE 1 (JOAN, JEAN, PIERRE)
B - JEAN. I give up.
E - JOAN. . . . a revelation from St. Margaret.

| | | | |
|---|---|---|---|
| ACT I, INTERLUDE IV (MASTERS, MARY, 4xM, 1xW) entire scene | S | 1 | 1 |

| | | | |
|---|---|---|---|
| SEPARATE TABLES—Terence Rattigan Fr. | S | 1 | 1 |

ACT I, SCENE 1 (JOHN, ANNE, 1xW)
B - JOHN. (*At length.*) Is this coincidence?
E - JOHN. Most, I suppose. Not all, though. Well, good night.

| | | | |
|---|---|---|---|
| STAGE DOOR—Edna Ferber and George S. Kaufman D.P.S. | C | 1 | 1 |

ACT I, SCENE 1 (KEITH, TERRY)
B - KEITH. Where's Jean Maitland?
E - KEITH. Sure . . . Onions . . . Say, what's your name, anyway?

| | | | |
|---|---|---|---|
| FIRST LADY—Katharine Dayton and George S. Kaufman D.P.S. | C | 1 | 1 |

ACT II, SCENE 1 (IRENE, HIBBARD)
B - IRENE. I never saw a room with so many books in it and nothing to read!
E - HIBBARD. (*Aghast.*) Really, my dear!
or
IRENE. I'm getting out of here.

| | | | |
|---|---|---|---|
| OF MICE AND MEN—John Steinbeck D.P.S. | S | 1 | 1 |

ACT III, SCENE 1 (LENNIE, CURLEY'S WIFE)

TYPE M W

B - CURLEY'S WIFE. What—what you doin' here?
E - LENNIE. . . . in the brush till he comes . . . that's what he said.

THE LITTLE FOXES—Lillian Hellman D.P.S. S 1 1
ACT III (REGINA, HORACE)
B - REGINA. We had agreed that you were to stay in your part of this house.
E - REGINA. He's had an attack. Come up here.

THE ROYAL FAMILY—George S. Kaufman and Edna Ferber Fr. S 1 1
ACT I (PERRY, GWEN)
B - PERRY. Come on get your bonnet on.
E - PERRY. Oh! . . . Yes . . . Well, I've got to get started, of course, if I'm going to get there. Goodbye.

PYGMALION—G. Bernard Shaw Fr. C 1 1
ACT V (HIGGINS, ELIZA)
B - HIGGINS. Well, Eliza, you've had a bit of your own . . .
E - HIGGINS. . . . everything you want me to.

ACT V (HIGGINS, ELIZA) C 1 1
B - HIGGINS. In short you want me to be as infatuated about you as Freddy?
E - ELIZA. I could just kick myself.

ACT V Final scene between Higgins and Eliza C 1 1

THE ADMIRABLE CRICHTON—J. M. Barrie Fr. C 1 1
ACT IV (LADY MARY, LORD BROCKELHURST)
B - LADY MARY. I am ready, George.
E - LADY MARY. I am so glad she was only a lady's maid.

THE MAN WHO CAME TO DINNER—George S. Kaufman and Moss Hart D.P.S. C 1 1
ACT I, SCENE 1 (SHERIDAN, MAGGIE)
B - MAGGIE. Hello there . . . Good evening, Sherry.
E - MAGGIE. That's my message to you, Big Lord Fauntleroy. (*And she is up the stairs.*)

| | TYPE | M | W |
|---|---|---|---|
| THE DEVIL'S DISCIPLE—Bernard Shaw Fr. | S | 1 | 1 |

ACT III (JUDITH, RICHARD, 1xM)
B - SERGEANT. You can have a quiet word with him here.
E - (*They go out, she sobbing convulsively.*)

| | | | |
|---|---|---|---|
| ELIZABETH THE QUEEN—Maxwell Anderson Fr. | S | 1 | 1 |

ACT II, SCENE 3 (ELIZABETH, ESSEX)
B - ELIZABETH. We are equal. I have made you so.
E - ELIZABETH. I shall take care. (End of scene)

| | | | |
|---|---|---|---|
| ACT III (ELIZABETH, ESSEX) | S | 1 | 1 |

B - ESSEX. You sent for me? Or so they said.
E - ELIZABETH. Take my kingdom. It is yours! (ESSEX, *as if not hearing, bows and goes on . . .*)

| | | | |
|---|---|---|---|
| THE GLASS MENAGERIE—Tennessee Williams D.P.S. | S | 1 | 1 |

SCENE 7 (LAURA, JIM)
B - JIM. Hello, there, Laura.
E - JIM. They're common as—weeds, but—you—well, you're—*Blue Roses!*

| | | | |
|---|---|---|---|
| AH, WILDERNESS—Eugene O'Neill Fr. | S | 1 | 1 |

ACT III, SCENE 2 (RICHARD, MURIEL)
B - RICHARD. Oh, hello. Is it nine already?
E - MURIEL. That'll be wonderful, won't it?

| | | | |
|---|---|---|---|
| BERKELEY SQUARE—John L. Balderston Fr. | S | 1 | 1 |

ACT III, SCENE 1 (PETER, HELEN)
B - PETER. (*Turns.*) And I was in love with the past.
E - HELEN. This little thing . . . *This* was our parting.

| | | | |
|---|---|---|---|
| I REMEMBER MAMA—John Van Druten D.P.S. | C | 1 | 1 |

ACT II (TRINA, PETER)
B - TRINA. Who's the most beautiful Norwegian baby in San Francisco?
E - TRINA. (*Overcome*). Yes, Peter. (*They hold hands.*)

| | TYPE | M | W |
|---|---|---|---|
| KISS AND TELL—F. Hugh Herbert D.P.S. | C | 1 | 1 |

ACT I, SCENE 1 (DEXTER, CORLISS)
B - DEXTER. What was Mildred snooping around for?
E - CORLISS. Okay.

| | TYPE | M | W |
|---|---|---|---|
| THE BARRETTS OF WIMPOLE STREET—Rudolph Besier D.P.S. | C | 1 | 2 |

ACT I, SCENE 2 (BELLA, BEVAN, ELIZABETH)
B - BELLA. Cousin Elizabeth.
E - ELIZABETH. Goodbye.

| | TYPE | M | W |
|---|---|---|---|
| THE MATCHMAKER—Thornton Wilder Fr. | C | 1 | 2 |

ACT I (MRS. LEVI, ERMENGARDE, AMBROSE)
B - (MRS. LEVI *enters up* RIGHT. *She stands listening.*)
E - MRS. LEVI. Mr. Vandergelder and I will be dancing at your wedding very, very soon.

| | TYPE | M | W |
|---|---|---|---|
| LIFE WITH FATHER—Howard Lindsay and Russell Crouse D.P.S. | C | 1 | 1 |

ACT III, SCENE 1 (VINNIE, FATHER)
B - VINNIE. I took a long walk and dropped in . . .
E - FATHER. Oh, God! (*Stamps out.*)

ACT I, SCENE 2 (VINNIE, FATHER)

| | TYPE | M | W |
|---|---|---|---|
| B - FATHER. Vinnie, I wish to speak to you before you go upstairs. | C | 1 | 1 |

E - FATHER. I am not a guide to Chinatown and the Bowery.

| | TYPE | M | W |
|---|---|---|---|
| THE REMARKABLE MR. PENNYPACKER—Liam O'Brien Fr. | C | 1 | 1 |

ACT I, SCENE 1 (KATE, WILBUR)
B - WILBUR. What does Laurie mean . . . "new woman"?
E - WILBUR. I love you so and I love—my feet.

| | TYPE | M | W |
|---|---|---|---|
| SABRINA FAIR—Samuel Taylor D.P.S. | C | 2 | 1 |

ACT III (DAVID, LINUS, SABRINA, 1xM, 1xW)
B - DAVID. You certainly were inquisitive.
E - end of act

| | TYPE | M | W |
|---|---|---|---|
| ARSENIC AND OLD LACE—Joseph Kesselring D.P.S. | C | 1 | 2 |

ACT I (MORTIMER, ABBY, MARTHA)
B - MORTIMER. Listen darlings, I'm frightfully sorry but I've got some shocking news for you.
E - MORTIMER. I couldn't eat a thing.

| | TYPE | M | W |
|---|---|---|---|
| MY SISTER EILEEN—Joseph Fields and Jerome Chodorov D.P.S. | C | 1 | 2 |

ACT I, SCENE 1 (RUTH, EILEEN, APPOPOLOUS)
B - APPOPOLOUS. Here you are! Come in my dear young ladies. Enter!
E - APPOPOLOUS. Good night, ladies. Sleep tight!

| | TYPE | M | W |
|---|---|---|---|
| THE RIVALS—Richard Brinsley Sheridan Fr. | C | 1 | 1 |

ACT III, SCENE 3 (MRS. MALAPROP, CAPTAIN ABSOLUTE)
B - beginning of scene
E - MRS. MALAPROP. For the present, capatain, your servant . . . elude my vigilance; yes, yes; ha! ha! ha! ha!

| | TYPE | M | W |
|---|---|---|---|
| CAVALCADE—Noel Coward Fr. | C | 1 | 1 |

PART II, SCENE 5 (EDWARD, EDITH)
B - EDITH. It's too big, the Atlantic, isn't it?
E - end of scene

| | TYPE | M | W |
|---|---|---|---|
| VICTORIA REGINA—Laurence Housman B. | S | 1 | 1 |

SCENE 9 Morning Glory (QUEEN VICTORIA, PRINCE ALBERT)
Entire scene

| | TYPE | M | W |
|---|---|---|---|
| BORN YESTERDAY—Garson Kanin D.P.S. | C | 1 | 1 |

ACT II (BILLIE, PAUL)
B - BILLIE. Hello.
E - PAUL. You know, I think I'm going to do that piece again. Plainer.

| | TYPE | M | W |
|---|---|---|---|
| ACT II (BILLIE, PAUL, BROCK) | C | 2 | 1 |

B - PAUL. Listen, who said this? "The proper study of Mankind is Man."
E - BROCK. I'll buy it for you.

| | TYPE | M | W |
|---|---|---|---|
| JENNY KISSED ME—Jean Kerr D.P.S. | C | 1 | 1 |

ACT II, SCENE 1 (FATHER, JENNY)
B - JENNY. Did you want me, Father?
E - FATHER. . . . until I've done some more research.

| | | | |
|---|---|---|---|
| GHOSTS—Henrik Ibsen Fr. | S | 1 | 1 |

ACT III (OSWALD, MRS. ALVING)
B - OSWALD. The sun is rising—and you know all about it.
E - OSWALD. The sun—the sun.

## ☆☆☆ SCENES FOR WOMEN

| | TYPE | W |
|---|---|---|
| THE LITTLE FOXES—Lillian Hellman D.P.S. | S | 2 |

ACT III (REGINA, ALEXANDRA)
B - REGINA. What do you want to talk to me about, Alexandra?
E - ALEXANDRA. Are you afraid, Mother?

| | | |
|---|---|---|
| OUR HEARTS WERE YOUNG AND GAY—Cornelia Otis Skinner and Emily Kimbrough D.P.C. | C | 2 |

ACT II, SCENE 1 (EMILY, CORNELIA)
B - EMILY. Gee, I bet if this boat sank, there'd be lots of flotsam and jetsam!
E - CORNELIA. (*Climbing to the top bunk.*) If you're going to be seasick, I'm going to sleep up!

| | | |
|---|---|---|
| TIME REMEMBERED—Jean Anouilh Fr. | C | 2 |

ACT I, SCENE 2 (DUCHESS, AMANDA)
B - DUCHESS. Well, child, I suppose you think I'm a mad old woman . . .
E - DUCHESS. (*Embracing her.*) Just say, "Excuse me, can you tell me the way to the sea?"

| | | |
|---|---|---|
| THE RELUCTANT DEBUTANTE—William Douglas Home Fr. | C | 2 |

ACT I, SCENE 1 (SHEILA, JANE)
B - SHEILA. (*On telephone.*) Hullo? Mabel? Darling, yes, it is.
E - SHEILA. (*At telephone.*) Mabel darling, keep it till tonight. Good-bye, my darling.

| | TYPE | W |
|---|---|---|
| WUTHERING HEIGHTS—Randolph Carter Fr. | S | 2 |

ACT II (ISABEL, CATHERINE)
B - ISABEL. Catherine, will you please shut that door?
E - ISABEL. Don't call me a girl, I'm a woman and I won't have you treat me as if . . .

| | | |
|---|---|---|
| BLITHE SPIRIT—Noel Coward Fr. | C | 2 |

ACT II, SCENE 2 (RUTH, MADAME ARCATI)
B - MADAME ARCATI. My dear Mrs. Condomine, I came directly I got your message.
E - RUTH. Damn—damn—damn!

| | | |
|---|---|---|
| ANASTASIA—Guy Bolton Fr. | S | 2 |

ACT II (EMPRESS, ANNA)
B - EMPRESS. Yes, I can see why the others have believed.
E - EMPRESS. . . . if it should not be you—don't ever tell me . . .

| | | |
|---|---|---|
| THE MATCHMAKER—Thornton Wilder Fr. | C | 2 |

ACT II (MRS. MOLLOY, MINNIE)
B - beginning of scene
E - MRS. MOLLOY. (*Running to workroom.*) Hurry, up, Minnie. Be quick, now.

| | | |
|---|---|---|
| OUR TOWN—Thornton Wilder Fr. | S | 2 |

ACT I (MRS. GIBBS, MRS. WEBB)
B - MRS. GIBBS. Here, chick, chick, chick.
E - MRS. GIBBS. . . . where they don't talk and think in English and don't even want to.

| | | |
|---|---|---|
| THE CHILDREN'S HOUR—Lillian Hellman D.P.S. | S | 2 |

ACT II, SCENE 2 (MARY, ROSALIE)
B - MARY. Whaoooooo. Whooooooooo. You're a goose.
E - MARY. Don't forget that.

| | | |
|---|---|---|
| DINNER AT EIGHT—George S. Kaufman and Edna Ferber Fr. | S | 2 |

ACT I, SCENE 1 (HATTIE, MILLICENT)
B - HATTIE. What's that? Covers for thirty again?
E - MILLICENT. I'll see what there is, and perhaps we can go to one of those . . .

TYPE W

THE GLASS MENAGERIE—Tennessee Williams D.P.S. S 2
ACT II, SCENE 7 (AMANDA, LAURA)
B - AMANDA. Why are you trembling so, Laura?
E - AMANDA. I've got to put courage in you, honey, for living.

MARY OF SCOTLAND—Maxwell Anderson Fr. S 2
ACT III (MARY, ELIZABETH)
B - MARY. I have seen but a poor likeness yet I believe this is Elizabeth.
E - ELIZABETH. You came here by your own road.

JUNIOR MISS—Jerome Chodorov and Joseph Fields D.P.S. C 2
ACT II, SCENE 1 (JUDY, FUFFY)
B - FUFFY. Merry Christmas, and here!
E - JUDY. Don't thank me, thank Kris Kringle.

LILIOM—Ferenc Molnar Fr. S 2
SCENE 1 (MARIE, JULIE)
B - MARIE. Are you sorry for him?
E - JULIE. Why—eh—he *said* we were to wait for him.

THE WOMEN—Clare Boothe D.P.S. C 2
ACT II, SCENE 2 (JANE, MAGGIE)
entire scene

TIGER AT THE GATES—Jean Giraudoux Fr. S 2
ACT I (ANDROMACHE, CASSANDRA)
B - ANDROMACHE. There's not going to be a Trojan War, Cassandra!
E - CASSANDRA. Whoever said it was not?

THE SKIN OF OUR TEETH—Thornton Wilder Fr. Fa 2
ACT III (SABINA, MRS. ANTROBUS)
B - SABINA. Puh! The terror of the world.
E - MRS. ANTROBUS. . . . and he's been dead five thousand years.

LITTLE WOMEN—John D. Ravold Fr. C 4
ACT I, SCENE 1 (JO, MEG, AMY, BETH)
B - JO. Christmas wouldn't be Christmas without any presents.
E - JO. "Roderigo, save me, save me!"

| | TYPE | W |
|---|---|---|
| GIGI—Colette (Dr-Anita Loos) Fr. | S | 2 |

ACT II, SCENE 1 (ALICIA, MME. ALVAREZ)
B - ALICIA. In the name of Heaven what's come over Gilberte?
E - ALICIA. But that's the way things go, in this life.

| | | |
|---|---|---|
| THE MADWOMAN OF CHAILLOT—Jean Giraudoux D.P.S. | C | 3 |

ACT II (CONSTANCE, GABRIELLE, COUNTESS, 1xW)
B - CONSTANCE. Aurelia! Here we are!
E - GABRIELLE. We are saved.

| | | |
|---|---|---|
| THE IMPORTANCE OF BEING EARNEST—Oscar Wilde Fr. | C | 2 |

ACT II (GWENDOLEN, CECILY,—MERRIMAN, few lines)
B - MERRIMAN. Miss Fairfax.
E - CECILY. No doubt you have many other calls of a similar character to make in the neighborhood.

## ☆☆☆ SCENES FOR MEN

| | TYPE | M |
|---|---|---|
| WITNESS FOR THE PROSECUTION—Agatha Christie Fr. | My | 3 |

ACT I (MR. MAYHEW, LEONARD VOLE, SIR WILFRID ROBARTS, 1xM)
B - MAYHEW. I wonder, Mr. Vole, if you are taking this business quite seriously enough.
E - LEONARD. (*Still unable to believe it.*) Then they really do suspect me.

| | | |
|---|---|---|
| ALL MY SONS—Arthur Miller D.P.S. | S | 2 |

ACT I (KELLER, CHRIS)
B - KELLER. What's she going to say? Maybe we ought to tell her.
E - CHRIS. I know that, Dad. Just you help me stay here.

| | | |
|---|---|---|
| THE EMPEROR JONES—Eugene O'Neill D.P.S. | S | 2 |

SCENE 1 (JONES, SMITHERS)
B - JONES. Who dare whistle dat way in my palace? Who dare wake up de Emperor?
E - SMITHERS. I 'opes they nabs 'im an' gives 'im what's what!

| | TYPE | M |
|---|---|---|
| DEATH OF A SALESMAN—Arthur Miller D.P.S. | S | 2 |

ACT II (HOWARD, WILLY)
B - HOWARD. Say, aren't you supposed to be in Boston?
E - HOWARD. Pull yourself together, kid, there's people outside.

ACT II (CHARLEY, WILLY) — S 2
B - WILLY. The Supreme Court! And he didn't even mention it!
E - WILLY. Charley, you're the only friend I got. Isn't that a remarkable thing?

THE HAPPY TIME—Samuel Taylor D.P.S. — C 2
ACT II, SCENE 2 (LOUIS, ALFRED)
B - LOUIS. Eh, bien?
E - ALFRED. None! not one!

INHERIT THE WIND—Jerome Lawrence and Robert E. Lee D.P.S. — S 3
ACT II, SCENE 2 (BRADY, HOWARD, DRUMMOND, 2xM)
B - BRADY. Go on, Howard. Tell them what else Mr. Cates told . . .
E - JUDGE. The witness is excused. Next witness.

OF MICE AND MEN—John Steinbeck D.P.S. — S 2
ACT I, SCENE 1 (GEORGE, LENNIE)
B - LENNIE. George?
E - end of scene.

ESCAPE—John Galsworthy Fr. — S 2
PART II, EPISODE 4 (MATT, OLD GENTLEMAN)
B - OLD G. (*approaching from* L.) Afternoon. Cleared up too well for you, I'm afraid.
E - OLD G. Do you know, that's been rather the effect on me. Original sin, I suppose. Good-day!

THE IMPORTANCE OF BEING EARNEST—Oscar Wilde Fr. — C 2
ACT I (ALGERNON, ERNEST)
B - ALGERNON. How are you, my dear Ernest? What brings you up to town?
E - ALGERNON. It is so shallow of them.

TYPE W

THE REMARKABLE MR. PENNYPACKER—Liam O'Brien Fr. C 4
ACT II (GRAMPA, WILBUR, PA, DR. FIFIELD)
B - PA. Come in, Doctor, Wilbur. Come in . . .
E - PA. . . . we merely protest different things.

LILIOM—Ferenc Molnar Fr. Fa 2
SCENE 6 (THE MAGISTRATE, LILIOM)
B - THE MAGISTRATE. Number 16,473.
E - THE MAGISTRATE. Go back to your seat. Number 16,474.

THE CAINE MUTINY COURT-MARTIAL—Herman Wouk Fr. S 3
ACT II, SCENE 1 (BLAKELY, MARYK, GREENWALD, 1xM)
B - GREENWALD. I call the accused.
E - GREENWALD. If the court concurs, I'll pass over the medical log.

THE TEAHOUSE OF THE AUGUST MOON—John Patrick D.P.S. C 3
ACT I, SCENE 1 (SAKINI, PURDY, FISBY)
B - (*Colonel Purdy moves around to the front of his desk.*)
E - end of scene

THE WINSLOW BOY—Terence Rattigan D.P.S. S 2
ACT II (SIR ROBERT MORTON, RONNIE WINSLOW)
B - SIR ROBERT. Will you stand at the table, facing me?
E - SIR ROBERT. I accept the brief.

SUNRISE AT CAMPOBELLO—Dore Schary D.P.S. S 2
ACT III, SCENE 1 (SMITH, F.D.R., 1xM)
B - SMITH. They tell me there's a lot of McAdoo money around town.
E - SMITH. It just occurred to me you were both too surprised to be surprised.

TIGER AT THE GATES—Jean Giraudoux Fr. S 2
ACT II (HECTOR, ULYSSES)
B - HECTOR. Now we come to the real tussle, Ulysses.
E - HECTOR. My guard will escort you.

## ☆☆☆SHAKESPEAREAN SCENES

| | TYPE | M | W |
|---|---|---|---|
| THE TAMING OF THE SHREW | | | |
| Act iv, Scene 5 (Katharina, Petruchio, Hortensio, Vincentio) | C | 3 | 1 |
| THE TWO GENTLEMEN OF VERONA | | | |
| Act i, Scene 2 (Julia, Lucetta) | C | | 2 |
| Act ii, Scene 7 (Julia, Lucetta) | C | | 2 |
| Act iv, Scene 4 (Julia, Silvia) | C | | 2 |
| AS YOU LIKE IT | | | |
| Act i, Scene 2 (Touchstone, Celia, Rosalind) | C | 1 | 2 |
| Act i, Scene 3 (Celia, Rosalind, Duke Frederick) | S | 1 | 2 |
| Act iii, Scene 2 (Celia, Rosalind) | C | | 2 |
| Act iii, Scene 2 (Orlando, Rosalind) | C-S | 1 | 1 |
| Act iii, Scene 4 (Corin, Rosalind, Celia) | C | 1 | 2 |
| Act iii, Scene 5 (Phoebe, Silvius) | C | 1 | 1 |
| Act iv, Scene 1 (Rosalind, Orlando) | C-S | 1 | 1 |
| Act v, Scene 1 (Touchstone, William, Audrey) | C | 2 | 1 |
| OTHELLO | | | |
| Act iv, Scene 2 (Othello, Desdemona, Emilia) | S | 1 | 2 |
| Act iv, Scene 3 (Desdemona, Emilia) | S | | 2 |
| Act v, Scene 2 (Othello, Desdemona, Emilia) | S | 1 | 2 |
| JULIUS CAESAR | | | |
| Act ii, Scene 1 (Brutus, Portia) | S | 1 | 1 |
| Act iv, Scene 3 (Brutus, Cassius) | S | 2 | |
| TWELFTH NIGHT | | | |
| Act i, Scene 3 (Sir Toby, Sir Andrew, Maria) | C | 2 | 1 |
| Act i, Scene 5 (Olivia, Viola) | S | | 2 |
| Act ii, Scene 2 (Sir Toby, Sir Andrew, Clown, Maria) | C | 3 | 1 |
| Act ii, Scene 5 (Sir Toby, Sir Andrew, Malvolio, Fabian) | C | 4 | |
| Act iii, Scene 1 (Olivia, Viola) | S | | 2 |
| Act iii, Scene 2 (Sir Toby, Sir Andrew, Fabian) | C | 3 | |
| Act iii, Scene 4 (Olivia, Maria, Malvolio) | C | 1 | 2 |

| | TYPE | M | W |
|---|---|---|---|
| THE MERCHANT OF VENICE | | | |
| Act I, Scene 2 (Portia, Nerissa) | S | | 2 |
| Act III, Scene 1 (Shylock, Tubal) | S | 2 | |
| Act III, Scene 2 (Bassanio, Portia) | S | 1 | 1 |
| ROMEO AND JULIET | | | |
| Act I, Scene 3 (Lady Capulet, Juliet, Nurse) | S | | 3 |
| Act II, Scene 2 (Romeo, Juliet) | S | 1 | 1 |
| Act III, Scene 2 (Juliet, Nurse) | S | | 2 |
| HAMLET | | | |
| Act I, Scene 3 (Laertes, Polonius, Ophelia) | S | 2 | 1 |
| Act II, Scene 1 (Polonius, Ophelia) | S | 1 | 1 |
| Act III, Scene 1 (Hamlet, Ophelia) | S | 1 | 1 |
| Act III, Scene 4 (Hamlet, Queen; Polonius x) | S | 1 | 1 |
| THE COMEDY OF ERRORS | | | |
| Act II, Scene 1 (Adriana, Lucina, Dromio of Ephesus) | C | 1 | 2 |
| Act II, Scene 2 (Antipholus of Syracuse and Dromio of Syracuse) | C | 2 | |
| Act III, Scene 2 (Luciana and Antipholus of Syracuse) | C | 1 | 1 |
| Act IV, Scene 2 (Adriana, Luciana, Dromio of Syracuse) | C | 1 | 2 |
| A MIDSUMMER-NIGHT'S DREAM | | | |
| Act I, Scene 1 (Hermia, Helena, Lysander) | S | 1 | 2 |
| Act III, Scene 2 (Helena, Lysander, Demetrius, Hermia) | S | 2 | 2 |
| Act V, Scene 1 (Pyramus, Thisbe, Wall, Lion, Moonshine) | C | 5 | |
| THE MERRY WIVES OF WINDSOR | | | |
| Act II, Scene 2 (Mistress Ford, Mistress Page) | S | | 2 |
| Act III, Scene 3 (Mistress Ford, Mistress Page, Falstaff, Robin) | C | 2 | 2 |
| MUCH ADO ABOUT NOTHING | | | |
| Act III, Scene 1 (Hero, Ursula) | C | | 2 |
| Act III, Scene 4 (Hero, Beatrice, Margaret, Ursula) | C | | 4 |
| Act IV, Scene 1 (Beatrice, Benedict) | C | 1 | 1 |
| Act V, Scene 2 (Beatrice, Benedict, Ursula) | C | 1 | 2 |

| | | TYPE | M | W |
|---|---|---|---|---|
| MACBETH | | | | |
| Act I, Scene 1 | (Three Witches) | S | | 3 |
| Act I, Scene 3 | (combine two scenes) | S | | 3 |
| Act I, Scene 5 | (Macbeth, Lady Macbeth, Messenger) | S | 2 | 1 |
| Act I, Scene 7 | (Macbeth, Lady Macbeth) | S | 1 | 1 |
| Act II, Scene 2 | (Macbeth, Lady Macbeth) | S | 1 | 1 |
| Act IV, Scene 1 | (Macbeth, Three Witches, Hecate) | S | 1 | 4 |
| Act V, Scene 1 | (Doctor, Lady Macbeth, Gentlewoman) | S | 1 | 2 |
| KING LEAR | | | | |
| Act I, Scene 1 | (Lear, Goneril, Regan, Cordelia) | S | 1 | 3 |
| Act III, Scene 2 | (Lear, Fool, Kent) | S | 3 | |
| Act IV, Scene 5 | (Regan, Oswald) | S | 1 | 1 |
| Act V, Scene 3 | (Edmund, Albany, Goneril, Regan) | S | 2 | 2 |

## ☆☆☆ONE-ACT PLAYS

| | TYPE | M | W |
|---|---|---|---|
| AFTERWARDS (2xM) Geraldine McGaughan Fr. | S | 1 | 1 |
| CATHERINE PARR (1x) Maurice Baring B. | C | 1 | 1 |
| ETHEL AND ALBERT COMEDIES (x's) Peg Lynch Fr. | C | 1 | 1 |
| MANIKIN AND MINIKIN Alfred Kreymborg Fr. | Fa | 1 | 1 |
| 'TWAS THE NIGHT BEFORE CHRISTMAS Lee Hendry Fr. | C | 1 | 1 |
| FINDERS KEEPERS George Kelly Fr. | S | 1 | 2 |
| IN THE SUDS Barnard and Rose Hewitt R.P. | Fa | 1 | 2 |
| SUPPRESSED DESIRES Susan Glaspell B. | C | 1 | 2 |
| TWELVE POUND LOOK, THE J. M. Barrie Fr. | S | 1 | 2 |
| BLUE BEADS Anne Coulter Martens R.P. | S | 1 | 3 |
| QUEENS OF FRANCE Thornton Wilder Fr. | S | 1 | 3 |
| RIDERS TO THE SEA (x's) J. M. Synge Fr. | S | 1 | 3 |
| WISDOM TEETH Rachel Field Fr. | C | 1 | 3 |
| SUNDAY COSTS FIVE PESOS Josephina Niggli Fr. | C | 1 | 4 |
| SOME WOMEN WERE TALKING John Kirkpatrick Fr. | C | 1 | 5 |
| ACE IS TRUMPED, THE H. H. Stimson Fr. | S | 2 | 1 |
| GRENACHIKA Merle Bouton Young R.P. | C | 2 | 1 |

| | TYPE | M | W |
|---|---|---|---|
| MARRIAGE PROPOSAL, THE Anton Chekhov Fr. | C | 2 | 1 |
| MINUET, A Louis N. Parker Fr. | S | 2 | 1 |
| RED CARNATIONS Glenn Hughes Fr. | C | 2 | 1 |
| CHANGING PLACES Ida Lublenski Ehrlich Fr. | C | 2 | 2 |
| CUP OF TEA, A Florence Ryerson Fr. | C | 2 | 2 |
| FIRST DATE J. T. Elias Fr. | C | 2 | 2 |
| FIRST DRESS SUIT, THE Russell Medcraft Fr. | C | 2 | 2 |
| LOVE ERRANT Russell Nail Fr. | C | 2 | 2 |
| MIND SET Merle Bouton Young R.P. | C | 2 | 2 |
| STEPS FROM BEYOND Jay Reid Gould R.P. | My | 2 | 2 |
| SUNNY MORNING, A Serafin and Joaquin Alverez Quintero Fr. | C | 2 | 2 |
| THIS WAY TO HEAVEN Douglass Parkhirst Fr. | Fa. | 2 | 2 |
| THREE ON A BENCH Doris Estrada R.P. | C | 2 | 2 |
| WHICH IS THE WAY TO BOSTON Ronald Lorenzen D.P.C. | S | 2 | 2 |
| HIGH WINDOW Verne Powers R.P. | S | 2 | 3 |
| HOUR OF HONOR Ralph Paul Joy R.P. | S | 2 | 3 |
| INFANTA Lewy Olfson R.P. | S | 2 | 3 |
| SHADOW OF A DREAM Roland Fernand D.P.C. | S | 2 | 3 |
| SENOR FREEDOM Jean Lee Latham R.P. | S | 2 | 3 |
| SUGAR AND SPICE Florence Ryerson and Colin Clements Fr. | C | 2 | 3 |
| WIENIES ON WEDNESDAY Edna Higgins Strachan R.P. | C | 2 | 3 |
| ZANORIN Catherine Brickenden Fr. | C | 2 | 3 |
| SPLINT FOR A BROKEN HEART John Kirkpatrick Fr. | C | 2 | 4 |
| CUP OF TEA, A Katherine Mansfield D.P.C. | S | 2 | 4 |
| GLORIA MUNDI Patricia Brown Fr. | S | 2 | 4 |
| BLUE STOCKING (Dr) Ruth Sergel D.P.C. | C | 2 | 5 |
| DARK BROWN Philip Johnson Fr. | My | 2 | 5 |
| LEPRECHAUN, THE Ruth Angell Purkey R.P. | Fa | 3 | 1 |
| ANDANTE Wesley Coutts R.P. | S | 3 | 2 |
| CRACKED ICE Guernsey Le Pelley R.P. | C | 3 | 2 |
| DARKEST HOUR, THE Charles George Fr. | S | 3 | 2 |
| FRIGHT James Reach Fr. | My | 3 | 2 |

| | TYPE | M | W |
|---|---|---|---|
| GROW UP Peggy Lamson Fr. | S | 3 | 2 |
| THANK YOU, DR. Gilbert Emery L.G. | C | 3 | 2 |
| THREE'S A CROWD Sara S. and E. Clayton McCarty R.P. | C | 3 | 2 |
| EARLY WORM, THE Anne Walters R.P. | C | 3 | 3 |
| ETERNAL LIFE Fred Eastman Fr. | S | 3 | 3 |
| FOG ON THE VALLEY Verne Powers R.P. | S | 3 | 3 |
| HAPPY JOURNEY, THE Thornton Wilder Fr. | C | 3 | 3 |
| REVOLT OF MOTHER, THE Mary Wilkins Freeman D.P.C. | C | 3 | 3 |
| SAFE HARBOR Douglass Parkhirst Fr. | S | 3 | 3 |
| SUNDAY'S CHILD Elizabeth Welch R.P. | C | 3 | 3 |
| TEAPOT ON THE ROCKS, THE John Kirkpatrick Fr. | C | 3 | 3 |
| TWO CROOKS AND A LADY Eugene Pillot Fr. | S | 3 | 3 |
| HER FIRST PARTY DRESS Hilda Manning Fr. | C | 3 | 4 |
| "MISTER VINCENT" Mari Bec R.P. | C | 3 | 4 |
| SOMETHING NEW IN MURDER Don Lathrop Fr. | C | 3 | 5 |
| RICH MAN, POOR MAN Bertha P. Burrill Fr. | C | 3 | 9 |
| ARIA DA CAPO Edna St. Vincent Millay B. | Fa. | 4 | 1 |
| YOUNG AMERICA Fred Ballard and Pearl Franklin Fr. | S | 4 | 1 |
| JINXED George Mosel Fr. | C | 4 | 1 |
| CURTAIN, THE Hallie Flanagan Fr. | S | 4 | 2 |
| PROOF OF A MAN Charles R. Love R.P. | S | 4 | 2 |
| FORGOTTEN MAN, THE Jewell Bothwell Tull D.P.C. | S | 4 | 2(x) |
| SHAKESPEARE Otto Asherman Fr. | C | 4 | 3 |
| TRYSTING PLACE, THE Booth Tarkington Fr. | C | 4 | 3 |
| UGLY DUCKLING, THE A. A. Milne Fr. | C | 4 | 3 |
| WEDDING, A John Kirkpatrick Fr. | C | 4 | 3 |
| BALCONY SCENE Donald Elser R.P. | S | 4 | 4 |
| I'M A FOOL Christopher Sergel D.P.C. | C | 4 | 4 |
| RED VELVET GOAT, THE Josephina Niggli Fr. | C | 4 | 5(x) |
| ELEVATOR, THE Herber Gardner Fr. | S | 5 | 1 |
| VALIANT, THE Holworthy Hall and Robert Middlemass L.G. | S | 5 | 1 |

| | TYPE | M | W |
|---|---|---|---|
| ALL AMERICANS Kenneth Pollard Fr. | S | 5 | 2 |
| INFORMER, THE John McGreevey D.P.C. | S | 5 | 3 |
| IMPORTANCE OF BEING EARNEST, THE Oscar Wilde (Ad) Harold G. Silker R.P. | C | 5 | 4 |
| LAMB IN THE WINDOW, THE Robert Finch R.P. | S | 6 | 3 |

## ☆☆☆ONE-ACT PLAYS FOR WOMEN

| | TYPE | W |
|---|---|---|
| AND A HAPPY NEW YEAR Hilda Manning Fr. | C | 7 |
| ALL ON A SUMMER'S DAY Ryerson and Clements Fr. | C | 4 |
| ANTI-CLOCKWISE Muriel and Sydney Box Fr. | C | 4 |
| BAD PENNY, THE Rachel Field Fr. | S | 4 |
| BRILLIANT PERFORMANCE Marjorie Allen Fr. | S | 4 |
| EARLY FROST Douglass Parkhirst Fr. | S | 5 |
| FOG Evelyn Neuenburg B. | S | 3 |
| GRATITUDE George Milton Savage, Jr. R.P. | S | 5 |
| GRAY BREAD Jean Lee Latham R.P. | S | 4 |
| HEARTS Alice Gerstenberg L.G. | S | 4 |
| IN A BOOKSHOP Elsie West Quaife Fr. | C | 5 |
| LADIES ALONE Ryerson and Clements Fr. | C | 3 |
| LITTLE PRISON George Milton Savage, Jr. R.P. | S | 5 |
| MURDER AT MRS. LORING'S S. Sylvan Simon Fr. | My | 5 |
| OVERTONES Alice Gerstenberg L.G. | S | 4 |
| SO WONDERFUL (in White) N. Richard Nusbaum Fr. | S | 9 |
| UNDERTOW Anne Weatherly R.P. | S | 9 |
| WALLFLOWERS James Reach Fr. | S | 5 |
| XINGU Thomas Seller D.P.S. | C | 5 |

## ☆☆☆ONE-ACT PLAYS FOR MEN

| | TYPE | M |
|---|---|---|
| DARK RIDER Robert Finch R.P. | S | 6 |
| FOUR ON A HEATH Foster Fitz-Simmons R.P. | S | 4 |
| FROM PARADISE TO BUTTE Robert Finch R.P. | C | 4 |

| | TYPE | M |
|---|---|---|
| GAME OF CHESS, THE Kenneth Sawyer Goodman Fr. | S | 2(2x) |
| IF MEN PLAYED CARDS AS WOMEN DO George S. Kaufman Fr. | C | 4 |
| LAZIEST MAN IN THE WORLD, THE Carl Webster Pierce Fr. | C | 4 |
| MAJOR MILLIRON REPORTS Robert Finch R.P. | S | 5 |
| MESSAGE FROM KHUFU, A H. Stuart Cottman and Le Vergne Shaw R.P. | S | 4 |
| MINOR MIRACLE Verne Powers R.P. | S | 4 |
| MOONSET Helen M. Clark Fr. | S | 6 |
| MOONSHINE Arthur Hopkins Fr. | C | 2 |
| NIGHT AT AN INN, A Lord Dunsany Fr. | My | 8 |
| NO CURTAIN CALLS John Rand Fr. | My | 5 |
| OPEN SECRET Robert Adler, George Bellak and Louis N. Ridenour Fr. | S | 7 |
| SEEKERS, THE Neil D. Greene R.P. | S | 8 |
| SKY-FODDER Jack Reynolds R.P. | S | 3 |
| SUBMERGED H. Stuart Cottman and Le Vergne Shaw R.P. | S | 6 |
| SUMMER COMES TO THE DIAMOND O Robert Finch R.P. | C | 8 |

## ☆☆☆THREE-ACT PLAYS

| | ROYALTY | TYPE | M | W |
|---|---|---|---|---|
| CHEAPER BY THE DOZEN (Dr) Perry Clark D.P.C. | $25 | C | 9 | 7 |
| CURIOUS SAVAGE, THE John Patrick D.P.S. | $35-25 | C | 5 | 6 |
| CURTAIN GOING UP Gregory Johnston Fr. | $25 | C | 7 | 10 |
| EVER SINCE EVE Ryerson and Clements Fr. | $25 | C | 6 | 5 |
| FATHER OF THE BRIDE (Dr) Caroline Francke D.P.S. | $35-25 | C | 10 | 7 |
| GEORGE WASHINGTON SLEPT HERE Moss Hart and George S. Kaufman D.P.S. | $25 | C | 9 | 8 |

| | ROYALTY | TYPE | M | W |
|---|---|---|---|---|
| JENNY KISSED ME Jean Kerr D.P.S. | $25 | C | 4 | 10 |
| JUNE MAD Ryerson and Clements Fr. | $25 | C | 7 | 6 |
| MELODY JONES Nathan and Ruth Hale Fr. | $25 | C | 6 | 9 |
| OUR HEARTS WERE YOUNG AND GAY (Dr) Jean Kerr D.P.C. | $25 | C | 8 | 9 |
| PEG O' MY HEART J. Hartley Manners Fr. | $25 | C | 5 | 4 |
| SABRINA FAIR Samuel Taylor D.P.S. | $50-25 | C | 7 | 7 |
| SEVENTEENTH SUMMER Anne C. Martens D.P.C. | $25 | C | 6 | 7 |
| TIME OUT FOR GINGER Ronald Alexander D.P.S. | $50-25 | C | 5 | 5 |
| YOU CAN'T TAKE IT WITH YOU Hart and Kaufman D.P.S. | $25 | C | 9 | 7 |
| YOUNG APRIL Aurania Rouverol Fr. | $25 | C | 7 | 9 |
| YOUNGEST, THE Philip Barry Fr. | $25 | C | 4 | 5 |

## More Difficult or Serious—Some Costume

| | ROYALTY | TYPE | M | W |
|---|---|---|---|---|
| BARRETTS OF WIMPOLE STREET, THE Rudolf Besier D.P.S. | $50-25 | S | 12 | 5 |
| BERKELEY SQUARE J. L. Balderston Fr. | $25 | S | 7 | 8 |
| BLITHE SPIRIT Noel Coward Fr. | $50 | C | 2 | 5 |
| CAPTAIN APPLEJACK William Hackett Fr. | $25 | C | 6 | 5 |
| CRADLE SONG, THE G. Martinez-Sierra Fr. | $50 | S | 4 | 10 (x) |
| EYES OF TLALOC, THE Agnes Emelie Peterson R.P. | $25 | My | 7 | 5 |
| HARVEY Mary Chase D.P.S. | $50-25 | C | 6 | 6 |
| HASTY HEART, THE John Patrick D.P.S. | $50-25 | S | 8 | 1 |
| IMAGINARY INVALID, THE Molière D.P.C. | 0 | C | 8 | 4 |
| IMPORTANCE OF BEING EARNEST, THE Oscar Wilde Fr. | 0 | C | 4 | 4 |

| | ROYALTY | TYPE | M | W |
|---|---|---|---|---|
| I REMEMBER MAMA John Van Druten D.P.S. | $50-25 | S | 9 | 13 |
| LARK, THE Jean Anouilh (Ad) Lillian Hellman | $50-25 | S | 15 | 5 |
| LIFE WITH FATHER Lindsay and Crouse D.P.S. | $50-25 | C | 8 | 8 |
| LOST HORIZON (Dr) Anne Coulter Martens and Christopher Sergel D.P.C. | $25 | S | 7 | 7 |
| MATCHMAKER, THE Thornton Wilder Fr. | $50-25 | C | 9 | 7 |
| MEET ME IN ST. LOUIS (Dr) Perry Clark D.P.C. | $25 | C | 9 | 7 |
| MISER, THE Molière Fr. | $25-20 | C | 11 | 5 |
| ON BORROWED TIME (Dr) Paul Osborn D.P.S. | $35-25 | S | 11 | 3 |
| OUR TOWN Thornton Wilder D.P.S. | $25 | S | 17 | 9 |
| PLAYBOY OF THE WESTERN WORLD, THE J. M. Synge Fr. | $25-20 | C | 7 | 5 |
| PYGMALION George Bernard Shaw B. | App. | C | 5 | 6 |
| QUEEN'S HUSBAND, THE Robert E. Sherwood L.G. | $25 | C | 11 | 4 |
| ROYAL FAMILY, THE Ferber and Kaufman Fr. | $35 | S | 11 | 6 |
| SEVEN SISTERS (Ad) Edith Ellis D.P.S. | $25 | C | 6 | 8 |
| SKIN OF OUR TEETH, THE Thornton Wilder Fr. | $50 | Fa | 5 | 5 (x) |
| SMILIN' THROUGH A. L. Martin Fr. | $35 | S | 5 | 5 |
| SONG OF BERNADETTE, THE (Dr) Jean and Walter Kerr D.P.C. | $25 | S | 7 | 11 |
| STAGE DOOR Ferber and Kaufman D.P.S. | $25 | S | 11 | 21 |
| TEAHOUSE OF THE AUGUST MOON, THE John Patrick D.P.S. | $50-25 | C | 18 | 8 (x) |

## Costume Plays—Large Casts

| | ROYALTY | TYPE | M | W |
|---|---|---|---|---|
| ADMIRABLE CRICHTON, THE J. M. Barrie Fr. | $25 | S | 13 | 12 |

| | ROYALTY | TYPE | M | W |
|---|---|---|---|---|
| AROUND THE WORLD IN EIGHTY DAYS (Dr) Rodney Dawes D.P.C. | $25 | C | 13 | 11 |
| CONNECTICUT YANKEE IN KING ARTHUR'S COURT, A (Dr) John G. Fuller B. | $25 | C | 6 | 6 |
| CYRANO DE BERGERAC Edmond Rostand Fr. | 0 | S | 30 | 16 |
| IF I WERE KING J. H. McCarthy Fr. | App | S | 20 | 9 |
| LITTLE WOMEN (Dr) John Ravold Fr. | $10 | S | 4 | 6 |
| PRIDE AND PREJUDICE (Dr) Helen Jerome Fr. | $25 | S | 10 | 16 |
| QUALITY STREET J. M. Barrie Fr. | $37-50 | S | 6 | 9 |
| RIVALS, THE R. B. Sheridan Fr. | 0 | S | 8 | 4 |
| SHE STOOPS TO CONQUER Oliver Goldsmith B. | 0 | S | 15 | 4 |
| VICTORIA REGINA Laurence Housman B. | App | S | 26 | 9 |

SHAKESPEARE A *Midsummer Night's Dream, The Taming of the Shrew, Romeo and Juliet, Julius Caesar, Macbeth, As You Like It, Twelfth Night.* Acting editions and streamlined versions—Fr.

## ☆☆☆ BOOKS

This carefully selected list of the most usable and, in the main, latest additions to theatre material covers the field of dramatic topics as presented in this book. Excellent bibliographies of older works are to be found in most drama books.

### History

Cheney, Sheldon. *The Theatre—3000 Years of Drama, Acting and Stagecraft.* New York: Longmans, Green & Co., Inc., Rev. ed. 1952.

Traces the development of drama and the physical theatre as well. One chapter on present-day theatre.

Hughes, Glenn. *The Story of the Theatre.* New York: Samuel French, Inc, 1928. Simply told and easy to understand. A good beginning history.

Freedley, George, and John A. Reeves. *A History of the Theatre.* New York: Crown Publishers, Inc., Rev. ed. 1955.
More complete; more emphasis on acting. Well illustrated.
Macgowan, Kenneth, and William Melnitz. *The Living Stage.* New York: Prentice-Hall, Inc., 1958. *Golden Ages of the Theatre* (Same as the above—abbreviated and cheaper.)
Sobel, Bernard. *Theatre Handbook and Digest of Plays.* New York: Crown Publishers, Inc., Rev. ed. 1959.
Practically a one-volume encyclopedia on actors, plays, theatres, and other dramatic topics. Very valuable for reference.
Wright, Edward A. *A Primer for Playgoers.* New York: Prentice-Hall, Inc., 1958. Written especially for the audience. *Understanding Today's Theatre* (Same as the above—abbreviated and cheaper. Includes Movies and Television.)

## Anthologies

Gassner, John, ed. *A Treasury of the Theatre.* (3 vols.) New York: Simon and Schuster, Inc. Rev. ed. 1951.
Representative plays from every period and country—from Æschylus to Arthur Miller. A real treasury.
Gassner, John. *Best Plays of the Modern American Theatre.* Five Series. New York: Crown Publishers, Inc., Latest 1958.
Contain modern plays you should be familiar with. They provide good scenes for acting.
Watson, E. Bradlee, and Benfield Pressey. *Comtemporary Drama—European, English, Irish, American Plays.* New York: Charles Scribner's Sons, 1941.
Contains *Abe Lincoln in Illinois, Elizabeth the Queen, The Emperor Jones.*
Cerf, Bennett A., and Van H. Cartmell, *16 Famous American Plays.* New York: Modern Library, Random House, Inc., 1941.
Cerf, Bennett A., and Van H. Cartmell, *16 Famous British Plays.* New York: Modern Library, Random House, Inc., 1942.
Cerf, Bennett A., and Van H. Cartmell. *24 Favorite One-Act Plays.* New York: Doubleday & Co., Inc., 1958.
Kronenberger, Louis, ed., *Best Plays*—by years. New York: Dodd, Mead and Company. (Formerly the *Burns Mantle Yearbook.*)
A review of the theatre season each year. Also short scenes from the so-called best plays, bridged by narration.

Stephens, Frances. *Theatre World Annual.* London: The Macmillan Company.

A pictorial record by years—the latest 1959.

## Acting

Blakelock, Denys. *Advice to a Player.* London: William Heinemann, Ltd., 1958.

Chekhov, Michael. *To the Actor.* New York: Harper and Brothers, 1953.

The "creative process" in acting presented by a master. Excellent.

Cole, Toby, and Helen Kritch Chinoy, eds. *Actors on Acting.* New York: Crown Publishers, 1949.

The views and methods of some of our best actors.

Eustis, Morton, *Players at Work.* New York: Theatre Arts Books, 1937.

Goodman, Edward, *Make-Believe—the Art of Acting.* New York: Charles Scribner's Sons, 1956.

Guthrie, Tyrone, *A Life in the Theatre.* New York: McGraw-Hill Book Company, Inc., 1959.

McGaw, Charles J., *Acting Is Believing.* New York: Rinehart & Company, Inc., 1957.

Redgrave, Michael, *The Actor's Ways and Means.* London: William Heinemann, Ltd., 1953.

Seyler, Athene, and Stephen Haggard. *The Craft of Comedy.* New York: Theatre Arts Books, 1957.

Stanislavsky, Constantin, *An Actor Prepares,* tr. Elizabeth Reynolds Hapgood. New York: Theatre Arts Books, 1936.

## Voice and Speech

Barnes, Grace. *General American Speech Sounds.* Boston: D. C. Heath and Company, 1946.

An analysis of and drill on the forty-three American speech sounds, with illustrations and charts showing their formation. Record to accompany book.

Woolbert, Charles H., and Severina E. Nelson. *The Art of Interpretive Speech.* New York: Appleton-Century-Crofts, Inc., 1956.

Clear and detailed treatment of interpretation.

## Production and Direction

Philippi, Herbert. *Stagecraft and Stage Design.* Boston: Houghton Mifflin Company, 1953.

Comprehensive. "Designed to develop sound and well-organized methods of work in shops and on stage." Very valuable.

Heffner, Hubert C., Samuel Selden, and Hunton D. Sellman. *Modern Theatre Practice.* New York: F. S. Crofts. 3rd ed. 1946. Rev. ed. 1959.
Each phase of production—direction, scenery, lighting—covered by an expert in that field. Excellent.

Hewitt, Bernard, J. F. Foster, and Muriel Wolle. *Play Production—Theory and Practice.* Philadelphia: J. B. Lippincott Company, 1952.
Covers all phases—construction, sound effects, backstage organization, costume, make-up.

Nelms, Henning. *Play Production.* New York: Barnes and Noble, Inc. College Outline Series, 1950.
"A guidebook for the student of drama—a handbook for backstage workers."

Hake, Herbert. *Here's How.* Evanston, Illinois: Row, Peterson and Company, 1942.
Practical, simple, clear directions for scenery construction.

Bailey, Howard. *ABC'S of Play Production.* New York: David McKay, Inc., 1955.

Gruver, Bert. *The Stage Manager's Handbook.* New York: Harper and Brothers, 1952.
A professional stage manager gives expert advice.

Selden, Samuel, and Hunton D. Sellman. *Stage Scenery and Lighting.* New York: Appleton-Century-Crofts, Inc., 1959.
A fairly short but comprehensive handbook of scenery and lighting for college, school, and community theatres.

Young, John Wray. *Directing the Play.* New York: Harper and Brothers, 1958. Excellent.

Jones, Margo. *Theatre-in-the-Round.* New York: Rinehart and Company, Inc., 1951.

Boyle, Walden P. *Central and Flexible Staging.* Berkeley and Los Angeles: University of California Press, 1956.

## Costume and Make-Up

Barton, Lucy. *Historic Costume For the Stage.* Boston: Baker, 1935.

Paterek, Josephine D. *Costuming for the Theatre.* New York: Crown Publishers, Inc., 1959.
Simple treatment of the subject.

Walkup, Fairfax Proudfit. *Dressing the Part.* New York: Appleton-Century-Crofts, Inc., 1950.
A history of costume for the theatre down to 1950. Well illustrated.

Davenport, Millia. *The Book of Costume.* New York: Crown Publishers, Inc., 1948.

Covers dress, jewelry, ornaments, coiffures and all other elements. It also records successive civilizations, cultures, and periods.

Corson, Richard. *Stage Make-up.* New York: Appleton-Century-Crofts, Inc., Rev. ed., 1960.

Features modeling with paint, with special attention to the planes of the face. Excellent.

Liszt, Rudolph G. *The Last Word in Make-up.* New York: Dramatists Play Service, Inc., 1942.

Covers all kinds of characters. Many photographs.

Factor, Max. *Hints on the Art of Make-up.* A set of nine illustrated booklets. Send for order blank and information on student's make-up kit to Max Factor Hollywood Make-up Studio.

Knapp, Jack S. *Technique of Stage Make-up.* Boston: Walter H. Baker Co., 1942.

"A practical manual for the use of Max Factor's Make-up." Small, very usable.

## Playwriting

Macgowan, Kenneth. *A Primer of Playwriting.* New York: Random House, Inc., 1951.

Rowe, Kenneth T. *Write That Play.* New York: Funk & Wagnalls, 1939.

## Shakespeare

Chute, Marchette. *An Introduction to Shakespeare.* New York: E. P. Dutton and Company, Inc., 1951.

Chute, Marchette. *Shakespeare of London.* New York: E. P. Dutton and Company, Inc., 1949. Paper ed. 1957.

"An attempt to show William Shakespeare as his contemporaries saw him, rather than as the gigantic legendary figure he has become since." Excellent.

Thorndike, Ashley H. *Shakespeare's Theatre.* New York: The Macmillan Company, 1928 (reprinted 1954).

A complete history in one volume, covering Shakespeare's London, the playhouses, the companies, the actors, and acting. Invaluable.

Hill, Frank Ernest. *To Meet Will Shakespeare.* New York: Dodd, Mead and Company, 1949.

For "readers who want to know Shakespeare—as a person, player, man of affairs, writer." Fictionalized episodes make delightful reading.

Watkins, Ronald. *On Producing Shakespeare.* New York: W. W. Norton and Company, Inc., 1950.

Explanations of different theories of production.

de Banke, Cecile. *Shakespearean Stage Productions: Then and Now.* New York: McGraw-Hill Book Company, Inc., 1953.

Covers production, staging, lighting, actors, and acting companies. Excellent chapter on costume, with sketches and illustrations. Chapter on music and dancing with extensive bibliography on music and recordings.

Chisman, Isabel, and Hester Emilie Raven-Hart. *Manners and Movements in Costume Plays.* Boston: Walter H. Baker Co., 1934.

Small but very valuable.

Onions, C. T. A *Shakespeare Glossary.* Oxford, at the Clarendon Press. Rev. ed. 1953.

Very complete. Very valuable.

Irvine, Theodora. A *Pronouncing Dictionary of Shakespearean Proper Names.* New York: Barnes and Noble, Inc., 1944.

Gives the pronunciations used by different actors.

Watt, Home A., Karl J. Holzknecht, and Raymond Ross. *Outlines of Shakespeare's Plays.* New York: Barnes and Noble, Inc., College Outline Series. Rev. ed. 1952.

Extremely usable for beginning drama students.

# Part 4

## METHODS

# Fourteen

## COURSES OF STUDY ☆☆☆

Courses of Study, methods of presenting the material in the classroom, help to achieve the following goals:

**OBJECTIVES IN EDUCATIONAL DRAMATICS**

I. Personal
 The maximum development of the individual so that
  A. he can live a happier and more complete life
   through specific improvement in posture, walk, and voice; in character traits; in English skills; in ability to evaluate; in self-confidence.
  B. he can make a greater contribution to society and thus to civilization
   through the development of a social conscience; of the qualities and habits of a good citizen; of poise and ease in social relationships; of the ability to work with others toward a common goal.

II. Dramatic
 The acquisition of essential habits and skills, knowledge and understanding, attitudes and appreciation, so that
  A. he can pursue a career in the theatre
   through the attainment of the basic techniques of theatre practice, acting technique, and knowledge of theatre history and literature.
  B. he can enjoy an avocation
   through the development of the ability to produce, direct, manage, or act in plays as a leisure-time activity.

C. he can continue as a student of drama in college
with a preliminary training established in acting and production techniques and an understanding of the responsibilities of a theatre worker.

The Courses of Study presented for Drama I, II, and III were used at University High School, Los Angeles, to show student teachers one way by which the material in the book may be used to cover three semesters of drama. The units may, of course, be modified to fit different situations and ability groups, or be disregarded completely where a Course of Study is already established.

The Drama I course, given the most detailed breakdown, served as a Demonstration Class for teachers, prospective teachers, administrators, and board of education members to observe. The beginning teacher may wish to drop one of the four acting projects at first, and only later include all four projects.

The philosophy underlying the treatment of the course studies is as follows:

1. Drama is primarily a creative activity, not an academic study. It gives the individual an opportunity to synthesize the various phases of learning, offering as it does direct practice in the skills of reading, writing, listening, and speaking. It also helps him to understand himself, his present environment and world, and his cultural heritage.
2. Since students enter the drama class with a desire to act, this ready-made motivation should be used by placing major emphasis on acting.
3. The maximum development of each student's personality and character traits is a primary aim in educational dramatics.
4. Directing activities toward this goal is not incompatible with teaching a sound course in theatre technique which will accord with the best practices of the professional theatre.
5. The various phases or elements of acting are learned most easily and are more meaningful when related to acting projects.
6. Good acting material is a necessary adjunct to such a course.
7. The skills of reading, writing, listening, and speaking are vital goals for any student. The study of drama gives a practical way to emphasize and reinforce these skills.

*On Stage, Everyone* is written and organized so that these goals can be achieved. The following courses of study for Drama I, II, and III offer suggestions for one way of using to full advantage the eighteen school weeks in each semester.

## DRAMA I

| UNIT | WEEKS | ACTIVITIES |
|---|---|---|
| I | 1 | Orientation, posture, walk |
| II | 3 | Modern Scene |
| III | 3 | Character-Opposite Scene |
| IV | 5 | Shakespearean Scene and Soliloquy |
| V | 6 | One-Act Play |

## DRAMA II

| UNIT | WEEKS | ACTIVITIES |
|---|---|---|
| I | 2 | Basic training: Senses and Emotions (Chapter 5)<br>Technique (Chapter 9) |
| II | 2 | Scene from Contemporary Drama (Chapter 13) |
| III | 2 | Basic training: Body (Chapter 6)<br>Voice (Chapter 7) |
| IV | 7 | Production techniques: Play Production (Chapter 10) Rehearsal, direction, and production of a one-act play or cut version of a three-act play |
| V | 5 | History and Horizons: (Chapter 8) Research, preparation, presentation of a period scene<br>Survey of modern acting mediums—stage, screen, television, radio |

## DRAMA III (Production)

A GROUP—Actors playing principal roles in the three-act play
B GROUP—Actors playing minor roles, or those not cast in the three-act play

| UNIT | WEEKS | ACTIVITIES |
|---|---|---|
| I | 2 | Reading, selecting, casting the three-act play |
| II | 8 | *Rehearsal (seven weeks)*<br>A Group: Daily rehearsal of three-act play following schedule<br>B Group: Rehearsal of minor parts as scheduled<br>Preparation of production duties (Chapter 10)<br>Preparation and rehearsal of additional scenes or one-act plays<br><br>*Production (one week)*<br>Entire class at every rehearsal:<br>Technical rehearsals<br>Dress rehearsals<br>Production of play<br>Photographs of play |
| III | 1 | Discussion of three-act play<br>Clean-up and return of all materials<br>Completion of prompt book<br>Workshop presentations of Group B |
| IV | 2 | Original scenes and improvisations (A and B) |
| V | 2 | Great roles or famous speeches from World Drama |
| VI | 3 | Selection, preparation, and presentation of final acting project: a ten- to fifteen-minute program of scenes, original material, pantomimes, or soliloquies |

## ☆☆☆ UNIT DEVELOPMENT OF DRAMA I

*On Stage, Everyone,* in Part I, Acting, gives intensive study in the beginning course to the four acting projects. Only those sections in Part II, Basic Training, with direct bearing on the learning project are used and threaded into the four acting units. Part III provides the acting materials. These four projects, however, may be repeated any number of times in advanced courses, if so desired, through the use of different and more difficult scenes.

| UNIT | WEEKS | ACTIVITIES |
|---|---|---|
| I | 1 | Discussion: elements of drama (Chapter 1)<br>definition of acting<br>nature of a play<br>survey of the Course of Study<br>Read the Prologue<br>Write "What I wish to accomplish in this course"<br>Study and observe people with special attention to posture and walk: Life Study<br>Evaluate each student on posture and walk; assign exercises for improvement (Chapter 6)<br>Staging, lighting vocabulary learned and tested (Chapter 9, pages 191-192) |

On the first day the group meets, discuss what the students wish to gain from their drama study and what the course should and will contain. In this way the students and teacher establish common goals and the direction of the course. It is effective to read the scene from *Abe Lincoln in Illinois* reprinted in the Prologue (page 1) in connection with class efforts to define drama, acting, and the nature of a play. This will lead naturally into the particular mediums of acting—the actor's body and voice, which are the instruments of dramatic expression that must be trained. Unlike a musician who must learn to play *on* an instrument, the actor must train *himself* as the instrument of dramatic expression (page 3).

No two classes are ever the same. It is important to learn as soon as possible something about the personalities of each class. After class discussion, ask each student to write a paper on "What I Wish to Accomplish in This Course." In such a paper students often expose their needs, problems, and aspirations. These are vital clues to the teacher in directing the students toward wholesome activities, planning for the individual personality needs, and analyzing the composition of the class.

Since characters will be drawn from life, the student should leave the first class period stimulated to observe people, paying particular attention to the way they walk. He should note posture, stance, and the carriage of different parts of the body. He must try to analyze the physical reasons for certain walks, such as a stiff ankle or a loose-jointed knee. He should be prepared to comment upon how much is revealed about a person by his posture and walk.

On the second day prepare the students for a posture-walk analysis. Then send the students across the stage one by one. Using the outline on pages 83-84, note the good points and the eccentricities of the posture and walk of each individual. However, do not make oral comments until all have finished. Then call attention to two or three of the most obvious faults, and give each student personal criticisms in writing. Refer to Chapter 6, where the exercises to correct the particular faults may be found. You may explain to the class, or demonstrate by using the sketches on page 88, common problems of posture. Group exercises may be practised, also. Assign the reading of Life Study, pages 63-64, to establish the importance of physical attitudes to acting. On the following day, you may combine a second posture review with learning to sit in and rise from a chair correctly according to the stage techniques explained on page 166.

The vocabulary of the theatre can be made more meaningful to students by a trip to the auditorium stage, where the terms may be illustrated. A quiz on staging and lighting vocabulary and technique terms should culminate the week's work.

| UNIT | WEEKS | ACTIVITIES |
| --- | --- | --- |
| II | 3 | *Modern Scenes* |
| | | Read Chapter 1<br>In class read and analyze one or more scenes (Chapter 11)<br>Select and rehearse a Modern Scene (Chapters 11 and 13)<br>Read the play from which the scene is taken<br>Study and discuss: Characterization (Chapter 1)<br>Plotting the stage<br>Technique of rehearsal<br>Memorization<br>Introduction of a scene<br>Critiques<br>Acting vocabulary studied and learned (pages 188-189)<br>Write a character analysis (page 10)<br>Design a stage plot for the scene<br>Write an introduction to the scene |
| | | Present Modern Scenes<br>Write critiques and discuss each presentation (page 23)<br>List all things learned from this project<br>Acting vocabulary tested (pages 188-189)<br>Summary test on Units I and II |

**CHAPTER 1—THE MODERN SCENE** The preparation of this project should be carefully planned and the *routines* firmly established for approaching the study of a role, rehearsing, and presenting a scene. These routines will be followed in each successive project during the rest of the semester. As a preliminary, assign the reading of Chapter 1. In class, scenes from Chapter 11 may be read and analyzed to prepare the students for the first acting assignment. Then sum up the objectives to be achieved. (See Call Board, page 6.)

On the second day, the students are ready to select a scene and partner and begin to relate the material in Chapter 1 to their specific roles. On the following days, discussions and drill on technique, scene development, and staging may precede rehearsal period. A full hour is usually too long for the rehearsal of a short scene. Ten or fifteen minutes at the beginning of each day and five to seven minutes at the close will provide time for presenting new vocabulary, clarifying problems in characterization, plotting the stage, establishing the Rehearsal Routine (page 14), preparing critiques.

Information for the Production Schedule (page 389) should be given to the teacher as soon as the scene has been selected and cast. This will include such material as is found on a theatre program—the name of the play, playwright, characters, and actors playing. A mimeographed program for production week which schedules three or four scenes a day will alert and train the students to meet deadlines in professional theatre tradition. The schedule should be followed exactly with no postponements. In case one actor is absent (and this must be for a very legitimate reason) his part is "read" by someone else, but the scene must be given on time, for "the show must go on." Excuses to extend performance dates are no more permissible than in professional theatre.

During the succeeding eight days of preparation, the teacher may space the dates on which written materials are due: (1) the stage plot, which should be drawn to scale (see page 388), (2) the character analysis, (3) the introduction to the scene, (4) the testing on acting vocabulary (pages 188-189), (5) the written critiques, and (6) the list of things learned from the project.

While students are rehearsing in groups in different parts of the room and stage, the teacher may aid students in movement, rearranging furniture, checking projection, and maintaining good rehearsal conduct. Students usually have to be prompted to keep moving and not just read lines. The beginning sessions may be organized disorder, but within a short time, students learn to concentrate sufficiently to block out the noise from the other scene groups. Although two weeks is a short time for preparing a scene, it is important that the actors participate in a performance as quickly as possible, for once the first scene is presented, students learn more effectively the techniques of acting. Therefore, pressure must be applied to meet this first deadline date. By rehearsals outside of class, by study and practice at home, and by insistence on accurate memorization, students can be stimulated to perform competently.

During the production week, the actors presenting the first scene of the day should set the stage immediately upon entering the classroom and be ready to play as soon as roll has been taken. Training in good audience attitudes is as much a part of the production week as is performance. An atmosphere of quiet, concentration, and appreciation for the students' performances should be created. As soon as the curtain closes and applause ends, the audience members may write individual notes and critiques while the next cast prepares its stage (page 23). Classes at the end of each day should first commend the performances and then analyze the performers' techniques and staging (page 25). Each actor should receive a brief appraisal of his work from the teacher, for students seek approval and help eagerly. Students learn so much from watching one another that usually the scenes become progressively better each day.

Written critiques from each student should be turned in to the teacher the day after all the scenes have been presented. Each successive set of critiques should show keener observation, greater understanding of what constitutes good acting, and an ever-expanding theatrical vocabulary.

In reviewing what has been achieved in this unit, evaluate the learning objectives and point toward the next acting project. Besides learning acting techniques and staging skills, students should begin to appreciate the necessity for organization in the management of props and costumes and preparation for and participation in rehearsal. They must learn to respect the vital role of discipline in theatrical training. By showing consideration and appreciation of the achievements of others, students can encourage each performer to do his best and build up the self-confidence of the group in performing before an audience. The performances themselves are the laboratory in which acting skills and techniques can be taught. Each student may discuss the technique he has found most helpful. Later, however, each should make a written list of everything he has learned. This will become a record of his achievement in each unit.

A written test covering the reading in Chapter 1, vocabulary, and scene work will enable the instructor to measure the students' comprehension of subject matter.

| UNIT | WEEKS | ACTIVITIES |
|---|---|---|
| III | 3 | *Character-Opposite Scenes* |

Introduction to Character-Opposite
Read Chapter 2
Write a character analysis of self (page 30)
Select and rehearse a Character-Opposite scene (Chapters 11 and 13)
Read play from which scene was taken
Study, discuss:
- Self-analysis
- Extroverts and introverts
- Body training (Chapter 6)
- Physical expression of emotional states (page 97)
- Daily Routine of Body Exercises (page 95)
- Creating the inner character (Chapter 5)
- Emotion (Chapter 5)

Write a character analysis (page 10)
Write a play analysis
Design a stage plot
Write an introduction to the scene
Prepare short pantomimes

Present Character-Opposite Scenes
Follow routine of Modern Scenes:
- Write critiques and discuss each presentation
- List all things learned from the project

Theatre conventions learned and tested (pages 215-216)

**CHAPTER 2—THE CHARACTER-OPPOSITE SCENE** To launch the more complex acting project of the Character-Opposite scene, illustrate on the board the diagram of "introvert, normal, and extrovert" characteristics found on page 99. The figures can easily be shown by stick-figure drawings. A discussion of these recognizable traits will focus students' attention on their own personal qualities. Have them analyze their own needs and select for production an appropriate character of opposite personality. This can be a most rewarding experience for young student actors, but requires considerable skill on the part of the teacher to clarify the personal analysis outline and to guide the students into challenging scenes. Although students are deeply interested in themselves, they are often confused and unwilling to discuss their own qualities, preferring instead *to be* analyzed.

The teacher can help each individual student to develop his personality and to adjust to people and situations. Sections from Chapters 5 and 6 may be used here to enrich the discussions and stimulate student thinking about how to develop into mature persons as well as creative actors.

Call Board (page 28) outlines the objectives and over-all design of the Character-Opposite scene. The unit begins with the individual student, but ends with each individual understanding others, in particular a dramatic character that is the extreme opposite of himself emotionally, socially, or in physical quality.

Once the students have completed their personal analyses, it is important that each select the right character to play. Since young actors do not have a wide acquaintance with dramatic literature, the instructor will have to be prepared to give expert guidance in the choice of appropriate scenes, by having extra plays available and by having noted some of the scenes in Chapters 11 and 13. Playing characters of advanced years is an excellent challenge for the students in this unit, especially since at this time emphasis is placed on body training.

The routine for rehearsal having been established, the words "Walk-Through, Think-Through, Follow-Through," may be placed on the board as reminders that movement and stage business must be rehearsed. The instructional periods at the beginning and close of the rehearsal hour should include physical training to develop responsive bodies (Daily Routine of Body Exercises, page 95) and the Physical Expressions of Emotional States (page 97). Pantomimes from Chapters 5 and 6 may be assigned or added when time allows. In addition, focus some attention on Creating the Inner Character (page 63) and Emotion (page 73), both of which relate to the advanced characterization. Different students may lead the class exercises, just as the cheer leader directs the yells. At this time, students should again concentrate upon individual posture and walk (Unit I). Each student may be asked to write (1) the criticism he received on posture and walk the first week of the semester, (2) the exercises that were suggested for improvement, and (3) the amount of time he has spent practicing them—minutes per day and total.

Space the due dates for the remaining written assignments throughout the two weeks. In addition, request that the students analyze in writing the entire play, specifying the theme, conflict, protagonist, antagonist, climax, mood, and relation of the selected scene to the plot development.

The students should be disciplined enough, and the rehearsal routine well enough established, to make it unnecessary to supervise all groups every day. Now, the rehearsal time can be divided so that two casts may work each day on the classroom stage under teacher direction. Every group needs some direct help. By the posting of a schedule, each scene group can be assured of one session to receive suggestions on characterization, interpretation, movement, and set arrangement.

Introducing Theatre Conventions (page 215) at this time will reinforce the professional attitude to be maintained during the rehearsal session.

During production week the procedure is as previously established. This time, however, the scene groups should be expected to move on and off stage more swiftly and smoothly, thus allowing a longer period for oral comments.

| UNIT | WEEKS | ACTIVITIES |
|---|---|---|
| IV | 5 | *Shakespearean Scenes* |
| | | Introduction to Shakespeare and Elizabethan England |
| | | Survey of theatre up to Elizabethan period |
| | | Shakespeare's London |
| | | Shakespeare's plays and characterizations |
| | | Shakespeare's productions and theatre |
| | | Read Chapter 3 and Chapter 8 through the Elizabethan Period |
| | | Select a Shakespearean research topic (page 41) |
| | | Receive a personal inventory of your voice and speech (pages 112-113) |
| | | Study and drill on voice training (Chapter 7) |
| | | Select and prepare a soliloquy |
| | | Select and rehearse a Shakespearean scene (Chapter 13) |
| | | Read entire play and write synopsis of plot |
| | | Write character analysis |
| | | Write an introduction |
| | | Design a stage plot |
| | | Improvise a Shakespearean costume from own wardrobe for scene |
| | | Present soliloquy |
| | | Present Shakespearean Scenes |
| | | Follow routine of Modern Scenes: |
| | | Critiques written and class discussion |
| | | List all things learned from the project |
| | | Summary test covering Units III and IV |

**CHAPTER 3—THE SHAKESPEAREAN SCENE**

The day you start the Shakespearean Unit, bring to the classroom all the theatrical excitement and visual aids you possess. The atmosphere you create by your own enthusiasm and appreciation must electrify the students and outweigh whatever dreary previous experiences the students may have had with reading Shakespeare's plays. Once you have set the stage, painted in their minds the living age and theatre in which Shakespeare wrote and performed, he will do the rest. However, perhaps no other unit in drama requires more energy and dramatic skill to teach than the Shakespearean material. Students often have an understandable fear of and resentment against his plays because of the way they were introduced to them. To overcome this, the teacher must stimulate the imagination of students so that they see spectacular actors performing before boisterous but critical and appreciative audiences which greeted brilliant performances with loud cheering demonstrations from the pit.

Allowing one week for preparation, two weeks for rehearsal, and two for production, you can in this unit challenge the superior student; additional research projects, the building of model stages or costume figures, and performing extra soliloquies or scenes all will appeal to him.

On the first day, have in the classroom pictures of Shakespearean productions (see Chapter 15, "Audio-Visual Aids: Shakespeare"), available stage models or blackboard diagrams, costumes, and books. Persuade the students to open their minds, "lend their ears," and let imaginations soar. Prepare a thirty- to forty-minute survey of theatre up to the Elizabethan period covering the beginning of drama, the stature of Greek plays, the changes in the physical stage, the medieval market place and wagon staging, the Commedia dell' Arte, and the beginning innyard performances outside of London. On the second day, make students aware of the city of London; visualize Queen Elizabeth, the robust excitment of audiences intoxicated with Shakespeare's people. Show the many theatres across the river from London, the people pouring into the playhouses, the shape and size of The Globe. (Use the film, *Shakespeare's Theatre: The Globe Playhouse*, to demonstrate the staging of plays. See Chapter 15, "Audio-Visual Aids: Shakespeare.") On the third day, focus on the story line of specific plays and the many-faceted, complex characterizations which Shakespeare created. Select a few characters of your choice, such as Hamlet, Shylock, Juliet, or Lady Macbeth, and describe the scope of their personalities, the flaws, and the greatness. Hamlet, the college student who broods over his father's death and mother's early remarriage, is especially understandable to modern students. Relate these great figures to modern counterparts whenever possible, illustrating the universality of Shakespeare's characterizations. Stress the fact that Shakespeare tailored parts for the most talented actors of his time to play, not for the scholars to study. Challenge the students to create the characters that great actors and actresses of all times aspire to play. Frankly admit that it is a difficult assignment. The language problems can be solved and will give each student a greater appreciation of words, an enlarged vocabulary, and poetic range. On the fourth and fifth days, present films, filmstrips, and recordings of productions. Summarize the week's introductory material with (1) a review of the Call Board objectives (page 38), (2) an assignment to read Chapter 3 along with the historical material found in Chapter 8, and (3) a selection of a research topic from one of the related areas found on page 41.

Since this is the logical unit in which to stress voice development, it is important to the student's training as well as to the success of the Shakespearean scene for him to prepare a soliloquy along with the scene. During the two weeks of rehearsal, spend the major part of the ten- to fifteen-minute instructional period on voice training. Give each student a personal inventory of his voice and speech (pages 112-113) and present the Daily Routine for Speech Practice (pages 118-119), stressing breathing, projection, articulation, and energy needed to gain command of the speeches. Relate the drill on interpretation techniques to their soliloquies and Hamlet's Advice to the Players (page 44) which you may want to have them all memorize. Some of the drill may be in the verse choir manner. Ask each student to write (1) the voice criticism which he has received in previous performances, (2) the exercises that were suggested for improvement, and (3) the amount of time spent practicing in minutes per day.

The last five or ten minutes of each rehearsal day may be used to *add* material relating to their scenes, to present exceptional research reports submitted by the students, to demonstrate the dictates of period costume on the actor's carriage and movement, and to show how to improvise an effective Shakespearean costume from their own wardrobes (pages 182-183). In addition, helpful instruction may be given on general research techniques and preparation of a bibliography.

In rehearsal, students with reading difficulties will need special help. Paraphrase each thought, if necessary, and guide the slower learners into serious scenes rather than comedy which demands greater insight and facility with language because of the puns, the word-play, and the more intellectual type of humor.

Assign dates for the completion in written form of a character analysis, plot synopsis, introduction, stage plot, research topic, critiques, list of things learned from the project, and record of voice practice.

In the fourth week the students present their soliloquies staged as they would be within the context of the given play. Give each student a detailed written analysis of his voice and interpretation, as well as suggestions on how to motivate movement from within the lines. At the close of each day, records of famous actors interpreting Shakespeare may be played. But at no time should students be allowed or encouraged to imitate intonations or phrasing. If the recordings of Laurence Olivier and John Barrymore as Hamlet are available, the differences in interpretation and technique may be illustrated; the subtleties marking Olivier's work are possible only in a motion picture, where the microphone is inches from the actor's face, while Barrymore's interpretation was meant to be projected from a stage.

In the fifth week, during production of Shakespearean Scenes, introduce improvised costumes. Arrangements will need to be made for a place in which the students may dress.

Follow the same production procedures as before. As students discuss what they have learned from this unit, their exchange of impressions of Shakespeare's drama will be a reward to each member of the class. Out of their own experience in performing in his plays, the students will undoubtedly list even more objectives than those on Call Board.

Outstanding scenes may be repeated for invited English classes. With successful class experiences in scene work, many teachers have been able to develop yearly Shakespeare festivals and within a few years to present a Shakespearean play to the entire student body and receive an enthusiastic and intelligent reception.

The close of the Shakespeare productions is a good time for a test on the Character-Opposite and Shakespearean scene material.

| UNIT | WEEKS | ACTIVITIES |
|---|---|---|
| V | 6 | *One-Act Plays* |
| | | Preparation for the One-Act Play<br>Assign the reading of one-act plays (Chapter 13)<br>Review analysis of a play (pages 7-9)<br>Discuss and relate fundamentals of play production in Chapter 10 to the one-act project<br>Read and discuss direction (Chapter 9, pages 175-178)<br>Discuss abilities and responsibilities of the director<br>Discuss and illustrate the director's prompt book (pages 199 and 52-53) |

| UNIT | WEEKS | ACTIVITIES |
|---|---|---|
| V | 6 | *One-Act Plays* |

Select directors
Read Chapter 4

Select plays and cast
Rehearse plays following routine in Chapter 4
Actors write character analysis
Directors write play analysis and supervise the development of prompt book
Select, design, and acquire production materials: ground plan, props, costumes, sound and music, make-up, publicity forms

Production of One-Act Plays (one or two each day)
Follow routine of Modern Scenes:
- Critiques written and class discussion
- List of all things learned from this project

Final examination
Reread first paper, "What I Wish to Accomplish in this Course," and write an evaluation to include:
- Success in achieving goals
- Summary of gains from entire course
- What was learned of greatest personal value

**CHAPTER 4—THE ONE-ACT PLAY** Acting in a one-act play presents special challenges in production techniques and demands from each individual more mature attitudes in group cooperation. In the last three projects, each student, working in groups of two or three, was able to play a leading character. Participation in the one-act play exposes the student to the stress of competitive casting. He must learn to accept graciously either the lead or the minor role. Besides creating a role, each student must share in the responsibilities involved in working with a larger group and assume production duties in the staging of the play. In short, each student must learn to be an all-around theatre worker and member of a well-organized team. The major objectives of the one-act assignment found on Call Board (page 48) center around a grasp of the increased scope of theatre training required in producing a complete play.

The instructor must carefully organize the preparation for the unit, for which at least five weeks should be allowed. If the unit is to develop smoothly and successfully, certain technical and organizational problems need to be solved.

(1) **Available plays to read** Have on hand a generous collection of individual plays for the students to read. Some teachers can obtain through the board of education all the plays listed in Chapter 13. Others must buy copies personally or use one-act anthologies from the library. Catalogues from each of the play firms should be on file so that students may send for new plays if they wish.

(2) **Securing scripts** Students should begin immediately to read and consider worthwhile plays for production. Since additional copies for each cast member will need to be ordered and purchased, the selections need to be made within a few days. Although there is no royalty charge when a play is used for classroom work only, in most cases it is a breach of the copyright laws to copy parts from a published script. While waiting for the scripts, the preparation, casting, and study for the unit can be developed.

(3) **Selection of directors** Since direction requires leadership qualities as well as technical skills, student directors should be chosen for their ability to guide the other cast members well. The instructor may wish to select the several directors and allow them to participate in the casting; or the class may divide itself into units, each selecting a play and choosing a director from its own group.

(4) **Casting** Depending upon the size of the group and other related factors, casting may be handled in one of several ways: (a) The students group themselves into companies, cooperatively select a suitable play, and cast the parts by mutual agreement. (b) The instructor selects the directors and assigns roles in accordance with the needs and ability of individual students. (3) Each director holds try-outs for his group's play; and casting is done with the help of the teacher. (See casting, pages 200-201.)

(5) **Production organization** While awaiting scripts, prepare a solid foundation for rehearsals and direction techniques (pages 175-178). Relate the fundamentals of play production found in Chapter 10 to the one-act plays. Assign the thorough study of Chapter 4. Give special emphasis to the responsibilities and duties of each technical worker or manager (pages 52-53), the explanation of the prompt book (pages 199-200), and the necessity of maintaining the rehearsal schedule (page 56).

During the rehearsal weeks, establish deadlines for the memorization of all parts, first run-throughs, and prompt book materials. Use the first ten to fifteen minutes of class time to clarify production details and check on rehearsal progress. Arrange a schedule by which a different group rehearses with you every day so that each has a chance to get some help on blocking and arranging stage pictures and on the collection of props, costumes, sound, and music materials. For production days, plan to present one to two plays daily, and prepare a mimeographed program. These productions should reflect the semester's training and provide incidental encouragement for student talent in art, organization and management, and music. As a summation, review the objectives of the entire course and discuss accomplishments and further needs before progressing to Drama II. Prepare a final examination, return the first paper of the semester, "What I Wish to Accomplish in This Course," and ask students to evaluate the following: (1) success in achieving goals, (2) summary of gains from the entire course, and (3) what was learned of greatest personal value. Add any other pertinent questions which may help you adapt the Course of Study more fully to your particular group.

## ☆☆☆ UNIT DEVELOPMENT OF DRAMA II

Because there is so much to be learned the first semester, Basic Training (Part II) is given only when it relates directly to the acting projects of Drama I. Students are ready in Drama II for more detailed instruction in each phase of the actor's training. The units of work in the Drama II Course of Study are centered around Chapters 5, 6, 7, 8, 9, and 10 of this book. The units of exercises, pantomimes, and improvisations, which provide drill in Body, Voice, Technique, and Senses and Emotions are designed to give the student greater variety in acting assignments and the chance to perform more often than is possible in whole scenes. After several weeks of study and performance, the student's mastery of these skills should be tested in scenes and plays which give the actor a chance to create and demonstrate more complete characterizations.

In Units II, IV, and V (See Courses of Study, pages 374, 376, 377), which provide for the performance of scenes or plays, special emphasis may also be given to direction and production. The final unit, History and Horizons, provides an opportunity to combine the study of theater history with the performance of a period scene.

In communities with access to live shows, symphonies, and other allied arts, it is profitable to consider the relationship of these arts to drama. Students may be asked to attend during the term (1) a concert by a symphony orchestra, (2) an art exhibit, (3) a ballet, (4) an opera, and (5) a play. Toward the end of the semester, have a session of reports and discussion comparing these art forms and analyzing the elements in each that relate to theatre.

| UNIT | WEEKS | ACTIVITIES |
|---|---|---|
| I | 2 | *Basic Training: Senses and Emotions, Technique*<br>Introduction to semester's work: Course of Study<br>Selection of research topic for History and Horizons to be presented at end of semester (Chapter 8)<br>Read and study Senses and Emotions (Chapter 5)<br>Prepare exercises and pantomimes in senses and emotions<br>Read and study Technique (Chapter 9)<br>Prepare exercises and pantomimes in technique |

**BASIC TRAINING: CHAPTERS 5 AND 9** In orienting the students to the five units of work and objectives in Drama II, spend some additional time in explaining the final unit of work, History and Horizons, and the need to review Chapter 8 immediately in order to select a topic for the semester's research project. It is advantageous if two, three, or more students study the same period of history, concentrating on different phases, so that they can work together in the final acting project, the presentation of a period scene.

At the first meeting of the class, assign Senses and Emotions, Chapter 5, to be read and studied. The motivation for the training and exercises to follow is a recognition that actors need a keen sense of awareness and an understanding of emotional drives. Spend a week of concentrated drill on the various exercises for developing and projecting vivid impressions. Students should prepare one exercise each day as carefully as they would any acting assignment. Assign each kind of exercise to several students. Limit performances to two minutes each, using a stop watch if necessary. During class time, do some of the group exercises such as those on pages 71, 77, 78, 79, and 80, which provide training in impromptu dramatization. You may assign, as a one-day experiment or a semester project, the recording of vivid sense impressions in a notebook.

During the second week, focus the training and instruction on Technique, Chapter 9. Most students recognize the need for additional drill and find the exercises interesting. From the pantomimes and exercises given the first week, list the stage techniques which students executed poorly. Have terms and techniques demonstrated by students in short scenes involving one or more techniques. Working in groups of three or more, the students can plan a series of stage pictures that show well-balanced, interesting groupings and tell a simple story. Review and test on stage vocabulary.

| UNIT | WEEKS | ACTIVITIES |
|---|---|---|
| II | 2 | *Scene from Contemporary Drama* |
| | | Read a contemporary three-act play |
| | | Select a scene for presentation |
| | | Select a partner |
| | | Rehearse and present scene |

After two weeks of drill, the students should prepare an acting assignment in a play to demonstrate the effectiveness of their skills and to show a sustained performance. If the students are encouraged or required to read plays from contemporary American, British, and European drama, they will build a background in dramatic literature from which to draw scenes for acting assignments. Chapter 13 lists plays and scenes for those students needing help.

Since the students have developed in Drama I the routine for giving a scene, each group should be able to proceed in rehearsal and performance without any instruction in class. Allow one week for rehearsal and one for performance. Require written material on ground plans, character and play analysis, and written critiques.

| UNIT | WEEKS | ACTIVITIES |
|---|---|---|
| III | 2 | *Basic Training: Body, Voice* |
| | | In class read the scene from *The Emperor Jones* (page 81) |
| | | Read and study *Body* (Chapter 6) |
| | | Do daily group drills in body exercises |
| | | Prepare pantomimes from Chapter 6 |
| | | Create original characterization pantomimes |
| | | In class read the scene from *Elizabeth the Queen* (page 107) |
| | | Read and study *Voice* (Chapter 7) |
| | | Do daily group drills in voice development |
| | | Prepare improvisations (pages 132-136) |
| | | Prepare interpretation selections (pages 137-139) |

**BASIC TRAINING: CHAPTERS 6 AND 7** The need for healthy, flexible, expressive bodies as instruments of dramatic projection is the motivation for specific drill in this unit. Begin the first lesson by reading the scene from *The Emperor Jones,* which dramatically demonstrates the physical agility demanded in acting; if you have used this before, select a comparable action scene from another play. Discuss the various sports and arts effective in body building. Lead into the exercises and drills for developing strength, flexibility, and control. Have each student make a personal inventory check (pages 83-84), and plan a variety of group exercises which the class can do in unison each day. Assign specific exercises to each student to correct individual problems, pointing out that professional actors do similar exercises systematically to keep fit, often under the direction of a gymnasium instructor. In this unit it is natural to stress the importance of health and vitality, with references to appropriate current articles. Collect pictures of professional actors and actresses in roles that demand exceptional physical grace, action, and feats of skill; inspire regular disciplined practice on the part of the students. Have the students prepare and demonstrate the exercises on pages 89-95.

The first section of Chapter 6 comprises exercises designed for the achievement and maintenance of physical fitness; the second section provides training for the dramatic application of this fitness in pantomimes. The appropriate division of class time between drill and creative pantomimes depends on the needs of the students.

Introduce the voice development work of Chapter 7 by reading the scene from *Elizabeth the Queen* and discussing the range of meaning and insinuation that may be achieved through vocal interpretation. A good voice is possibly an actor's greatest single asset. It will compensate for many other deficiencies; in radio it is all-important. Few people are born with the vocal equipment to have a great voice, but everyone can develop a more pleasing one. As in Chapter 6, the first section is concerned with exercises to develop skill, while the second contains dramatic material for practice in projecting the thought from the printed page to an audience.

Using the chart on page 114, explain the physiology of how sound and voice are produced in the human body. Spend some time on the drills for correcting faulty production. In the beginning stress relaxation and good posture as the foundation of vocal control. Review the Daily Routine for Speech Practice, adding other specific drills each day dealing with projection, pitch, melody, resonance, and articulation. In explaining the forty-three speech sounds (page 121), you can illustrate how the science of phonetics is used by playing records from *My Fair Lady*, in which the training of Liza to speak like a lady was accomplished through daily speech lessons and phonetic drills. Have each student take the voice and speech inventory (page 112) and do specific exercises to correct or develop his voice; then stress emphatically the necessity of daily practice to achieve any success. Use records to illustrate beautiful speech. Discuss good voices heard on radio, television, in the movies, and on the stage. Assign the preparation and performance of improvisational scenes and selections for interpretation on pages 132-139.

| UNIT | WEEKS | ACTIVITIES |
|---|---|---|
| IV | 7 | *Basic Training: Production* |
| | | Read and study Play Production (Chapter 10) |
| | | Select either a group of one-act plays or a cut version of a three-act play |
| | | Participate in organizational techniques, rehearsal, direction, and production |

**BASIC TRAINING: CHAPTER 10** The techniques and skills necessary in organizing and producing a play are best learned through experience. This unit is focused on two levels of study and performance: (1) the creation of a characterization, and (2) the preparation and execution of a unified, finished production. Seven weeks are allowed for the project so that rehearsals may alternate with periods of teaching. Every student should learn how to prepare each section of the prompt book and to understand the responsibilities and duties of all the technical assistants involved in a production. The unit is designed to train the students to assist the director in a three-act play production, as well as to produce their own plays with little or no supervision. All the material in Chapter 10 may be related to the unit.

If the one-act plays are selected as the nucleus for training, follow the teaching procedure used in Drama I for the one-act project, Chapter 4. In choosing a single play or a condensed version of a three-act play which can be presented in one or two class periods, consider a play written by a major playwright which would be interesting and challenging to the entire class. Even though it may not have wide audience appeal, a period or Shakespearean play is a good medium. Double cast, if necessary, or double in roles, and assign a student director to each act. Although the three-act play may not give many students an opportunity to practice direction, it does bring the whole group into a single cast working toward a unified production.

The entire class should discuss the play from the standpoint of the director, and participate in working out the production factors: preliminary planning, tryouts, rehearsal schedule, technical responsibilities, and finished prompt book.

It is suggested that every Monday be used for instruction, planning, and clarification of characterization and acting problems. Create exercises for demonstrating and teaching the principles of direction, grouping, and stage balance. The directors can be referred to more advanced books on direction. You may have the directors prepare their blocking in advance. From this, you can use the difficult situations and incorrect movement patterns as a basis for class instruction, allowing the class to help solve blocking problems. In rehearsal, you should conduct the first sessions in order to teach the proper method by example. Later, conduct each kind of rehearsal—blocking, polishing, run-through, and others—at least once. While scenes are in rehearsal, give the production staff not on stage at the time such individual training and reference books on the subject as they need to develop their work.

For the finished production, costumes may be created, improvised, or borrowed from wardrobe, but no expense should be entailed; simple pieces of scenery can be constructed from available set pieces. If time permits, demonstrate the fundamentals of make-up application, so that the students may apply their own for the production.

With students assigned to a variety of jobs, it is desirable to keep a close check on each one's activities. A teaching device which has proved successful is the weekly Work Schedule (page 391); the student records his acting and work assignments, indicating the number of hours spent and completion dates. These may be graded weekly.

| UNIT | WEEKS | ACTIVITIES |
| --- | --- | --- |
| V | 5 | *Basic Training: History* |
| | | Submit research project in written form |
| | | Review survey of History (Chapter 8) |
| | | Participate in additional reading assignments and class lectures |
| | | Prepare and present period scene |
| | | Survey Modern Acting Mediums: stage, radio, screen, television |

**BASIC TRAINING: CHAPTER 8** To prepare the final unit of work, evaluate and grade the research papers assigned the first week of the term on which each student has been working throughout the semester. Plan a three-week series of lectures, using available audio-visual teaching aids (see Chapter 15), so that the students can clearly grasp the essential feeling, facts, and contributions of each historical period. The instructor, being best informed, should lead the lectures, but every student should be expected to participate and contribute highlights of information gleaned from his study. Select a few outstanding student papers for oral presentation, spacing these reports over the three weeks of lectures and study. To enrich the students' understanding, prepare a reading list of books and articles which may be placed temporarily on reserve in the library and assigned as additional reading. Interweave sections taken from the student reports, giving individuals credit; also share pictures from their reports as well as those from your files. At the close of three weeks the students should be able to explain the cultural and social background of each period and its major contributions to world drama, as well as to identify its leading playwrights, plays, and actors, and the characteristics of its physical stage.

The fourth week, the students perform scenes taken from plays written in their period of history study. Stimulate the class to improvise period costumes and stage their scenes in the style and manners of the age. A short introduction to each scene should identify the period, acquaint the audience with special features of the play, and briefly explain the plot circumstances.

In the final week, survey modern acting mediums in stage, radio, screen, and television. Use current articles from newspapers, theatre magazines, and books to explore the trends and opportunities in these acting mediums. If you have assigned the five art projects of reporting on allied arts, expand the discussions to include these related forms. This is also the time to answer student questions concerning careers in one or more of the theatre arts and the necessary preparation and training required.

A final examination covering all the work of the semester is usually desirable.

## ☆☆☆ UNIT DEVELOPMENT OF DRAMA III (Play Production)

One semester, preferably two, should be spent on dramatic training before a student appears in a major production. Plays should be the outgrowth of a systematic course of instruction if they are to have great educational value. Just "putting on a play" is not teaching drama, nor does it use the dramatic medium to its fullest capacity as an educational tool.

If the class play or yearly production is cast from schoolwide tryouts and rehearsed outside of class time, the techniques and organizational plans for producing a play found in Chapter 10 will be of great help to the director and students. The units of study suggested here, however, apply to a class in Play Production. They are flexible, depending upon the number of weeks scheduled for preparing the play. In this Course of Study ten weeks are allotted. Less than ten weeks does not allow for the gradual growth of the individual which is so essential in learning. If students are to create and mature their characterizations *with* the guidance of a director and to have a great share of responsibility, through which they will learn much, they may be expected to take longer for the whole process than more highly skilled persons would take. In addition, the rehearsal schedule must allow students to keep up their other school work.

| UNIT | WEEKS | ACTIVITIES |
|---|---|---|
| I | 2 | Play reading<br>Play selection<br>Casting |

In many instances, the teacher has in mind the play most suitable for a given production group. However, often the number of students enrolled and available talent is not known until the first day of the class. In this case, it is desirable to have at hand three or four possible plays. A good learning experience can be provided if the students are allowed to read, evaluate, and help in the selection. Once the script is chosen, every student should have a copy as quickly as possible, and all should participate in the play-reading experience. Comments on characterization and play structure will prepare them for tryouts. (See pages 195-197, Selection of the Play.)

The primary considerations in casting are given in Chapter 10, pages 200 to 203. Many teachers select the cast without help. Others have found a judging committee a successful device in the tryout period, with other teachers, administrators, and drama alumni serving as an advisory group. However, each judge must have read the play before casting and in the final decision rely on the director to set the cast.

| UNIT | WEEKS | | ACTIVITIES |
|---|---|---|---|
| II | 7 | | *Rehearsal (seven weeks)* |
| | | A. Group: | Daily rehearsal of three-act play following the schedule |
| | | B. Group: | Rehearsal of minor parts as scheduled<br>Preparation of production duties (Chapter 10)<br>Preparation and rehearsal of additional scenes or one-act plays |

| UNIT | WEEKS | ACTIVITIES |
|---|---|---|
| II | 1 | *Production (one week)* |
| | | Entire class at every rehearsal:<br>Technical rehearsals<br>Dress rehearsals<br>Production of play<br>Photographs of play |

One big problem in the drama production class is how to provide for those students not cast in the play and those having minor roles a worthwhile dramatic experience and also an opportunity to earn a superior grade for college entrance credit. This can be done through the establishment of Drama Workshop groups in which each student is responsible for the presentation of a program the week after the three-act play is completed. Activities may consist of one-act plays, scenes, or programs of readings, original skits, pantomimes, and improvisations. Originality, initiative in organization, and production quality can be evaluated. Each group may have a name, a Master of Ceremonies, and as elaborate a presentation as imagination and industry can provide.

Because the class will be divided much of the time in using the workshop system, you must devise schemes to keep a certain amount of class unity. Devote part of the class time each Monday to creating *esprit de corps* toward the larger production. The entire group may drill together on projection, articulation, and basic techniques which need to be strengthened in cast members. Every Friday, or periodically, the Drama Workshop groups can be asked to serve as a critical audience, giving both written and oral comments which may be graded.

The Work Schedules (page 391) may prove valuable for checking the activities of the entire group. They may be mimeographed and checked each week for work done both in class and outside: rehearsal, production duties, reading, written work, voice and body exercises, tutoring students in Drama I and II.

The techniques for planning and developing the rehearsal periods of the production are clearly outlined in Play Production (Chapter 10). Sample mimeographed forms used in the rehearsal procedure are given in Chapter 15, pages 390-391. It may be helpful to recapitulate the following: the direction of a major production requires tremendous energy, technical skill, and artistic decisions. In a school situation, it is imperative that the teacher-director be well-organized, responsible in meeting all deadlines (particularly in regard to printed copy), and able to maintain professional and harmonious relationships with administrators and faculty members.

| UNIT | WEEKS | ACTIVITIES |
|---|---|---|
| III | 1 | Discussion and evaluation of three-act play<br>Clean-up and return of all materials<br>Completion of prompt book<br>Workshop group presentations |

Following the production, the entire class should be given the opportunity to discuss freely the play, the comments by friends and relatives, the personal achievements, and the learning values. In addition, the group should be given critical evaluations of the performances with all criticism directed toward improving future productions. The Drama I and II classes should be assigned written critiques, which may then be shared with the cast, though the authors' names should be kept anonymous.

An important part of the students' training, and one often overlooked, is the job of clean-up after the production is over. Every member of the cast should be responsible for returning materials, rented props, and costumes, and for putting the make-up and dressing rooms in proper order. The technical staff is responsible for submitting the records of the production to the director for the completion of the prompt book.

The remainder of the week can be devoted to the Drama Workshop groups and the presentation of their programs; the cast should be strongly motivated to use this respite from assignments in drama to catch up on any school work they have been postponing.

| UNIT | WEEKS | ACTIVITIES |
|---|---|---|
| IV | 2 | Original scenes and improvisations |
| V | 2 | Great roles or famous speeches from World Drama |
| VI | 3 | Selection, preparation, and presentation of final acting project: a ten- to fifteen-minute program of scenes, original material, pantomimes, or soliloquies |

Units IV, V, and VI outlined in the Course of Study are merely suggestive of a few activities that can be used in the remaining weeks of school after the major production has been completed. The so-called letdown after the play is over must be counteracted with a project or series of activities that is stimulating, creative, and educational. Units not covered in the Drama II Course of Study may be used; experiments in central and flexible staging (see pages 184-187) may capture the enthusiasm of the group. If the production was of a serious nature, a project involving scenes from comedy would provide interest, such as Humor Through the Ages, illustrating comedy techniques from the Greek, Middle Ages, Shakespeare, Restoration, French, melodrama, and modern theatre.

# Fifteen

# TEACHING-LEARNING AIDS ☆☆☆

The materials and suggestions given in this chapter are intended to:

1. implement the Courses of Study given in Chapter 14
2. provide new ideas or sources for enriching an already established Course of Study
3. share techniques for building public relations in the community

## ☆☆☆ AUDIO-VISUAL AIDS: GENERAL

Two general references are (1) *Film Strip Guide* and (2) *Educational Film Guide*. Both are published periodically by H. W. Wilson Company, 950 University Avenue, New York 52, New York. Each gives a description of the aid, its source, and other information.

The list below will be helpful in establishing a library of aids.

### Records

Recordings of scenes from plays, entire plays, soliloquies, and interpretive readings may be purchased from:

Linguaphone Institute, 32 Rockefeller Plaza, New York, New York
The Gramaphone Shop, Inc., 18 East 48th Street, New York 17, New York
Caedmon Sales Corp., 277 Fifth Avenue, New York 16, New York
Harvard Film Service, 4 Lawrence Hall, Cambridge 38, Massachusetts

### Films

Educational films designed for teaching may be rented or purchased from:

Educational Film Sales Department, University Extension, University of California, Los Angeles 24, California
Comma, 1104 Fair Oaks Avenue, South Pasadena, California

### Filmstrips

Filmstrips on history of the theatre, lighting, costume, scenery construction, acting, and the dramatic arts may be purchased from:

The Stanley Bowmar Company, 513 West 166th Street, New York 32, New York

Comma, 1104 Fair Oaks Avenue, South Pasadena, California

### Life Magazine

For picture display and articles that have appeared in *Life* during the last year, write to *Life Magazine*, 9 Rockefeller Plaza, New York 20, New York. When sending a request, specify the exact dates of copies needed by consulting *The Readers' Guide to Periodical Literature* or the *Life Index.*

## ☆☆☆AUDIO-VISUAL AIDS: SHAKESPEARE

A vast amount of material is available on Shakespeare, his works and time, and the London he knew. In teaching a unit on Shakespearean acting such as is given in Chapter 3 of this book, the instructor will find helpful the following selective list of materials which may be rented, purchased, or collected at nominal cost.

1. Pictures and articles from *Life Magazine.* (See listing above.)
2. Pictures and prints of Shakespeare's London and playhouses. Write Folger Shakespeare Library, Washington, D.C.
3. Stills of current Shakespearean motion pictures. Write the studio producing the film.
4. Photographic records of productions in book form:
   The *Shakespeare Memorial Theatre Yearbooks,* published by Reinhardt and Evans, London, England.
   The *American Shakespeare Festival,* John Houseman and Jack Landau, New York: Simon and Schuster, 1959.
5. Filmstrips to introduce Shakespeare and pictures from the film versions of his plays. (See listing above, Stanley Bowmar Company.)
6. The film, *Shakespeare's Theatre: The Globe Playhouse.* (See listing above, Educational Film Sales Department.)
7. Records made by professional British and American actors. (See listing above, Records.)
8. Models and blueprints of Shakespeare's Globe playhouse. Write Loomis Laboratory, 17 Miller Avenue, Cambridge, Massachusetts.

## ☆☆☆STAGE EQUIPMENT

Plette, W. Fredric. *Directory of Stage Equipment and Supply Houses.* Published by The National Thespian Society, College Hill Station, Cincinnati, Ohio, 1950.

## ☆☆☆ SCRIPTS

The play publishers and their addresses are given in Chapter 13, pages 328 to 329. Catalogues will be sent free upon request and should be available to students for reference in the classroom. A supply of new desirable three-act and one-act plays should be added each year to either the school library or the classroom files.

## ☆☆☆ CLASSROOM EQUIPMENT

It is strongly recommended that the instructor have in the classroom a portable record player, tape recorder, and filmstrip projector so that audio-visual aids may be used quickly and effectively as needed. Most vital of these is the record player, which is used for both teaching and productions.

## ☆☆☆ SUPPLEMENTARY ACTING GAMES AND EXERCISES

Many teaching days are interrupted by assembly schedules, shortened class periods, and holidays that interfere with regular lesson plans. For such days or periods when regular plans must be altered, the teacher needs to have on hand stimulating activities. There are many creative acting exercises and games which the students enjoy. The following are activities that are not only fun, but worthwhile and challenging as well:

1. **Verse choir.** Mimeograph copies of dramatic and humorous selections such as "The Congo," by Vachel Lindsay; "The Highwayman," by Alfred Noyes; "The Listeners," by Walter de la Mare; "Miniver Cheevy," by Edwin Arlington Robinson; "The King's Breakfast," by A. A. Milne; "The Owl and the Pussy-Cat," by Edward Lear; and "Hamlet's Advice to the Players," (page 44).
2. **Grab-bag box.** Fill a box with thirty or forty small objects such as a baby's shoe, comb, pipe, compact, dance program, football ticket, glove, etc.; have each student draw an object from the box and create a pantomime that tells a story centered on the object.
3. **Animal characterizations.** Have a collection of animal pictures or a list of animals. Each student selects one and creates a pantomime in which the person possesses distinctive animal-like movements and characteristics that the class can identify. Examples are a woman with sleek, graceful feline motions, or a man with the arrogant, proud stride of a race horse.

4. **Improvisations.** Make a list of phrases which can be used as **tag lines.** Have groups of students create improvised situations and dialogue that lead up to and finish with the given tag line.
5. **Object scenes.** Organize a series of cards each bearing the names of three objects, such as (1) pen, (2) mirror, and (3) flower. In groups of three or more, have the students build a scene in which each of the objects contributes to the story. These may be pantomimed scenes or improvisations.
6. **Shakespearean quotations.** Collect a list of some of Shakespeare's famous quotations. Give the quote and have the students identify the play, the character who says the line, the character addressed, and (briefly) the situation involved.
7. **Identification quiz.** Make a series of flash cards with theatre terms, vocabulary, famous actors, actresses, plays, characters from classical and other well-known plays, and playwrights. Divide the class into teams for an identification contest in spelling-bee fashion.
8. **"Who Am I?" quiz.** Create a series of "clues" (about five for each) on famous theatre personalities, plays, and characters from plays. Give the clues one at a time until students can make the identification.

## ☆☆☆ CLASSROOM STAGE EQUIPMENT

Some carefully selected and flexible stage equipment is desirable to give an opportunity for the design and development of movement and business. The following suggested unit furniture and set pieces will prove helpful and easy to build or collect:

1. Screens (two or more) hinged to fold either way provide a background for practically any scene. Each panel should be no larger than 6′6″ by 2′, covered on both sides with canvas (muslin is not sufficiently durable). One side may be painted to match the walls of the room, the other side decorated with a colorful design or an outdoor scene. For variety, butcher's paper can be painted and temporarily thumbtacked onto the screens.
2. A few pieces of furniture that are sturdy (reinforced or built extra strong) will be needed. A couch, armchair, and tables of different sizes made with simple, straight lines may be built by the woodshop classes. A very useful piece is a combination unit with a bookcase on one side and a fireplace on the other; on the bookcase side, the back of the fireplace opening is a decorated panel.

3. A few props, such as lamps, pillows, slip covers, a telephone, a few dishes, and a tablecloth, are decorative and help to make a set realistic. However, since storage space is always limited, the prop supplies should be kept at a minimum and students expected to augment them by bringing extra articles from home for their scenes.

## ☆☆☆ CLASSROOM COMMITTEES

In large classes of thirty or forty students, much of the routine work can be done by committees of students. Duties could include checking in and out of scripts, plays, props, and books; recording of class papers such as plots, introductions, critiques, and character analyses; caring for the stage and props, the bulletin board, publicity for the school paper, the class scrapbook, and supplementary material. A system of keeping records that is simple, but accurate, should be used by the committees. A typing committee—to keep script copies fresh, to supply new scenes, and to prepare material for mimeographing—is essential.

## ☆☆☆ THEATRE PARTIES, TOURS, AND SPEAKERS

It is surprising, even in theatrical centers such as New York and Los Angeles, how many students in a drama class have never seen a play or have seen only school productions. So much can be learned from seeing and evaluating together plays produced by professional, educational, and community groups that it is well worth the effort to plan and organize theatre parties. Usually student rates can be arranged. In most schools, parent permits in writing are necessary for students to attend whether the activity is during school hours or in the evening; be sure to protect yourself and the students by securing releases and approval through the board of education. Exchange theatre parties with other high schools are popular and create interschool interest in drama. Universities and colleges are usually happy to cooperate with the school drama groups in making student rates available or even extending invitations to dress rehearsals.

Tours either in your area or to neighboring cities are worthwhile experiences. Some useful places for students to visit are: community and professional playhouses, make-up studios, costume houses, lighting companies, and scenery houses.

Invite personalities associated with theatre to speak before classes or an assembly. Among those who will be stimulating and informative speakers are professional actors, actresses, producers, directors, technicians, representatives from theatrical supply houses, and business managers of community theatres.

## ☆☆☆ PUBLIC RELATIONS IN THE COMMUNITY

The play produced for the community audience (and student body) is in many schools the only other major contact besides sports that brings the community members to the school. With the growing number of recreational offerings to adults for their leisure hours, not to mention the time spent watching television, building audience attendance for the school play is an ever-increasing problem. It is, perhaps, most pronounced in large cities where there is so much entertainment from which to choose. The budget allowed for a production, the type of play possible to produce, and the number of performances are all conditioned by the potential audience attendance. Building community relations and support of the plays involves more than newspaper publicity, posters, and mailing lists. While there is no one formula to ensure attendance, there are techniques that consistently prove successful and fundamental in building community support and pride in the drama programs:

1. Select and produce quality plays that do not offend the tastes or standards of the community. It is better to do one finished and technically polished production than two or three "satisfactory" ones.
2. Use all the available media in regard to printed publicity and word of mouth promotion that "works" in your community and discard those that are ineffectual. One method of discovering what media bring results in your area is to insert in the play program a separate questionnaire sheet asking guests who *are* there to check the sources from which they learned about the play.
3. Seek opportunities throughout the year to serve community organizations with programs. As the drama teacher, you are the primary promotional agent for the program. Send selected scenes, interpretations, one-act plays, and specially designed programs to the civic service organizations, church groups, PTA meetings, children's hospital, elementary and junior high schools. But make sure that all work is of the highest quality, with the finest trained talent, for this contact may make a lasting impression on the adult group, one on which the merit and reputation of the entire drama program is judged. Although these activities require additional time, they are one of the most important contacts in serving the community and building future audience support.

## ☆☆☆ MODEL FORMS

On the following pages are a few of the forms previously referred to which may be used as models. The stage plots for your scenes will be as simple as the one shown here for *Holiday*. Acting area and furniture should be drawn to scale. Note that this arrangement of furniture has been used in developing the movement and business indicated in the script, page 219.

## ☆☆☆ STAGE PLOT AND INTRODUCTION
## HOLIDAY by Philip Barry

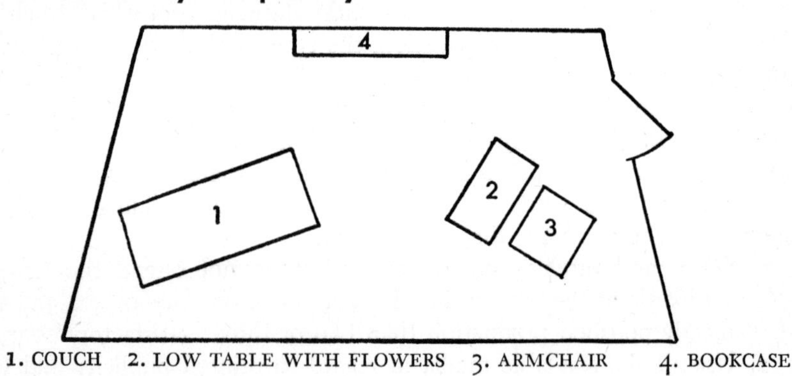


1. COUCH  2. LOW TABLE WITH FLOWERS  3. ARMCHAIR  4. BOOKCASE

### INTRODUCTION

This scene from Act I of *Holiday* by Philip Barry takes place in the third floor sitting-room of Edward Seton's house in New York. You are to imagine it as the playwright describes it—"a handsome room, and quite a comfortable room, but rich, very rich."

It is about twelve o'clock on a bright, cold Sunday in mid-December.

Johnny Case, a brilliant, self-made young lawyer, has just become engaged to Julia Seton, member of an extremely wealthy and socially prominent family. In this scene Julia introduces him to her sister Linda, who is just returning from church.

The characters are:

Julia Seton, played by—
Johnny Case, played by—
Linda Seton, played by—

## ☆☆☆ PRODUCTION SCHEDULE

### DRAMA I—PERIOD II

***presents THE MODERN SCENE***

*Monday, September 21, 19—*

HOLIDAY—Barry
JULIA—Patty Elton
JOHNNY—Bill Heath
LINDA—Beth Rowan

EVER SINCE EVE—Ryerson-Clements
SPUD—Ray Dennison
JOHNNIE—Bud Bailey

OUR TOWN—Wilder
GEORGE—Jack Ryan
EMILY—Bonnie Foster

*Tuesday, September 22, 19—*

STAGE DOOR—Kaufman-Ferber
TERRY—Irene Johnson
JEAN—Lois Banning

OUR HEARTS WERE YOUNG AND GAY—Skinner-Kimbrough
EMILY—Marjorie Blaine
CORNELIA—Carol Jensen

*Wednesday, September 23, 19—*

THE LARK—Anouilh
CHARLES—Jim Fleming
JOAN—Barbara Dale

VISIT TO A SMALL PLANET—Vidal
KRETON—John Wright
POWERS—Tom Denton
ROGER—Stuart Hughes

TIME OUT FOR GINGER—Alexander
AGNES—Charlotte Sawyer
JEAN—Judy Pierce

*Thursday, September 24, 19—*

THE ROYAL FAMILY—Kaufman-Ferber
JULIE—Gloria Douglas
GWEN—Susan Benefiel
FANNY—Mary Jean Mayer

CRITIQUE PERIOD

In like manner prepare Production Schedules for The Character-Opposite Scene, The Shakespearean Scene, and The One-Act Play.

WORK ASSIGNMENTS FOR THREE-ACT PLAY

| COMPLETION DATE | JOB | MANAGER | CREW |
|---|---|---|---|
| Fri. Apr. 7 | set design | Bob James | |
| Wed. Apr. 12 | scene plot | " | |
| Fri. May 5 | set construction | Alan Taylor | Phil Jones |
| Fri. May 12 | set painting | " | Dick Hansen |
| (etc.) | | | Clem Baker |

## ☆☆☆ IF I WERE KING

A portion of the rehearsal organization for a three-act play is given here. In this Breakdown of Scenes the first column indicates the number of pages of script to be covered in a single rehearsal. Later several of these sections are combined in one day's rehearsal, as would be shown on the completed schedule.

BREAKDOWN OF SCENES

| NO. | PAGES | CHARACTERS |
|---|---|---|
| | | Act I |
| (7) | 9-16 | Vagabonds, Robin, Louis, Tristan, Francois |
| (6) | 17-23 | Same |
| (6) | 23-29 | Same, Mother Villon, Katherine, Page |
| (5) | 29-32 | Same, Katherine, Thibaut, Captain, 5 French Soldiers |
| | | Act II |
| (5) | 34-40 | Louis, Astrologer, Tristan, Katherine, Olivier, Villon, Pages |
| (4) | 40-44 | Villon, Noel, French Soldiers, Huguette, Vagabonds |
| (5) | 45-49 | Villon, Noel, Huguette, Katherine, Olivier |
| (4) | 49-53 | Villon, Noel, Katherine, Olivier, Louis, Ladies, Musicians, Courtiers, French Soldiers, Archers, Burgundians, Toison d'Or, Astrologer, Tristan |
| | | Act III |

.......................

A portion of the Rehearsal Schedule for the same three-act play.

REHEARSAL SCHEDULE

| DATE | IN CLASS | AFTER SCHOOL 3:30 TO 5:30 | EVENING 7:00 TO 9:30 |
|---|---|---|---|
| Mon. Apr. 10 | 9-16 | | |
| Tues. Apr. 11 | 17-23 | 9-23 | |
| Wed. Apr. 12 | 23-29 | | |
| Thur. Apr. 13 | 29-32 | 23-32 | |
| Fri. Apr. 14 | 34-40 | | Act I |
| Mon. Apr. 17 | 40-44 | | |
| Tues. Apr. 18 | 45-49 | 34-44 | |
| Wed. Apr. 19 | 49-53 | | |
| (etc.) | | | |

Work Schedules should be turned in for checking each week by every member of the Drama Production class except those playing the leading roles in the three-act play.

WORK SCHEDULE FOR DRAMA PRODUCTION CLASS

NAME: ____________________

PRESENT ASSIGNMENTS: ____________________

____________________

____________________

DATE:

MONDAY:
TUESDAY:
WEDNESDAY:
THURSDAY:
FRIDAY:

TOTAL NUMBER OF OUTSIDE HOURS ____________

## ☆☆☆ SET DESIGN AND PLOT

For the One-Act Play it may be desirable to make both a scene design and a more detailed stage plot, as sketched below. These may serve as a basis for the construction of a model stage. Note that both are drawn to the same scale.

# INDEX ☆☆☆